# ANCIENT INDIAN TRADITION AND MYTHOLOGY

*Translated by*
A Board of Scholars

*Edited by*
Prof. J.L. Shastri

**VOLUME 27**

# ANCIENT INDIAN TRADITION AND MYTHOLOGY SERIES

[PURĀṆAS IN TRANSLATION]

*Volumes Released*

ŚIVA 1-4
LIṄGA 5-6
BHĀGAVATA 7-11
GARUḌA 12-14
NĀRADA 15-19
KŪRMA 20-21
BRAHMĀṆḌA 22-26
AGNI 27-30
VARĀHA 31-32
BRAHMA 33-36
VĀYU 37-38
PADMA 39-48
SKANDA, PARTS I-XXIII, 49-71
VĀMANA 72-73

*Volumes Under Preparation*

BHAVIṢYA
BRAHMAVAIVARTA
DEVĪBHĀGAVATA
KĀLIKĀ
MĀRKAṆḌEYA
MATSYA
VIṢṆU
VIṢṆUDHARMOTTARA

# THE AGNI-PURĀṆA

**PART I**

*Translated and Annotated by*

N. GANGADHARAN

MOTILAL BANARSIDASS PUBLISHERS
PRIVATE LIMITED • DELHI

*2nd Reprint: Delhi, 2013*
*First Edition: Delhi, 1984*



ISBN: 978-81-208-0359-6

MOTILAL BANARSIDASS
41 U.A. Bungalow Road, Jawahar Nagar, Delhi 110 007
8 Mahalaxmi Chamber, 22 Bhulabhai Desai Road, Mumbai 400 026
120 Royapettah High Road, Mylapore, Chennai 600 004
236, 9th Main III Block, Jayanagar, Bangaluru 560 011
Sanas Plaza, 1302 Baji Rao Road, Pune 411 002
8 Camac Street, Kolkata 700 017
Ashok Rajpath, Patna 800 004
Chowk, Varanasi 221 001

UNESCO COLLECTION OF REPRESENTATIVE WORKS—*Indian Series*
*This book has been accepted in the Indian Translation Series of the UNESCO Collection of Representative Works, jointly sponsored by the United Nations Educational, Scientific and Cultural Organization (UNESCO) and the Government of India*

*Printed in India*

by RP Jain at NAB Printing Unit,
A-44, Naraina Industrial Area, Phase I, New Delhi–110028
and published by JP Jain for Motilal Banarsidass Publishers (P) Ltd,
41 U.A. Bungalow Road, Jawahar Nagar, Delhi-110007

## PUBLISHER'S NOTE

The purest gems lie hidden in the bottom of the ocean or in the depth of rocks. One has to dive into the ocean or delve into the rocks to find them out. Similarly, truth lies concealed in the language which with the passage of time has become obsolete. Man has to learn that language before he discovers that truth.

But he has neither the means nor the leisure to embark on that course. We have, therefore planned to help him acquire knowledge by an easier course. We have started the series of Ancient Indian Tradition and Mythology in English Translation. Our goal is to universalize knowledge through the most popular international medium of expression. The publication of the Purāṇas in English Translation is a step towards that goal.

# PREFACE

The present volume contains the *Agni Purāṇa* Part I (Chapters 1-100) in *English Translation.* This is the twenty-seventh Volume in the Series on *Ancient Indian Tradition and Mythology.*

The project of the Series was envisaged and planned in 1970 by Lala Sundar Lal Jain of Messrs Motilal Banarsidass. Hitherto twentysix volumes of the Series (comprising English translation of *Śiva, Liṅga, Bhāgavata, Garuḍa, Nārada, Kūrma* and *Brahmāṇḍa Purāṇas*) have been published and released for sale.

The present Purāṇa, like all other Purāṇas is of encyclopaedic character. The early chapters which open this Part describe glories of lord Viṣṇu in his different forms. There are legends of Viṣṇu as Fish saving Manu from drowning in the Cosmic Flood, as Tortoise supporting Mount Mandara at the churning of the ocean, as Boar slaying Daitya Hiraṇyākṣa, as Man-lion killing Hiraṇyakaśipu, as Dwarf cheating Bali, as Paraśurāma destroying Kṣatriya rulers, as Rāma assassinating Rāvaṇa, as Kṛṣṇa beheading Kaṁsa, as Buddha preaching the gospel of meditation, as Kalki to slay Mlecchas.

Going ahead, we find that a considerable portion of this Part deals with the Tantrika ritual for the installation and consecration of images of Viṣṇu, Śiva and other deities in their respective temples. A number of chapters relate to the initiation of a novice to the cult and the rites of initiation. The rites are described in detail. They are interspersed with the mystic syllables of Tantras which impart efficacy to the ritual concerned. A number of chapters throw light on the characteristics of images, mode of their installation and worship. Scattered here and there are the chapters on creation, on purification of oneself and others, on the positions of fingers (*mudrās*) in worship and on scores of other topics with details not found in other Purāṇas.

As to the date of this Purāṇa, nothing can be said with certainty. It being a compilation from various works written in different periods, no single date can be assigned to the Purāṇa as a whole. But, what is certain is the fact that a number of sections were written long before the Mahommedan invasion.

For instance, chapters on archery and arms, civil administration and military discipline are purely of Hindu character and can claim antiquity. Chapters on medicine and grammar are also old. Summaries of the Rāmāyaṇa and Mahābhārata indicate that the sections were written when Hinduism was in flourishing condition and the epic tradition had become sacred. Sections on *Avatāras*, on polity and judicature, on genealogy and history of ancient kings and distinguished personages also belong to pretty olden times. Sections on religion are also old as they seem to have been written when there was no rift among various sects.

But, the Purāṇa contains sections which are obviously later in date. For instance, a considerable number of chapters which deal with the mystic rules, mantras and ceremonies cannot claim antiquity. They might have been written after the tantric form of worship had become popular in India.

*Acknowledgement of Obligations*

It is our pleasant duty to put on record our sincere thanks to Dr. R. N. Dandekar and the UNESCO authorities for their kind encouragement and valuable help which rènder this work more useful than it would otherwise have been. We are extremely grateful to Dr. N. Gangadharan of Sanskrit Department, University of Madras for his critical Introduction, lucid translation and comprehensive annotations. We also thank those persons who have offered suggestions for improving the same.

—*Editor.*

## CONTENTS

### PART I

# ABBREVIATIONS

Common and self-evident abbreviations such as Ch(s)-Chapter(s), p—page, pp—pages, V—Verse, VV—Verses, Ftn—footnote, Hist. Ind. Philo—History of Indian Philosophy are not included in this list.

| | |
|---|---|
| ABORI | *Annals of the Bhandarkar Oriental Research Institute*, Poona |
| AGP | S. M. Ali's *The Geography of Purāṇas*, PPH, New Delhi, 1973 |
| AIHT | *Ancient Indian Historical Tradition*, F. E. Pargiter, Motilal Banarsidass (MLBD), Delhi. |
| AITM | *Ancient Indian Tradition and Mythology* Series MLBD, Delhi, 1972 onwards. |
| AP | *Agni Purāṇa*, Guru Mandal Edition (GM), Calcutta, 1957 |
| Arch.S.Rep. | Archaeological Survey Report |
| AV | *Atharva Veda*, Svadhyaya Mandal, Aundh |
| Bd. P. | *Brahmāṇḍa Purāṇa*, (MLBD), Delhi 1973 |
| BG | *Bhagavadgitā* |
| Bh. P. | *Bhāgavata Purāṇa*, Bhagavat Vidyapeeth, Ahmedabad |
| Br. | *Brāhmaṇa* (preceded by name such as Śatapatha |
| BS. P. | *Bhaviṣya Purāṇa*, Vishnu Shastri Bapat, Wai. |
| BV. P. | *Brahma Vaivarta Purāṇa*, GM, 1955-57 |
| CC. | *Caturvarga Cintāmaṇi* by Hemādri |
| CVS | *Caraṇa Vyūha* Sūtra by Śaunaka; Com. by Mahidāsa |
| DB | *Devi Bhāgavata*, GM, 1960-61 |
| De or GDAMI. | *The Geographical dictionary of Ancient and Mediaeval India*, N. L. De, Orienta Reprint, Delhi, 1971 |
| Dh. S. | *Dharma Sūtra* (preceded by the author's name such as Gautama) |
| ERE | *Encyclopaedia of Religion and Ethics*—Hastings. |
| GP | *Garuḍa Purāṇa* Ed. R. S. Bhattacharya Chowkhamba, Varanasi, 1964 |

| | |
|---|---|
| GS | *Gṛhya Sūtra* (Preceded by the name of the author such as Āpastamba) |
| HD | *History of Dharma Śāstra*, P. V. Kane, G. O. S. |
| IA | *The Indian Antiquary.* |
| IHQ | *The Indian Historical Quarterly* |
| JP | *Purāṇa* (Journal of the Kashiraj Trust) Varanasi |
| KA | *Kauṭilya Arthaśāstra* |
| KP | *Kūrma Purāṇa*, Veṅkaṭesvara Press Edt. Bombay, also Kashiraj Trust Edt., Varanasi 1971 |
| LP | *Liṅga Purāṇa*, GM, 1960; also MLBD, Delhi, 1981 |
| Manu. | *Manusmṛti* |
| Mbh. | *Mahābhārata*, Gītā Press, Gorakhpur, VS 2014 |
| MkP | *Mārkaṇḍeya Purāṇa* |
| MN | *Mahābhārata Nāmānukramaṇi*, Gītā Press Gorakhpur, VS 2016 |
| MtP. | *Matsya Purāṇa*, GM, 1954 |
| MW | *Monier Williams Sk. English Dictionary* MLBD, Delhi, 1976 |
| NP. | *Nāradiya or Nārada Purāṇa*, Veṅkaṭeśvar Press, Bombay |
| PCK | *Bhāratavarṣiya Prācina Caritrakośa*, Siddheshwar Shastri, Poona, 1968 |
| Pd. P. | *Padma Purāṇa*, GM, 1957-59 |
| PE | *Puranic Encyclopaedia*, V. Mani, English, MLBD, Delhi, 1975 |
| PR or PRHRC | *Puranic Records on Hindu Rites and Customs* R. C. Hazra, Calcutta, 1948 |
| ṚV | *Ṛg-Veda*, Svādhyāya Mandal, Aundh |
| Śat. Br. | *Śatapatha Brāhmaṇa* |
| SC or SMC | *Smṛti Candrikā*—Devanna Bhaṭṭa |
| SEP | *Studies in Epics and Purāṇas*, A.D. Pusalkar Bharatiya Vidya Bhavan (BVB), Bombay |

# INTRODUCTION

*The Term Purāṇa*

According to the definition of the grammarian Pāṇini, the etymologist Yāska and the *Purāṇas* themselves, the word *Purāṇa* is that which is existing from long time past. *Itihāsapurāṇa* is held as the fifth *Veda* in the *Chāndogyopaniṣad* (VII.i.4). The *Vedas* do not use the word *Purāṇa* as referring to the class of literature now known as the *Purāṇas*. The *Brāhmaṇas* refer to the practice of recitation of the *Purāṇas* at the sacrifices. The plural usage *Purāṇāni* in the *Taittiriya āraṇyaka* leads us to infer that during the days of the *Āraṇyakas* the idea of many *Purāṇas* had come into vogue. The *Rāmāyaṇa* of *Vālmiki* refers to the class of literature known as *Purāṇas*. According to *Mahābhārata*,[1] the *Itihāsapurāṇa* had to be used as supplement to *Vedas*. It also declares that the *Veda* is afraid that men of little learning would misinterpret it. The *Arthaśāstra* of Kauṭilya names the *Atharvaveda* and *Itihāsa* as *Vedas* after naming the three *Vedas*—*Ṛg*, *Yajus* and *Sāman*.

According to a tradition found in *Skanda*, *Padma* and *Matsya purāṇas*, the *Purāṇas* were one single literary piece consisting of the three topics *dharma*, *artha* and *kāma*.

From the *Nyāyasūtrabhāṣya* of Vātsyāyana we find that the following three broad divisions of the literature existed—(1) the *Vedas* consisting of the formulae for sacrificial rites and rules relating to them, (2) the *Itihāsa* and *Purāṇa* dealing with the history of world or people and (3) the *Dharmaśāstra* for the determination of *puṇya* and *pāpa* in the world. It seems the last section was also incorporated in the *Purāṇas* in C. 5th or 6th century A.D.

---

1. yo vidyāc caturo vedān sāṅgopaniṣado dvijaḥ /
na cet purāṇaṁ saṁvidyān naiva sa syād vicakṣaṇaḥ //
itihāsapurāṇābhyāṁ vedaṁ samupabṛṁhayet /
bibhetyalpaśrutād vedo mām ayaṁ prahariṣyati //
*Mbh.* 1.2. 645; 1.1. 260

*The Origin of the Purāṇas*

The *Purāṇas* hold identical views regarding the origin of the *Purāṇas* from the mouth of Brahmā, the only point of difference is regarding the time of their origin either before or later to the *Vedas*[1]. While the *Vedas* came out of Brahmā in order, the *Purāṇas* came out at the same time.[2]

The *Purāṇas* are unanimous in their view that Vyāsa made the *Purāṇasaṁhitā* and instructed his pupil Lomaharṣaṇa whom he entrusted the work of spreading it. This is considered to have been at a time when the *Vedas* were divided into four. Vedavyāsa who had the knowledge of the *Purāṇas* is said to have composed the *Purāṇasaṁhitā* based on the *ākhyāna*, *upākhyāna* and *gāthā* etc. While the *ākhyāna* is the narration about an incident which the speaker himself has witnessed, the *upākhyāna* is that which was heard from somebody and retold. *Gāthās* are the metrical quotations found in the *Vedas*, *Brāhmaṇas* etc.

*The definition of the term Purāṇa*:

We also find a traditional definition[3] in some of the *Purāṇas*[4] according to which a *Purāṇa* should comprise the five topics, namely, (1) the primary creation; (2) the secondary creation; (3) the genealogy of gods and sages; (4) the periods of Manu and (5) the accounts of royal genealogy. While some of the *Purāṇas* satisfy this definition, most of them do not.

Almost all the *Purāṇas* contain either briefly or in detail these topics. The first topic Sarga (creation) concerns with the creation of the categories divided into three groups—*Prākṛta*, *Vaikṛta*

---

1. purāṇaṁ sarvaśāstrāṇām prathamam brahmaṇā kṛtam /
anantaraṁ ca vaktrebhyo vedāstasya vinirgatāḥ //
*Mat. P.* 53.3

ṛgyajus sāmātharvākhyān vedān pūrvādibhirmukhaiḥ /
śāstramijyāṁ stutistomam prāyaścittaṁ vyadhāt kramāt //
*Bhāg. P.* III.12.37

2. itihāspurāṇāni pañcamaṁ vedamiśvaraḥ /
sarvebhya eva vaktrebhyaḥ sasṛje sarvadarśanaḥ //
*Bhāg. P.* III.12.39

3. sargaśca pratisargaśca vaṁśo manvantarāṇi ca /
vaṁśānucaritaṁ caiva purāṇam pañcalakṣaṇam //

4. viz. *Mat. P.* 53. 64.

and *Ubhayātmaka*. The first group consists of the following—(1) *mahat*; (2) *ahaṅkāra*; (3) *bhūtatanmātrās*; (4) *indriya* (*jñāna* and *kriyā*); (5) *manas*; (6) *tamas* (*tāmisra, andhatāmisra, tamas, moha* and *mahāmoha*). The second group consists of—(1) *ūrdhva-srotas* (higher orders); (2) *tiryaksrotas* (lower orders) and (3) *arvāksrotas* (middle orders). The last group consists of *Kaumāra-sarga*—creation of Sanaka, Sanandana, Sanātana and Sanat-kumāra.

The second topic, namely, the Pratisarga, describes the different kinds of *pralaya*[1]—*naimittika prākṛtika, nitya* and *ātyantika.* The *naimittika* is that which takes place at the end of Brahmā's one day, i.e., a *kalpa*. It lasts during the period of Brahmā's night. The *prākṛtika* is that in which the seven *prakṛtis* (mahat, ahaṅkāra and the five tanmātrās) merge in that one which was the cause of their origin at the end of *parārdha* (fifty years) of Brahmā's life. The *nitya* is that which takes place every day (nityaḥ sadaiva bhūtānāṁ yo vināśo divāniśam) during the night when all beings go to sleep. The *ātyantika* takes place at the end of hundred years of Brahmā's life.

The third one, the *vaṁśa*, is that which gives an account of the genealogy of the kings and sages belonging to the past, present and future: rājñāṁ brahmaprasūtānāṁ vaṁśastraikāliko'nvayaḥ. (*Bhāg. P.* XII. vii. 16).

The fourth one, the *manvantara* gives the names of Manus, their periods, the names of sages, Indra etc. (manvantaram manurdevā manuputrāḥ sureśvarāḥ / ṛṣayo' ṁśāvatārāśca hareḥ ṣaḍvidhamucyate // (*Bhāg. P.* XII. vii. 15.)

The fifth one, the *vaṁśānucarita* describes the lives of great sages and kings born in a particular lineage (vaṁśānucaritaṁ teṣāṁ vṛttaṁ vaṁśadharāśca ye (*Bhāg. P.* XII. vii. 16.)

However, these topics are very meagrely represented in most of the *Purāṇas*. The above subjects are dealt with in a comparatively abridged form in *Agni P.* and *Gar. P.* and paraphrased in *Vi. P.* There are only three cases of complete description of

1. nityo naimittikaścaiva prākṛto' tyantikastathā /
caturdhāyam purāṇeṣu procyate pratisañcaraḥ //
naimittikaḥ prākṛtikastathaivātyantiko dvija /
nityaśca sarvabhūtānām pralayo'yaṁ caturvidhaḥ //
*Vi. P.* VI. iii.2

these five topics in the *Purāṇa* literature, namely, in the *Brahma. P.*, *Brahmāṇḍa P.*, *Vāy. P.*, and *Mat. P.* Pargiter[1] opined that there was one complete harmonious account from which others were reproduced.

Almost all the *Purāṇas* have a sectarian character according to the cult of the deity they adhere to. This gave rise to new definitions for the *Purāṇas*. According to the *Brahmavaivarta*,[2] the five characteristics are applicable to the *Upapurāṇas* and the *Mahāpurāṇa* must have ten characteristics. The *Bhāgavata*[3] also prescribes ten characteristics for a *Purāṇa*. These are "creation, details of creation, duties of sentient beings, protection of devotees, ages of Manu, dynasties of kings and sages, career of individuals, dissolution of the world, cause of creation and Brahmā". The *Matsyapurāṇa*[4] adds in addition to the above ten characteristics, the following characteristics also—"The glorification of Brahmā, Viṣṇu, Sūrya and Rudra, dissolution and preservation of the world and the four *puruṣārthas*". The *Jayamaṅgalā*, a commentary on the *Arthaśāstra* of Kauṭilya quotes a verse from some old work giving a new set of five topics such as "the creation, existence, destruction, the pursuit of righteousness and liberation" for a *Purāṇa*.

Besides the five topics described above, the *Purāṇas* also contain topics relating to these and flowing legitimately from them. These topics which we generalise as the *dharmaśāstra* teach man about his duties as a student, householder and as an ascetic. Man's ultimate aim is to know about the purpose of his creation and the ultimate goal he has to reach. To achieve this he has to traverse the three purposes of life, namely, the *dharma*, *artha* and *kāma*. One has to follow the path of righteous living and earn wealth for his existence and for distribution to the needy and satisfy his just desires. All these ideals are explained in detail in the *Purāṇas*.

*The eighteen Purāṇas* :

The *vidyās* are counted as eighteen consisting of the four *Vedas*,

---

1. *Parg*. p. 36.
2. IV. 13. 6-9.
3. XII. 7. 9-10.
4. 53. 65-66.

four *Upavedas—Āyurveda* (medicine), *Dhanurveda* (archery), *Gandharvaveda* (music) and *Sthāpatyaśāstra* (mechanics, architecture), six *Vedāṅgas* (auxiliary texts to the *Vedas*), *Purāṇa*, *Nyāya* (dialectics) *Mīmāṁsā*, and *Dharmaśāstra*. The number of *Purāṇas* and *Upapurāṇas* are given as eighteen. The number of sections in the *Mahābhārata* is eighteen. The *Bhagavadgītā* also contains eighteen chapters. The significance for counting their number as eighteen is explained as follows: The functional organs of the body are spoken to be eighteen—the five sense-organs, the five organs of action, the mind, the five vital air, intellect and ego. These are the instruments in the performance of good and bad acts. That is why the branch of learning concerning the rules governing one's acts are reckoned to be eighteen. Moreover the ancient literature[1] and the *Purāṇas* divide the globe into eighteen sections known as *dvīpas*. The *Purāṇas* describe also the creation of eighteen principles *mahat*, *ahaṅkāra*, five sense-organs, five organs of action, mind and five elements.

The sequence in which the *Purāṇas* are enumerated is almost unanimous. There is a short couplet in the *Devībhāgavata*[2] indicating the names of the eighteen *Purāṇas* according to which the eighteen *Purāṇas* are *Matsya*, *Mārkaṇḍeya*, *Bhāgavata*, *Bhaviṣyottara*, *Brahma*, *Brahmavaivarta*, *Brahmāṇḍa*, *Viṣṇu*, *Vāyu*, *Vāmana*, *Varāha*, *Agni*, *Nārada*, *Padma*, *Liṅga*, *Garuḍa*, *Kūrma* and *Skanda*. Although some enumerations read *Śivapurāṇa* instead of *Vāyupurāṇa*, *Vāyupurāṇa* is the genuine *mahāpurāṇa*. Similarly the *Bhāgavata* is the *mahāpurāṇa* and not the *Devībhāgavata*. The *Nārada-purāṇa* (I. 92-109) enumerates their names and also gives an index of their contents, in 18 chapters. The *Matsyapurāṇa* (53), *Agnipurāṇa* (272) and *Skandapurāṇa* (Prabhāsa, 2.28-76) also have similar indices. The traditional order of the enumeration of the *Purāṇas* are also given in some of the *Purāṇas*. The *Brahma* or the *Matsyapurāṇa* is given as the first *purāṇa*. There is no speciality in the uniformity of order in the enumeration of the *Purāṇas*.

---

1. *navadvayadvīpa* in *Naiṣadhīya* I.5 and *aṣṭādaśadvīpanikhātayūpaḥ* in *Raghuvaṁśa* VI. 38.
2. madvayaṁ bhadvayaṁ caiva bratrayaṁ vacatuṣṭayam /
   anāpaliṅgakūskāni purāṇāni pṛthak pṛthak // I.iii.2

The number of verses in the individual *Purāṇas* is also given in some of the *Purāṇas*. On the whole the total number of verses in all the *Purāṇas* together comes to four lakhs.

*The classi cation of the Purāṇas* :

The *Purāṇas* themselves and also the modern scholars have attempted to classify these *Purāṇas* on the basis of the subject matter of the *Purāṇas*[1].

On account of the varied subject matter, the *Agni*, *Garuḍa* and *Nārada purāṇas* are classified as encyclopaedic.

*The Date of composition of the Purāṇas* :

The *Purāṇas* are believed to have been composed during the Gupta rule. The earliest of the *Purāṇas* could have come into existence around the 2nd century, while the latest of them around the 12th century, some of them also have been revised subsequently.

*Philosophy in the Purāṇas* :

Besides the five topics, the *Purāṇas* contain many other topics useful for man's existence and to elevate his thoughts. The philosophical discussions of the different schools are blended together and we have a theistic *Sāṅkhya* and *Aṣṭāṅgayoga*.

*Aṣṭāṅgayoga* :

It is well-known that the *Itihāsapurāṇa* literature has generally the background of a theistic type of *Sāṅkhya-yoga*. It is this prevailing terminology; it has sometimes oriented towards Viṣṇu or Śiva or Devī according to the deity to which the *Purāṇa* is affiliated more specifically.

The *Purāṇas* describe the Trinity of Gods consisting of Śiva, Viṣṇu and Brahmā as a manifestation of one of these three. That God is held as the cause of creation, preservation and destruction. While He is the cause, He is not affected by these activities. He is the form of the universe (*Viśvarūpa*), the immanent soul of the universe (*viśvātman*) and transcending the

1. See Dr. N. Gangadharan, *Liṅgapurāṇa—A Study*, pp. 49-50

universe (*viśvādhika*). Following *Sāṅkhya*[1], *avyakta, mahat, ahaṅkāra, pañcabhūta, pañcatanmātra, pañcakarmendriya, pañcajñānendriya* and mind are the twentyfour *tattvas*. The twenty-fifth *tattva* is the worshipper himself. The twenty-sixth *tattva* is lord Śiva or Viṣṇu as the case may be. Then we find in the *Purāṇa* a good deal of *Sāṅkhya* terminology in the course of the description of the process of creation.

The knowledge of the utilisation of the *Bhagavadgitā* by the *Purāṇas* goes without saying. Dr. Raghavan has made[2] a comprehensive survey and bibliography of *Gitā* thought and expression as found in other parts of the *Mahābhārata* and the *Purāṇa* and *Upapurāṇa* literature.

For example, the *Garuḍapurāṇa* has the following verses:

daivī hyeṣā guṇamayī harermāyā duratyayā /
tāmeva ye prapadyante māyāmetāṁ taranti te // I.219. 30
nainaṁ chindanti śastrāṇi nainaṁ dahati pāvakaḥ /
na cainaṁ kledayantyāpo na śoṣayati Mārutaḥ // II. 1.4.

and

Vāsāṁsi jīrṇāni yathā vihāya
navāni gṛhṇāti naro'parāṇi /
tathā śarīrāṇi vihāya jīrṇā-
nyanyāni gṛhṇāti navāni dehī // II.88. 42

These are the same as *Bhagavadgitā* verses 7.14; 2.23 and 2.22 respectively. The *Liṅgapurāṇa* (ch. 58) mentions the chief of each class of beings which is a patent echo of the *vibhūtiyoga* chapter (X) of the *Bhagavadgitā*.

*Purāṇas of Encyclopaedic nature* :

As already mentioned the *Agni*, *Garuḍa* and *Nāradapurāṇas* are classified as encyclopaedic. They contain varied matter treating of different subjects.

1. iha ṣaḍviṁśako dhyeyo dhyātā vai pañcaviṁśakaḥ /
caturviṁśakamavyaktaṁ mahadādyāstu sapta ca //
mahān tathā tvahaṅkāraṁ tanmātram pañcakam punaḥ /
karmendriyāṇi pañcaiva tathā buddhindriyāṇi ca /
manaśca pañcabhūtāni śivaḥ ṣaḍviṁśakastataḥ //
*Liṅg. P.* I. 28. 7-9a

2. See *Journal of Oriental Research*, Madras II. pp. 86-122. See also N. Gangadharan, The Gitā and the Garuḍapurāṇa, *Dr. Raghavan Ṣaṣṭyabdapūrti Felicitation Volume*, pp. 218-20.

The *Agnipurāṇa* counted as the eighth in the traditional list found in the *Viṣṇupurāṇa*, contains 383 chapters in the Veṅkaṭeśvara Press edition and 382 chapters in the other editions. This is because the Veṅkaṭeśvara Press text contains one extra chapter on the Saṅgrāmavijayavidyā numbered as the 135th chapter. Dr. R. C. Hazra has shown[1] that this *purāṇa* is spurious one. This spurious one has been composed between 700 and 1000 A.D. In spite of its spurious nature it serves as an invaluable piece of document throwing light on the culture of that period. In about 8000 verses it treats of varied topics such as dharma, mantra and tantra, physiognomy, political expediency, genealogy of kings, medicine, equinology, veterinary science, science relating to elephants, metrics, poetics, grammar, lexicography, philosophical inquiries, brief accounts of the epics and the manifestations of lord Viṣṇu, archery and account of Vedic literature. Although the treatment of topics of the five characteristics is very meagre, there is no second thought about the valuable nature of this *Purāṇa*.

The *Agnipurāṇa* follows the general Puranic scheme and embodies theistic *Sāṅkhya* theory of evolution. This we find described in chapter 20. It follows the general scheme and describes the secondary creation in chapters 18 and 19. The creation made by Dakṣa is also narrated herein. So also, it gives an account of the fourteen Manu-periods together with the respective sons, gods, seven sages and Indras in one chapter (chapter 150). Genealogies of the kings of the solar and lunar races are dealt with in six chapters (chapters 273-78). This portion has been pointed out[2] as late recompilation of the material in early *Purāṇas* restating the genealogies in fresh verses in a condensed form. We find here bald pedigrees with hardly any incidental allusions. This is said to follow the *Matsyapurāṇa* tradition.

It is interesting to note that there are many interlocutors such as Agni, Nārada, Hayagrīva, Īśvara, Puṣkara, Rāma, Samudra, Dhanvantari, Pālakāpya, Śālihotra, Skanda, Kumāra and Yama.

We know from Dr. Hazra's scholarly work[3] which of the ver-

1. *Pur. Rec.* pp. 134-140.
2. *Parg.* p. 80.
3. *Pur. Rec.* pp. 318-19 and 338.

ses on dharma quoted by the nibandha writers are traceable or untraceable in the *Agnipurāṇa*.

A brief account of some of the important topics dealt with in this *Purāṇa* would show its utility.[1] It devotes 15 chapters to the description of the manifestations of lord Viṣṇu. It makes use of this opportunity to introduce a summary of the epics, the *Rāmāyaṇa* and the *Mahābhārata*. As in other *Purāṇas*, we find a detailed description of geographical matters in 14 chapters (chapters 107-120). The material on dharma mainly based on the *Manu*, *Nārada* and *Yājñavalkya smṛtis* is spread over 24 chapters (chapters 151-174). This *Purāṇa* describes the various religious observances in chapters 175-200. Political expediency consisting of coronation, duties of the king and council of ministers, law and order, six constituents of state and the like, is explained in chapters 218-242. Medicine based on Suśruta is dealt with in chapters 278-97. Moreover, summary of Piṅgalasūtras on metrics (chapters 323-35), Pāṇini's Śikṣā (phonetics) (chapter 336), Poetics (chapters 337-46), Summary of *Amarakośa* (chapters 359-366), vyavahāra (chapters 253-57) are some of the other important topics dealt with here.

---

1. For a general survey of its contents see S. D. Gyani, *Agnipurāṇa A Study*, Varanasi, 1964 and for individual topics the following : (1) on the *vyavahāra* portion see S. C. Banerji, *Purāṇa* XX. No. 1 (Jan. 1978), pp. 38-56. (2) On the mantras see Andre Padoux, *Purāṇa* XX. No. 1., pp. 57-65. (3) On the Temple Architecture see Tahsildar Singh, *Purāṇa* XXIII. No. 2 (July 1981), pp. 188-200. (4) On the date of composition of the *Agni. P.* see Parasnath Dvivedi, *Agra University Journal of Research* (Letters) Vol. XIX. Pt. II (July 1971), pp. 75-86.

# CHAPTER ONE

## *Introductory*

1. I bow to (goddesses) Śrī (Lakṣmī), Sarasvatī, Gaurī (Pārvatī) and gods Gaṇeśa, Skanda, Īśvara (Śiva), Brahmā, Vahni, Indra and other celestials and Vāsudeva (Kṛṣṇa).

2. Śaunaka and other sages (staying at the sacred forest) of Naimiṣa, conducting a sacrifice devoted to Hari (Viṣṇu), welcomed Sūta (the reciter of ancient lores) on his arrival there after a pilgrimage.

*The sages said* :

3. O Sūta ! You are adored by us. Tell us the quintessence of all things, by knowing which alone one gets omniscience.

*Sūta said* :

4. The illustrious Viṣṇu (who is) the Supreme Being (and) the Creator, is the quintessence. By know ng that 'I am *Brahman*', one gets omniscience.

5. Two *Brahmans* are to be known, the *Śabdabrahman* (the *Vedas*) and *Parabrahman* (the Supreme Spirit). The *Ātharvaṇī Śruti* (*Muṇḍakopaniṣad*) refers to this as the two (kinds of) knowledge to be learnt.

6. Myself, (sage) Śuka (son of sage Vyāsa), (sage) Paila (disciple of sage Vyāsa) and others bowed Vyāsa having resorted to the hermitage at (holy) Badarikāśrama. He imparted to us the quintessence (of all things).

*Vyāsa said* :

7. O sūta, listen in the company of Śuka and others what Vasiṣṭha has said to me about the excellent quintessence of the *Brahman*, when he was requested by the sages.

*Vasiṣṭha said* :

8. O Vyāsa, Listen, in entirety, to the two (kinds of) knowl-

edge, which (god) Agni narrated to me in the company of the sages and the celestials.

9. The excellent *Purāṇa* (known as) the *Āgneya* (or *Agni*) and the two (kinds of) knowledge, *Parā* (the superior) and *Aparā* (the inferior) signifying respectively the knowledge about the *Brahman* and the knowledge about the *Ṛgveda* and so on, which satisfies all the celestials (will be narrated to you).

10. The *Purāṇa* spoken by Agni and designated as the *Āgneya* by Brahmā and which gives *bhukti* (enjoyment) and *mukti* (release from mundane existence) for those who read it or hear it (will be narrated to you).

11. Being requested by the sages (I will also describe) (god) Viṣṇu in the form of the destructive Fire at the end of the world (who is) the effulgent *Brahman* (and) the most Supreme Being (who is) worshipped by means of knowledge and action (religious rites and so on).

*Vasiṣṭha said* :

12. O *Brahman* (Agni), point out to me the masterly way of crossing the ocean of mundane existence, by knowing the quintessence of which knowledge one becomes omniscient.

*Agni said* :

13. Viṣṇu is the destructive Fire at the end of the world (in the form of) Rudra (Śiva). I shall tell you the essence of knowledge (in the form of) this *Purāṇa*, which represents all learning and is the cause of all things.

14. (Lord) Viṣṇu, who assumes the form of a fish, a tortoise (and other beings), is the cause of the primary creation, the secondary creation, the genealogy of the sages, the cycles of Manu-periods and the genealogy of the kings.

15-17. O Twice-born ! (Lord) Viṣṇu (is the cause of) the two kinds of knowledge *Parā* (the superior) and *Aparā* (the inferior). Here the *Aparā* is represented by the *Ṛgveda*, *Yajurveda*, *Sāmaveda*, *Atharvaveda*, the six supplementary texts, (namely)—*Śikṣā* (phonetics), *Kalpa* (rules governing rituals), *Vyākaraṇa* (grammar), *Nirukta* (etymological science), (the science dealing with) the movement of the luminary bodies, *Chandovidhāna* (metrics), *Mīmāṁsā* (investigation of the interpretation of the ritual of the *Vedas*), *Dharmaśāstra* (law -books), *Purāṇas* (18 in number), *Nyāya* (logical philosophical system), *Vaidya* (medical science), *Gāndharva* (science of music), and *Arthaśāstra* (polity). The *Parā-Vidyā* (superior knowledge) is that through which the *Brahman* is known.

18. I shall narrate to you (that *Purāṇa*) which was told to me by Viṣṇu and the celestials by Brahmā and which deals with that invisible, incomprehensible, not having a cause for itself and eternal (form of Viṣṇu) which is the cause of the forms such as the fish and others.

## CHAPTER TWO

### *Manifestation of Viṣṇu as Fish*

*Vasiṣṭha said* :

1. O Brahmā ! Describe unto me the manifestations of Viṣṇu, such as the Fish etc., which are the cause of creation. Also narrate to me the *Agni Purāṇa* as heard from Viṣṇu in the days of yore.

*Agni said* :

2. O Vasiṣṭha ! I shall describe to you the manifestation of Hari as a Fish. Listen. The manifestations are for the destruction of the wicked and for the protection of the pious.

3. At the end of the past *kalpa* (of 432 million years), there was a periodical dissolution. Brahmā was its instrumental cause. O sage ! the earth and the people were submerged under the rising water.

4-5. Vaivasvata Manu was practising penance for gaining objects of enjoyment and for release from mundane existence.

Once when he was offering waters of libation in the (river) Kṛtamālā, a small fish came in the waters in his folded palms. As he desired to throw it into the waters, it said "O excellent man ! do not throw me away.

6. Now I have fear from the crocodiles (and others)." Having heard this (Vaivasvata Manu) put it into a vessel. When

it had grown there in size, it requested him, "Get me a bigger vessel".

7. Having heard these words, the king put the fish in a bigger vessel. Growing there again in size it requested the king, "O Manu ! Get me a bigger place".

8. When it was put into a tank, it soon grew in size as big as it (the tank) and said, "Get me to a bigger place". Then (Manu) put it into the ocean.

9. In a moment, it grew in size extending to a lakh of *yojanas* (one *yojana* 8 or 9 miles). Seeing that wonderful fish, Manu got surprised and said :

10. "Who are you, but Viṣṇu ? O Nārāyaṇa (Viṣṇu) I salute you. Why do you stupefy me with your illusory power, O Janārdana (Viṣṇu)".

11. Having heard the words of Manu, the Fish replied Manu who had been engaged in the protection (of the world), "I have manifested for the protection of this universe and for the destruction of the wicked."

12-13. On the seventh day, the ocean would flood the earth. Having put the seeds (of creation) etc. in the boat that would approach you, you would spend the night (of 1000 mortal years) of Brahmā on it being encircled by the seven sages. (You) bind this boat to my horn with the big serpent.".

14. Saying thus, the fish disappeared. Manu, who was waiting for the appointed hour, boarded the boat as the ocean commenced to swell.

15. The fish now appeared with a single golden horn of one million *yojanas* in length. He tied the boat to its horn.

16-17. After having praised it with adoration, he heard from the fish the *Purāṇa* known as the *Matsya* which is capable of destroying the sins. Keśava (Viṣṇu) killed the demon Hayagrīva,[1] the destroyer of the *Vedas* of *Brahman* and thus protected the vedic *mantras*. And when the *Varāhakalpa* (one of the periods of time) set in, Hari (Viṣṇu) assumed the form of a tortoise.

---

1. Hayagriva was the name of a powerful demon, who carried away the *Vedas* during Deluge. He was killed by Viṣṇu manifesting as a fish and the *Vedas* were rescued. *Bhāg. P.* VIII. xxiv. 8 and 57 *P. Index* III. p. 742.

# CHAPTER THREE

## *Manifestation of Viṣṇu as a Tortoise*

*Agni said* :

1. I shall describe unto you (now) about the manifestation (of Viṣṇu) as a tortoise, by hearing which one's sins will be destroyed. In days of yore the celestial gods were defeated by the demons in a battle between them.

2. On account of the curse of sage Durvāsas,[1] the celestials were deprived of all their prosperity. Then they praised Viṣṇu who was (reclining) in the milky ocean and said, "Protect us from the demons".

3. Hari said to Brahmā and others, "You make a treaty of peace with the demons for churning the ocean for securing ambrosia.

4. In the interest of an important work even the enemies should be sought for union. I will make you get the ambrosia and not the demons.

5. Making the (Mount) Mandara as the churning rod and (the serpent) Vāsuki as the rope, you vigilantly churn the milky ocean with my help".

6. Concluding an agreement with the demons as suggested by Viṣṇu, (the celestials) came to the milky ocean. The celestials began to churn the ocean (from that side) where the tail of the serpent was.

7. The celestials who were afflicted by the sighs of the serpent, were comforted by Hari (Viṣṇu). As the ocean was being churned the mountain being unsupported entered into the water.

8. Then Viṣṇu assumed the form of a tortoise and supported the (Mount) Mandara. From the milky ocean which was being churned, first came out the poison known as *Hālāhala*.

9. That poison being retained by Hara (Śiva) in his neck, Śiva became (known to be) Nīlakaṇṭha (blue-necked). Then the goddess Vāruṇī (The female energy of the celestial god

---

1. Name of an irascible sage, son of Sage Atri and Anasūyā. Once he met a Vidyādhara maid with a garland. He took that garland and presented it to Indra. Indra put it on his elephant, which in turn threw it on the ground and trampled upon it. Enraged at this the sage cursed him that he would lose all his fortune. See *Vi.P.* I. ix. 1 ff.; *P. Index* II. p. 106.

Varuṇa), the *Pārijāta* (tree) and the *Kaustubha* (gem) came out of the ocean.

10. Then came out the (celestial) kine and the nymphs. Then came out Lakṣmī, who became the consort of Hari (Viṣṇu). Beholding her and adoring her all the celestials regained their lost prosperity.

11. Then Dhanvantari, (a form of Viṣṇu) and founder of the (science of) *Āyurveda* rose up holding a water-pot full of ambrosia.

12. Taking the ambrosia from his hands the demons Jambha and others having given half of it to the celestials went away with the other half. Then Viṣṇu assumed the form of beautiful damsel.

13. Having seen that beautiful form, the demons became fascinated and said, "O fair-faced one ! Be our wife, take this ambrosia and make us drink it."

14-15. Hari (Viṣṇu) said, "Let it be so", and took it from them and made the celestials drink it. As Rāhu assumed the form of the Moon and drank a portion, he was detected by the Sun and the Moon and was brought to the notice of (Viṣṇu). His head was severed by his enemy Hari (Viṣṇu). That severed head of Rāhu then said to Hari, the bestower of gifts (by whose grace) it had attained immortality.

16. "When the intoxicated Rāhu would seize the Sun and the Moon, may the charities made on that occasion be imperishable."

17. Viṣṇu in the company of all the immortals said, "Be it so" and cast off his female form. He was then requested by Hara to show that form (again).

18. (Lord) Hari (Viṣṇu) showed the feminine form to Rudra (Śiva). Śambhu (Śiva) being captivated by the illusory power, renouncing Gaurī (Pārvatī) sought that feminine form.

19. Becoming nude and behaving like a mad man, he held the damsel by her hair. She got herself freed and ran away. He too followed her.

20. Wherever the seminal fluid of Hara dropped, there came into being sacred places of liṅgas and gold.

21. Then knowing her as illusory, Hara (Śiva) assumed his original form. Then Hari (Viṣṇu) told Śiva, "O Rudra (Śiva) My illusory power has been conquered by you.

22-23. There is no other male on the earth besides you, who is capable of conquering this illusory power of mine." Then the demons, who had not got the ambrosia were defeated by the celestials in battle. The celestials got back to their celestial home. One who reads this account goes to the celestial region.

## CHAPTER FOUR

### *Manifestations of Viṣṇu as the Boar*

1. I describe (unto thee) the manifestation as a Boar (which) removes (one's) sins. Hiraṇyākṣa[1] was a demon chief. He conquered the celestials and got established in the heavens.

2. Viṣṇu being praised by the celestials (who had) gone (to him), (he) assumed the form as Yajñavarāha (boar). Having killed that demon along with the (other) demons (he made the earth) devoid of thorns (difficulties).

3-4. (That) Hari, the protector of righteousness and the celestials (then) disappeared. Then (the demon) Hiraṇyakaśipu,[2] brother of Hiraṇyākṣa after conquering the celestials (was grabbing a share of the offerings) exercised control over all the celestials. (Viṣṇu) assumed the form of Narasiṁha (human body with lion's face) (and) killed him along with the (other) demons.

---

1. Hiraṇyākṣa, a demon, was one of the sons of Kaśyapa and Diti. He waxed eloquent and entered the underworld in search of Viṣṇu. Viṣṇu assumed the form of a boar and after severe combat slew the demon. See *P. Index* III. *C.* 774.

2. Hiraṇyakaśipu, a demon, was the other son of Kaśyapa and Diti. He had got a boon that he could not be killed either by a man or by a beast or during the day or the night or inside or outside the house. He conquered the celestials. His son Prahlāda was a devotee of Viṣṇu. All the attempts of Hiraṇyakaśipu to wean Prahlāda from his devotion to Viṣṇu were of no avail. Hiraṇyakaśipu subjected Prahlāda to many ordeals. Prahlāda emerged unscathed. The desperate Hiraṇyakaśipu challenged Prahlāda whether that Viṣṇu would be present everywhere and Prahlāda could show him in the pillar in front of them and kicked the pillar. Viṣṇu manifested in the form of a man with lion's face from that pillar and killed Hiraṇyakaśipu placing him on his lap and at the thresh-hold during the twilight. See *P. Index* III. pp. 769-70.

5-7. (He) re-established the celestials in their original places and was praised by the celestials. Once in the battle between the celestials and the demons, the celestials were defeated by (demon) Bali[1] and other demons (and) were driven away from the heaven (and) sought refuge in Hari (Viṣṇu). Having given refuge to the *devas* he being praised by Aditi (wife of the latter) (and mother of the celestials) and Kaśyapa (a sage) became a Dwarf (as a son) of Aditi (and) went to the sacrifice (performed by Bali) (and) recited the *Vedas* at the royal gates of Bali the sacrificer.

8-9. Having heard him reciting the *Vedas*, the bestower of the wanted things (Bali) said to the Dwarf in spite of being obstructed by Śukra (the preceptor of the demons), "Whatever (you) desire I shall give (you)". The Dwarf asked Bali, "Get (me) three feet of space for the sake of the preceptor. (Bali) said to him, "I shall give (you)".

10-11. When the water was poured on the hand the Dwarf became a Giant (and) measured the worlds of *Bhūḥ*, *Bhuvaḥ* and *Svar* with the three strides and (sent) Bali to *Sutala* (a nether world) and (then) Hari (Viṣṇu) gave the worlds to Śakra (Indra). Śakra (Indra) praised Hari (Viṣṇu) along with the celestials (and) remained happy as the ruler of the world.

12-13. "I shall describe (unto you) the manifestation as Paraśurāma." "Hear, O twice-born" ! Considering the *kṣatriyas* (ruling clan) as haughty, Hari (Viṣṇu), the protector of the celestials and the brahmins manifested as Bhārgava, son of Jamadagni and Reṇukā and proficient in arms for removing the pressure on the earth and for the sake of peace. [Manifestation of Viṣṇu as Paraśurāma]

14. Kārtavīrya became a king by the grace of Dattātreya (considered as a manifestation of the Trinity as son of Atri and Anasūyā). He had thousand arms. He was the lord of the entire world. (Once) he went for hunting.

1. Bali was a powerful demon. He was a son of Virocana and grandson of Prahlāda. Being oppressed by him, the celestials sought refuge in Viṣṇu. In deference to their wishes, Viṣṇu assumed the form of a dwarf and approached Bali and requested him to give as much earth as he could cover in three steps. Bali readily conceded to his request. The dwarf soon grew into a mighty form, covered the earth and heaven in two strides and as the third stride placed his foot on the head of Bali and subdued him. See *Rām.* I. xxvii.; *P. Index* II. pp. 469-70

15. (He) being tired, was invited by the sage Jamadagni. The king was fed along with his retinue (by the sage) by the grace of the *Kāmadhenu* (divine cow).

16-20. (The king) sought for the *Kāmadhenu*. When he (the sage) did not give (the cow) the king took it away. Then Rāma (Paraśurāma) cut off (the king's) head with his axe in the battle. The cow returned to the hermitage. Jamadagni was killed by the sons of Kārtavīrya on account of revenge, when (Paraśu) Rāma had gone to the forest. Seeing his father slain (and) getting angry on account of the loss of his father the great man made the earth devoid of the warrior clan for 21 generations. Making out five pits (*kuṇḍa*) at Kurukṣetra and satisfying his manes, having given the earth to Kaśyapa, (he) stationed himself at the Mahendra mountains. (One) who hears (the story of) the manifestations as a Fish, a Boar, a Lion and Rāma (Paraśurāma) goes to the celestial regions.

## CHAPTER FIVE

### *Manifestation of Viṣṇu as Rāma* :

*Agni said* :

1. I shall describe (unto you) the (story of) Rāmāyaṇa, as it (was) once described by Nārada to Vālmiki (and which) if read in that manner yields enjoyment and release (from mundane existence).

*Nārada said* :

2. Brahmā (was born) from the lotus in the navel of Viṣṇu. (Sage) Marīci (was) the son of Brahmā. (Sage) Kaśayapa (was) then (born) from Marīci. The Sun (god) (and) Vaivasvata Manu (were born successively in the line).

3. Then from him (Vaivasvata Manu), Ikṣvāku (was born). Kakutstha (was born) in his line. Raghu (was the son) of Kakutstha. Aja (was born) to him. Then Daśaratha (was born).

4-7. Hari (Viṣṇu) manifested himself in the four (forms) for the sake of the annihilation of Rāvaṇa and others. Rāma was born from Daśaratha to Kauśalyā, Bharata to Kaikeyī and Lakṣmaṇa and Śatrughna to Sumitrā simultaneously from partaking of the sweet gruel obtained from (the performance) of the sacrifice of the father. The king being requested by (the sage) Viśvāmitra for the annihilation of those who impede (the performance) of the sacrifices sent Rāma and Lakṣmaṇa along with the sage. Rāma who had gone (with the sage) (and) was taught in the use of the weapons (*astra*[1] and *śastra*)[2] (became) the killer of (the demoness) Tāṭakā.[3]

8. (Rāma) made (demon) Mārīca[4] stupefied by the missile (known as) *Mānava* and led him far away. The valiant killed also (the demon) Subāhu, the destroyer of sacrifices along with his army.

9. Residing at the (place) Siddhāśrama[5] along with (the sages) Viśvāmitra and others, (Rāma) went along with his brother to see the sacrifice (test for prowess) of Maithila (King Janaka).

10-12. At the instance of (the sage) Śatānanda[6] and on account of the glory of Viśvāmitra, that sage being shown due respects by the king at the sacrifice and Rāma being informed sportively pulled the bow and broke it. (King) Janaka gave Sītā, the girl not born of the womb, and associated with a prize bid, to Rāma. And when the parents had come, Rāma also

---

1-2. The word *astra* denotes a weapon discharged along with the repetition of the mystic syllables, whereas '*śastra*' is any ordinary missile.

3. Tāṭakā was a female fiend, daughter of Suketu. She was the wife of Sunda and mother of Mārica. She had been changed into a fiend by the sage Agastya when she had disturbed his austerities.

Although Rāma was at first reluctant to raise his bow against a woman, she was later killed by him, at the instance of Viśvāmitra, when she disturbed the sacrificial performances of Viśvāmitra. See *Rām*. I.xxv-xxvi.

4. Mārica was a demon, son of Sunda and Tāṭakā. He was the uncle of Rāvaṇa. *Rām*. I.xxiv. 26-27

5. Siddhāśrama was the place where Viṣṇu manifested as the Dwarf to subdue the demon Bali, and also where the aspirants realized their ambitions. See *Rām*. I. xxix.

6. Śatānanda was the son of sage Gautama and Ahalyā and was the family priest of Janaka. See *Rām*. I.li.1.

married that Jānakī (Sītā). In the same way Lakṣmaṇa (also married) Urmilā.

13-14. Then Śatrughna and Bharata married Śrutakīrti and Māṇḍavī, the two daughters of the brother of Janaka. Rāma after conquering Jāmadagni (Paraśurāma, son of Jamadagni) went to Ayodhyā with (sage) Vasiṣṭha and others and Bharata with Śatrughna went towards (the country of) Yudhājit (uncle of Bharata).

## CHAPTER SIX

### *Manifestation of Viṣṇu as Rāma (continued)* :

*Nārada said* :

1-2. After Bharata had gone, Rāma saluted the parents and others. King Daśaratha said to Rāma, "Rāghava (Rāma) ! listen to me, you have been anointed mentally by the people as ruler on account of (your) qualities. I shall make you the heir-apparent (next) morning."

3-4. "In the night you observe (the necessary) rites (vows) along with Sītā." And the eight ministers[1] of the king—Sṛṣṭi, Jayanta, Vijaya, Siddhārtha, Rāṣṭravardhana, Aśoka, Dharmapāla and Sumantra and also Vasiṣṭha spoke.

5. After hearing the words of the father and others, Rāghava said that he will do accordingly. He worshipped the gods and informed the news to Kauśalyā.

6. The king told Vasiṣṭha and others to gather the materials required for the coronation of Rāma and went to Kaikeyī.

7. After seeing the decoration of the city of Ayodhyā and knowing that the coronation of Rāma is to take place, Mantharā informed her friend Kaikeyī (accordingly).

8. Having been pulled by Rāma by the foot by mistake, on account of that enmity she desired of Rāma's sojourn to the forest.

1. Some of the names of the ministers are little different from those found in the *Rāmāyaṇa*. Instead of the name Dṛṣṭi, Arthasādhaka and Mantrapāla in the *Rāmāyaṇa* we have Sṛṣṭi, Rāṣṭravardhana and Dharmapāla here. See *Rām*. I. vii.3.

9. "O ! Kaikeyī ! you get up (and see) the anointment of Rāma. There is no doubt (that it is) death (itself) for your son, to me and to you" (said Mantharā).

10-11. She (Kaikeyī) heard the words of the *kubjā* (hunch-backed) (Mantharā) and gave her an ornament. She said "Just as Rāma is (my son) so also Bharata is my son. I do not find any plan, by which Bharata may get the kingdom." The angry Mantharā after rejecting the ornament (given by Kaikeyī) said to Kaikeyī :

12. "O ! stupid girl you protect Bharata, yourself and me from Rāghava. Rāghava will be the king in future and then his son."

13-15. O Kaikeyī, "The royal lineage will be taken away from Bharata. Once when the people were persecuted by Śambara[1] at the time of the battle between the gods and demons, when the king went there for (rendering help), you protected him by your art and skill. Then the king gave you two boons. (You) ask for them now from the king. (The boons are) the stay of Rāma in the forest for fourteen years and the conferment of the heir-apparentship on Bharata. These (the king) will give."

16. She (Kaikeyī) being encouraged by the deformed lady (Mantharā), who saw meaning in the worthless thing, said (to her), "(Tell) me a good plan which would make it work."

17-18. (Kaikeyī) having entered the anger apartment (remained) in a swoon fallen to the ground. Then the king Daśaratha having honoured the twice-borns (came there and) saw the angry Kaikeyī (and) said, "How (is) she such ? Is she sick or agitated by fear," (and said) "I shall do as you wish".

19. "Without which Rāma, I cannot live (even) a moment, I swear by him that I will do as you wish O beautiful woman !"

20-22. "Speak the truth", said she to the king (and added), "The two boons (you) granted me formerly, you give me (now) (as you swear) by truth, O King ! Let Rāma live in the forest for fourteen years being self-controlled (and) with these preparations let Bharata be installed here this day itself (and) if you

1. Śambara was a demon chief, son of Kaśyapa and Danu. At the time of the battle between the celestials and the demons Śambara was harassing the people. Indra sought help from Daśaratha. Daśaratha who lost his consciousness in the battle was safely charioted back by Kaikeyī. See *Rām.* I. ix. 11 ff.

do not grant (these boons) O King ! I shall die (after) drinking poison." Having heard these (words) the (king) fell into a swoon on the earth as if struck by a mace.

23-25. After a moment he regained his consciousness and said, "What (harm) was done to you by Rāma or by me, O lady, determined to do sins ! What you tell me in this manner is unpleasant to all the people. By merely doing (something) pleasing to you, I will be censured. What a kind of wife (you are) like the night of destruction[1] at the end of the world. Bharata is not such a kind of son. (You) rule the kingdom as a widower after I have died and the son has gone."

26-29. Being bound by the noose of truth, (he) called Rāma and said (to him), "O ! Rāma, I have been cheated by Kaikeyī; restraining me (you) rule the kingdom. You have to live in the forest and Bharata, (the son of) Kaikeyī (is to be) the king." Having saluted his father and Kaikeyī, after doing a circumambulation, and bowing down to Kauśalyā and having consoled her and with Lakṣmaṇa, with (his) wife Sītā and with Sumantra in the chariot and having made the gifts for the brahmins, poor and destitutes, he left the city with the mothers, brahmins and others stricken with grief.

30. Having spent the night on the banks of the (river) Tamasā (he went away) leaving the people. Not finding him in the morning they all returned to Ayodhyā again.

31. The lamenting king also went to the apartments of Kauśalyā extremely grief-stricken. Being separated from the king all the citizens and women wept.

32. Rāma, being seated in the chariot and wearing the bark-garments went to Śṛṅgaberapura. Being entertained by Guha[2] there, he resorted to the foot of the Iṅdgudī (tree).

33-34. And during the nights Lakṣmaṇa and Guha kept awake. Leaving Sumantra together with the chariot in the morning, Rāma, Lakṣmaṇa and Sītā crossed the river Jāhnavī (Ganges) by boat and reached Prayāga. (They) paid their obeisance to (the sage) Bharadvāja (and then) reached the Citrakūṭa mountain.

---

1. *Kālarātrī*, the night of destruction at the end of the world is identified with the Goddess Durgā.

2. Guha, a hunter chief was reigning at Śṛṅgaberapura. He was an admirer of Rāma. See *Rām.* II.1.33.

35. Then (they) having performed the *Vāstupūjā* (propitiatory rites at the house site), stayed on the banks of the Mandākinī (Ganges). And (then) Rāghava showed the Citrakūṭa (mountain) to Sītā.

36. With an arrow (Rāma) plucked one of the eyes of the crow which was tearing her (Sītā) with (its) nails. Then the crow sought refuge in the celestials.

37-40. On the sixth day after Rāma had gone to the forest, the king told Kauśalyā in the night the past story of how in (his) youth he had killed unknowingly with (his) *Śabdabheda*[1] (weapon) the ascetic youth Yajñadatta as (he was filling) the pot raising asound. Lamenting his father cursed (Daśaratha). His mother felt grief-stricken and wept again and again and the (two) said, "We will die without the son. You will also die of grief." "O Kauśalyā ! without the son and remembering (the past) my death (will come off now) on account of grief." After narrating this story and uttering (the words) "Alas ! Rāma !", the king passed away.

41-42. Thinking that the king was sleeping, Kauśalyā also slept on account of pangs of grief. Early in the morning the singers and bards such as the *sūtas*, *māgadhas*, the awakeners attempt ed to wake him up. He did not wake up and was dead. Knowing him as dead, Kauśalyā said, "O I have been ruined."

43. The men and women then wept. Then Bharata along with Śatrughna was hurriedly brought to the city from the royal palace by Vasiṣṭha and others.

44. Having seen the grief-stricken Kaikeyī he reproached (her) out of grief. "(You) have made censure fall on the head" and praised Kauśalyā.

45-46. Having done the funeral rites of his father (whose body was kept preserved) in oil in oval vessel on the banks of the river Sarayū, when (he) was asked by Vasiṣṭha and others to rule the kingdom, he said, "I go now to bring back Rāma. Rāma is the king stronger than myself". (He went) to Śṛṅgavera and to Prayāga where he was entertained by Bharadvāja.

47-48. Having saluted Bharadvāja, (Bharata) came to

1. *Śabdabheda* was a missile capable of reaching a mark merely by the sound associated with the mark, the object itself not being perceived.

Rāma and Lakṣmaṇa (and said), "O Rāma ! Our father has reached the heaven. You become the king of Ayodhyā. I will go to the forest adhering to your command." Having heard this, Rāma (after) giving him water asked him to go (back) taking the sandals.

49. (Bharata said), "I will not go to the city. I swear, I will be remaining with matted locks." On being urged by Rāma, Bharata returned to Nandigrāma and stationed there with his army, leaving the sandal at Ayodhyā and worshipping it ruled over the kingdom.

## CHAPTER SEVEN

### *Manifestation of Viṣṇu as Rāma (continued)* :

*Nārada said* :

1-2. Rāma bowed to Vasiṣṭha, the mothers, (sage) Atri and his wife Anasūyā, (sages) Śarabhaṅga[1] and Sutīkṣṇa, the brother of Agastya and Agastya and reached the Daṇḍaka forest having obtained the bow and sword by the grace of (Agastya).

3. He was staying at Pañcavaṭī in the Janasthāna on the banks of the (river) Godāvarī. The awful (demoness) Śūrpaṇakhā[2] came there to devour them all.

4-5. Seeing the beautiful form of Rāma, that lustful (woman) said to him, "Who are you ? Whence have you come ? You become my husband being entreated by me. I shall eat these two." So saying to him she approached them. On the words of Rāma, Lakṣmaṇa cut off her nose and ears.

6-7. She returned to her brother Khara with blood oozing out (and) said, "I shall die without a nose. I would live, O Khara ! only when you would make me drink the hot blood of Sītā, the wife of Rāma and Lakṣmaṇa, his brother.

8. Khara said to her that he will do so and went there with

---

1. Śarabhaṅga was a sage who entered the fire in the presence of Rāma and ascended heavens with a glowing body by the merits of his austerities. On his advice Rāma met another sage Sutīkṣṇa. *Rām*. III. v. and vii.

2. Śūrpaṇakhā was the sister of Rāvaṇa, the king of Laṅkā and of Khara, the ruler of Janasthāna.

Dūṣaṇa, Triśiras and 14000 demons in order to fight (with Rāma).

9-10. Rāma also fought well and killed the demons with his arrows and led the army consisting of the elephants, cavalry, chariots and infantry together with the fighting Triśiras, Khara and Dūṣaṇa[1] to death. Śūrpaṇakhā went to Laṅkā and fell down on the earth in front of Rāvaṇa.

11-13. (And) said to Rāvaṇa angrily, "You are neither a king, nor a protector. You abduct Sītā, the wife of Rāma, the killer of Khara and others. I will live only after drinking the blood of Rāma and Lakṣmaṇa and not by anything else." Having heard her Rāvaṇa also said yes and said to Mārīca, "You move in front of Sītā in the form of a golden deer drawing Rāma and Lakṣmaṇa away. I will carry her away. Otherwise you will be dead."

14-15. Mārīca[2] said to Rāvaṇa, "Rāma with his bow is verily the god of death himself." "Either I have to die at the hands of Rāvaṇa or at the hands of Rāghava (Rāma). If I have to die, it is better (to die at the hands of) Rāma than Rāvaṇa. Having thought so (Mārīca) became a deer and roamed in front of Sītā again and again.

16. Being entreated by Sītā, Rāma (ran after that deer and) then killed that with an arrow. As it was dying, the deer said "O Sītā and O Lakṣmaṇa."[3]

17-20. Then Saumitri (Lakṣmaṇa) being told inconsistent (words) by Sītā went (in search) of Rāma. Rāvaṇa also abducted Sītā, having wounded the vulture Jaṭāyu,[4] and being wounded by Jaṭāyu, carrying Sītā on the lap reached Laṅkā, kept (her) guarded in the *Aśoka* (grove) and said (to her), "You become my wife. You will be kept as the foremost." Having killed Mārīca, Rāma saw Lakṣmaṇa and said (to him), "O Saumitri ! this is a phantom deer. By the time you had come here, Sītā

1. Dūṣaṇa and Triśiras were the commanders of Khara.

2. Mārīca remembered his past miserable experience at the sacrificial site of Viśvāmitra. See V. 8 above.

3. Mārīca imitated the voice of Rāma while crying aloud.

4. Jaṭāyu, the vulture was an intimate friend of king Daśaratha. He obstructed the path of Rāvaṇa on hearing the wails of Sītā, and was fatally wounded and died after being seen by Rāma and Lakṣmaṇa.

would have been taken away certainly." Then he did not find her as he returned (to that place).

21. He lamented with grief (and said), "Where have you (Sītā) gone discarding me?" Being comforted by Lakṣmaṇa, Rāma began to search for Jānakī (Sītā).

22. Having seen him, Jaṭāyu told that Rāvaṇa had carried her away. He (Jaṭāyu) then died. (Rāma) performed his obsequies. He then killed (the demon) Kabandha.[1] Getting free from a curse, he (Kabandha) said to Rāma, "You go to Sugrīva."

## CHAPTER EIGHT

### *Manifestation of Viṣṇu as Rāma (continued)*

*Nārada said* :

1. Having gone to the lake of Pampā, Rāma stayed there (that) night thinking (of what to do). Then he was (met and) taken to Sugrīva by Hanūmat. Rāma made friendship (with Sugrīva).

2. After having pierced the seven *Tāla* trees with a single arrow and (even as others) were seeing, threw away the body of Dundubhi[2] by his foot to a distance of ten *yojanas*.

3-4. Having killed Vālin,[3] his (Sugrīva's) enemy, who had been the cause of enmity, he bestowed on him the monkey-kingdom of Kiṣkindhā (as well as) Rumā and Tārā on the Ṛṣya-

---

1. Kabandha was a heavenly being at first and was later cursed by the sage Sthūlaśiras and Indra to become an ugly-shaped demon as he tormented the other ascetics and was told that he would regain his original form after he met Rāma and died at his hands. See *Rām*. III. lxxi. 1-16.

2. Dundubhi was a powerful demon slain by Vālin, the brother of Sugrīva. When Sugrīva showed to Rāma the skeleton of this demon to show how powerful Vālin was, Rāma gently kicked it and threw it many miles away. See *Rām*. IV. xi. 24 ff.

3. When Māyāvin, the eldest son of Dundubhi, a demon, challenged Vālin, Vālin chased him. Māyāvin entered a cave and Vālin also followed suit. Sugrīva, who had gone with his brother and was asked by his brother to

mūka (mountains). That ruler of Kiṣkindhā (Sugrīva) told (Rāma), "I will do in such a way, O Rāma ! by which you will be getting back Sītā".

5-7. Having heard that, he (Rāma) spent the four months on the Mālyavat (mountain). As Sugrīva had not come to Kiṣkindhā to see (Rāma), Lakṣmaṇa (met him and) spoke to him the words of Rāma, " (You) go to Rāghava. The way in which Vālin was killed is not yet closed. O Sugrīva ! You stand by at this juncture. Do not take to the course of Vālin." Sugrīva said, "I did not realize the elapse of time on account of my preoccupation."

8-9. Saying so, he (Lakṣmaṇa) went away. The lord of the monkeys (Sugrīva) (approached) Rāma, bowed and said, "All the monkeys have been brought in order to search for Sītā. As desired by you, I shall send them. Let them search for Jānakī in the (direction of) east etc. Let them return in a month. (If they come) after a month I will kill them."

10. So saying (he sent monkeys in all directions). The monkeys sent towards the eastern, western and northern routes came (back) to Rāma and Sugrīva not finding Jānakī.

11. Having taken the signet ring of Rāma, Hanūmat together with other monkeys searched in the south in the caves of Suprabhā (mountain).

12-16. And being engaged for more than a month and not being able to find Jānakī, they said, "We will die in vain. Jaṭāyu is fortunate. For the sake of Sītā, he gave his life being wounded by Rāvaṇa in the battle." Having heard this, (the eagle) Sampāti, abandoning (his intention of) eating the monkeys (said), "This brother of mine, Jaṭāyu, was protected by me from the heat of the Sun as he was flying in the solar region. Hence, I had my wings burnt as I was flying in the clouds. On account of hearing the story of Rāma, the wings have grown again. I see Jānakī

---

guard at the entrance to the cave, took his brother to have been slain when he had not returned even after a long time. Sugrīva closed the entrance to the cave with stones, returned to Kiṣkindhā and assumed charge. As Vālin returned, the entreaties of Sugrīva were of no avail . Sugrīva retreated to Ṛśyamūka mountains to escape the wrath of Vālin as Vālin dreaded to enter that region on account of a curse. Tārā, the wife of Sugrīva, was also taken away by Vālin, but was restored to her husband after Vālin was slain by Rāma. See *Rām*. IV. ix.x

gone to *Aśoka* grove in Laṅkā in the Trikūṭaka (mountain) in (the middle of) the salt ocean of an extent of hundred *yojanas*. Knowing this let the monkeys tell Rāma and Sugrīva."

## CHAPTER NINE

### *The Story of Rāma (continued)*:

*Nārada said* :

1. Having heard the words of Sampāti, Hanūmat, Aṅgada, (son of Vālin) and others having seen the ocean said, "Who may cross the ocean and make us live?"

2. For the survival of monkeys and accomplishing the task of Rāma, that Māruti (Hanūmat) crossed the ocean extending to hundred *yojanas*.

3-5. Having seen the rise of Maināka (mountain), having killed (the demon) Siṁhikā and having seen Laṅkā and searching the houses of the demons and those of the women and the houses of the tenheaded (Rāvaṇa), Kumbha, Kumbhakarṇa, Vibhīṣaṇa, Indrajit, and other demons, he did not find (Sītā) (also) in the place for drinking wine. Becoming anxious and having gone to the *Aśoka* grove he found Sītā at the foot of the Śiṁśapā tree.

6. Remaining on the Śiṁśapā tree he saw Sītā being guarded by the demonesses, (and) Rāvaṇa asking her to become his wife and Sītā replying him that she could not.

7-9. The monkey (also saw) the demonesses asking Sītā to become the wife of Rāvaṇa, After Rāvaṇa had gone he said, "Daśaratha was a king. His sons Rāma and Lakṣmaṇa, the two excellent brothers came to the forest. You, Jānakī, the wife of Rāma were forcibly taken away by Rāvaṇa. Rāma became a friend of Sugrīva, sent me to search for you, (and) (you) take this signet ring of identification given by Rāma."

10-12. Sītā received the ring. Having seen Māruti seated on the tree and again in front of her, (she) asked him, "If (he) lives, how Rāma does not take me away?" The monkey said to her who was doubtful, "O Sītā ! Rāma does not know. Knowing now he will take you away after killing Rāvaṇa along with his army. O Devī (queen) ! Do not worry. You get me an identity." Sītā gave the crest jewel to the monkey.

13. (And) said, "You do in such a way that Rāma would take me away quickly. O dispeller of grief ! You retell him the story of the removal of the eye of the crow."

14-15. Getting the jewel and (listening to) the story, Hanumat said, "The Lord will be taking you away. Otherwise, if you feel some hurry, O auspicious one !' You get on to my back. I shall show you Sugrīva and Rāghava today." Sītā said to Hanūmat, "Let Rāghava take me away."

16-18. Then Hanūmat made a stratagem in order to see Daśagrīva (Rāvaṇa). He destroyed the grove, having killed the guards (of the grove) with his teeth and nails, and all the attendants, the sons of seven ministers, prince Akṣa. Śakrajit (Indrajit) (son of Rāvaṇa) bound him with the Nāgapāśa and took him to the red-eyed Rāvaṇa.

19. Rāvaṇa asked him, "Who you are". Māruti (Hanūmat) said to Rāvaṇa, "I am the messenger of Rāma. You return Sītā to him. Otherwise you will certainly die along with the other demons in Laṅkā being hit by the arrows of Rāma."

20-25. (Hearing these words) Rāvaṇa was intent on killing (Hanūmat) but was prevented by Vibhīṣaṇa. He (Rāvaṇa) made his (Hanūmat's) tail set fire to. Having burnt Laṅkā and the demons with the blazing flames Māruti, met Sītā again and saluted her. He crossed the ocean and informed Aṅgada and others that he had seen Sītā. Having drunk honey in the honey-garden along with Aṅgada and others, overpowering Dadhimukha and other guards, they met Rāma and told him that Sītā was seen. Rāma also being happy asked Māruti, "How Sītā was seen by you ? And what (message) did she send for me ? Sprinkle me who am tormented by the fire of passion, with the nectar of the story of Sītā. Hanūmat said to Rāma (how) he had come after crossing the ocean and seeing Sītā, burning the city (of Laṅkā) and taking jewel from Sītā. "O Rāma ! Do not worry. You will get back Sītā after having killed Rāvaṇa."

26-28. Receiving that jewel Rāma being grief-stricken wept and said, "Having seen this jewel (I feel) I have seen my Jānakī. (Sītā) ! (You) take me (there). I cannot live without her."

Being consoled by Sugrīva and others (Rāma) reached the banks of ocean. Vibhīṣaṇa who was forsaken by his wicked brother Rāvaṇa for having advised him to return Sītā to Rāma, came there alone to Rāma.

29-31. Rāma anointed his friend Vibhīṣaṇa as the ruler of Laṅkā. He requested ocean for (making) a way. When he had not come, then he split the (ocean) with an arrow. And the (king of the) ocean who had appeared before Rāma, said, "by building a bridge in the ocean by Nala you reach Laṅkā. I have been made great by you in the past." Rāma also reached the other banks of the mighty ocean by means of the bridge constructed by Nala with trees and rocks. Along with the monkeys he saw Laṅkā, himself remaining on the Suvela mountain.

## CHAPTER TEN

### *Manifestation of Viṣṇu as Rāma (continued)* :

*Nārada said* :

1. Being asked by Rāma, Aṅgada went to Rāvaṇa (and) said, "Let Jānakī be returned to Rāghava immediately, otherwise you will die."

2. Rāvaṇa was intent on killing (Aṅgada). The ten-headed demon who was ready to fight sent words to Rāma that war was the only way thought of.

3-5. After hearing these words, Rāma came to Laṅkā with the monkeys for the sake of battle. The monkeys were Hanūmat, Mainda, Dvivida, Jāmbavat, Nala, Nīla, Tāra, Aṅgada, Dhūmra, Suṣeṇa, Keśarī, Gaya, Panasa, Vinata, Rambha, Śarabha, Krathana the strong, Gavākṣa, Dadhivaktra, Gandhamādana and others and Sugrīva. With these and other innumerable monkeys (Rāma came to Laṅkā).

6. There was a disorderly battle between the demons and monkeys. The demons killed the monkeys with arrows, spears and mace".

7. The monkeys killed demons with nails, teeth and stones. The force of the demons consisting of elephants cavalry, chariots and infantry was destroyed.

8. Hanūmat killed the enemy Dhūmrākṣa with a big rock. Nīla killed the fighting Akampana and Prahasta.

9. Rāma and Lakṣmaṇa fainted on account of the arrow discharged by Indrajit. Regaining their consciousness after perceiving Tārkṣya (the chief of the eagles), they killed the forces of demons.

10. Rāma made Rāvaṇa shattered in the battle by means of arrows. And the grief-stricken Rāvaṇa woke up Kumbhakarṇa.

11-12. Then being awakened, Kumbhakarṇa, drinking thousands of pots of wine, and having eaten buffaloes and other (animals), said to Rāvaṇa, "You have done the sin of abducting Sītā and because (you are) my master, I shall go now for the war and kill Rāma along with the monkeys."

13. So saying, Kumbhakarṇa crushed all the monkeys. Being seized by him, Sugrīva cut off his ears and nose.

14. Having lost ears and nose he was eating the monkeys. then Rāma cut off the arms of Kumbhakarṇa with the arrows.

15-17. Then having cut off the feet, (Rāma) made (his) head fall on the earth. And then the demons Kumbha, Nikumbha, Makarākṣa, Mahodara and Mahāpārśva, the arrogant, Praghasa, Bhāsakarṇa, Virūpākṣa, Devāntaka, Narāntaka, Triśiras, Atikāya (were killed) in battle by Rāma, Lakṣmaṇa and the monkeys in the company of Vibhīṣaṇa.

18-21. And other demons, as they were fighting were made to fall down. Fighting by conceit, Indrajit bound Rāma and others with the *Nāgāstra* got as a gift. After they were made secure and free from wounds when Māruti had brought the mountain. Hanūmat bore him (Lakṣmaṇa) to that place where (Indrajit) was doing homa and offering āhuti-s unto the fire at Nikumbilā· Lakṣmaṇa killed the valiant Indrajit in battle. Being burnt by grief, Rāvaṇa was intent on killing Sītā.

22. The king although obstructed by the women, went (to fight) seated on a chariot and accompanied by the army. Being directed by Indra, Mātali[1] made Rāma seated on a chariot.

---

1. Mātali is the charioteer of Indra.

23. The fight between Rāma and Rāvaṇa was none the second. Rāvaṇa attacked monkeys and Māruti and others attacked Rāvaṇa.

24-26. Just as a cloud, Rāma showered on him (Rāvaṇa) arrows and weapons. He cut off his flagstaff along with his chariot, horses and charioteer as well as the bow, arms and heads. The cut-off heads grew again (on his body). Rāvaṇa was made to fall down to the ground by Rāma by piercing (his) heart with the *Brahmāstra* (weapon of the Pitāmaha). The (*rākṣasa*) women wept along with other demons. After consoling them, Vibhīṣaṇa cremated him as directed by Rāma.

27-28. Rāma made the pure Sītā to be brought (to him) by Hanūmat. He accepted her who was (declared) pure by her entry into the fire and (he) was praised by Indra, Brahmā, Daśaratha and others as, "You are Viṣṇu, the killer of the demon." Indra being propitiated, revived the monkeys by a shower of nectar.

29-30. They all (Brahmā and o hers) being worshipped by Rāma returned to heavens after witnessing the battle. Rāma entrusted Laṅkā to Vibhīṣaṇa. Having honoured the monkeys, being seated in the (aerial chariot) Puṣpaka in the company of Sītā, Rāma returned by the same route by which he had gone (to Laṅkā) showing the forests and mountains to Sītā and having a happy mind.

31. Having paid obeisance to Bharadvāja, he reached Nandigrāma. Being revered by Bharata there, he reached Ayodhyā and settled there.

32. Having saluted Vasiṣṭha and other sages, Kauśalyā, Kaikeyī and Sumitrā and having obtained the kingdom he honoured the twice-born.

33. He worshipped Vāsudeva (Viṣṇu), his own self, with the *Aśvamedha* (sacrifice). He conferred gifts on the deserving men). He protected (the welfare) of his subjects.

34. (He protected) *dharma* (righteousness), *kāma* (desire for worldly enjoyments) etc. just as his sons. (He) was bent on subduing the wicked. The world was abound with all righteous activities. The earth was abound with all grains. As Rāma was ruling, there was no premature death.

## CHAPTER ELEVEN

### *Manifestation of Viṣṇu as Rāma (continued)*:

*Nārada said* :

1. The well-honoured sages Agastya and others went to Rāghava, who was ruling the country (and said), "You are fortunate and are victorious because you have killed Indrajit.

2. Pulastya was the son of Brahmā. Viśravas was (the son of Pulastya). Kaikasī (was his wife). (His ) first (wife) was Puṣpotkaṭā.[1] The lord of wealth (Kubera) was her son.

3. Rāvaṇa was born to Kaikasī (possessing) 20 arms and 10 faces. By means of (his) penance he got a boon from Brahmā and conquered celestials.

4. Kumbhakarṇa was always sleeping, Vibhīṣaṇa became deep-rooted in *dharma*. Their sister (was) Śūrpaṇakhā, Meghanāda (was born) from Rāvaṇa.

5. Having conquered Indra, he became Indrajit. He was stronger than Rāvaṇa. Desirous of welfare of the celestials, (he) was killed by you (and) Lakṣmaṇa".

6-7. Having told (thus) those sages Agastya and others had gone after being prostrated by (Rāma). Śatrughna directed by Rāma as per desires of celestials, became the killer of Lavaṇa at some place (known as) Mathurā. Being directed by Rāma, Bharata killed three crores of sons of Śailūṣa with sharp arrows.

8-9. (Having killed) Śailūṣa, the wicked Gandharva, a resident on the banks of (the river) Sindhu and having established his sons Takṣa and Puṣkara in those countries, Bharata went to Rāghava along with Lakṣmaṇa and remained worshipping him after having killed the wicked in the battle and protected the pious.

10. The two sons Kuśa and Lava, the excellent brothers were born in the hermitage of Vālmīki to Sītā abandoned on

1. The name of the first wife of Viśravas is given as Devavarṇinī, daughter of Bharadvāja. See *Rām.* VII.ii.

Viśravas blessed Kaikasi, the daughter of Sumālin, when she had come to him desirous of progeny. But the progeny would be dreadful as she had come to him at twilight, said the sage. When she again entreated him, he blessed her that her next son would be like himself pursuing righteous life. See *Rām.* VII. ix.

account of rumour among the people; and were known from the hearing of (their) good episode.

11. After having been anointed in the kingdom and being bent on contemplation with (the attitude of) "I am brahman", (and then) the son of Sītā after having ruled for 11,000 years and after performing sacrifices went to heaven along with the citizens and (his) brother, and being attended to by the people and honoured by the celestials.

*Agni said* :

12. Vālmīki composed the Rāmāyaṇa in elaborate (form) after hearing from Nārada. One who hears this will go to heaven.

## CHAPTER TWELVE

### *Manifestation of Viṣṇu as Kṛṣṇa*

*Agni said* :

1. I shall describe the genealogy of Hari (Kṛṣṇa). Brahmā (was born) from the lotus in the navel of Viṣṇu. (Sage) Atri (was born) from Brahmā. Then Soma (was born). Purūravas was born from Soma.

2. Āyu was (born) from him (Purūravas). From him (was born) Nahuṣa and then Yayāti. From whom Devayānī[1] gave birth to Yadu and Turvasu.

3. Śarmiṣṭhā, the daughter of Vṛṣaparvan (gave birth to) Druhyu, Anu and Puru (through Yayāti). The Yādavas (came) in the race of Yadu. Vasudeva was the foremost among these.

1. Devayānī was the daughter of Śukra, the preceptor of demons. When her love for Kaca, the pupil of her father was not reciprocated by him, she cursed him and he in turn cursed her that she would become the wife of a warrior. Once when Devayānī and her companion Śarmiṣṭhā were bathing, their dresses got exchanged, and the irate Śarmiṣṭhā slapped Devayānī and threw her into the well. Devayānī was later rescued from the well by Yayāti, who married her with the consent of her father. As cursed by Devayānī, Śarmiṣṭhā became her servant. See *Apte SD.* and *M Bh.-Nam.* p. 151.

4-7. From Vasudeva through Devakī (was born Kṛṣṇa) in order to remove oppression on the earth. Once the sons of Hiraṇyakaśipu (became) the six embryos in the womb of Devakī being led by the meditative-sleep cast by Viṣṇu. The seventh child in the womb of Devakī that was strong was transferred to (the womb of) Rohiṇī and (was born) as the son of Rohiṇī.[1] Then Hari the four-armed (manifested) in the sky on the eighth day of the dark fortnight and being adored by Devakī and Vasudeva (was born) as a child with two arms. Vasudeva took (the child) to the couch of Yaśodā, being afraid of Kaṁsa.

8-10. Yaśodā carried the daughter (born to her) and left it at the couch of Devakī. Having heard the cries of the child, Kaṁsa (came there and carried the child) and smashed it on the stone slab in spite of being obstructed by Devakī. Having heard the voice in the heavens that, "My eighth birth would be your death", and being infuriated all the children born were killed (by him) after they were left with him by Devakī as promised (by Vasudeva) at the time of their marriage. The girl who was thrown (on the slab) (bounced) to the sky and said:

11. "O Kaṁsa ! What is the use of throwing me (to kill me). One who would kill you, that lord of all the celestials had born (already) for the removal of oppression on the earth."

12-13. Having told so she (disappeared). And she having killed Śumbha[2] and other demons and being praised by Indra (was known differently as) the Āryā, Durgā, the source of the *Vedas*, Ambikā (the mother), Bhadrakālī (beneficent Kālī), the beneficent, Kṣemyā (bestower of peace), propitious, (and) multi-armed. I bow unto her. Whoever reads these names at the three twilights will get all cherished desires fulfilled.

---

1. Vasudeva had two wives—Devakī and Rohiṇī. The six sons born of yogic sleep were carried off by Hiraṇyakaśipu's yogic power. They were again born to Devakī and were killed by Kaṁsa. The seventh child in the womb of Devakī was transferred to the womb of Rohiṇī, hence was known as Saṅkarṣaṇa *alias* Balarāma. See *Bhāg. P.* X.lxxxv. 46-49; *Vi.P.* V. i. 70; *P. Index* III. p. 769.

2. Śumbha and his brother Niśumbha, the two demons, propitiated Brahmā and requested him that they should have no death. When Brahmā declined to grant their request as impossible, they again requested that they should not die at the hands of mortals, celestials, animals or birds. They excluded women, as they thought that women are not so much powerful to fear death at their hands. When they oppressed all beings, the goddess killed them. See *Devi Bh. P.* V. xxi. xxx. xxxi.

14-15. Kaṁsa also sent Pūtanā and others in order to kill the boy. (Bala) Rāma and Kṛṣṇa, being entrusted by Vasudeva to the custody of Nanda, the husband of Yaśodā, for their protection from the fear of Kaṁsa and others, were living at Gokula with the cows and shepherds.

16. They (two), the protectors of the entire world became the protectors of cows. (Once the boy) Kṛṣṇa was tied to the mortar with a rope by the bewildered Yaśodā (to contain his sportive mischiefs).

17-20. He went in between the two Arjuna- trees[1] and uprooted them. And the cart[2] was made to roll away by a kick of the foot. Pūtanā, who was intent on killing (him) was killed by that seeker of the breast (milk) by sucking her breast. Kṛṣṇa, who had gone to Vṛndāvana (grove of holy basil), drew out the (serpent) Kāliya, resident in the waters, from the waters of (the river) Yamunā and conquered it and was praised by (his brother) Bala. (He) made the Tālavana (palymyra grove) secure after killing (the demon) Dhenuka (in the form of) an ass (and) after having killed (the demons) Ariṣṭa (in the form of) a bull (and) Keśi in the form of a horse. Abandoning the festivity for Śakra (Indra), the ritual of protecting the cows was made to be observed.

21. The mountain was borne and the rain (caused to fall) by Indra, was warded off. (Then) Govinda (Kṛṣṇa) was saluted by Indra and offered with the peacock (plumes).

22. Festivities for Indra were again caused to be done by Kṛṣṇa, after being pleased. Riding a chariot he went to Mathurā and was praised by Akrūra, as directed by Kaṁsa.

23. Being attended to by the devoted and sportive shepherd women, he having killed the washerman who did not get (the clothes), seized the clothes.

24-26. Wearing the garland along with Rāma (Balarāma) he blessed the garland-maker. He made upright the hunchbacked woman who had given him unguent. He killed the demon Kuvalayāpīḍa (in the form of) an intoxicated elephant. Even as Kaṁsa and others were looking on, he entered the (wrestling) court and fought with those (wrestlers) on the dais.

---

1. Arjuna trees, later personified as two demons.
2. The name of a demon, who assumed the form of a cart.

Much strength was shown by the wrestler Cāṇūra and Muṣṭika. The wrestlers Cāṇūra and Muṣṭika and others were killed by them.

27-28. Having killed Kaṁsa, the ruler of Mathurā, Hari (Kṛṣṇa) made his father as the ruler of Yādavas. Asti and Prāptī, the wives of Kaṁsa were the two daughters of Jarāsandha. Being entreated by them Jarāsandha besieged Mathurā and fought with the Yādavas with arrows.

29-31. (Bala) Rāma and Kṛṣṇa came to Gomantaka leaving Mathurā. After conquering Jarāsandha, the despiser of Vāsudeva (Kṛṣṇa) and of Pauṇḍraka,[1] he made Dvārakā as his capital and stayed there being surrounded by Yādavas. Having killed (the demon) Naraka, the son of the Earth, he (Kṛṣṇa) brought 16000 daughters of the celestials, *gandharvas and yakṣas* (kinds of semi-divine beings) and married them, as well as the eight (girls) Rukmiṇī and others.

32-34. (Then) the killer of Naraka, (seated) on the (bird) Garuḍa, in the company of Satyabhāmā and with the jewel-store and other jewels after having conquered Indra in the heavens and brought the (divine tree) Pārijāta planted (it) in the house of Satyabhāmā. Having learnt the (science of) *astra* and *śastra* (use of weapons) from Sāndīpanī (rescued) his son and brought him (to him) after conquering the demon Pañcajana and was well-worshipped by Yama (the god of death). He killed (the demon) Kālayavana[2] (by a ruse) and was worshipped by (the king) Mucukunda.[3]

35. He worshipped Vasudeva and Devakī the devotees and

1. Pauṇḍraka was the King of Kāśī and the son of Vasudeva and Sutanu, the daughter of Kāśirāja. When he became the king, he asserted that he was the real Vāsudeva. Kṛṣṇa invaded Kāśī and killed him. See *Vi.P.* V. xxxiv. 4-28; *Bhāg. P.* X lxi. 1-23; *P. Index.* II. p. 393.

2. Kālayavana was a king of the Yavanas. He was an enemy of Kṛṣṇa and an invincible foe of the Yādavas. Kṛṣṇa found it impossible to vanquish him. He cunningly decoyed him to the cave where Mucukunda was sleeping. Mucukunda's sleep being disturbed, he burnt him down.

3. King Mucukunda, son of Māndhātṛ, assisted celestials in their war against demons and got as a boon a long and unbroken sleep and that whoever dared to disturb his sleep would be burnt to ashes. Accordingly when Kālayavana disturbed his sleep, he was burnt to ashes. See note 2 above and *Apte SD*.

brahmins. Niśaṭha and Ulmuka were born to Revatī through Balabhadra.

36. Sāmba (was born) through Jāmbavatī and other sons were (born) through other (wives) to Kṛṣṇa.

37-39. Pradyumna was born through Rukmiṇī (to Kṛṣṇa) and was forcibly taken away on the sixth day by Śambara[1] and thrown into the ocean. A fish seized him. A fisherman (caught) that fish and brought it to Śambara[1] and Śambara (gave it) to Māyāvatī (the maid). Māyāvatī having found her husband inside the fish, nourished him with respect. She also said to him, "I am Rati. You are my husband. You are Kāma (cupid) and made bodiless by Śambhu (Śiva). I was forcibly taken a (captive). I am not his wife. You (are) knower of magic. You kill Śambara."

40. Having heard that Pradyumna killed Śambara and went to Kṛṣṇa along with (his) wife Māyāvatī. Then Rukmiṇī was happy.

41-42. From Pradyumna Aniruddha was born, who was the husband of Uṣā and was highly intelligent. Bāṇa (was) the son of Bali (and) his daughter (was) Uṣā. (His city was known) as Śoṇitapura. By (his) penance (he) was (treated as) son of Śiva. "Bāṇa ! You will be waging a war (as indicated) by the fall of flagstaff," said Śiva to Bāṇa, becoming pleased.

43-44. Having seen Gaurī (Pārvatī) sporting with Śiva, Uṣā was desirous of (getting) a husband. Gaurī said to her, "The person seen by you in your dream on the twelfth day in the month of Vaiśākha (the second month in the Hindu new year) will become you husband". Uṣā becoming happy on these words of Gaurī, saw him (that person) (in dream) while she slept in her house.

---

1. Śambara was a companion of Kaṁsa. He took away the child Pradyumna a couple of days after the birth of the child, knowing that it would be his slayer and threw him into the ocean. A giant fish swallowed it. When the fishermen caught the fish and brought to Śambara, the fish was sent to the kitchen. When the cooks cut the fish and found the beautiful child, they informed Māyāvatī, the mistress of Śambara's household. Māyāvatī knew that she was none other than Rati and Kāma was reborn as Pradyumna. She nourished and brought up Pradyumna. Aftei he grew up she revealed the truth to him. The two got married. Atlast Śambara was killed by Pradyumna after a severe battle. See *Bhāg. P.* X. xxxvi. 36 and lv. 3-24.

45-46. Knowing (that person) united with herself, she (identified) Aniruddha from the drawn portraits (of princes) through (the assistance of) her friend Citralekhā (and) brought that grandson of Kṛṣṇa from Dvārakā (to her place) by the daughter of Kumbhāṇḍa, the minister of Bāṇa. Aniruddha went and made marry with Uṣā.

47-48. (Bāṇa was) informed (of this) by his mobile guards. Aniruddha had a fierce fight with Bāṇa.[1] Having heard this from Nārada, Kṛṣṇa (went along) with Pradyumna (and) Balabhadra (and) remaining on the Garuḍa (vehicle of Viṣṇu) conquered the fires and the fever related to Maheśvara (Śiva).

49. There was a fight between Hari and Śaṅkara (Śiva) with arrows. Nandi, Vināyaka, Skanda and others were conquered by Tārkṣya (Garuḍa) and others.

50. When Śaṅkara (Śiva) yawned, Viṣṇu (employed) the missile *Jṛmbhaṇa* and cut the thousand arms (of Śaṅkara). Protection was sought by Rudra (Śiva).

51-53. Bāṇa was animated by Viṣṇu. The two-armed (Viṣṇu) said to Śiva, "What protection was offered by you to Bāṇa (is identical with) that (offered) by me. There is no difference between us and one who (thinks of) any difference goes to hell. Viṣṇu was propitiated by Śiva and others. Aniruddha in the company of Uṣā and others, having gone to Dvārakā, amused himself along with Ugrasena and other Yādavas. Vajra (was) the son of Aniruddha. He learnt all knowledge from Mārkaṇḍeya.

54-55. Balarāma was the killer of (the demon) Pralamba[2] (by whom) there was the dragging of the river Yamunā. The destroyer of the monkey Dvivida[3] and the destroyer of the pride

---

1. As Bāṇa was a devotee of Śiva, the forces of Śiva came to assist him in the war. See verse 42 above. See *Bhāg. P.* X. lxiii. 23.

2. Pralamba, an *asura* friend of Kaṁsa went in the guise of a cowherd to the place where Kṛṣṇa and Balarāma were playing with their companions. Being admitted to the games, while carrying Balarāma on his back, he grew into a huge form and was killed by Balarāma. See *Bhāg. P.* X. xviii. 17-29; *M. Bh.-Nam.* p. 209b; *Vi. P.* V. ix. 1-38.

3. Dvivida, a counsellor of Sugrīva and brother of Mainda, was also a friend of the demon Naraka. In order to avenge the death of his friend, he burnt the cities and villages and caused much havoc. He was finally killed by Balarāma after a hard combat. See *Bhāg. P.* X. lxvii; *Vi.P.* V. xxxvi. 1-23 and *P Index* II. p. 150.

of Kauravas, Lord Hari amused himself in many forms along with Rukmiṇī and others. He produced many sons and innumerable Yādavas. Whoever reads the account of the lineage of Hari, that person would have his desires fulfilled and attain Hari.

## CHAPTER THIRTEEN

### *Origin of the Kauravas and Pāṇḍavas* :

*Agni said* :

1. I shall narrate the (story of) Bhārata (which has) the description of the greatness of Kṛṣṇa. Viṣṇu removed heavy oppression on the earth having Pāṇḍavas as the instrumental cause.

2. Brahmā was born of the lotus in the navel of Viṣṇu. (Sage) Atri was the son of Brahmā. From Atri was born Soma. From Soma, Budha was born. From him (Budha) was born Aila—Purūravas.

3-4. Āyu (was born) from him. King Nahuṣa was then (born). Then Yayāti, then Puru (were born successsively). In his race (was born) Bharata. Then king Kuru (was born). In that race (was born) Śantanu. From him (was born) Bhīṣma (as) the son of the Ganges. (His) brothers Citrāṅgada and Vicitra (vīrya) were born to Śantanu through Satyavatī.

5-8. After Śantanu's death, Bhīṣma who had no wife, (governed and) protected his brother's kingdom. The young Citrāṅgada was killed by the Gandharva Citrāṅgada. The two daughters of Kāśirāja, Ambikā and Ambālikā brought (as captives) by Bhīṣma, the conqueror of the foes, (became) the wives of Vicitravīrya,. He (Vicitravīrya) died on account of consumption. With the consent of Satyavatī, from Vyāsa, King Dhṛtarāṣṭra was (born) through Ambikā and Pāṇḍu through Ambālikā as sons. From Dhṛtarāṣṭra through Gāndhārī hundred sons (were born) with Duryodhana as the first.

9. By the curse of a sage[1] then he (Pāṇḍu) died on account of union with his wife at the hermitage of Śataśṛṅga, then Yudhiṣṭhira (was born) to Pāṇḍu through Kuntī from Dharma (Yama).

10. (Similarly) Bhīma from Vāta (God of wind), Arjuna from Śakra (were born) and through Mādrī, Nakula and Sahadeva from the Aśvinī kumāra. Pāṇḍu died when (he was) in union with Mādrī.[1]

11. Karṇa, born to Kuntī, when she was a virgin, became a dependent of Duryodhana. By destiny there was enmity between the Kurus (Kauravas) and Pāṇḍavas.

12. The wicked Duryodhana burnt the Pāṇḍavas in the lac house. The Pāṇḍavas escaped from the burnt house along with their mother as the sixth.

13. Then at (the place) Ekacakrā, in the house of a brahmin, they all remained in the attire of an ascetic after killing the demon Baka.[2]

14. They went to the fair at Pāñcāla and in the *svayamvara* (self-choice) of Draupadī. The well adorned Draupadī was obtained by the five Pāṇḍavas.

15. Then (they) were known to have got half of the kingdom by Duryodhana and others. The divine bow Gāṇḍīva and the excellent chariot were obtained from the Fire god.

16. And in the battle, Arjuna got Kṛṣṇa as the charioteer and inexhaustible arrows and similarly the missiles (known as) Brahmā and other weapons (were obtained) from Droṇa. All were proficient in (the use of) arms.

17-18. (Acting on the words of) Kṛṣṇa, Arjuna put out the fire at the Khāṇḍava forest. And the Pāṇḍava (Arjuna) having obstructed rains (caused by Indra) with the shower of arrows, conquered the countries in different) directions. Yudhiṣṭhira ruled the country along with the (other) Pāṇḍavas. (He per-

1. The sage Kindama, who was sporting with his wife, both assuming the form of a deer, was hit along with his wife by the arrows of Pāṇḍu, who had gone there for hunting. The sage cursed Pāṇḍu that he would also die while copulating with his wife. See *M. Bh.* I. cxvii. 5-31.

2. Baka was a demon living in the city Ekacakrā. Under an agreement the residents were supplying his daily food consisting of a buffalo, a man etc. from each family in turn. When the five Pāṇḍavas were staying in that place disguised as ascetics, Bhīma killed the demon to relieve a poor brahmin resident, who was lamenting his fate as it was his turn that day. *M. Bh.* I. clxvi ff.

formed) the Rājasūya (sacrifice) (spending) plenty of gold. Suyodhana (Duryodhana) could not bear that.

19-20. Being directed by brother Duḥśāsana and by Karṇa who had been enriched by him, he won over Yudhiṣṭhira in dice, (being assisted) by Śakuni in playing the dice. His kingdom was also won by conceit. Those in the court laughed at him. Yudhiṣṭhira being won, went to the forest along with the brothers.

21-24. He spent twelve years in the forest as promised (by him) along with (the sage) Dhaumya and Draupadī as the sixth, feeding 88000 twice-borns as before. Then (he) went to the King of Virāṭa, with the other names, the king (Yudhiṣṭhira) unrecognised as the brahmin Kaṅka, Bhīma as the cook, Arjuna as Bṛhannalā, (their ) wife (Draupadī) as Sairandhrī and the twins. And Bhīmasena killed Kīcaka[1] in the night as he was desirous of winning over Draupadī. And Arjuna conquered the Kurus, who were engaged in seizing and lifting the cows. (Hence) they were recognised as Pāṇḍavas (by the Kurus).

25-28. (Then) Subhadrā, the sister of Kṛṣṇa, gave birth to Abhimanyu, from Arjuna. And (King) Virāṭa gave his daughter Uttarā to him. Dharmarāja (Yudhiṣṭhira), the master of seven *akṣauhiṇī*[2], was (ready) for the war. That Kṛṣṇa, the messenger, having gone to the intolerant Duryodhana said to that lord of eleven *akṣauhiṇī*, "Give half the kingdom or five villages to Yudhiṣṭhira. Or else (you) fight (with him)." Hearing (these) words, Suyodhana (Duryodhana) said to Kṛṣṇa, "I will not give land (even of the size) of a needle tip. I will fight engaged in seizing it."

*Agni said* :

29. Having shown the invincible omnipresent form (and) being honoured by Vidura, (Kṛṣṇa) returned to Yudhiṣṭhira and said to Yudhiṣṭhira, "Fight with this Suyodhana (Duryodhana)."

---

1. Kīcaka was the commander-in-chief and brother-in-law of King of Virāṭa. *M. Bh.—Nam.* pp. 68-69

2. The army consisted of 21,870 chariots, as many elephants, 65,610 horses and 109,350 foot-soldiers. *Apte SD.*

## CHAPTER FOURTEEN

### *Story of the Mahābhārata*

*Agni said* :

1-3. The armies of Yudhiṣṭhira and Duryodhana went to Kurukṣetra. Having seen Bhīṣma, Droṇa and others, (Arjuna said) that he would not fight with his preceptors. The Lord (Kṛṣṇa) said to Pārtha (Arjuna), "You need not worry about Bhīṣma and prominent men. The bodies are perishable. But the soul does not perish. This soul is the supreme *Brahman*. You know that (by realizing that), 'I am *Brahman*.' Being neutral towards success and defeat and as a *yogin* you protect the duties of a king."

4-6. Being told thus by Kṛṣṇa, Arjuna fought (the battle). He sounded drums remaining in the chariot. Bhīṣma was the first commander for the army of Duryodhana. And Śikhaṇḍi (was the commander) for the Pāṇḍavas. There was a fight between these two armies. (The armies) of the son of Dhṛtarāṣṭra along with Bhīṣma killed the armies of Pāṇḍavas. The Pāṇḍavas in the company of Śikhaṇḍī[1] and others killed (the army) of the sons of Dhṛtarāṣṭra. The battle between the armies of Kurus and Pāṇḍavas was similar (to the battle) between *devas* and *asuras*.

7-10. It was (a cause) for the growth of delight of the *devas* in the heavens who were watching it. For ten days Bhīṣma destroyed the army of Pāṇḍavas with *astras*. On the tenth day Arjuna showered arrows on the valiant Bhīṣma. On the words of Drupada, Śikhaṇḍī[2] showered *astras* just as a cloud would do. The elephants, horses, chariots and infantry were brought down by the *astras* (of the two armies) mutually. Bhīṣma, able to die at his own will, after having shown the mode of war and being told by the *Vasus* (a class of deities), was remaining in the bed of arrows awaiting to reach *Vasuloka*, and for the (com-

---

1. Śikhaṇḍi, son of Drupada, was at first a woman known as Śikhaṇḍini and was later transformed into a man and was known as Śikhaṇḍin. M.Bh. V. xci.

2. Bhīṣma had pledged not to fight against eunuchs. As Arjuna had Sikhaṇḍī as his charioteer, it was easy for him to kill Bhīṣma as Bhīṣma would not fight against Śikhaṇḍi, a woman transformed into a man.

mencement of the) summer solstice all the while remaining contemplating on Viṣṇu and praising Him.

11. As Duryodhana was grief-stricken, Droṇa became the Commander. As the army of Pāṇḍavas was jubilant, Dhṛṣṭadyumna (was made) the Commander.

12. There was a fierce battle between the two which made the domain of Yama (the god of death) extensive. Virāṭa, Drupada and others were drowned in the ocean of (arrows of) Droṇa.

13. The huge army of Duryodhana (consisted of) elephant, horse, chariot and infantry. Droṇa became just like Kāla (death himself) for the (army) headed by Dhṛṣṭadyumna.

14-15. When it was proclaimed that Aśvatthāman was killed, Droṇa abandoned his *astras*. Overcome by the arrow of Dhṛṣṭadyumna he fell on the earth on the fifth day, (himself being) unassailable and after having killed many warriors. As Duryodhana was grief-stricken, Karṇa became the commander.

16. And Arjuna (became the commander) of the Pāṇḍava forces. There was combat between them, between weapons and weapons, very fierce and resembling a war between *devas* and *asuras*.

17. In the war known as the Karṇārjuna, Karṇa killed the enemies with his arrows. On the second day, Karṇa was killed by Arjuna.

18. Śalya fought for a day and Yudhiṣṭhira killed him. Suyodhana (Duryodhana), whose army had been destroyed, fought with Bhīmasena.

19. Having killed many men (in their army) (he) challenged Bhīmasena. Bhīmasena killed him, who was attacking with the mace.

20-21. (Bhīmasena) killed his brothers with his mace. On that eighteenth day, in the night, the very strong Aśvatthāman killed the sleeping army of Pāṇḍavas of the extent of an *akṣauhiṇī*, the Pāñcālas and the sons of Draupadī. He also killed Dhṛṣṭadyumna.

22. Then Arjuna seized his crest-jewel with an arrow (and gave it) to that Draupadī who had lost her sons and was lamenting.

23. Hari (Kṛṣṇa) revived (all of them) who were burnt by the arrows of Aśvatthāman. That embryo of Uttarā became a king (known as) Parīkṣit.

24. Kṛtavarman, Kṛpa and Drauṇi (son of Droṇa) (Aśvatthāman) survived in the battle. The five Pāṇḍavas, Sātyaki and Kṛṣṇa survived and none else.

25-26. Then that Yudhiṣṭhira having pacified the grief-stricken women, in the company of Bhīma and others, having done the obsequies for the killed warriors and having offered waters and money and after having heard the peace-yielding *dharmas*, the royal duties, *dharma* relating to final emancipation, *dharma* relating to charity, became a king.

27. The destroyer of his enemy (Yudhiṣṭhira) gave away charities to the brahmins at the *Aśvamedha* (sacrifice). Having heard about the destruction of Yādavas[1] caused by the club and having installed Parīkṣit in the kingdom, (he) reached heavens along with the brothers.

## CHAPTER FIFTEEN

### *Ascendance of Pāṇḍavas to heaven* :

*Agni said* :

1. O Brahmin ! When Yudhiṣṭhira was ruling the kingdom, Dhṛtarāṣṭra went to the forest along with Gāndhārī and Pṛthā (Kuntī) and passed from one stage of life to another.

2-5. Vidura was burnt by the forest fire and ascended heavens. Thus, Viṣṇu removed the oppression of demons and others on the earth, for the sake of *dharma* and for the destruc-

1. This alludes to the curse of sages when the Yādava boys dressed up Sāmba, son of Jāmbavatī, as a woman and requested sages to tell what kind of child would be born to her. The sages cursed that an iron mace would be born. When it happened accordingly, the mace was powdered and thrown into the sea. They were washed ashore and later grew into reeds. The Yādavas under the influence of liquor quarrelled with each other and destroyed themselves by beating with the uprooted reeds. See *Vi.P.*V. xxvii. 9-10; *M. Bh.* XVI. i. 15-22.

tion of *adharma* and having the Pāṇḍavas as an apparent cause. Having the curse of a brahmin, as a pretext, he destroyed with the club, the race of Yādavas who were oppressing (the world) Then (he) installed Vajra (son of Aniruddha) in the kingdom. On the directive of celestials, Hari himself having discarded his body at Prabhāsa, is being worshipped by the residents of heavens at the worlds of Indra and Brahmā. Balabhadra, (who was) a form of Ananta, reached heavens in the nether world.

6. Hari, the imperishable lord, is always to be contemplated upon by those who meditate (on him). Without him (at Dvārakā), the ocean flooded the city of Dvārakā.

7-8. Pārtha (Arjuna), having performed the obs quies of Yādavas, and having offered the waters of oblation and money, felt grief-stricken when the women, who were the wives of Viṣṇu (Kṛṣṇa), were carried away by the shepherds (using) the clubs as weapons and defeating Arjuna on account of the curse of Aṣṭāvakra.[1]

9-12. Being consoled by Vyāsa, he thought, "My strength remains only in the presence of Kṛṣṇa." Having come to Hastināpura, Pārtha then informed Yudhiṣṭhira, his brothers and the guards of the people. That bow, those weapons and the chariot and those horses were lost in the absence of Kṛṣṇa, just as a charity made to a person not well learned (would be lost). Having heard that (news), the intelligent Dharmarāja (Yudhiṣṭhira), having established Parīkṣīt in the kingdom, set out on his final journey to relinquish this world along with Draupadī and his brothers, after having realized the transitory nature of the mundane existence and repeating 108 (names) of Hari.

13. Draupadī, Sahadeva, Nakula, Phālguna[2] (Arjuna), Bhīma had fallen on the way (of their march). The king was grief-stricken.

---

1. Once when a brahmin Aṣṭāvakra was doing penance standing in neck-deep water, the heavenly nymphs who happened to pass that way bowed to him and sought his blessings to get a good husband. Being pleased he blessed them that they would become the wives of the Lord when he manifested as Kṛṣṇa. Later, when they began to mock at him, on seeing his crooked form as he came out of waters, he got enraged and cursed them that they would be forcibly taken away by thieves. See *Vi.P.* V. xxxviii. 71-82.

2. On account of his birth on the Himalayan peaks as the moon was in asterism Uttarā Phalgunī, Arjuna was known by this name.

14. Mounting the chariot brought by Indra he reached heavens along with his brothers, having seen Duryodhana and others and Vāsudeva and becoming happy. This is (the story of) Bhārata told to you. Whoever reads this, goes to heaven.

## CHAPTER SIXTEEN

*Manifestation of Viṣṇu as Buddha and Kalki* :

*Agni said* :

1. I am describing the manifestation (of Viṣṇu) as Buddha, by reading and hearing which one gets wealth. Once in the battle between *devas* and *asuras, devas* were defeated by the *daityas* (demons, sons of Diti).

2. They sought refuge in the lord saying, "Protect us ! Protect us !". He (Viṣṇu), who is of the form of illusory delusion became the son of Śuddhodana.

3-4. He deluded those demons. Those, who had abandoned the path laid down in the *Vedas*, became the Bauddhas and from them others who had abandoned the *Vedas*. He then became the *Ārhat* (Jaina). He then made others as *Ārhats*. Thus the heretics came into being devoid of vedic *dharmas*.

5-6. They did such a work deserving hell (as reward). They would receive even from the vile. All of them became mixed *Dasyus* and devoid of good conduct at the end of Kaliyuga. Of the *Vājasaneyaka veda* (*Śuklayajurveda*) only fifteen sections will be existing.

7. Non-aryans in the form of kings would devour men who wear the costumes of righteousness and have a taste for unrighteous thing.

8-9. Kalki, as the son of Viṣṇuyaśas, (and having) Yājñavalkya as the priest would destroy the non-Aryans, holding the

---

*Continued from previous page*

उत्तराभ्यां फल्गुनीभ्यां नक्षत्राभ्यामहं दिवा ।
जातो हिमवतः पृष्ठे तेन मां फाल्गुनं विदुः ।।

*M. Bh.* IV. xliv. 16.

*astra* and having a weapon. He would establish moral law in four-fold *varṇas* in the suitable manner. The people (would be) in the path of righteousness in all the stages of life.

10. Hari, after discarding the form of Kalki, would go to heaven. Then would come the Kṛtayuga as before.

11-13. O Most virtuous person ! Men would remain devoted to their respective duties of castes and stages of life. Thus, in all the *Kalpas*[1] and *Manvantaras*,[2] the manifestations (of Viṣṇu) are innumerable, some already past and some yet to come off. Whoever reads or hears the stories of the manifestations of Viṣṇu would get all desired things, become pure, and attain heaven along with his race. In this way, Hari settles the righteousness and unrighteousness. Hari is the cause of creation etc. and after manifesting (in different forms) he has returned.

## CHAPTER SEVENTEEN

### *Description of Creation* :

*Agni said* :

1. I shall describe now the creation of the universe. which is the sport of Viṣṇu.[3] He who creates heaven etc. is the beginning of the creation and is endowed with qualities and is without qualities.

2. Brahmā, the unmanifest, was the existent being. There was no sky, neither the day nor the night etc. Viṣṇu having entered the nature (*Prakṛti*) and the soul (*Puruṣa*), then agitated them.

---

1. *Kalpa* is a day of Brahmā or thousand (*catur* ) *Yugas* being a period of 432 million years of mortals and measuring the duration of the world.

2. Manvantara is the age or the period of Manu, being equivalent to 1/14th of a day of Brahmā or 71 *catur yugas*.

3. According to the Sāṅkhya system of philosophy the involuntary union of soul and nature causes creation, while others hold creation as due to the sport of Brahmā.

3. At the time of creation, the intellect (*Mahat*) (emanated first). The ego (Ahaṅkāra) came into being then, and then the evolutes (*Vaikārikas*),[1] the lustre (*taijasa*), the elements etc. and the darkness (*tāmasa*).[2]

4. Then emanated the ether, the sound-principle from the ego. Then the wind, the principle of feeling and the fire, the colour-principle came into being from it.

5. The water, the taste-principle (came into being) from this. The earth is known as the smell-principle. From the darkness (born of) ego, the senses (came into being) (which) are lustrous.

6. The evolutes are the ten celestials and the mind, the eleventh sense. Then the lord Svayambhū[3] Brahmā became desirous of creating different types of beings.

7. He created waters first. The waters are referred to as *nārāḥ* because they are the creation of the Supreme spirit.

8. Since his motion was first in them, he is known as Nārāyaṇa. That egg lying in the water was golden in colour.

9-10. From that, Brahmā was born of his own accord, whom we know as the self-born (Svayambhū). Having lived (in it) for one full year, the Hiraṇyagarbha,[4] made that egg into two, the heaven and the earth. Between those two pieces, the lord created the sky.

11-13. The ten directions supported the earth floating on the waters. Then the lord of the beings (Prajāpati) desirous of creation, created time, mind, speech, desire, anger, attachment and other counter-parts. From the lightning he created thunder and clouds, the rain-bow and birds. He first created Parjanya (Indra). Then he created the *Ṛk* hymns (*Ṛcaḥ*), Yajur hymns (*Yajūṁṣi*) and the Sāman hymns (*Sāmāni*) for accomplishing the sacrifice.

14. Those who want to accomplish, worship *devas* with these (hymns). The higher and lower beings (were created) from the arms. He created Sanatkumāra and Rudra, born of anger.

---

1. *Vaikārikas* are the first creation from the natural state.
2. *Tāmasa* is the creation of ignorance.
3. Brahmā is known as Svayambhū, as he was self-born. See verses 9-10 below.
4. Hiraṇyagarbha denotes Brahmā, as he was born from the golden egg.

15. He then created the sages Marīci, Atri, Aṅgirasa, Pulastya, Pulaha, Kratu, Vasiṣṭha, who are regarded as the seven mind-born sons of Brahmā.

16. O ! Excellent one ! these seven (sages) procreated (many) beings and the Rudras. Having divided his body into two, he became a male with one half and a female with another. Then Brahmā procreated children through her (the female half).

## CHAPTER EIGHTEEN

### *Genealogy of Svāyambhuva Manu* :[1]

*Agni said* :

1. Śatarūpā of ascetic disposition (becoming) desirous gave birth to two sons Priyavrata and Uttānapāda and a beautiful daughter[2] from Svāyambhuva Manu.

2-3 From (Devahūti) the wife of Kardama, (were born) (two daughters) Samrāṭ and Kukṣi.

Uttama was born as the son of Uttānapāda through Suruci. And Dhruva* was born as the son (of Uttānapāda) through Sunīti. O Sage ! Dhruva did penance for three thousand celestial years for gaining fame.

4. Becoming pleased (with him) Hari conferred on him a firm position[3] above the sages. Having seen his progress Uśanas[4] recited the (following) verse :

---

1. An epithet of the first Manu was Svāyambhuva Manu, as he was a son of Brahmā.

2. The *Bhāg. P.* specifies the name of the daughter of Svāyambhuva Manu as Devahūti and describes in detail her marriage with Kardama. See *ibid.* III. xxi-xxii.

* For a detailed account of the story of Dhruva see *Vi.P.* I. Chs. 11-12.

3. The young boy Dhruva was one day contemptuously treated by his step-mother as he tried to sit on his father's lap. On the advice of his mother he retired to the forest and did penance steadfastly devoted to Viṣṇu. At last he was raised to the status of a pole-star. See *Vi. P.* I. xi-xii.

4. Uśanas also known as Śukrācarya or Kāvya was the preceptor of Asuras.

5. O what a strength his penance had! How well-heard of! What a wonderful thing that the seven sages[1] are situated, placing Dhruva in front of them.

6-7. Śambhu gave birth to Śiṣṭi and Bhavya from Dhruva. Succhāyā bore five blemishless sons from Śiṣṭi, (namely), Ripu, Ripuñjaya, Ripra, Vṛkala, Vṛkatejasa. Bṛhatī bore the brilliant Cākṣuṣa from Ripu.

8. Cākṣuṣa begot Manu through Puṣkariṇī (also known as Vīriṇī) (daughter of Vīraṇa Prajāpati). Ten excellent sons were born to Manu through Naḍvalā.

9. (They were) Ūru,[2] Puru, Śatadyumna, Tapasvin, Satyavāk,[3] Kavi[4], Agniṣṭu[5], Atirātra, Sudyumna, and Abhimanyu.

10. Āgneyī bore six great sons to Ūru—Aṅga, Sumanas, Khyāti, Kratu, Aṅgīras, (and) Gaya[6].

11. Sunīthā bore only Vena[7] from Aṅga. He, who was not a protector, and was delighted in doing sins was killed by the sages with their *kuśa* grass.

12. Then for the sake of progeny, the sages churned his right hand. When the hand of Veṇa was churned King Pṛthu came into being.

13. Having seen him, the sages said, "This person will make the subjects happy and will attain great valour and fame.

14. He was born with a bow and an armour as if consuming (everything) by his lustre. Pṛthu, the son of Vena, the predecessor of the *kṣatriyas*, protected the subjects.

15. That lord of the earth is the first among those coronated after the Rājasūya (sacrifice). From that (ceremony) were born the clever (singers) *sūta* and *māgadha*.

---

1. The seven sages are Marīci, Atri, Aṅgiras, Pulastya, Pulaha, Kratu and Vasiṣṭha.
2. Kuni, see *Vi. P.* I. xiii.5.
3. Satyavat, see *ibid.*
4. Śuci, see *ibid.*
5. Agniṣṭoma, see *ibid.*
6. Śibi, see *Vi. P.* I. xiii.7.
7. Vena born to Sunīthā, the daughter of Mṛtyu was of wicked nature since childhood. When he became the king he proclaimed himself as the lord of sacrifices and did not allow sages to propitiate Viṣṇu by doing sacrifices. Their entreaties being of no avail they killed him by employing *kuśa* grass purified by the chant of mystic syllables. *Vi.P.* I. xiii. 11 ff.

16-17. The two heroes praised him. He became a king by pleasing the people. For the sake of (getting)grains and for the existence of the subjects, the cow (earth) was milked by him along with the celestials, sages, *gandharvas*, nymphs, manes, demons, snakes, plants, mountains and people.

18. The earth being milked in their respective vessels gave milk as much as (they) wished. (All) sustained their lives with that.

19. Antardhāna and Pālita[1], the two righteous sons were born to Pṛthu. From Antardhāna, Sikhaṇḍinī begot Havirdhāna.

20. Dhiṣaṇā, of the family of Agni gave birth to the six sons—Prācīnabarhiṣ, Śukra, Gaya, Kṛṣṇa, Vraja and Ajina from Havirdhāna.

21. (He was known as Prācīnabarhis) because the *kuśa* grass were facing the east as he was praying on the earth.[2] The lord Prācīnabarhis was a great progenitor.

22. Savarṇā, the daughter of Samudra (the lord of the ocean) bore ten Prācīnabarhis. All of them were known as Pracetas and were proficient in archery.

23. Practising the same religious austerities, they all did severe penance, remaining in the waters of the ocean for ten thousand years.

24. Having got the status of a progenitor and pleased Viṣṇu, they came out (of waters) (and found) that the earth and the sky were overspread with trees. They burnt them down.

25. Beholding the destruction of trees by the fire and wind produced from their mouths, Soma, the king (of plants) approached these progenitors and said :

26-27. "Renounce (your) anger, I will get you this most excellent maiden Māriṣā, (born to) (the nymph) Pramlocā and the ascetic sage Kaṇḍu (who was nourished) by me. Having known the future (I have) created (her). Let (she) be your wife, capable of multiplying the family. Dakṣa will be born to her who will multiply progeny."

28-30. The Pracetas married her and Dakṣa was born through her. That Dakṣa, having mentally created the immov-

1. Vādi, see *Vi.P.* I. xiv. 1
2. i.e., the sacrifices were performed all over the earth.

ables, movables, bi-footed beings and the quadrupeds, then created the (sixty) daughters (of whom) he gave[1] ten to Dharma, thirteen to Kaśyapa, twenty-seven to Soma, four to Ariṣṭanemin, two to Bahuputra, two to Aṅgiras.

31. By mental intercourse the celestials, serpents and others (were born) to them in the past. I shall describe (you) the creation of Dharma through his ten wives.

32. The Viśvedevas (were born) to Viśvā, Sādhyā gave birth to the Sādhyas. The Maruts came into being from the Marut and the Vasus from Vasu.

33. The Bhānus (were) the sons of Bhānu and the Muhūrtas (were born) to Muhūrtā. Ghoṣa (was born) to Dharma through Lambā. Nāgavīthī was born of Yāmī.

34. All that belonged to the earth were born of Arundhatī. Saṅkalpā (was born) from Saṅkalpā. The stars were the sons of moon.

35. The eight Vasus[2] are known by the names—Āpa, Dhruva Soma, Dhara[3], Anila, Anala, Pratyūṣa and Prabhāsa.

36. Vaitaṇḍya, Śrama, Śānta, and Muni[4] (were) the sons of Āpa. Kāla, the destroyer of the Universe (was the son) of Dhruva. Varcā was the son of Soma.

37. Dhara had the sons Draviṇa, Hutahavyavāha, Śiśira, Prāṇa and Ramaṇa through Manoharā.

38. Purojava[5] was (the son) of Anila and Avijñāta of Anala. Kumāra, the son of Agni, was born in a clump of reeds.

39. Śākha, Viśākha and Naigameya were his younger brothers. (He was known as) Kārttikeya (as he was the son) of Kṛttikā. (He is also known as) the ascetic Sanatkumāra.

40. Devala was born from Pratyūṣa. Viśvakarman (was born) from Prabhā, and was the architect of thousands of sculptures and the architect of celestials.

41. Men earn their livelihood by this art of architecture and of (making) ornaments. Surabhi begot eleven Rudras[6] from Kaśyapa.

---

1. For a detailed account see *Vi.P.* I. xv. 103b ff.
2. Vasus are a class of semi-divine beings.
3. Dharma, see *Vi.P.* I.xv. 111a.
4. Dhvani, see *Vi.P.* I. xv. 112a.
5. Manojava, see *Vi.P.* I. xv. 114b.
6. Following the Brahmāṇḍa P. narration, Rudras are given here as sons of Surabhi and Kaśyapa.

42. O Most pious man! By the favour of Mahādeva (Śiva) (who was) thought of (by her) in her ascetic observances Satī gave birth to Ajaikapād, Ahirbudhnya, Tvaṣṭṛ and Rudra.

43-44. Viśvarūpa, the great illustrious and fortunate (was) the son of Tvaṣṭṛ. Hara, Bahurūpa, Tryambaka, Aparājita, Vṛṣākapi, Śambhu, Kapardin, Raivata, Mṛgavyādha, Sarpa and Kapālin were the eleven forms by which the entire world, both movable and immovable were pervaded by hundreds and thousands of Rudras.[1]

## CHAPTER NINETEEN

### *Description of secondary creation : the progeny of Kaśyapa*

*Agni said* :

1-3. O Sage! I describe the creation (made) by Kaśyapa through Aditi and others. Those devas who were (known) as Tuṣita in the Cākṣuṣa manvantara, again became (the sons) of Kaśyapa through Aditi in the Vaivasvata manvantara as the twelve Ādityas (with the names) Viṣṇu, Śakra, Tvaṣṭṛ, Dhātṛ, Aryaman, Pūṣan, Vivasvat, Savitṛ, Mitra, Varuṇa, Bhaga, and Aṁśu. The progeny of the wives of Ariṣṭanemi were sixteen.

4. The four lightnings were the daughters of the learned Bahuputra. Those born of Aṅgiras were excellent. (The progeny) of Kṛśāśva were the celestial weapons.[2]

5. Just as the sun rises and sets, similarly these (do) in every *yuga*. From Kaśyapa, Hiraṇyakaśipu and Hiraṇyākṣa (were born) through Diti.

6. Siṁhikā was also their daughter, who was married by Vipracitti. Rāhu and others born to her were known as Saiṁhikeyas.

---

1. The names of Eleven Rudras are not the same in the enumerations in different Purāṇas. On the Eleven Rudras see *Annals of Ori. Res.* XXIV. Pt. II

2. According to the science of *Jyotiṣa*, these four lightnings are *kapilā*, *atilohitā*, pitā and *asitā* indicating respectively wind, heat, rain and famine.

7-8. The four sons of Hiraṇyakaśipu (were) very effulgent. (They were) Anuhrāda, Hrāda, Prahrāda a staunch devotee of Viṣṇu; and Saṁhrāda was the fourth (son). Hrada (was) the son of Hrāda. Āyuṣmat, Śibi, and Bāṣkala (were) the sons of Hrada.

9. Virocana (was) the son of Prahrāda. Bali was born to Virocana. Bali had hundred sons. Bāṇa was the foremost among them, O great sage !

10. Having propitiated the consort of Umā (Śiva) in the past *kalpa*, a boon was obtained by Bāṇa from the lord that he would always wander by the side (of the lord).

11. The sons of Hiraṇyākṣa were five.[1] Śambara, Śakuni[2], Dvimūrddhan, Śaṅkurārya[3] were (the prominent among) the hundred sons of Danu.

12. Suprabhā was the daughter of Svarbhānu (a son of Danu). Śacī was known as the daughter of Puloman (a son of Danu). Upadānavī, Hayaśirā, and Śarmiṣṭhā (were) the daughters of Vṛṣaparvan (a son of Danu).

13. Pulomā and Kālakā were the two daughters of Vaiśvānara. They both married Kaśyapa and they had crores of sons.

14-16. In the family of Prahrāda (were born) four crores (of sons) (known as) the *nivātakavaca* (protected by armour). Tāmrā had six daughters—Kākī, Śyenī, Bhāsī, Gṛdhrikā, Śuci and Sugrīvā. The crows and (other birds) were born from them. The horses and camels (were born in the line) of Tāmrā. Aruṇa and Garuḍa (were born) from Vinatā. Thousands of serpents (were) born of Surasā. Thousands of serpents (such as) Śeṣa, Vāsuki, Takṣaka and others were born of Kadrū.

17. Animals having tusks, other earthly beings and the aquatic birds were born to Krodhā. The cows, buffaloes and other animals (were born) from Surabhi. The grass and other things were the production of Irā.

---

1. They are Utkura, Śakuni, Bhūtasantāpana, Mahānābha, Mahābāhu and Kālanābha. See *Vi.P.* I. xxi. 1-3,.
2. Given as the son of Hiraṇyākṣa. See *ibid.*
3. Śaṅkuśirāḥ. See *ibid.*

The reading given in the text here mixes the progeny of Hiraṇyākṣa and that of Danu.

18. The Yakṣas (semi-divine beings) and the demons (were born) of Khasā. The nymphs came into being from Muni. The Gandharvas (a class of semi-divine beings) (were born) to Ariṣṭā. Thus the stationary as well as the movable are born of Kaśyapa.

19-21. Innumerable are the offspring of these. The Dānavas (the progeny of Danu) (the demons) were conquered by the celestials. Diti, who had lost her offspring, propitiated Kaśyapa, desirous of (getting) a son capable of destroying Indra. (She) achieved (her object) from Kaśyapa. Indra, seeking to find a fault (found out that she) had slept without washing her feet[1] and destroyed (cut off) the embryo. They became celestials (known as) Maruts, fifty one (in number) radiant with lustre and the allies of Śakra (Indra).[2]

22. All these (are) forms of Hari. Having installed Pṛthu as the ruler, Hari duly set apart kingdoms for others.

23. The moon (was made the king) of the twice-born and the plants, Varuṇa (as) the king of waters, Vaiśravaṇa (Kubera) (as) the king of kings, Viṣṇu (as) the lord of Suns.

24. Pāvaka (fire) as the king of Vasus; Vāsava (Indra) (as) the lord of Maruts and then Dakṣa (as the king) of Prajāpatis (patriarchs), Prahlāda (as) the ruler of demons.

25. Yama (was made) the king of manes, Hara (Śiva) (as) the lord of goblins, Himavat (as the ruler) of mountains, the ocean (as) the lord of rivers.

26. Citraratha (was made the ruler) of Gandharvas, and then Vāsuki (as the ruler) of Nāgas, Takṣaka (as) the king of serpents, and then Garuḍa, among the birds.

27. The Airāvata (was made the ruler) among the lords of elephants, bull of the kine and the tiger, of the animals, (and) Plakṣa (the Indian fig-tree) (as) the lord of trees.

28. And Uccaiḥśravas (was made the ruler) among the horses.[3] Sudhanvan (son of Vairāja Prajāpati) became the regent of the east, Śaṅkhapād (the son of Kardama Prajāpati) (the

1. Failure to observe the necessary hygiene deprived her desire to get a vanquisher of Indra. For a detailed account of this episode see *Vi.P.* I. xxi. 30-41; *P. Index* II. pp. 87-88.

2. *Cf. Vi. P.* I. xxi. 11-14.

regent) of the south, Ketumat (son of Rajas) as the protector of the waters (on the west), Hiraṇyaromaka (son of Parjanya Prajāpati) on the Saumya (the north).

## CHAPTER TWENTY

### *Primary creation*

*Agni said* :

1. The intellect (*mahat*) is the first creation of Brahmā. The second (creation) is that of the subtle principles (*tanmātrās*),[1] known as the *bhūtasarga* (creation of elements).

2. The third is the creation of evolutes (*vaikārikas*) known as the sense-organs. These are the primary creation (*prākṛtasarga*) produced out of the intellect.

3. The fourth, is the main creation (*mukhyasarga*). The immobile things are known as the main (creation). That (creation) which is spoken as (the creation of) the lower order (*tiryaksrotas*) is known as that of the sub-human beings (animals, birds etc.).

4. Then the sixth creation is that of the higher orders (*ūrdhvasrotas*), known as the creation of the celestials. Then the seventh creation is that of the middle orders (*arvāksrotas*), the man.

5-6. The eighth is the creation (known as) the *anugraha* (compassionate divinities), composed of the qualities (*sāttvika* and *tāmasa*. These (latter) five are known as the *Vaikṛtasarga* (creation subject to transformation). The ninth creation is the Kaumāra (the creation of Sanatkumāra etc.) These are the nine creations[2] of Brahmā which are the main cause for the universe.

7-8. Bhṛgu and others married Khyāti and other daughters of Dakṣa. Creation has been described as three-fold by the people. They are usual (*nitya*), subject to some cause (*naimittika*), (and)

---

1. The *tanmātrās* or the subtle principles are related to the sense-organs.

2. The puranic cosmology divides creations into nine classes. See *Śiva P.* (English translation) p. 248 note 214.

daily (*dainandini*).[1] (The creation) after the intermediate dissolution is known as the daily (dainandinī). The constant creation that takes place everyday is considered as *nitya*.

9. From Bhṛgu, Khyāti gave birth to the celestials Dhātṛ and Vidhātṛ. Śrī (Lakṣmī) (was) the consort of Viṣṇu, and was praised by Śakra (Indra) for multiplying the progeny.

10. The sons of Dhātṛ and Vidhātṛ were Prāṇa and Mṛkaṇḍuka successively. Vedaśirā gave birth to Mārkaṇḍeya from Mṛkaṇḍu.

11-12. A son (by name) Paurṇamāsa was born to Marīci through Sambhūti. Sinīvālī, Kuhū, Rākā and Anumati were the sons of Aṅgiras through Smṛti. With Atri, Anasūyā gave birth to Soma, Durvāsas, and Dattātreya *yogin*.

13. A son (by name) Dattoli was born to Prīti, the wife of Pulastya. Sahiṣṇu and Kramapādika[2] were born to Kṣamā from Pulaha.

14. The highly radiant Bālakhilyas were born to Sannati[3] from Kratu. They, who were 60000, were of the size of a joint of the thumb.

15. To Urjā from Vasiṣṭha (were born) Raja, Gātra, Urdhvabāhu, Savana, Alaghu[4], Śukra and Sutapāḥ, the seven sages.

16. Pāvaka, Pavamāna and Śuci were born of Agni and Svāhā. The manes Agniṣvāttāḥ, devoid of fire and Barhiṣada, with fire (were born) from *aja* (Brahmā, the unborn).

17. Menā and Dhāriṇī were the daughters of the manes through Svadhā. Hiṁsā was the wife of Adharma. Then Anṛta was born to them.

18. Nikṛti (was their) daughter. Bhaya and Naraka (were born) from them, who had Māyā and Vedanā as their wives.

19. Of those two, Māyā gave birth to Mṛtyu, the destroyer of living beings. And also Vedanā gave birth to a son Duḥkha from Raurava (Naraka).

20. Vyādhi, Jarā, Śoka, Tṛṣṇā and Krodha were born from Mṛtyu. (Rudra) was born wailing from Brahmā and (was known as) Rudra by name on account of the wailing.

---

1. The minor dissolution of the world after 15 years of Brahmā's life is known as the *dainandina pralaya*. *MW*. p. 497b.
2. *Vi.P.* I. x. 10 reads Kardama and Urvarūpa.
3. Santati. *Vi.P.* I.x.11.
4. Anagha. *Vi.P.* I.x.14.

21. O twice-born ! the grandfather (Brahmā) said to (him) (called him as) Bhava, Śarva, Īśāna, Paśupati, Bhīma, Ugra (and) Mahādeva.

22. His wife Satī gave up her life on account of the wrath of Dakṣa and having become the daughter of Himavat again became the wife of Śambhu (Śiva).

23. (I will now describe) the methods of worship of Viṣṇu etc., preceded by bathing and other (rites) and yielding enjoyment and emancipation, by doing which Svāyambhuva (Manu) (had the benefit), as told by Nārada and others to the sages.

## CHAPTER TWENTYONE

### *Method of worshipping Viṣṇu and other gods*

*Nārada said* :

1. I will (now) describe the general method of worshipping Viṣṇu and others as well as the *mantras* (mystic formulae) which yield good to all. One has to worship (him by saying) "Salutations to Acyuta (Viṣṇu) and to (his) entire family (of gods).

2-4. (Salutation to) Dhātṛ, Vidhātṛ,[1] Gaṅgā, Yamunā, the two *nidhis* (treasures), the fortune of Dvāra(kā), the Vāstu-deity (the presiding deity of the housesite), Śakti (female divinity), Kūrma (tortoise), Ananta (the serpent), the Earth, righteous knowledge, detachment from the world, the omnipotence (of the lord), the unrighteousness etc. the root, stalk, filament and pericarp of the lotus, *Ṛgveda* and other (*Vedas*), Kṛta and other (*yugas*), *sattva* and other (qualities), the solar and other regions, the pure and elevating union of knowledge and action. One has to worship these.

5. Joy, truth, the goddess benevolently placed, Durgā (Pārvatī), speech, goblins, field and Vāsudeva and others are worshipped.

---

1. Dhātṛ and Vidhātṛ are the two sons of Brahmā.

6. The heart, head, coat of mail, eye and weapons, conch, disc, mace, lotus, Śrīvatsa (sacred mark on Lord Kṛṣṇa's chest) and the Kaustubha gem are worshipped.

7. The garland of wood-flowers (worn by Kṛṣṇa), Śrī (Lakṣmī), *Puṣṭi* (nourishment), Garuḍa (vehicle of Viṣṇu), and the preceptor are worshipped. Indra, Agni, Yama, Rakṣa (Nairṛta), water, wind, lord of wealth (Kubera) (are also worshipped).

8. That Īśāna, the unborn, and weapons, vehicles, Kumuda and others (are worshipped next). By the worship of Viṣvaksena (all-pervasive) (Viṣṇu) in a circle first, one gets his desires accomplished.

9. Then the general worship of Śiva (is described). One has to worship Nandin at first. (Then) Mahākāla (Śiva), Gaṅgā, Yamunā, Gaṇas, and others (are worshipped).

10-11. (Then) the speech, the goddess of prosperity, the preceptor, the Vāstu (deity), the different female energies and Dharma (the lord of death) and other gods (are worshipped). (The female energies) Vāmā, Jyeṣṭhā, Raudrī, Kālī, Kalavikariṇī, Balavikariṇī, Balapramathinī, Sarvabhūtadamanī, Manomanī and Śivā (are worshipped) in the due order.

12. (Saying) Hām, Hum, Ham (salutation) to the form of Śiva, Śiva is worshipped along with his limbs and mouth. Haum, (salutation) to Śiva, Haum and Hām (salutations) to Īśāna (one of the Pañcabrahman forms of Śiva) and other faced (forms of Śiva).

13. Hrīm (salutation) to Gaurī (Pārvatī), Gam (salutation) to Gaṇa, face of Śakra (Indra), Caṇḍa, heart and others. The mystic syllables in the worship of the sun (are described now). The tawny-coloured Daṇḍin is to be worshipped.

14. One should adore Uccaiḥśravas (the horse of Indra), the very much pure Aruṇa (younger brother of the Sun-god). The moon and the twilight, the other faces and Skanda (progeny of Śiva) in the middle are worshipped.

15. Then (the female divinities) Dīptā, Sūkṣmā, Jayā, Bhadrā, Vibhūti, Vimalā, Amoghā, Vidyutā and Sarvatomukhī are worshipped.

16. Then the mantra Ham, Kham, Kham for the firebrand (is used for the worship) of the seat of the sun and (his) form. Hrām, Hrīm, salutation to the sun, Ām, salutation to the heart.

17. (Salutation) to the (rays of the) sun, to his head, and similarly to the flames reaching up the regions of demons, wind, earth, ether, and heavens. Hum is remembered as the mystic amulet.

18-19. (Salutations are made) to the lustre, eye, Hraḥ, to the weapons of Sun, Rāji, Śakti, and Niṣkubha. Then Soma (Moon), Aṅgāraka (Mars), Budha (Mercury), Jīva (Jupiter), Śukra (Venus) and Śani (Saturn) as well as Rāhu, Ketu, *tejas*, Caṇḍa are worshipped in order in brief. Then the worshipper (should worship) the seat of the image (of the deity) and the heart etc.

20. (The *mantra*) for the seat of Viṣṇu for the image of Viṣṇu (is) "Rām, Śrīm, Śrīm, Śrīdhara, Hari." Hrīm (is) the mystic syllable for the images (of all deities) which is capable of captivating the three worlds.

21. Hrīm, Hṛṣīkeśa (master of the senses) (Viṣṇu), Klīm, Viṣṇu. With long vowels (one should adore) the heart and other things. (The performance) of worship on the fifth day (pañcamī) with all these (mystic syllables) yields victory in battles.

22-23. Worship of the disc, mace, conch, pestle, sword, Śārṅga (the bow), noose, goad, Śrīvatsa (mark on the chest of the lord), with the garland of wood-flowers and with the *mantra* Śrīm, worship of Śrī, Mahālakṣmī, Tārkṣya (vehicle of Viṣṇu), the preceptor, Indra etc. (are made) in order. With the (mystic) syllable Aum, Hrīm, Devī (goddess) Sarasvatī (one has to worship) the seat of (Goddess) Sarasvatī.

24. The Hṛt etc., Lakṣmī, Medhā, Kalā, Tuṣṭi, Puṣṭikā, Gaurī, Prabhāvatī, (and) Durgā (the different female divinities), goblins, preceptor and the presiding deity of the field (are worshipped).

25. Then (one has to say) Gaṁ, (salutation) to the lord of the *gaṇas*, Hrīm to Gaurī, Śrīm to Śrī, Hrīm to Tvaritā, Aim, Klīm, Saum to Tripurā using the fourth declensional endings and ending with salutations.

26. All the mystic syllables are pronounced preceded by the Praṇava (syllable Om), adding *bindu* (the nasal sound marked by a dot), either while offering adorations or the performance of repetition.

27. By the offer of a *homa* (offer unto the fire) with sesamum and ghee and other things, (these *mantras*) become bestowers of

*dharma*, *kāma*, *artha* and *mokṣa* (four principal objects of human life). Whoever reads these syllables of adoration reaches heaven after enjoying pleasures.

## CHAPTER TWENTYTWO

### *Procedure for bathing prior to a religious rite*

*Nārada said* :

1. I will (now) describe the (mode of) bathing preceding (any religious) act. Having taken a clod of earth accompanied by (meditation on) the man-lion form (of Viṣṇu), and making it into two parts, (one has to do) mental bathing with one part of it.

2. Having immersed (one's body in waters) and having partaken (three drops of) water and assigning (on the body) with the lion (man-lion) one has to get himself protected. Then one has to do bathing as laid down, being preceded by the control of the breath.

3. Meditating on Lord Hari in one's heart with the eight-syllabled *mantra* (Oṁ namo Vāsudevāya, Oṁ namo Nārāyaṇāya or Oṁ namo Narasiṁhāya), the clod of earth (is made) into three parts on the palm and protection in (all) the quarters (is achieved) with the recitation of (the *mantra*) for the lion (man-lion).

4-7. With the recitation (of the *mantra*) of Vāsudeva, having mentally resolved the sacred water and having rubbed the body with *vedic mantras* and having adored the image of deity and having remembered the *aghamarṣaṇa* (*sūkta*) which destroys sins) and putting on a cloth, perform the (following) rite. Putting water on the palm, accompanied by *mantras* and wiping off waters on the palm, controlling with the Nārāyaṇa (*mantra*), the air is inhaled and water is let off. Then contemplating on Hari, offering waters (of oblation) and reciting the twelve-syllabled (mantra), appeasing all others with devotion commencing in order with the seat of meditation, the *mantras* upto all the guardian deities of the quarters, the sages, clans of manes, men, all beings and ending with the mobile (beings) are placed.

8. Then having assigned limbs (for the different deities), withdrawing the *mantras* one has to go to the house for performing rites. In this way, one has to bathe with the *mūlamantra*[1].

## CHAPTER TWENTYTHREE

### *Mode of performing worship*

*Nārada said* :

1-2. I will now describe the mode of worship, O brahmins ! by doing which one gets all (objects of life). Having washed feet, sipping waters, and controlling his speech and having guarded (himself like this), facing the east, and having seated in the *svastika* or *padmāsana* or other posture (one has to meditate) on (the syllable) *yam* at the centre of the navel, having tawny colour and of the form of terrible wind.

3. Then meditating on the syllable *kṣaum* of abundant lustre at the centre of the heart, burn down all impurities from the body.

4-5. One has to burn the impurities with the flames surging upwards and downwards. One has to meditate on the (*mantra*) of the shape of the moon situated in the sky. An intelligent person has to sprinkle his own body with the nectar-like waters pervading the lotus in the heart through (the artery) *suṣumnā* and passing through the nerves.

6. Having purified materials (for worship) one has to assign (them). Then (one has) to purify hands as well as implements. Commencing with the thumb of the right hand, (the fingers) of the two hands are made to rest on the principal limbs.

7-8. (Then) with sixtytwo *mantras* (sacred syllables) one has to assign to the body the twelve limbs—heart, head, tuft of hair, armour, weapons, eyes, belly, hinder part, arms, thighs, knees and feet. Having offered the *mudrā* (special posture of the

1. *mūlamantra* is the basic subtle mystic syllable.

arms and body), one has to meditate on Viṣṇu, and having repeated (his name) one hundred and eight times, one has to worship him.

9. Having placed the water-jar on the left and the materials for worship on the right and having washed (them) with the implements and water offerings, they are placed together with flowers and scents.

10-11. Having sprinkled the radiant (form) of consciousness and omnipresence with waters (purified) by the repetition (of the *mantra* of the lord) eight times (and) having sprinkled the hand with *mantra* ending with *phaṭ* and then having meditated on Hari, with his face directed towards the (south-east) direction (presided over by) Agni, (one has to pray) for virtue, knowledge, detachment, (and) supremacy. (Facing) the east (and other directions), (one has to get rid) of his sins and physical impurities remaining in yogic postures.

12. (Remaining) in *Kūrma* (tortoise) posture, one should adore Ananta, Yama, the solar and other luminous regions and other planets (occupying) the filament and pericarp (of the lotus).

13-14. Having first meditated (on them) in one's heart and having invoked and worshipped in a circle, (offerings) of waters of respect, waters for washing feet, waters for rinsing, *madhuparka*[1] (respectful offering), bath, cloth, sacred thread, scents, flowers, incense, lamp and eatables (are made) (along) with the formula (known as) Puṇḍarīkākṣa.

15. First, one has to worship the limbs and then Brahmā at the doorway in the eastern (direction), the disc and the club in the southern (direction); the conch, and the bow have to be assigned in the corner (governed by) the moon.

16. One should assign the quiver and sword to the left and right side of the deity, the armour and nourishment on the left, and the prosperity on the right in front.

17. One has to worship with respective sacred syllables, the garland of wild-flowers, (the mark) *śrīvatsa*, (the gem) *kaustubha* and the presiding deities of the quarters outside and all (the attendant gods) of Viṣṇu as well either partially or wholly.

18-19. One has to worship with the limbs with the sacred

1. It consists of curd, clarified butter, water, honey and sandalpaste.

syllables partially or wholly. After having repeated (the sacred syllables), doing circumambulation and adoration and offering waters of adoration and the offerings, one has to assign in the heart and after having meditated, "I am the brahman and Hari", (one has to repeat the words) 'come' used in (the ceremony of) invocation and "forgive me" in dismissal (at the conclusion).

20. Having worshipped in this manner with the *mantra* of eight letters (one becomes eligible) to get liberation. The (mode of) worship of one form (of a deity) has been described. Listen to the (mode of) worship in the structure of nine (apartments).

21-23. Having assigned Vāsudeva, Balarāma) and others to the two thumbs and then at first to the fingers, then to the body, head, forehead, face, heart, navel, organ of generation, knees, (and) between the feet, one has to worship in order, single seat of the deity consisting of nine parts and then the nine seats and of the nine forms consisting of nine parts in nine lotuses as before. Then in the midst of the lotus one has to worship Vāsudeva.

## CHAPTER TWENTYFOUR

### *Mode of constructing the sacrificial pit and the oblations unto fire*

*Nārada said* :

1-2. I shall describe the mode of oblation to fire, by which (one) gets all his desires fulfilled. One has to dig a square pit after having measured out with a thread, four times, twenty-four thumbs in length. Leaving a space of the breadth of two thumbs a girdle is to be made (around) the pit.

3. (One seat) of twelve thumbs in length, and eight, two and four thumbs respectively in extent (should be made) in the east.

4. (One) beautiful (seat) of ten, six and four thumbs in extent and with a mouth, two thumbs in width and tapering gradually should be made in the west.

5. It should be of the form of a leaf of the holy fig tree and

should enter a little into the pit. A drain, quarter of a thumb in breadth and fifteen thumbs in length (should then be dug).

6. The base (of the drain) at the seat (will be) three thumbs and the fore part six. (This is) the characteristic (of a pit) of one cubit (hand). (The characteristic of a pit) of two cubits is twice (this).

7. I have thus described to you (about) the pit surrounded by three altars. I will now describe (about) the circular pit. A thread is to be fixed in half of the pit, the remaining portion being fixed at an intermediate point.

8-9. Having placed half the rope in the pit, if (the rope) is moved around it would be a circle. After having marked out the centre, (if one makes) a crescent-shaped pit east-west, and away from the northern direction, half (the size) of the pit and half the angular portion, it indicates auspiciousness.

10. (In pits of) circular (shape) the girdles would be of the shape of the petals of a lotus. The ladle for the sake of oblation is to be made of the size of an arm.

11. Then one has to make (ready) a site (of the length) of thirteen thumbs and four (in breadth). A pit of three-fourths (of the site) is dug and a beautiful circle (is made).

12-13. One has to purify (the space) outside the pit evenly, horizontally and upwards (to the extent of) half a thumb (and) one-fourth of a thumb. A beautiful boundary line is to be made with the remaining (space) (around) the pit.

14-15. Or it may be half a thumb more. The mouth would be at the front (having) a width of four or five thumbs. Its central part might be three times two thumbs and beautiful. The extent (on all sides) (might be) of equal (measurement) (and) its central portion is lowered.

16. There must be a hole at the neck portion (of such a size) that the little finger would enter. The other pit should be beautifully made according to one's liking.

17. The (sacrificial) ladle should have a handle of the length of one hand. A beautiful spoon (having) circumference of two thumbs has to be made.

18-19. Just as the cow's foot (would) sink in a little mud, so also after having drawn a line (of the length) of a thumb (known as) *vajranāsikā*, (one has to draw) first a line with a fine tip, (then) two lines between it and the east (and) then three lines in the middle from the south onwards in order.

20. Having drawn (the lines), (and) consecrating, with the syllable *Om*, one who knows the *mantras*, has to make a seat in which the energy of Viṣṇu rests.

21-22. Having adorned the incarnate form (of energy), one has to throw fire after having remembered Hari. Having offered twigs of the size of a span (between the thumb and the fore-finger)and having sprinkled water and having spread around on the three sides in the east etc. with the *darbha* grass, the fire from the fuel as well as the ladle for pouring clarified butter, (*sruk*) and sacrificial ladle (*sruva*) are to be placed on the ground.

23-26. (One should then place) vessels (for keeping) clarified butter, (and) (*caru*) (oblation of rice, barley and pulse boiled together), *kuśa* grass and clarified butter. The *prokṣaṇi*[1] vessel being sprinkled with water with the *praṇitā*[2] vessel, (and) taken up and filled with water (and) that water being enclosed in the hand with the *pavitra* (*darbha* grass) placed in between and having taken the *prokṣaṇi* vessel towards the east and having placed it in front of the radiant fire (and) having sprinkled (all the vessels) thrice with water and having placed the fuel in front, (and) having meditated on Viṣṇu in the *praṇitā* vessel containing a flower and having then filled vessel for (keeping) clarified butter with clarified butter and having placed it in front, the purification of the clarified butter is made by straining and sprinkling clarified butter on the fire.

27. One should take up two *kuśa* grass with unbroken tips, not being filled in, and of the measure of a span (between the thumb and the fore-finger) with the thumb and the nameless finger (ring-finger) of the palm facing upwards.

28-30. Having taken with them the clarified butter twice and having carried them, (they) must be cast downwards thrice. And again having taken the ladles (*sruk* and *sruva*) (and) having sprinkled them with water with them (the *kuśa* grass) and having heated and wiped them with the *darbhas* and again having sprinkled (water) and burnt and having placed along with the syllable

1. Small vessel used at the time of religious rites.
2. Small vessel used at the time of religious rites.

*Om*, the aspirant must perform fire oblation commencing with the syllable *Om* and ending with salutation. (One has to perform) *garbhādhāna* and other rites as much as it is laid down.

31. One has to do upto the naming ceremony, the undertaking of a vowed observance, observance marking the conclusion of study of the student, (and) investiture of authority in due manner.

32. The aspirant must everywhere do the worship with the syllable *Om*. One has to do offering unto fire with the auxiliaries befitting one's means.

33-34. *Garbhādhāna*[1] is the first one. Then *puṁsavana*[2] is remembered. Then the *simantonnayana*[3], *jātakarma*[4], *nāma (karaṇa)*[5], *annaprāśana*[6], *cūḍākṛti*[7], *vratabandha*[8], and many more are the vedic observances. One who has the right to do these rites should perform these in the company of his wife.

35. Having contemplated (on the deity) in the heart and other limbs and worshipping him, one has to offer sixty-four oblations for every one of the rites again.

36. The worshipper has to offer the final oblation with the sacrificial ladle, chanting loudly with sweet intonation the mystic formula ending with the word *vauṣaṭ*.

37. After having purified the fire of Viṣṇu, the food intended for Viṣṇu has to be boiled. After having worshipped Viṣṇu in the altar and remembering the mystic formulae one has to seek his protection.

38-39. Having worshipped in order his seat and other things along with the enclosures with fragrant flowers and contemplating on the most excellent lord of all deities, and placing the fuel and then the support, the oblations of clarified butter

1. One of the purificatory rites performed to ensure conception.

2. One of the purificatory rites performed to get a male child when the embryo has not yet begun to move.

3. The parting of hair, another purificatory rite performed on the eighth month after conception.

4. rite performed soon after the birth of a child.

5. rite performed to name the child.

6. first partaking of food by a child.

7. tonsure at the age of three.

8. Undertaking a religious observance.

(should be poured) in order (on fires) placed in the south-east, north-east, north-west and south-west.

40. Then having poured portions of the clarified butter in the south and north, one has to offer oblation in the middle reciting the mystic formulae in the order of worship.

41-42. One has to offer oblation with clarified butter to the deity and a tenth part to the limbs. (Having offered) oblations of clarified butter and other things hundred times or thousand times, or of the twigs or of the sesamum, and concluding the worship ending with the oblation and calling the disciples who are pure, and placing the fed beasts in front, (they are) sacrificed by means of weapons.

43-45. Having united the disciples with one's own self with the fetters of knowledge and action and the consciousness which follows the *liṅga*[1] and which is protected along with the *liṅga*, having been consecrated by means of contemplation, (they) have to be purified by the syllables of Vāyu. Then the creation of the whole egg (the universe), consumed by the fire (and) reduced into a heap of fire is contemplated upon with the syllables of the Fire god. (Then one should sprinkle ashes on the water and meditate on the world.

46. Then one has to assign the creative power which is known as the seed of the earth and which is enveloped by all the subtle principles.

47. Then one has to meditate on the egg produced out of it, (which) is its base and identical with the self. Then one has to meditate on the form of the *puruṣa* (the Supreme Being) identical with the *praṇava* (the syllable *Om*) at its centre (centre of the egg).

48. The *liṅga*, situated in one's self, (and) (which) has been purified earlier, is then to be transferred. Then the positions of the different important organs are to be thought of.

49. Then, having remained for one year, the egg is split. The heaven and earth (are placed) in a part. Prajāpati (the creator) (is placed) in between the parts.

50. Having meditated on his form and again having consecrated that child with the *praṇava* (syllable *Om*) and having made his body made up of the mystic for-

1. Situated in one's own self, representing the Supreme Being

mulae, (one has to do) the assignment (of limbs to different deities) as described before.

51-52. Then having placed the hand of Viṣṇu on the head and contemplated on one or many (forms) of Viṣṇu in this way, (and) having muttered mantras (remaining) in meditative posture, (and) seizing the hands with the basic mystic formula, one who knows the mystic formula having covered the eyes with a cloth (has to sprinkle) water with a new cloth.

53. After having performed worship, the preceptor, who knows perfectly well the nature of the god of gods, should make his disciples sit facing the east and with folded palms holding flowers.

54-55. Having been instructed by the preceptor in this way, they (the disciples) also must adore Hari. Having offered the handful of flowers there (and) then having offered worship with flowers without (the recitation of) any mystic formula and saluted the feet of the preceptor, (the disciples) must give (him) the fee, either all his possession or half of them.

56. The preceptor has to instruct the disciples thoroughly. Hari must be worshipped by them by (the recitation of his) names. The Lord Viṣvaksena[1] (whose powers go everywhere), who bears the conch, disc and mace has to be worshipped.

57. (Then that deity) stationed in a circular altar, (and who is frightening) (is worshipped) with the fore-finger and is requested to leave.

58-59. The entire remnants of offerings to Viṣṇu, must be offered to Viṣvaksena. Then having bowed down and sprinkled (with waters), (their own persons), (the disciples) having placed the fire of the pit on their own person, Viṣvaksena is permitted to leave. One who is desirous of enjoyment gets all things. One who is desirous of release from mundane existence gets merged in Hari.

---

1. A form of that deity to whom the fragments of a sacrifice are offered; also used as an attribute of Viṣṇu. *MW*. p. 998. col. 1

## CHAPTER TWENTYFIVE

*The formulae and mode of worship relating to Vāsudeva, Saṅkarṣaṇa, Pradyumna and Aniruddha*

*Nārada said* :

1. I shall now describe to you the characteristics of the adorable formulae related to Vāsudeva and others. Vāsudeva, Saṅkarṣaṇa, Pradyumna and Aniruddha (are the four forms).

2. (The words) salutations to the lord (are said) at first along with the mystical letters a, ā, am, aḥ. (Then) beginning with the syllable 'Om' (and) ending with (the word) salutations and then (the words) salutations to Nārāyaṇa (are uttered).

3. Om, salutations to the eternal Brahmā, Om, salutations to Viṣṇu, Om, Kṣaum, Om, salutations to the Lord Narasiṁha (are uttered).

4-6. Om, *bhūḥ*[1], salutations to lord Varāha. The lords of men having the colour of *japā* (flower) (red), brown, yellow, blue, black, red, the colour of a cloud, fire, honey, (and) tawny, (are) the nine lords of vowels (and) mystical letters. The heart and the different limbs are resolved in order along with their respective names being well divided by those proficient in the *tantras* (branch of literature dealing with the magical and mystical worship of different deities). The characteristics of those mystical letters which are consonants are different.

7. They are divided by long vowels ending with (the word) 'salutation'. The limbs situated in between yoked with short (vowels) are described. as minor limbs.

8. The mystic syllable situated at the end of the last letter of the name which is divided is excellent. The principal and minor limbs (are composed)of long and short vowels inorder.

9-10. This is the method (of use) of consonants for arrangement in the heart (and) other (limbs).One has to repeat according to his accomplishment (the mystic formula) divided into the mystic basic syllable and their ending names (along with) the names of limbs, after having resolved the yoked twelve (limbs) beginning with the heart etc.

11. The heart, head, tuft, armour, eye, weapons (are)

---

1. The mystical syllable representing the earth.

the six limbs of the mystic basic syllables of the basic (mystic formula) constituting twelve parts.

12. One should then assign in order to (the limbs)—the heart, head, tuft, hands, eyes, belly, back, arms, thighs, knees, shank, (and) feet, (the following syllables and gods).

13. (The letters) kam, ṭam, pam, śam are for Vainateya[1]. (The letters) kham, ṭham, pham, ṣam (are) for the brother of mace-bearer (Kṛṣṇa). (The letters) gam, ḍam, vam, sam (form) the mystic formula for the nourishment. Gham, ḍham, bham, ham salutations to Śrī (Goddess of wealth).

14. (One has to worship) Pāñcajanya[2], (with the mystic letters) vam, śam, mam, kṣam. (The mystic letters) cham, tam, pam (are for the worship of) Kaustubha (gem worn by Viṣṇu on his head), jam, kham, vam for the Sudarśana (the disc in the hands of Viṣṇu), sam, vam, dam, cam, lam for Śrīvatsa (the mark on the chest of Viṣṇu).

15. Om, dham, vam salutations to the garland of wild flowers (worn by Viṣṇu) and to the great Ananta.[3] The limbs are set forth with the words of the mystic formula consisting of words without the mystic letters.

16. Along with the names ending with the caste (names), the heart and other (limbs) (are set forth). The *praṇava* (letter Om) (is repeated) five times. Then the heart and other (limbs) are mentioned five times.

17. With the *praṇava* (one should adore) the heart first. (With the word) 'for the supreme', the head (and) the tuft and with one's name, the armour (are adored). The end of the name would be (to worship) the weapon.

18. Om, the supreme weapon is the first. (Then) one's own name ending in the fourth case (is to be said). Then (the word) 'salutations' (comes) at the end. This consists of one to twentysix parts.

19. One should worship *prakṛti* (nature) at the tips of the little and other fingers of the arms in (one's) body. (That one) consisting of *prakṛti* (nature) is the second form of the supreme being consisting of *puruṣa* (soul).

---

1. Garuḍa, the eagle vehicle of Viṣṇu; born to Vinatā and sage Kaśyapa.
2. The name of the conch of Kṛṣṇa.
3. Without end; may denote Lord Viṣṇu as well as Śeṣa Nāga.

20-21. Om (salutation) to the supreme being, the foremost or the first soul. The air and the sun (are his) two forms. The fire the third form having been assigned to pervade hands and the body, wind and the sun in the fingers of hand, this is embodied in the three parts in the two arms, left and the other arm, in the heart, in the body forming the fourth state.

22. The *Ṛgveda* (is made) to pervade hand. The *Yajus* (*Yajurveda*) is assigned to fingers. The form of *Atharva* (is assigned) to two palms. Thus (assignments are made) in (different limbs) head, heart, upto the feet.

23. As before having assigned the extensive sky to his arm and body, wind and other (elements), to fingers, head, heart, generative organ and the feet.

24. The wind, fire, water, earth (and sky or ether) are spoken as his five forms. The mind, ear, skin, eye, tongue (and) nose are said to be the six forms.

25-28. The extensive mind is assigned from the thumb onwards to the head, mouth, generative organ and the organ of excretion. The prime form is said to be consisting of compassion. It is known as the *jiva* (life) (which is) all pervasive. The seven (words), earth, ether, heaven, *mahas*, *jana*, *tapa* and *satya*[1] are assigned duly to hands and the body beginning with thumb. The Lord of the world, the seventh one and existing in the palm (is taken) gradually to the body, head, forehead, mouth, heart, generative organ and feet. This is said to be the *Agniṣṭoma*.[2] (Next follows the description of) the *Vājapeya*[3] (and) the *Ṣoḍaśi*[4] rites.

29-32. *Atirātra*[5] and *Aptoryāma*[6] (rites will also be described). The soul of the sacrifice which has seven forms extending to the intellect, ego, mind, sound, touch, colour, taste, smell, comprehension, should be assigned duly to the fingers and the body. A person has to assign it to the teeth, palms, head, forehead,

1. The seven worlds earth etc. are situated one above the other successively.
2. A sacrificial rite lasting for several days in spring forming part of the *Jyotiṣṭoma*, a *soma* sacrifice.
3. One of the soma sacrifices performed by kings or by a brahmin aspiring for higher position.
4. A rite forming part of the *soma* sacrifice.
5. An optional part of the *Jyotiṣṭoma* sacrifice.
6. A particular way of offering the *soma* sacrifice.

face, heart, navel, the generative organ and the feet. These are remembered as the eight *Vyūhas* (parts). The life which consists of nine parts—life, intellect, ego, mind, sound, quality, wind, colour, and taste, is assigned to two thumbs. They (are placed) in order on the left hand by means of the forefinger and other fingers.

33. Indra remains pervading the ten (limbs) consisting of body, head, forehead, mouth, heart, navel, the generative organ, two knees and feet.

34-35. The fire (is assigned) to two thumbs. Mind consisting of eleven parts—ear, skin, eye, tongue, smell, speech, hand, foot, anus is assigned to head, forehead, face, heart, navel, the generative organ, two knees and feet with the forefinger.

36. The mind is made to pervade the male organ. The two thumbs (are made to pervade) the ear. Commencing with the fore-finger in order, the eight fingers (are assigned). The (two fingers) left over are assigned to palm.

37. The head, forehead, month, heart, navel (are assigned) in order to generative organ, two thighs, shanks, ankles and feet.

38-39. Viṣṇu, Madhuhara (killer of the demon Madhu), Trivikrama, Vāmana, Śrīdhara, Hṛṣīkeśa, Padmanābha, Dāmodara, Keśava, Nārāyaṇa, Mādhava, Govinda (are the names of Viṣṇu). Viṣṇu is made to pervade.

40. The thumb (and other fingers), palms, feet, two knees, waist are assigned to head, crown of head, waist, knees and feet.

41-43. There are twelve, twentyfive or twentysix parts—the supreme being, intellect, ego, mind, thinking, touch, taste, colour, smell, ears, skin, eyes, tongue, nose, speech, hand, feet, anus, generative organ, earth, water, light, wind and sky. The pervasive Supreme Being is assigned and then in the thumbs and other fingers.

44-46. The remnant are assigned in the palm, head, or forehead and then face, heart, navel, generative organ, thigh, knee, and feet are assigned to feet, knee, thing, generative organ, heart and head in order. A wise man has to meditate upon the great soul of the Supreme Being in these twentysix things as before and then the nature has to be worshipped in a circular (altar). The heart and other (limbs) have to be worshipped in the east, south, west and north.

47. As before the weapons (of Viṣṇu, Vainateya (the vehicle bird of Viṣṇu) (are adored) in the corners of south-east etc. (One should adore) the guardian deities of the quarters also. In (the worship of) three parts, the fire (will be) at the centre.

48. The directions east etc. are decorated with the strength, abode and kingdom.

49-50. The omnipresent form (of Viṣṇu), endowed with all parts and the five constituents Garuḍa etc. as well as Indra and others, should be adored (by one) for conquering kingdoms and for firmness of all (objects). One may get all desires (fulfilled). Viṣvaksena (an epithet of Viṣṇu) is worshipped by (his) name, the mystic letter being placed in the ether.

## CHAPTER TWENTYSIX

### *A description of different positions of fingers in worship*

1. ( I now) describe the characteristic of (the different) positions of fingers (*mudrā*) (which) bring (the worshipper) nearer (to the object of worship). *Añjali* (folding of hands) is the first *mudrā*. (The second) is the *Vandanī* (fingers interlocked) to be placed near the heart.

2. With the left fist folded and the thumb erect, the right thumb interwoven with the erect left thumb is said to be (the third one).

3. (These are) the three common formations. The (following are) not common. By the unyoking of the smallest and other fingers eight positions (are formed) in order.

4. The first eight basic syllables are repeated in order. One has to bend the three fingers commencing with the little finger, with the thumb.

5. One has to raise up the hand to the face for the ninth

mystic syllable. Then the left hand is raised up and bent half slowly.

6. These are the *mudrās* of the limbs of *Varāha*[1] in order. Then the left fist having been kept closed, the fingers are released one by one.

7. The same position is held by the right hand also and the previous position is bent down. The left fist (is held) with the thumb erect. This results in the accomplishment of the *mudrā*.

## CHAPTER TWENTYSEVEN

*Mode of performing the initiation rite* :

*Nārada said* :

1-2. I shall describe the initiation rite, which yields everything. Hari should be worshipped in the lotus in a circle. Having gathered the articles (required) for the sacrifice on the tenth (lunar) day, assigning and consecrating hundred times with the (basic syllables) of the man-lion (*Narasiṁha*) (form), one should scatter on all sides the mustard seeds, destructive of demons, ending (the act) with the syllable *phaṭ*.

3. The female energy, contained in every being, in the form of grace is assigned there. Having collected all the herbs and spread, they are consecrated.

4. A worshipper has to accomplish the five products[2] of the cow hundred times in pure vessels by means of the five basic forms.

5. Having sprinkled the earth (with the basic syllable) ending with (the word) Nārāyaṇa, with the tips of *kuśa* (grass), those scattered (things) are thrown with the raised hand with the (basic syllable of) Vāsudeva.

---

1. If the two palms are placed together so as to form a cavity it represents the *Varāha Mudrā*.
2. Milk, curd, butter and the solid and liquid excreta.

6. Then standing with the face facing the east one has to meditate on Viṣṇu in the heart. One has to worship Viṣṇu in the waterpot along with the *vardhani*[1].

7. Having recited hundred times the sacred syllables for the weapon and having sprinkled the *Vardhani* (vessel) with a continuous shower (of water) it should be taken to the north-east quarter.

8. Taking the jar on his back one has to place it on the scattered (mustard seeds). Then having gathered them by means of the *Kuśa* (grass) one has to adore the presiding deity of the jar and the *karkari*[2].

9. One has to worship Hari adorned with clothes (and) five jewels, on a piece of ground (made ready), offering oblations to fire (for his sake) and reciting the sacred syllables, as before.

10. Sprinkling with a lotus and anointing with unguents the worshipper has to fill the boiling vessel with clarified butter and cow's milk.

11. Having looked at it with the Vāsudeva and the Saṅgharṣaṇa (basic syllables), rice mixed with clarified butter should be thrown into milk well-cooked.

12. After stirring it with the (basic syllable of) Pradyumna the worshipper has to mix it slowly with the ladle and then the cooked food is lifted with the (basic syllable of) Aniruddha.

13. Having washed him and besmearing (with sandals), the vertical mark is made on the forehead with the ashes. The food thus prepared well is placed by the side with the (basic syllable of) Nārāyaṇa.

14. A part of it has to be offered to the deity, the second part to the jar, and with the third part he should offer three oblations.

15-17. The preceptor has to partake of the fourth part in the company of his disciples for the sake of purification. Having consecrated seven times (the stick) got from the milky tree, the piece of wood for cleaning the tree being made use of and discarded and being conscious of one's sins and having offered oblations to the hundred auspicious and most excellent lions lying in

1. A water-jar of a particular shape.

2. A water-jar with small holes at the bottom as in a sieve.

the north, northeast, east and southeast, having done the *ācamana*[1] and having entered the chamber of worship, the knower of the mystic syllables should assign Viṣṇu in the east and do circumambulation.

18. You are, alone, O Lord ! the refuge of the beings immersed in the ocean of mundane existence, for the release from the fetters. You are always kind towards your worshippers.

19. "O Lord of Lords ! (you) permit (me). (I will) free these beings by your grace from their earlier fetters by which they are bound".

20-21. Having submitted thus to the lord of the celestials and having made the animals enter (the place), (they) have to be purified then by holding them as before and to be consecrated with the fire. Having yoked them with the deity their eyes should be closed. Their eyes are covered. Handful of flowers are offered there and their names are added.

22. Worship is made duly as before without reciting any basic syllable (*mantra*). That particular name of the idol on which the flower falls that is pointed out.

23. One should then take up a red thread spun by a maiden and measure it six times from the tuft of the hair to the toe and again multiply it three times.

24. Then one should meditate on the *Prakṛti* in which the universe lies and from which the universe is born, as being present there,.

25. Having tied the nooses of *Prakṛti* proportional to the number of principles, that thread is placed on an earthen vessel near the pit.

26. Then having meditated upon the principles commencing with the *Prakṛti* to the earth, following the order of creation, the spiritual teacher should assign them to the body of the disciple.

27. Those (principles), one, five, ten or twelve[2] may be tied individually and given by those who devote their thought on the principles.

---

1. *Ācamana* consists of sipping three drops of water, followed by touching of different parts of body reciting the different names of Viṣṇu.

2. *Prakṛti* is represented by one, the subtle principles by five, the organs of perception and action by ten, and these ten together with *Prakṛti* and mind by twelve.

28-29. With the five organs of action (one has to create) the entire universe in the order of evolution. Having drawn the subtle principles into one's self and (having placed) the rope of illusion on the animal, the nature is taken as the creative power, the intellect or the mind as the agent, the five subtle principles as born of intellect and the five elements from the organs of action.

30-31. One has to meditate on these twelve principles in the rope as well as in the body according to his desire. Having made oblations with the residue of offerings according to the order of creation, and hundred oblations to each and every (principle) and then the final oblation, the earthen vessel is covered and is dedicated to the presiding deity of the pot.

32-33. Having duly performed the initial consecration, the devoted disciple is initiated. Then in a place where the wind blows, an arrow of a particular shape and a knife made either of silver or iron as well as all necessary materials are placed; and touched with the principal mystic syllable he should perform the initial consecration ceremony.

34. He should then say "Salutations,. (I offer) the food to the goblins on the *kuśa* grass". Then having contemplated upon Hari, the sacrificial yard is adorned with multitudes of vessels of sweet meats.

35. Viṣṇu is then worshipped in a circular altar. Then after offering oblations to the fire, the pupils who are seated in the *Padmāsana*[1] posture are called upon and are initiated.

36-37. Having sprinkled water on Viṣṇu, and touching the head gradually, all the principles from the primordial down to the transformations as well as their presiding deities, the entire divine creation is conceived in the heart and all the subtle principles which have become one with the soul are absorbed gradually

38-40. Then the preceptor has to pray the presiding deity of the pitcher and draw the thread. Then having come near the fire and placing it (the thread) by the side of the fire, he (should offer) hundred oblations to the passive Lord of creation with the principal mystic syllable. Then the preceptor having reached

---

1. Sitting with crossed legs, the feet placed over the thigh of the opposite leg.

him, and having offered the final oblation, has to collect the white dust and strike the heart with that sanctified by the basic mystic syllable and ending with the syllables *hum* and *phaṭ*.

41. Then oblations are separately offered in order to the earth and other principles with mystic syllables made up by subtracting syllables.

42. When Hari has been uttered unto the fire which is the abode of all principles, the wiseman has to remember the method that is being followed there.

43. Separating by means of beating and collecting (them) one has to remain quiet. Then after collecting by the Primordial, an offering is made into the fire as instructed.

44. After offering eight oblations each (in favour) of (*Garbādhāna*[1], *Jātakarma*[2], enjoyment and dissolution, he should offer them for purification.

45. The preceptor should take up pure materials and bring together the two excellent principles in order in such a way they are not broken.

46. Then the soul, freed from fetters is immersed in the supreme soul in the supreme undecaying position.

47. A learned person has to think of the peaceful, supreme, blissful, pure intellect and offer the completing oblation. Thus ends the (rite of) initiation.

48. I shall describe the mystic syllables for the application with which the oblation (relating to) the initiation is closely associated:

*Oṃ*, *Yam*, the goblins, the pure *hum*, *phaṭ*. By this one should strike and separate the two.

49. *Om*, *yam*, I destroy the goblins. After having seized this (syllable) (you) hear (the mode of) yoking it with the nature. *Om*, *am*, the goblins and the males. I shall describe the mystic syllable for the oblation as well as the final oblation.

50. *Om*, destroy the goblins; oblations. *Om*, *am*, *Om*, salutations to the Lord Vāsudeva, *vauṣaṭ*. After the final oblation the disciple has to be accomplished. In this way the wiseman has to purify the principles.

1. The rite performed for facilitating conception.
2. The ceremony performed at the birth of a child.

51. Ending with (the word) salutation and with the basic syllable *sva* and preceded by beating (one has to say) *Om, vām,* the organs of action, *Om, dem,* the organs of intellect (sense). With the syllable *yam* similar beating etc. are done.

52. *Om, sum,* to the principle of smell, separate, *hum, phaṭ*. *Om,* protect, *hā*. *Om, svam, svam,* unite with the primordial. *Om, sum, hum,* to the principle of smell, destroy oblations. Then the final oblation is to be applied in the northern direction as follows: *Om, rām,* to the principle of taste. *Om, bhem,* to the principle of colour. *Om, ram,* the principle of touch. *Om, em,* to the principle of sound. *Om, bham,* salutations. *Om, som, egoism. Om, nam,* to intellect. *Om, Om,* to the primordial. This method of initiation has been described in brief in the case of the deity of a single form. The procedure for the nine-vyūhas etc. are also remembered to be of the same kind.

53. A person after having consumed (all the things) should consign the primordial thing to eternal bliss. Then a person has to consign the primordial thing to the Lord devoid of transformation.

54. Then having purified the elements, one has to purify the instruments of action, the intellect, the principles, mind, knowledge and egoism.

55-56. After having purified the soul of the body, he should again purify the primordial principle at the end. The supreme being and the pure primordial principle stationed in the Lord (which is) held under control and has been rendered an abode after being freed from bondage is contemplated upon and the final oblation is offered. This is the (mode of) initiation for a person (who is) fit.

57-58. Having worshipped with the constituents of the mystic syllables, the principles are uniformly carried and gradually purified. Having meditated (on the Lord) endowed with all accomplishments, the final oblation is made. This is the (mode of) initiation for an aspirant in case if there is no abundance of articles and no capacity for a person.

59. Having worshipped the lord as before endowed with all the materials, the excellent preceptor has to initiate (the disciple) on the *dvādaśi* (the 12th day) from the beginning of the rite.

60. The disciple must be devoted, humble, endowed with all physical qualities, not very rich. Such a person is initiated after the worship of the deity in the altar.

61-62. Having contemplated the entire path, divine, pertaining to the elements or to the self, in the order of their creation in the body of the disciple, the preceptor, desirous of creation, having offered first sixteen oblations to Vāsudeva and other (gods) who are radiant, with their respective mystic syllables, (they are) allowed to go.

63-65. Then purification is made by oblation in the order of destruction. Having released all the fetters of deeds, the preceptor, has to purify the principles, having drawn them in order from the body of the disciple. Having dissolved in the fire, the primordial Viṣṇu and the Supreme Spirit, the pure principle is accomplished by (offering) final oblation with impure principle. After the disciple had attained his natural state, he has to consume all the qualities of the primordial being.

66. The preceptor has to release or bind the children. Or the preceptor remaining in his natural state has to perform a different kind of initiation (called) *Śaktidikṣā*[1].

67-69. Having worshipped Viṣṇu placed nearby with the lad in an altar and (who) is being adored with the devotion of ascetics and mendicants, the pupil remains facing the deity, the self (preceptor) facing obliquely. After having contemplated upon the entire course which has been resolved by him (the preceptor) according to the phases of the moon, (the preceptor) has to think deeply with contemplation on the Lord, the supreme spirit, stationed in the body of the disciple.

70. As before all the principles have to be purified gradually by beating etc. on the altar of Hari. Then (he) who is bent on the inquiry of the self has to set them aside after having taken them, and beating.

71. He should purify them befitting their nature and unite them with the deity. They are then collected with pure mental disposition and yoked in order.

72-73. By means of contemplative mood and the pose of knowledge (*jñānamudrā*) (they) are all purified. When all the

1. Initiation rite relating to the female energy or goddess.

principles have been thus purified and the Supreme lord remains as the main, the principles have to be burnt and (the fire) extinguished and the disciples have to be engaged in the service of the Lord. Then the excellent preceptor should conduct the aspirant on the path of accomplishment.

74. In the same manner, a householder becomes qualified by remaining vigilant in (the performance of) the rites. One has to remain purifying his self until there is dissipation of anger.

75. After having known himself as shorn of anger and purified from sins, a self-controlled person should confer the right on (his) son or the disciple.

76. After having burnt the noose composed of illusion, renouncing and remaining in (the contemplation) of the self, he, who possesses the unmanifest form, should remain waiting for the decay of his body.

## CHAPTER TWENTYEIGHT

### *Mode of anointment for the preceptor*

1-2. I shall describe the anointment of the preceptor as the son would do and by which an aspirant would become accomplished and a diseased would get rid of the disease, the king (would get his) kingdom, a woman would get a child and also destruction of impurity. Pictures made of earth and endowed with gems are to be placed in the middle, the east etc.

3. Thousands or hundreds (of them are placed) in a circular form and Viṣṇu in the east and north-east at an elevated place in an altar.

4. Having placed all of them the aspirant (should assign) his son in parts. After having worshipped well the anointment should be performed preceded by songs etc.

5. Men should offer yogic seats etc. requesting his favour. The preceptor also should announce the terms and the pupil (initiated) into the secrets then becomes the recipient of all (that he wants).

# CHAPTER TWENTY-NINE

*Mode of worshipping Hari in the figure called Sarvatobhadra*

*Nārada said* :

1. The aspirant has to accomplish the mystic syllable in the temple of the deity after having worshipped the Lord Hari in a circular figure in a purified ground.

2. One has to draw circles etc. in a square piece of ground, the *Sarvatobhadra*[1] is drawn in the compartments of *rasa*, *bāṇa* and *akṣi*.

3. A lotus seat containing thirty-six apartments should be outside in a row. Among these two (squares are set apart) for the path-way and two for the doors in the quarters.

4. A lotus figure is drawn in front outside and a circle is drawn around it. Half of the lotus is divided into twelve compartments.

5. Having thus divided it one should draw four circles, one around the other. The first one is that of the pericarp and the second, that of the filaments.

6-7. The third (is) that of the joints of the petals and the fourth, that of the tips of the petals. The joints of the petals are marked by stretching the threads from the angular points upto the middle of the side facing the angle and placing them on the tips of the filaments. Then the threads are made to lie (fall) and then an eight-petalled lotus is drawn.

8. Having allowed a measure (equal to) the space between the joints of the petals, the tops of the petals are drawn in front of it and afterwards.

9. Having allowed in the middle a measure of space (equal to that) of the interstices between the petals, two filaments are drawn in between every two petals.

10. This is the ordinary lotus circle said to be of twelve petals. Circles are drawn in order in the east of the measure of half the pericarp.

11. By this drawing there will be six circles on its side. In this way there will be twelve fish and twelve petals.

---

1. It is so called because it brings about all round happiness.

12. Having drawn a fish with five petals of a lotus for the sake of success, the skyline (is made) outside the seat (altar). The compartments are (cleanly) swept.

13. Four other places for the feet (are made ready) in the angular points. Besmeared vessels are kept in the four quarters.

14. Two rows are marked in the quarters for the sake of pathway. Doors are made in all the four quarters.

15. A wise man has to make eight ornaments of graceful expressions by the side of the doors. An equal number of ornaments are also to be made by their side.

16. Then corners of ornaments should be made. In each one of the middle compartments in all the four directions, two figures are drawn.

17. The four outer compartments are cleansed, as well as one on each side. Three figures are drawn on each side of the petal for beautifying it.

18. Similarly, three ornaments are to be drawn on the opposite direction inside the angular point as well as outside without any difference between the two.

19. In this way, sixteen compartments are formed and in the same manner another circle is formed. In the (figure having) twelve compartments a lotus figure with thirtysix petals (is drawn).

20. As before one line is drawn at each door for beautification. In the circular altar of one cubit a lotus should be drawn (having) twelve finger-breadth.

21. A door should be drawn of the measure of two cubits by one cubit. The altar should be a square. The disc of the lotus should be of two cubits.

22. Half the lotus is drawn with nine (finger breadth), the navel with three, the radius with eight (breadth), the circumference with four.

23. Having divided the ground into three parts, an inner figure is marked with two (breadth). For the sake of accomplishing (one's object) one has to mark the five vowels inside and the radii.

24. Then according to his desire, one has to draw figures of the petals of lotus or citron leaves or of the shape of lotus leaves.

(as above). The subtle principle of touch has to be absorbed in the principle of sound by meditative *yuga*.

28. *Om, hrim, haḥ, phaṭ, hrūm* I absorb the subtle sound principle. Salutations, with the single incantation one has to absorb the etherial space of the colour of pure crystal and pervading the space in between the nose and tuft.

29. One has to perform purification of the body by desiccation etc. Then the dry body from the foot to the tuft has to be meditated upon.

30-31. After having meditated upon the drop which has come out of the cavity of brain with the syllable *ram* and on the body covered by a garland of flames with the syllables *yam* and *vam*, one has to besmear the body with the ambrosia of ashes. Then with the syllable *lam*, it should be converted into a sacred body.

32. Having made the *nyāsa*[1] on the hand and body one has to do mental worship. Viṣṇu is adored with his retinue in the heart-lotus with mental flowers.

33. The lord of lords who yields enjoyment and liberation has to be worshipped with the principal mystic syllable. "O lord of gods, welcome to you. O Keśava ! be present here."

34. "Accept my excellent mental adoration properly." Then the Tortoise, the supporting power, then Ananta and then the earth have to be worshipped.

35-36. The righteousness, un-righteousness etc. (have to be worshipped) in the middle of fire etc., the lotus in the middle of *sattva* (goodness) etc., the principle of time, the solar and other regions and the king of birds, in *māyā* (illusion) and *avidyā* (ignorance). Then (the deities) of the quarters commencing with north-west and ending with north-east as well as the line of preceptors.

37. The attendant gods, Sarasvatī, Nārada (sage), Nalakūbara (son of Kubera), the preceptor, the sandals of the preceptor's preceptor and of the preceptor have to be worshipped.

38-39. The perfections already accomplished and the later perfections, the female energies—Lakṣmī, Sarasvatī, Prīti, Kīrti

1. The assignment of fingers on the different parts of the body by touching them.

as before beautification is made. Seven of the corners outside and three apartments inside are cleansed.

39. The supreme brahman is to be worshipped in the auspicious twenty-five (compartment) formation. Then in the lotus (drawn) in the middle commencing with east, Vāsudeva and other deities are worshipped in order.

40. Having worshipped the boar-form in the lotus in the east the formation is worshipped in order until the thirty-six (forms are finished).

41. With the effort that it has to be worshipped, (one has to worship) all formations in the order in the single lotus as described. The progenitor is regarded as the sacrifice.

42. Acyuta divided into many forms is regarded as 'truth'. Forty cubits of the ground in the north has to be divided in order.

43-44. Each one (of these divisions) are again (first) divided into seven parts and then into two. Then of one thousand seven hundred and sixty-four apartments we will have a *bhadraka* (figure) (formed) by the central sixteen apartments. There will be a pathway on the side, then eight *bhadra* apartments and a pathway.

45-46. Then sixteen (figures) of lotuses and twenty-four lotuses for the rows and thirty-two for the pathway and forty rows and a passage with the remaining three rows (are drawn). The doors are provided with ornaments and minor beautifications in the directions, omitting the centre.

47. For accomplishing, two, four and six doors (space) is cut off in the four directions and five, three and one outside (are set apart) for accomplishing the adornment of the doors.

48. In the same manner, six or four (compartments) are omitted outside the door and four inside. There will be six minor adornments.

49-50. There should be four doors on one side or three doors specifically in each direction. One has to draw five apartments at the angular points (as well as) in the rows in order. An auspicious altar dear to a mortal has to be (drawn) in this manner.

# CHAPTER THIRTY

*Mode of worship of different gods in specially drawn lotus figures*

*Nārada said :*

1. One has to worship Brahmā in the lotus at the centre, the lotus-navelled (Viṣṇu) with all his retinue in the east, the nature (primordial matter) in the lotus in the south-east and the supreme spirit in the lotus in the south.

2. (One has to worship) the fire-god (in the lotus) at the south of the supreme spirit, the wind-god in the south-west and west, the sun in the lotus of the moon, the Ṛg- (Veda) and Yajur- (Veda) in the lotus of the lord.

3-4. Indra and other gods are to be worshipped in the sixteen (lotuses) in the second (row) then, (along with) the Sāma- (veda), Atharva (veda), sky, wind, lustre, water, earth, mind, ear, skin, (and) eye. One should also worship the tongue, nose, (the worlds) Bhū, (and) Bhuva.

5-7. Having worshipped (the worlds) Mahas, Janas, Tapas (and) Satya and (also the sacrifices) Agniṣṭoma, Atyagniṣṭoma, Uktha, Ṣoḍaṣī, Vājapeya, Atirātra, one has to worship Aptoryāma, mind, intellect, ego, sound, touch, colour, taste, (and) smell in order in twenty-four lotuses. (One has to worship) the soul, ego, the lord of the mind, (and) the sound principle of the primordial matter.

8-9. (One should then worship) the images of Vāsudeva and others, having worshipped the (following) ten—the soul, mind, ear, skin, eye, tongue, nose, speech, hand, (and) foot in thirty-two lotuses. One has to worship these in the fourth enclosure along with their attendants and retinue.

10. Having worshipped the anus and penis one has to worship the lords of the twelve months as well as the twentysix forms commencing with Puruṣottama in the external enclosure.

11. Among these the Lords of the months are to be worshipped in the lotus of the disc. Then the eight, six, five or four (total twentythree) principles of the primordial matter (are to be worshipped) in another (lotus).

12-13. Then one has to dust in a drawn circular altar. (You) hear. The pericarp should be of yellow colour, and all the lines equal and white. (They) should be two cubits long and one thumb in breadth. Half the length are white. The joints (should be coloured) white, black or dark-blue.

14. The filaments should be red and yellow-coloured. The corners should be filled with red. The yogic seat should be bedecked with any of the colours according to one's own desire.

15. The pathway is decorated with canopy of creepers and leaves. The entrance to the altar (should be painted) white, bright-red and yellow.

16. Ornamentation of all the white corners (is done) with blue (colour). It has been said that the altar *bhadraka* should be filled (with the colours) and in this way the other (altars) are filled.

17. The three corners should be decorated with pale, red and black, the two corners with red and yellow (and) the centre of the circle by black.

18. The black (coloured) radii (should be decorated) by yellow and red, the circumference with red, the lines outside (being drawn) in white, brown, red, black and yellow.

19. The powder of rice (is) white. The dust of saffron is red. It (becomes) yellow with turmeric. From burnt grains (we get) black (colour).

20. (It becomes) black with *śamī* leaves and other (leaves). By the repetition of the basic mystic letters lakh times and of the basic syllables four lakh times, a lakh of mystic learning is accomplished.

21. Ten thousand times of the science of intellect and thousand times of the hymns (are repeated). The purification of the self by means of a lakh of the basic syllables is done prior to this.

22. Then with another lakh, the basic syllable would get established. It has been well advocated that oblation of the mystic letters is similar to the prior service.

23. The prior service has been advocated to be performed with a tenth part of the mystic syllables. The monthly austerity has to be performed with the preparatory mystic syllable.

24. The left foot should be placed on the ground and the donation should not be accepted. In this way by the repetition, twice or thrice (one gets) mediocre and excellent accomplishments.

25. I shall describe the (mode of) contemplation of the mystic syllable, by which (one gets) the benefits got from the basic syllable. The gross form is composed of sound and is laid down as the outward deity.

26. The subtle form composed of lustre becomes the mental (figure) made up of thoughts in the heart. That (form) which is beyond thinking, is declared as the supreme.

27. The potential of the bear, lion and other forms are principally gross. The form of Vāsudeva is declared as that beyond the reach of thought.

28. The other forms are remembered always as existing in the thoughts of the heart. The gross (form) is said to be *vairāja* (belonging to Brahman) and the subtle form would be marked.

29-32. The form beyond thought is declared as that of Īśvara (the lord). One has to contemplate on the lustrous, undecaying consciousness residing in the lotus of the heart, (namely) the basic letter, the soul of the basic letter of the shape of a *kadamba* flower. Just a lamp lies obstructed inside the pitcher, so also the lord of the mystic syllable lies restrained in the heart. There are many holes in the pitcher. The beams of the light come out through them. In the same way the beams of the mystic letters come out through the tubular organs. Then uniting themselves with the power of the deity they exist in the body.

33. The tubular organs, having come out from the heart, come within the ken of the sense of sight. Among those (tubular organs) the two tubular organs Agni and Soma are (those which) remain at the tip of the nose.

34. Then having conquered the wind in the body the reciter of the basic syllable engaged in the repetition and contemplation enjoys the benefits of the basic syllable.

35. With the gross elements and subtle principles purified, contented (and) practising *yoga*, (one) gets *aṇimā*[1] etc. (Remaining) detached and depending on the lord of the soul one gets free from the gross elements and subtle principles and seizure of the organs.

---

1. The first among the eight kinds of superhuman powers by which one is able to become very minute.

# CHAPTER THIRTYONE

## *Mode of cleansing oneself and others*

*Agni said* :

1. I will now describe (the rite) known as the cleansing for the protection of one's self and others, by which a man would become freed of miseries and get happiness.

2-3. *Om*, salutations to the greatest object, the soul, the great soul, the formless and many-formed, the all-pervading, supreme soul, blemishless, pure and (person) engaged in meditative contemplation. Having saluted I shall expound. May my words prove true.

4. (Salutations) to the Boar, Man-lion and Dwarf (forms of Viṣṇu), the great sage. Having saluted I shall expound. May my words prove true.

5. (Salutations) to Trivikrama (a form of Viṣṇu, as he measured the three steps and removed the pride of the demon Bali), Rāma, Vaikuṇṭha (abode of Viṣṇu), the (Supreme) man. Having saluted I shall expound. May my words become true.

6. O Boar, Lord as Man-lion, Lord as Dwarf, Trivikrama, Hayagrīveśa (Lord as Horse-necked), Lord of all beings, Hṛṣīkeśa (Viṣṇu) (the Lord of all senses) destroy my impurity.

7. With these four most excellent weapons, the ever victorious disc and others of unbroken power, you become destroyer of all wicked things.

8. You remove the calamity of such a person and do (him) all good and also (remove) the fear of distress due to fetters of death which is the fruit of sins.

9. (You) destroy the magical incantations set up by others with meditation for working evils, causing diseases and decrepitude.

10. *Om*, salutations to Vāsudeva, Kṛṣṇa, bearer of sword. Salutations to lotus-eyed, Keśava (and) the first holder of the disc.

11. Salutations to the wearer of clean dress made yellow by the filaments of lotuses (and) the disc (of Viṣṇu) hurled on the shoulders of the enemies at the great battle, (and) the wielder of the same.

12. Salutations to the one who lifted the earth on his tusk[1], who has the three forms embodied in him, the great Yajña-varāha,[2] and the one who reclines on the hood of (the serpent) Śeṣa.

13. Salutations to you, the divine lion having manes of the hue of molten gold, eyes bright like the burning fire, (and) claws (harder) than thunder-bolt to touch.

14. Salutations again and again to you, Kāśyapa, the shortest statured, adorned with the *Ṛg*, *Yajur* and *Sāma* (*veda*) (and) the Dwarf form which covered the earth.

15. O Boar, One with huge tusks, you crush all evils completely, their effects and also the effects of sins.

16. O Man-lion, having a dreadful face (and) the burning fire in between the teeth, the destroyer of distress, you break-down all evils by your cry.

17. May Janārdana (Viṣṇu), the one who assumed the form of a Dwarf, dispel all grief of this person by words embedded with the *Ṛg*, *Yajur* and *Sāma* (*veda*).

18-19. O Govinda ! (You) destroy quickly this person's sufferings. Destroy fevers—quotidian occurring on alternate days, tertian, quartan and also the terrible *satata*, those arising out of derangement (of humours), the *sannipāta* (caused by the derangement of three humours), as well as accidental.

20-24. The diseases of the eye, the afflictions of the head, diseases pertaining to the stomach, (difficulty) in breathing in, excessive breathing, burning (sensation) in the body along with trembling, diseases in the anus, nose, feet, leprosy as well as consumption, and diseases like jaundice and very dreadful urinary disease, fistula, all kinds of dysentry, diseases of the mouth, chest (diseases), stone in the bladder, strangury, and other dreadful diseases, diseases caused by wind, biles and phlegm and others like *sannipāta*, accidentally afflicting diseases, (poison due to) spiders and boils etc.

25. May all these be destroyed by the recitation of (the name of) Viṣṇu. Being struck down by the disc of Hari, may all these (ailments) be completely destroyed.

---

1. This refers to the lifting of earth from waters assuming the form of a boar by Viṣṇu.
2. The boar-form of Viṣṇu.

26. I am uttering verily the truth. Being scared by the recitation of the names Acyuta (undecaying), Ananta (unending), Govinda (cowherd) (all are synonyms of Viṣṇu), all the diseases are destroyed.

27-28. On his (name) being recited, may Janārdana destroy the poisons of animate and inanimate objects, as well as artificially made, those caused by teeth, by nails and those arising from the sky as well as those caused by (insects like) spider and others which cause grief.

29-31. May the life of boyhood of Viṣṇu (Kṛṣṇa) destroy the evil forces which afflict mothers and children, such as, planets, evil spirits, female goblins, vampires, ghosts, *gandharvas*, *yakṣas*, demons, the impeding forces such as Śakuni Pūtanā and others, (the female forces such as) Mukhamaṇḍī, Revatī and the terrible Vṛddharevatī, and the fierce forces known as Vṛddhaka.

32. May these evil forces which afflict at the old age, and the children and the youth be scorched by the looks of the Man-lion.

33. May the dreadful face of the Man-lion of enormous strength destroy these evil forces completely for the welfare of the world.

34. O Man-lion, O Great lion, possessor of garland of flames, Fiery-mouthed, Possessor of fiery eyes, Lord of all, devour the evil forces completely.

35-37. May the Lord of all (beings), Supreme Lord, Janārdana destroy diseases, great portents, poisons, great evil forces, the fierce beings, the afflictions due to the planets whichever is cruel, the injuries caused by weapons, and *jvālāgardabhaka*[1] etc., assuming any one of the forms of Vāsudeva and hurling the Sudarśana disc which is dreadful like a garland of fire. O Acyuta, the foremost among gods (you) destroy the evil forces.

38. O Sudarśana, the huge fire and great sound (you) destroy (all evils). O Vibhīṣaṇa (one who frightens) ! may all the evil demons get destroyed.

---

1. a kind of disease in which pimples appear on the body. See *MW*. p. 420a.

39. May the Man-lion (deity), the soul of all beings, possessing terrific roars protect me in the east, west, south and north.

40. May Lord Janārdana of manifold forms protect me in heavens, on the earth, in the sky, behind me, on the sides and in front of me.

41. As Viṣṇu (protects) the entire universe (consisting of) the celestials, demons and mortals, may the evils of this person be put down by that truth.

42. As the sins get destroyed atonce by the remembrance of Viṣṇu, may all evil of this person get destroyed by that truth.

43. As the Supreme Lord Viṣṇu has been extolled in the *vedānta* (the philosophical inquiry is known as it forms the concluding portion of the Vedas) may all the evils of this person get destroyed by that truth.

44. As Viṣṇu, the lord of sacrifices is exolled among the celestials, may what all has been uttered by me become so by that truth.

45-46. May there be peace. May there be good. May the evil of this man get destroyed, being agitated by me with the *kuśa* (grass) originating from the body of Vāsudeva. May Govinda, the Nara-Nārāyaṇa[1] cleanse me. May there be remo. l of all miseries by the chant (of the names) of Hari in the same manner.

47. This is the weapon which cleans and which wards off all diseases. I am Hari. The *kuśa* grass is Viṣṇu. Your diseases have been destroyed by me.

## CHAPTER THIRTYTWO

### *Narration about the purificatory rites*

*Agni said* :

1. An intelligent man has to do forty-eight purificatory

1. Form of Kṛṣṇa; originally conceived as identical; spoken as representing Kṛṣṇa and Arjuna in later epics and *kāvyas*. See *Apte SD*. p. 281.

rites[1] among the initiatory rites for attaining liberation. You hear them, by which one may become a celestial.

2. One has to perform *garbhādhāna* as soon as the conception takes place, then the *puṁsavana*[2] rite, the *simantonnayana*[3], the *jātakarma*[4], and the naming ceremony.

3. (One has to perform the rites of) giving food (to the new born child), then the tonsure, and the *brahmacarya* (the life of celibacy practised by a boy while studying the *Vedas*). (One has to perform) the four (rites)—the *vaiṣṇavi*, *pārthi*, *bhautiki* and *śrauti*[5], and making a gift of cows, entering the life of a householder after completing one's vedic studies.

4-7. The seven kinds of *Pākayajñas*[6] are *aṣṭakā*, *pārvaṇaśrāddha śrāvaṇi*, *āgrayaṇi*, *caitri* and *āśvayuji*. The *Haviryajñas*[7] are seven. (You) hear them. (They) are (*agni*) *ādhāna*, *agnihotra*, *darśapūrṇamāsa*, *cāturmāsya*, *paśubandha*, and *sautrāmaṇi*. (You) hear the seven kinds of *Somasaṁsthās*[8] *agniṣṭoma* the excellent sacrifice *atyagniṣṭoma*, *uktha*, *ṣoḍaśi*, *vājapeya*, *atirātra and aptoryāma*. These are of thousand kinds.

8-9. They are *hiraṇyāṅghri*, *hiraṇyākṣa*, *hiraṇyamitra*, *hiraṇyapāṇi*, *hemākṣa*, *hemāṅga*, *hemasūtraka*, *hiraṇyāsya*, *hiraṇyāṅga*, *hemajihva*, and *hiraṇyavat*. The *aśvamedha* is the excellent among them. Now you hear the eight virtues.

10-11. They are—compassion towards all beings, forbearance, sincerity, purity, ease, wishing the welfare of all, liberality and freedom from avarice. A hundred oblations are to be offered with the basic mystic syllable. The same procedure is to be followed in the initiation (ceremony) related to Saura, Śakti (the female deity) and Viṣṇu.

---

1. The purificatory rites are referred to as twelve. See *Manu* 2.27.
2. The rite performed after the conception of a child to ensure the birth of a son.
3. The rite of parting the hair performed on the fourth. sixth and eighth month of pregnancy.
4. The rite performed soon after the birth of a child.
5. These are special rites performed as a mark of respect to the four sages who are like the guardian deities for the different *kāṇḍas* of the Vedas.
6. This is a simple or domestic sacrifice. The text has omitted the *sthālīpāka* and names only six.
7. Sacrifices in which oblations of clarified butter are offered.
8. Sacrifices in which *soma* is pressed for oblation.

12. Being purified by these purificatory rites, one may get enjoyment, release (from bondage). Such a man becoming free from diseases remains like a god. By the recitation (of the names of god), by offering oblations and by worship and meditation on the deity one gets his cherished desire.

## CHAPTER THIRTYTHREE

*Mode of investiture of the sacred thread for the deity and the installation of the deity*

*Agni said* :

1. I shall describe the (mode of) installation of Hari and the benefits of worship for a year. The first day (of the lunar fortnight) at the commencement of (the month of) *āṣāḍha* and the concluding part (of the month) of *Kārttika* yields riches.

2-3. Commencing with the second day (of the lunar fortnight) (the installation) of Śrī, Gaurī, Gaṇeśa, Sarasvatī, Guha (son of Śiva), Mārtaṇḍa (Sun), the divine mothers, Durgā, Śiva and Brahmā are performed in order. To which deity one is devoted, the lunar day of that deity is sacred to him.

4-5. The mode of installation is the same (for all the deities). Only the sacred syllables are different. A thread spun by a brahmin woman (made of ) gold, silver, copper, silk or cotton etc. or in its absence a purified one is made into nine folds. The investiture is done with that.

6-7. It is excellent if it is longer than one hundred and eight (finger-length) or half of it. "Whatever has been prescribed by you, O Lord, for the warding off of the discontinuance of the rite, that is being done by me O Lord. May there be no impediment here in the *pavitraka* rite. O Lord of undiminishing success ! Grant me this".

8-10. Having prayed (in this way), one has to tie it to the circular altar at first with the Gāyatrī[1] *Oṁ nārāyaṇāya vidmahe*

1. The Gāyatri is a vedic metre consisting of 24 letters. Sacred syllables consisting of 24 letters in the form of a Gāyatrī and addressed to a particular deity is known as the Gāyatrī of that deity and 24 such Gāyatrīmantras are reckoned.

*vāsudevāya dhimahi tanno viṣṇuḥ pracodayāt.* A garland made of one thousand and eight wood-flowers is consecrated to the Lord of lords extending upto the feet and the *pavitraka* (sacred thread) upto the knees, thighs, and navel of the idol befitting him. The garland should be made thirty-two fingers length.

11. In the circular lotus of one finger (breadth) the pericarp, filament, leaf, the first basic syllable and the outer circumference of the circle are consecrated.

12-13. By the measure of one's fingers the threads for the preceptors (are consecrated) on the models of the parents on the ground. Twelve knots made fragrant are consecrated to the end of the navel. Then two garlands are made ready at first containing one hundred and eight flowers.

14. O twice born one! Otherwise twenty-four or thirty-six garlands should be consecrated to the sun with the ring and middle fingers by those who desire for a daughter.

15. There may be twelve knots in the sacred thread for the pot of the Sun, and the fire as in the case of Viṣṇu.

16. According to one's ability the knots of the sacred thread should be placed in the midst of the articles for the worship of Viṣṇu on the altar in the pit encircled by a girdle.

17-18. One who has bathed and performed the twilight worship should dye the seventeen strings divided into three parts, with *rocanā* (yellow pigment), agallochum, camphor, turmeric, saffron or sandal. Then one has to worship Hari on the eleventh lunar day at the sacrificial yard.

19. One has to offer food to all the subordinate deities at the altar. *Kṣaum*, to the guardian deity at the end of the door. And (one should then worship) Śrī on the garland.

20. (Adorations) to Dhātā, Vidhātā (names of Brahmā), (the rivers) Ganges, Yamunā. And after having worshipped the two *nidhis*[1] *śaṅkha* and *padma* at the middle, the *vāstu*[2] is removed. (Adorations) to *śārṅga* (the bow of Viṣṇu). Then one has to perform the purificatory rites for the elements remaining standing.

1. The nine treasures of Kubera, the lord of wealth.
2. Evidently the *vāstupuruṣa* governing the site of a dwelling place.

*Om, hrūm, haḥ, phaṭ, hrūm*, I absorb the subtle principle of smell. Salutations. *Om, hrūm, haḥ, phaṭ, hrūm*. I absorb the subtle principle of taste. Salutations. *Om, hrūm, haḥ, phaṭ, hrūm* I absorb the subtle principle of touch. Salutations. *Om, hrūm, haḥ, phaṭ, hrūm* I absorb the subtle principle of sound. Salutations.

21-22. With the five incantations (as above) one has to meditate on the yellow-coloured, hard quadrangle of earth of the form of subtle principle of smell and governed by Indra with the mark of holding the thunder-bolt in between his feet. Then the worshipper has to spread the pure subtle principle of taste and absorb the subtle principles of taste and colour in this way.

*Om, hrim, haḥ, phaṭ, hrūm*, I absorb the subtle principle of taste. Salutations.*Om, hrim, haḥ, phaṭ, hrūm*, I absorb the subtle principle of colour. Salutations, *Om, hrim, haḥ, phaṭ, hrūm*, I absorb the subtle principle of touch. Salutations. *Om, hrim, haḥ, phaṭ, hrim* I absorb the subtle principle of sound. Salutations.

23. One has to meditate on the presiding deity Varuṇa placed in between the two thighs, holding a white lotus jar, white-hued and crescent-shaped.

24. With the four incantations (as above) one has to absorb the pure subtle principle of taste in the subtle principle of colour. The subtle principle of colour is absorbed.

*Om, hrūm, haḥ, phaṭ, hrūm*. I absorb the subtle principle of colour. Salutations. *Om, hrūm, haḥ, phaṭ, hrūm*. I absorb the subtle principle of touch. Salutations. *Om, hrūm, haḥ, phaṭ, hrūm* I absorb the subtle principle of sound. Salutations.

25. Having meditated on the Fire, the presiding deity which is red triangular fire-column pervading the space between the navel and neck and having the mark of a *svastika*, that pure (sound principle) is absorbed in the principle of touch with these three incantations.

*Om, hrim, haḥ, phaṭ, hrūm* I absorb the subtle principle of touch. Salutations. *Om, hrim, haḥ, phaṭ, hrūm* I absorb the subtle principle of sound. Salutations.

26-27. One has to meditate on the grey-coloured circular column of air pervading the space between the neck and nose, and bearing the mark of the pure moon with the two incantations (as above). The subtle principle of touch has to be absorbed in the principle of sound by meditative *yuga*.

28. *Om*, *hrim*, *haḥ*, *phaṭ*, *hrūm* I absorb the subtle sound principle. Salutations, with the single incantation one has to absorb the etherial space of the colour of pure crystal and pervading the space in between the nose and tuft.

29. One has to perform purification of the body by desiccation etc. Then the dry body from the foot to the tuft has to be meditated upon.

30-31. After having meditated upon the drop which has come out of the cavity of brain with the syllable *ram* and on the body covered by a garland of flames with the syllables *yam* and *vam*, one has to besmear the body with the ambrosia of ashes. Then with the syllable *lam*, it should be converted into a sacred body.

32. Having made the *nyāsa*[1] on the hand and body one has to do mental worship. Viṣṇu is adored with his retinue in the heart-lotus with mental flowers.

33. The lord of lords who yields enjoyment and liberation has to be worshipped with the principal mystic syllable. "O lord of gods, welcome to you. O Keśava ! be present here."

34. "Accept my excellent mental adoration properly." Then the Tortoise, the supporting power, then Ananta and then the earth have to be worshipped.

35-36. The righteousness, un-righteousness etc. (have to be worshipped) in the middle of fire etc., the lotus in the middle of *sattva* (goodness)etc., the principle of time, the solar and other regions and the king of birds, in *māyā* (illusion) and *aviḍyā* (ignorance). Then (the deities) of the quarters commencing with north-west and ending with north-east as well as the line of preceptors.

37. The attendant gods, Sarasvatī, Nārada (sage), Nala-kūbara (son of Kubera), the preceptor, the sandals of the preceptor's preceptor and of the preceptor have to be worshipped.

38-39. The perfections already accomplished and the later perfections, the female energies—Lakṣmī, Sarasvatī, Prīti, Kīrti

1. The assignment of fingers on the different parts of the body by touching them.

Śānti, Kānti, Puṣṭi, Tuṣṭi, Mahendrā etc. have to be worshipped in the middle. Hari, Dhṛti, Śrī, Rati, and Krānti etc. have to be invoked in the middle. Acyuta is established with the principal mystic syllable.

40. Having prayed by saying "*Om*, have (your) face towards me and come near me," and having placed the articles of worship *and offered scents etc.* one has to worship with the principal (mystic syllable).

41. *Om* (you) frighten, (you) frighten. Again terrorise the heart and head. (You) pound the tuft, commencing with the flames and from the *śastra*[1] to the *astra*.[2]

42. (You) protect. (You) destroy. Salutations to the armour. *Om*, *hrūm*, *phaṭ*. Salutations to the missile. (One should worship) the parts of the body with the principal mystic letter.

43-44. At first one should worship different forms of idols in the east, south, west and north. Vāsudeva, Saṅkarṣaṇa, Pradyumna, Aniruddha, Agni, Śrī, Dhṛti, Rati and Kānti (are) the forms of Hari. The conch, disc, mace, lotus and Agni (should be worshipped) in the east.

45. The bow, club, sword, and garland of wild flowers (should be worshipped) outside it. Indra and others as well as Ananta, and Varuṇa (should be worshipped) in the south-west.

46-48. Brahmā and Indra (should be worshipped) in the north-east and their hosts of weapons on the outside. The Airāvata (the elephant of Indra), goat, buffalo, monkey, fish, deer, hare, bull, tortoise, and *haṁsa* (should be worshipped) and Kṛṣṇa on the outside. The gate-keepers Kumuda and others (should be worshipped) in pairs from the east to the north. After saluting Hari, the food (is offered) outside. Salutations to the attendants of Viṣṇu. The offering should be made on the altar.

49. One should worship the Universal Being, the All-pervading on the north-east. The protective thread should be tied on the right arm of the lord.

---

1. An ordinary missile.
2. Any missile discharged after the repetition of appropriate mystic syllables.

50. (One should say), "*Om* salutations to the one who confers full benefits of worship done through the whole year. You wear this thread for the purpose of installation."

51. One should observe the vow of fasting etc. in the presence of the deity (saying), "I am pleasing the deity by observing fasting etc."

52. "May not lust, anger, and all other (qualities) reside in me ever. O lord of gods from this day onwards it is the last of them."

53. If the worshipper is unable (to do as described), he should observe the vow eating only in the night. Having made oblations, the *visarjana* (dismissal) is done, after laudation. This is the (mode of) daily worship which yields riches. *Om*, *hrim*, *śrim*, salutations to Śrīdhara the enchanter of the three worlds.

## CHAPTER THIRTYFOUR

### *Mode of performing oblation*

*Agni said* :

1-2. One has to enter the sacrificial ground with the following mystic syllable and adorn it. "Salutations to the brahman, the lord, Śrīdhara (and) undecaying self, the form of *Ṛg*, *Yajur* and *Sāma* (*veda*), (possessing) a body (composed) of sound (and) Viṣṇu. Having drawn the circular altar in the evening, one has to bring materials for the sacrifice.

3. Having washed hands and feet and made assignment, and taken the *arghya* (respectful offering) in the hands one should sprinkle the *arghya* on the head and the gate-way.

4. He should then begin sacrifice at the gateway. He should worship the presiding deity of the arch. The *aśvattha*[1], *udumbara*[2], *vaṭa*[3] and *plakṣa*[4] are the trees of the east.

1. Ficus religiosa (fig. tree).
2. Ficus glomerata.
3. Ficus indica (banyan tree).
4. Ficus infectoria (a large tree with small white fruit).

5. The Ṛg (*veda*) is the ornament of Indra on the west. The *Yajur* (*veda*) is auspicious for Yama. The *Sāma* (*veda*) is of the water-god and is known as Sudhanvan. The *Atharva* (*veda*) is of Soma (and is called) Suhotraka.

6. The edges of the gate, flags, (gate-keepers) Kumuda etc. and two pitchers should be adored at every door by their respective names, as well as a pitcher full of water in the east.

7. Then one should worship the guards of the doors — Ānanda, Nandana, Dakṣa, Vīrasena, Suṣeṇaka, Sambhava and Prabhava in the north (Saumya)[1].

8. One should enter after having removed obstacles by throwing flowers and the repetition of names of weapons. Having performed purificatory rites of the elements and the assignment (of limbs) one should show the posture of hands.

9-10. Having recited the mystic syllable ending with *phaṭ* one should scatter mustard seeds in different directions. (One should sanctify) the cow's urine with Vāsudeva, cow's dung with Saṅkarṣaṇa, the milk with Pradyumna and the curd got from it with Nārāyaṇa. The ghee should be one part and the others respectively one part more.

11. When these are mixed in a vessel of ghee it is known as the *pañcagavya*[2] (the five products got from a cow). A part of it is for the sprinkling of the temple building and the other for eating.

12. One should worship Indra and other guardian deities of the world in ten pitchers which have been brought. Having worshipped them one has to make them hear command. They must be installed by the command of Hari.

13. Having kept the articles of sacrifice well-protected, one must scatter those which must be scattered. Having recited the basic mystic syllable eight hundred times one should take *kuśa* grass.

14. Then one should place there a pitcher and (the vessel) *vardhani* at the north-east. Having worshipped Hari along with

1. Soma means Kubera, the regent of the north.
2. These are—the dung, urine, milk, curd and ghee.

the attendant gods in the pitcher one should worship weapons in the (vessel) *vardhani*.

15. (Having made) a circumambulation of the sacrificial place, water is sprinkled in broken streams by the *vardhani*. Then the pitcher should be taken and worshipped at a fixed place.

16. Hari should be worshipped with perfumes etc. in the pitcher adorned with five gems and cloth and the weapons (should be worshipped) at the left in the *Vardhani* in which gold has been placed.

17. One should worship the goddess of the building and the presiding deity of obstacles near it. In the same way, one should arrange for the consecration of Viṣṇu on the days of movement (of the sun from one stellar place to another), and other days (of importance).

18. Nine dentless jars full of water should be placed in the nine corners. One should offer water for washing the feet, *arghya* for rinsing the mouth and the *pañcagavya*.

19. The five sweet things, water etc. (are placed) in the east, north-east etc. The curd, milk, honey and hot water are the four constituents for the worship of the feet.

20. The lotus, *śyāmāka* (a kind of grain), *dūrvā* (grass) and the consort of Viṣṇu are for the worship of the feet. Together with barley seeds, perfumes, fruits and unbroken rice, this is spoken as constituting the eight articles for the worship of the feet.

21. The *kuśa* (grass), flowers of white mustard, sesamum (are) the articles (used) for adoration. One should offer waters for rinsing the mouth together with cloves and *kaṅkola* (berries).

22. One should bathe the deity with the five sweet materials along with (the recitation of) the principal mystic syllable. One should pour pure water on the head of the deity from the central pot.

23. The worshipper should touch water poured from the pitcher and the tip of the *kūrcha* (bunch of *kuśa* grass). One should offer pure water for washing the feet and *arghya* for sipping.

24. After having wiped the body with a cloth, the deity (adorned) with a cloth should be taken to the altar. Having worshipped him there, one should offer oblations in the sacrificial pit after having controlled breath.

25. Having washed hands, three lines running towards the east from the south to the north and three running towards the north are drawn.

26. Having sprinkled them with the waters of *arghya*, one has to show *yonimudrā*.[1] Having meditated on the fire of the form of the self in the *yoni* one should throw it in the pit.

27. Then one should place vessels together with *darbha* grass and wooden ladles. The twigs and saw (should be) at arm's distance.

28. (Then one must bring) vessels *praṇitā*, *prokṣaṇi* and *sthāli* for (holding) the clarified butter (and offering) ghee etc. Two *prasthas*[2] of rice (are spread) evenly with face downwards.

29-30. The *kuśa* (grass) with its tip (facing) eastwards should be placed in the *praṇitā* and *prokṣaṇi* vessels. Having filled *praṇiṭā* (vessel) with water and having meditated on the deity and worshipping, the *praṇitā* (vessel) should be placed in the midst of materials in front. Having filled the *prokṣaṇi* (vessel) with water and worshipping it, it should be placed on the right side.

31. The oblation should be consigned to the fire. Brahmā should be assigned to the south. Having spread the *kuśa* (grass) in the east etc. the (line of) enclosure should be drawn.

32. Rites relating to Viṣṇu should be done with (the rites) such as *garbhādhāna* etc. The *garbhādhāna*, *puṁsavana*, *simantonnayana*, and (the rite performed after) the birth (are the rites).

33. Eight offerings to the fire are made commencing with naming (ceremony) and ending with *samāvarta* (rite performed on the completion of one's studies). The final oblation is made with the sacrificial ladles for each act.

34. The oblation is made after having meditated on the lustrous (goddess) Lakṣmī at the middle of the pit. (She) is known as Kuṇḍalakṣmī (Lakṣmī of the sacrificial pit), the source of the material world composed of the three qualities.

35. She is the source of all beings as well as mystic learning and collection of mystic syllables. The fire is the cause of liberation. The supreme soul (Viṣṇu) is the conferer of emancipation.

---

1. On this *mudrā* and other *mudrās* see *Kāli. P.* 70.36-56. This is one of ten *mudrās* in the worship of the goddess. See *Brahmāṇḍa P.* IV. 36.62; 42.1-19.

2. A measure equivalent to 32 *palas*.

36. (His) head is spoken as at the east, the two arms are situated at the corners north-east and south-east, the two thighs at the north-western and south-western corners.

37-38. The belly is called (the sacrificial) pit. The organ of generation is said to be the source. The three qualities are the girdle. Having meditated thus fifteen twigs should be placed in the fire (after reciting) *Om* by showing *muṣṭi mudrā*[1]. Oblations should be made again to the vessels and worship is offered (to the vessels) on the north-west to south-east.

39. Parts of oblations are offered (for the directions) upto the north-east with the basic mystic syllable. (Oblations are made) in the north with (the syllables) (forming) the end (of the) twelve syllables[2] and with the middle (of the mystic syllable) in the south.

40. The consecrated fire of Viṣṇu, possessing seven tongues and having the radiance of crores of sums and having the moon as its face and sun as the eye and situated in the middle of the lotus should be meditated upon with the *vyāhṛtis*.[3] Then one should offer one hundred and eight oblations (to this form). Then fiftyeight oblations (should be offered) and a tenth of it for the limbs.

## CHAPTER THIRTYFIVE

### *Mode of consecration of an image*

*Agni said* :

1. Having sprinkled with the residual offering one should perform consecration of the sacred, subtle, and chanted mystic formulae of the manlion form.

2-3. Consecration of the vessels covered by the clothes should be done with mystic syllables. The vessels on which water is sprinkled once or twice with bel (leaves), should be placed

1. This is formed by holding a clenched fist.
2. *Om namo bhagavate Nārāyaṇāya.*
3. The basic syllables forming part of the Gāyatri-mantra.

near the pitcher. Having pronounced the protective spell the priest should place stick for (cleansing) the teeth and myrabolan on the east with (the recitation of syllable for) Saṅkarṣaṇa.

4. The ashes, sesamum, and cowdung-mixed earth (should be consecrated)on the south with (syllable for) Pradyumna, in the west with (that of) Aniruddha and in the north with that of Nārāyaṇa.

5. Then the waters along with the *kuśa* grass (should be assigned) to the south-east with the heart, the saffron and pigment on the north-east with the head, the incense on the south-west with the tuft.

6. Then the principal beautiful flowers (should be assigned) to the north-west with the armour. The sandal, water, unbroken rice, curd, and *dūrvā* (grass) are placed in small cups (made of leaves).

7-8. The chamber having been encircled by three threads, the articles kept ready should be thrown again. Then in one's own order of adoration one should offer perfumes and (other) articles, at the foot of the gate or at the pitcher of Viṣṇu with sacred syllables. One should then worship the radiant, beautiful form of Viṣṇu capable of destroying all sins.

9. "I conceive on thy limbs, the deity who grants all coveted things". After having worshipped him by (showing) the incense, lamp etc., one should approach the gate-way.

10. One should offer *pavitra*[1] along with perfumes, flowers and unbroken grains. The radiant *pavitra* of Viṣṇu (is capable) of destroying all sins.

11. I hold on my limbs (the *pavitra*) for the accomplishment of virtue, desire and worldly benefits. The *pavitra* is offered to the other attendant deities and to the preceptor (seated) on a seat.

12. After having worshipped well with perfumes, one has to offer to Hari along with perfumes, flowers etc. and saying, "May these become the energy of Viṣṇu".

13-14. Having offered to the deity stationed in the fire one should pray to the deity (saying), "O lord couched on the great

1. It means the sanctified articles. It also means the twining of the *darbha* grass in a particular shape so that it could be worn on the finger.

serpent in the milky ocean. I shall worship you in the morning. You (please) be present here O Keśava." Then having offered offerings to Indra and others one should dedicate them to the attendants of Viṣṇu.

15. Then one should place a pitcher covered by two cloths and filled with water mixed with perfumes, *rocanā*, camphor and saffron in front of the deity.

16-18. Having adorned the deity with perfumes and flowers, one should worship him with the mystic formula. Having come out of the hall one should place in three circular enclosures the five products obtained from the cow, the sacrificial offering (*caru*) and wood for cleansing the teeth. One should read *purāṇas* and recite hymns and along with servants, a women and children remain awake. Then the consecration rite should be performed immediately without sacred perfumes.

## CHAPTER THIRTYSIX

*Mode of performing the investiture of sacred thread*

*Agni said* :

1. Having bathed in the morning and worshipping the guardian deities, (the worshipper) should enter the secret chamber and gather (articles) and place.

2. The articles (are) the dress, ornaments and perfumes which were offered in the consecration ceremony earlier. Having discarded the remnants (of articles for worship), the deity should be well-installed and worshipped.

3. One should offer the *pañcāmṛta* (five sweet articles), the unguents, pure and perfumed waters as well as dress, perfumes and flowers.

4. Having offered unto the fire as done everyday one should pray to the deity and bow down. Having submitted one's actions to the deity one should perform the *naimittika* (periodical) ceremony.

5. One should worship the gate-keeper, the pitcher of Viṣṇu and the *varddhani* (vessel) and Hari. The pitcher (should be consecrated) with the sacred syllable '*ato deva*' (and the following).

6. "O Kṛṣṇa ! Salutations to you. You accept this sacred thread for the sake of purifying all and which yields fruits of a year's worship.

7. You purify sins that had been committed by me. O God ! the lord of celestials I will be purified by your grace."

8. Having sprinkled mentally the sacred thread and the self, and having sprinkled the pitcher of Viṣṇu, one should go near the deity.

9-10. One should offer a sacred thread to the self, after having discarded the protective thread (tied on the hand). O Lord ! Accept the sacred thread that has been made ready by me, for the sake of accomplishing rites so that there may not be any fault on me. The sacred thread (should be offered) to the gate-keepers, the seat and to the chief preceptors.

11. The garlands of forest flowers (should be offered) to the gods of inferior order with the basic formula. The articles should be offered to the heart etc. and ending with Viṣvaksena (an epithet of Viṣṇu).

12. Having offered to the fire the oblations placed near the fire for Viṣṇu and other (gods), and having worshipped, the final oblation should (then) be made with the basic formula for the expiation (of one's sins).

13-16. O Lord ! having Garuḍa as your emblem ! Let this be your annual adoration with one hundred and eight or five *Upaniṣads*[1] (and) with garlands of gems and corals, the flowers *mandāra* and others.

"O Lord ! Just as the garland of wild flowers and the *kaustubha* gem (are) (worn) always on the chest, so also bear the sacred thread and the worship on the chest. Whatever has been done wantonly or unwantonly in the regulations of the worship let it become complete by the rite shorn of impediments." Having worshipped, bowing down, and requesting them the purified article should be placed on one's own head.

---

1. The mystical writings ascertaining the meaning of the *Vedas*.

17. Having made offering to Viṣṇu the preceptor should be satisfied by (giving) the fees. The brahmins should be satisfied) by (giving) food, clothes and other things either for a day or for a fortnight.

18. At the time of bathing, having gone down into the waters, the sacred thread should be offered. Without any restriction, food and other things should be given (to others) and then one has to eat.

19-22. Having worshipped fire at the (rite of) dismissal the threads are removed. (One should then say) "Having thus duly accomplished my annual adoration O thread ! you now go to the world of Viṣṇu having been permitted by me. Having worshipped Someśa and Viṣvaksena at the centre and having worshipped the sacred threads one should dedicate them to the brahmins. As many knots as there are in that thread (one will) live gloriously for so many thousands of years in the world of Viṣṇu. One will get release (from bondage) after having redeemed hundreds of his ancestors the ten preceding and the ten succeeding and having established them in the world of Viṣṇu.

## CHAPTER THIRTYSEVEN

### *The investiture of sacred thread for all gods*

*Agni said* :

1. Listen to (the description of the mode of) investiture for all deities. The thread is the primary characteristic as well as its yellow orpiment.

2. O the cause of the universe ! come here along with the attendant gods. I invite you in the morning and offer this sacred thread.

3. O the creator of the universe. Salutations to you ! Accept this sacred thread for the sake of purification (and which) conveys the fruits of the annual worship.

4. O God Śiva ! Salutations to you ! Accept this sacred

thread along with garlands of gems and corals and *mandāra* flowers.

5-6. O lord of the learned in the *Vedas* ! Let this be your annual worship. After having accomplished this annual worship of mine according to the rules, O articles of worship ! go to heavens after being discarded by me. O lord Sun ! Salutations to you. Accept this article of worship.

7. O Lord Śiva ! Salutations to you. Accept this article of worship which is capable of yielding fruits of annual worship for the sake of purification.

8. O lord of gaṇas ! Salutations to you. Accept this article of worship which is capable of yielding fruits of annual worship for the sake of purification.

9. O goddess Śakti ! Salutations to you. Accept this article of worship which is capable of yielding fruits of annual worship for the sake of purification.

10-14. I dedicate unto you this excellent thread verily the same as (lord) Nārāyaṇa and (lord) Aniruddha and which is capable of yielding fruits of annual worship for the sake of purification and which yields wealth, grains and health. I dedicate unto you this excellent thread verily the same as Kāmadeva and Saṅkarṣaṇa, which yields learning, progeny and welfare. I dedicate unto you this thread verily the same as Vāsudeva, which yields *dharma*, *artha*, *kāma*, and *mokṣa* and which is the cause for transport over the ocean of mundane existence. This thread verily the universal form is the donor of all things, the destroyer of sins and elevates past and future lineage. I offer in order to the four younger deities with the mystic syllables.

## CHAPTER THIRTYEIGHT

### *Benefits of constructing temples*

*Agni said* :

1. I will now describe the benefits of erecting the

1. These are the four objects of human life, namely, righteousness, pleasures, desires and release from bondage.

temples of Vāsudeva and others. One who is desirous of constructing the temples of gods gets freed from sins incurred in thousand births.

2-5. Those who conceive of building a temple get the sins accrued in hundreds of births destroyed. Those who approve the building of a temple for lord Kṛṣṇa, also become free from their sins and go to the world of Acyuta (Viṣṇu). Having built a temple for Hari, a man immediately conveys a lakh of his ancestors both past and future to the world of Viṣṇu. The manes of a person who builds a temple for Viṣṇu having seen it remain in the world of Viṣṇu well-honoured and relieved of their sufferings in hells. The erection of the abode for the deity destroys sins such as the killing of a brahmin.

6. Whichever benefit could not be obtained by doing sacrificial rites, could be got by the erection of an abode (for the god). He who erects an abode for the god reaps fruits of bathing in all holy waters.

7. Even the making of a temple by perfidy with dust one would reach heaven. It gets more benefits than those (got) being slain in the battle.

8. One who builds one temple goes to heaven. One who builds three temples goes to the world of Brahmā. The builder of five abodes reaches the world of Śambhu (Śiva). By building eight abodes one remains in the world of Hari.

9-17. One who builds sixteen abodes gets enjoyment and emancipation. Having built a small, medium or excellent temple for Hari one gets heaven or the world of Viṣṇu or emancipation respectively in order. Which merits a rich man would get by erecting an excellent temple of Viṣṇu, a poor man would get by (erecting) a small temple itself. Having acquired riches and built a temple for Hari even with a small portion of it one would get excellent and enormous merits. By erecting a temple of Hari with a lakh or thousand or hundred or fifty (units of money) one would reach the place of that person who has the eagle in his banner. Those who play in their childhood with (the building of) abodes of Hari with earth also go to the world of Vāsudeva. The building of temples of Viṣṇu at holy places, within temples, accomplished place or hermitage (yields) threefold benefit than those already described. Those who decorate (the temple) of Viṣṇu with the *bandhūka* flowers and anoint with fragrant paste, also reach the place of the lord. (Having erected the temple of Hari), a person obtains two-fold merits after having elevated the fallen, the falling and half-fallen. He who brings about the fall of a man is the protector of one fallen.

18-19. By (erecting) a temple of Viṣṇu one reaches his region. As long as the bricks remain in the temple of Hari, the founder of that family is honoured in the world of Viṣṇu. He becomes pious and adorable in this world as well as the next.

20. He who builds a temple for Kṛṣṇa, the son of Vasudeva is born as a man of good deeds and his family gets purified.

21. He who builds an abode for Viṣṇu, Rudra, Sun or the goddess etc. acquires fame. What is the use of the hoarded riches for an ignorant person?

22-23. If one does not cause an abode for Kṛṣṇa to be built (with wealth) acquired by hard (work) (and) if one's wealth could not be enjoyed by manes, brahmins, celestials and relatives, his acquisition of wealth is useless. As death is certain for a man so also the destruction of wealth.

24. One who does not spend his riches for charities or for enjoyments is stupid and is being bound even while alive, while the riches are flickery.

25. Is there any merit in being the lord of wealth acquired either accidentally or by one's effort, if it is not spent for acquiring fame or for philanthropy?

26-31. One may give to the foremost brahmins and also do (such acts) which would glorify him. More than the charities and more than the acts which would glorify him, one has to build the temples of Viṣṇu and other gods. The temple of Hari being set up by devoted great men, the three worlds, the movable and immovable things and the entire objects get established. All the things beginning with Brahmā to the Pillar, that has already born, that is being born, that is to be born, the gross, the minute and the other things are born of Viṣṇu. Having set up an abode for that lord of lords, the omnipresent, the great Viṣṇu, one is not born again in this world. By building temples for the celestials, Śiva, Brahmā, Sun, Vighneśa (lord of impediments), Caṇḍī (Pārvatī), Lakṣmī and others (a man) reaps the same benefit as he would get for building an abode for Viṣṇu. Greater merit (is acquired) by installing images of gods.

32. In the rites (relating to) installation of an idol there is no limit for the fruits (gained). An image made of wood gives greater merit than that made of clay. One made of bricks yields greater merit than that made of wood.

33. One made of stones gives (greater merit) than that made of bricks. (Images made) of gold and other metals yield more benefits. Sins committed in seven births get destroyed even at the very commencement of installation.

34. One who builds a temple goes to heaven and never goes to hell. Having elevated a hundred of his ancestors he conveys them to the world of Viṣṇu.

35. Yama (god of death) said to his emissaries :

*Yama said* :

"Those men who build temples of gods and adore the idols are not to be brought to hell.

36. Bring them to my view who have not built temples and other things. Move around in the befitting way and execute my directive.

37. Except those who have resorted to Ananta, the father of the universe, no other beings would at any time disregard the command.

38. Those who are devotees of Viṣṇu and have their mind fixed on him have to be avoided by you. They are not to live here.

39-49. Those who always adore Viṣṇu should be avoided by you from a distance. Those who sing the glories of Govinda while standing or sleeping or walking or standing behind or stumbling or remaining (at a place) are to be avoided by you from a distance. Those who worship Janārdana with obligatory and occasional rites are not to be beheld by you. Those who follow this course attain good position. Those who worship (the god) with flowers, incense, raiments, favourite ornaments, (and) those who have gone to the abode of Kṛṣṇa are not to be seized by you. Those who besmear with unguents, and those who are engaged in sprinkling his body, their children and their descendants should be left in the temple of Kṛṣṇa. Hundreds of men born in the family of one who has built the temple of Viṣṇu should not be seen by you with evil mind. Whoever builds a temple of Viṣṇu with wood or stone or earth gets free from all sins. One who builds the temple of Viṣṇu gets that great benefit which (one would acquire) by doing sacrificial rites everyday. By building a temple for Viṣṇu (one) conveys hundreds of his discendants and hundreds of his ancestors to the world of Acyuta. Viṣṇu is identical with the seven worlds. One who builds a house for him saves the endless worlds and also obtains endlessness. One who builds (a temple) for him, lives for so many years in heaven as the number of years the set up bricks would remain. The maker of the idol (would reach) the world of Viṣṇu.One who consecrates it would get absorbed in Hari.

One who builds a temple, makes an idol and installs it goes within his range.

*Agni said* :

"I have not brought one who has installed Hari as told by Yama". Hayaśiras told Brahmā for the installation of gods.

## CHAPTER THIRTYNINE

### *Preparations of ground for constructing temples*

*Hayagriva said* :

1. O Brahman ! Listen to me speaking about the installation of (images of) Viṣṇu and others. (The principles of) *Pañcarātra*[1] and *Saptarātra* have (already) been described by me.

2-5. They have been divided by the sages into twentyfive (books) in this world. *Hayaśirṣa tantra* is the first one. *Trailokya-*

1. The word *rātra* means knowledge and the *Pañcarātra* means the collective knowledge of five kinds according to the *Nar. Sam.* I.1.

However the *Ahir. Sam.* the earliest text of this class of literature would take it to mean the fivefold manifestation of Lord Vāsudeva, viz. *Para*, *vyūha*, *vibhava*, *arcā* and *antar yāmin.*

*mohana*, *Vaibhava*, *Pauṣkara*, *Prahlāda*, *Gārgya*, *Gālava*, *Nāradiya*, *Śrīpraśna*, *Śāṇḍilya*, *Aiśvara*, spoken by Satya, *Śaunaka*, *Vāsiṣṭha*, *Jñānasāgara*, *Svāyambhuva*, *Kāpila*, *Tārkṣya*, *Nārāyaṇiyaka*, *Ātreya*, *Nārasiṁha*, *Ānanda*, *Aruṇa*, *Baudhāyana*, and the one spoken by Viśva as the quintessence of that (the preceding), having eight parts (or the other books).

6-7. A brahmin born in the middle country may perform installation (rite). Those who were born in Kaccha (Cutch), (in the regions of the river) Kāverī, Koṅkaṇa, Kāmarūpa, Kaliṅga, Kāñcī, Kāśmīra, Kosala should not (do installation). The sky, wind, radiance, water, and earth are the *pañcarātra*.

8. Those other than the *pañcarātra* are inanimate and engulfed in darkness. He is the preceptor who has the knowledge "I am brahman and stainless Viṣṇu".

9. Even though deficient in all characteristics he who is a master of the *tantras* is (to be looked upon as) the preceptor. The image of the deity should be placed facing the city and never turned backwards.

10. At Kurukṣetra, Gayā and other places and near the rivers, (the image of) Brahmā at the centre of the city and (the image of) Indra on the east are auspicious.

11-12. (The images) of Agni, mothers, goblins, and Yama (should be placed) in the south-east. (The images) of Caṇḍikā (should be placed) in the south and those of the manes and demons in the south-west. The temples of Varuṇa and others should be built in the west. (The images) of Vāyu and Nāga (serpent) (should be) on the north-west and those of Yakṣa and Guha (Kārttikeya) on the north.

13-15. (Those) of Caṇḍīśa (the lord of Caṇḍī), the great lord and Viṣṇu (are) always (placed) in the north-east. One should not knowingly construct a temple of a reduced size or equal in size or bigger in size than another temple already constructed so as to encroach upon it. A wise-man would leave between them a space measuring twice the elevation and erect a new temple without affecting both the temples. After having examined the ground one has to take possession of it.

16. The offerings to the (presiding) goblins should be offered upto the outer enclosing wall (with a mixture of) black

gram, turmeric powder, fried grains, curd and flour.

17-18. Having dropped the flour in all directions along with (the recitation of) eight syllables: (one has to say), "The demons and goblins who remain on this ground may go away. I am making a place for Hari." Having cleaved the earth with the plough one should cleave it with oxen.

19. Eight *Paramāṇus* make one *rathāṇu*. Eight *rathāṇus* are said to make one *trasareṇu*. Eight times that (makes) one *bālāgra* and eight times that is known as *likhyā*. Eight times that is known as *yūka*. Eight times that is a *yavamadhyama*. Eight times *yava* (makes) one *aṅgula*. Twenty-four *aṅgulas* (make) one *kara*. Four *aṅgulas* make one *padmahastaka*.

## CHAPTER FORTY

### *The mode of making the respectful offering to the god*

*The Lord said* :

1. In days of yore that material principle was dreadful among all principles. It being placed on the earth it was known to be the lord of that place.

2. At a place (divided) into sixty-four compartments Īśa occupying a half of the corner square is worshipped with ghee and unbroken rice. Then the (god) Parjanya (the rain god) occupying a square (is worshipped).

3. The god Jayanta, who occupies two squares (is worshipped) with lotus (flowers) and water, and the lord Mahendra, who remains in one square (is worshipped) with a banner. The Sun god (is worshipped) in a square with all red things.

4. The (god of) truth occupying half a square at the bottom is worshipped with canopy and profuse offering of ghee. The lord of the sky occupying half the angular square (is propitiated) with the bird's flesh.

5. The fire-god in half a square (is worshipped) with the

1. The mantra of eight syllables: *Oṁ namo nārāyaṇāya*.

sacrificial ladle and the god Pūṣan in a square with fried grains, the lord of untruth in two squares with gold, churning rod and unbroken rice in the house.

6. The lord Dharmeśa stationed in two squares is worshipped) with meat and cooked food, the Gandharva in two squares with incense and the tongue of a bird.

7. Mṛga occupying one upper (square) (is) then (worshipped) with blue cloth. The manes (are worshipped) with a dish composed of milk, sesamum and rice in half a square and sticks of tooth-brush in another square.

8. The (two) door-keepers Sugrīva and Puṣpadanta occupying two squares (are worshipped) with barley grains and a clump of grass respectively, and Varuṇa with lotus flowers in a square.

9. The *asura* (demon) in two squares (is propitiated) with wine, (the serpent) Śeṣa in a square with ghee and water, the sin in half a square with barley grains, the disease in half a square with *maṇḍaka* (a kind of baked flour).

10. The Nāga (serpent) (is worshipped) in a square with the *nāga* flowers and the chief serpent in two squares with edibles The Bhallāṭa (a kind of superhuman being) (is worshipped) in a single square with rice mixed with kidney-bean, and the moon (with the same offering) in the next square.

11. The sage placed in two squares (is worshipped) with honey, sweat gruel and nutmeg, Diti in a square with anointments and Aditi in one and a half squares.

12. Āpas (is propitiated) in a square below in the north-east with milk and cake and then Apavatsa remaining in a square below with curd.

13. Marīci (is propitiated) in four squares in the east with balls of sweet-meat and for (the god) Savitṛ, the red flowers (are placed) in the lower angular square.

14. In the square below that, water along with *kuśa* grass is offered to Savitṛ, red sandal paste is offered to Aruṇa in four squares.

15. Respectful offering along with turmeric (is made) to Indra in the lower square in the south-west and rice mixed with ghee (is offered) in the corner square below Indrajaya.

16. Sweet gruel (mixed) with jaggery (is offered) to Indra

in four squares and cooked meat (is offered) to Rudra in the corner square in the north-west.

17. In the corner square below that wet fruit (is offered) to Yakṣa, rice meat and black-gram (are offered) to Mahīdhara in four squares.

18. Rice and sesamum should be placed in the central square for Brahmā. Carakī (is worshipped) with black-gram and clarified butter and Skanda with a dish composed of milk, sesamum and rice and a garland.

19. Vidārī (a demoness) (is worshipped) with red lotuses, Kandarpa (god of love) with cooked rice and meat, Pūtanā (a demoness) with meat and bile and Jambaka (a demon) with meat and blood.

20. The Īśa (is appeased) with bile, blood and bones, Pilipiñja (a demon) with a garland and blood. Other deities are worshipped with blood and meat and in their absence with unbroken rice.

21. Sacrificial offerings are made to demons, divine mothers, manes and guardian deities of the ground in due order.

22. One should not build temples and other things without offering to these (deities) or appeasing them. Hari, Lakṣmī, Gaṇa (the attendant deity of Śiva) should be worshipped at the place (set apart) for Brahmā.

23-24. The final offering is then made to Brahmā in the central pitcher and to Brahmā and other deities as well as Maheśvara, the presiding deity of the ground with a pitcher together with a small vessel. After having made benediction, and holding well the water-jar with small holes at the bottom an auspicious circumambulation is made.

25. O Brahman ! the drop of water is rotated (to fall) in a line. As before in the same line seven kinds of seeds are sown.

26. The excavation should begin in the same way. Then a hole of the measure of a hand should be dug at the centre.

27. Then having made (the pit) smooth to a depth of four fingers' breadth and having contemplated on the four-armed Viṣṇu (waters of adoration) should be offered from the pitcher.

28. Then the hole is filled (with water) from the water-jar having holes at the bottom, white flowers are placed. The excellent conch-shell (known as the) Dakṣiṇāvarta (curved to the

right) has to be filled with seeds and earth.

29. After having performed the offering of water, one should present the preceptor of cows, clothes and other things and honour the sculptor, and the *vaiṣṇavas* who know the proper time.

30. One should then dig carefully till water is found. The substance lying below the presiding deity under the building would not have any beneful influence.

31. The bone or substance below if broken, the broken thing forebodes baneful influence for the inmate. Whatever kind of sound one would hear, (it is to be known) as due to the substance lying below.

## CHAPTER FORTYONE

### *Mode of performing consecration*

*The Lord said* :

1. I shall narrate the mode of consecration of the foundation and (the rites relating to) the laying down of the foundation stone. A shed is erected at first and four (sacrificial) pits (are made).

2. The placing of pitchers (of water) and bricks, the erection of the doors and pillars (are finished). The dug up pit is filled to a quarter (of its depth) and the presiding deity is worshipped at the same time.

3. The bricks should be of twelve fingers in length, with a breadth and width of four fingers respectively, and well-burnt.

4-8. Stones measuring a cubit (in length) would be best in the case of stone slabs. Nine copper pitchers and bricks should be placed. The pitchers (should be filled) with water, (substance known as *pañcakaṣāya*[1], waters of all herbs and fragrant waters.

1. A decoction from the fruits of five plants *jambū*, *śālmali*, *vāṭyāla*, *bakula* and *badara* (*MW*. p. 575).

Then with the pitchers filled well with waters (and containing gold and rice and anointed by fragrant sandal, and having placed the stones along with (the recitation of) the mystic syllables —the three-footed *āpo hi ṣṭhā*[1], *śanno devī*[2], *tarat sa mandiḥ*[3], *pāvamānī*[4], *uduttamaṁ varuṇa*[5], *kayā naḥ*[6], *varuṇasya*[7], *haṁsaḥ śuciṣat*[8], *śrīsūkta*[9].

9. Hari should be worshipped in a bed in the shed in the eastern part of the (drawn) diagram. Then having kindled the fire twelve twigs should be offered (as oblation).

10. The primary offering and the offering with clarified butter should be done with the syllable *om*. Then subsequently eight offerings and again eight offerings with clarified butter (should be offered) with the syllables (known as)*vyāhṛtis*[10] duly.

11. After that offer oblation (in the fire) to the gods, Agni, Soma and Puruṣottama separately with *vyāhṛtis*.

12-13. The preceptor (officiating at the rite) should do the expiatory rite facing the eastern quarter offering to the image, meat, and sesamum along with ghee separately in the pitchers with the vedic syllables or the mystic formula of twelve syllables. Having scattered (sesamum) in the eight directions a stone and a pitcher should be placed at the centre and the following divinities (should be invoked) in order.

14. *Padma*[11], *mahāpadma*, *makara*, *kacchapa*, *kumuda*, *nanda*, *padma*, *śaṅkha* and *padminī* (are the divinities).

15. The pitchers should not be moved. Eight bricks should be placed in them duly beginning with the eastern direction and ending with the north-east.

16. The female energies Vimalā and others, the presiding deities of these bricks, should be invoked in their proper pitchers.

---

1. *ṚV.* 10.9.1a.
2. *ṚV.* 10.9.4a.
3. *ṚV.* 9.58.1a.
4. *G. Dh.* 19.12.
5. *ṚV.* 1.24.15a.
6. *ṚV.* 4.31.1a.
7. One of the many hymns beginning with this word See *Ved. Con.*
8. *ṚV.* 4.40.5a.
9. This is the *sūkta*, '*hiraṇyavarṇām hariṇīm*', *ṚV Kh.* 5.87.1a.
10. The three syllables bhūr, bhuvas, svar. *Manu* 2.76.
11. This and the following are the different treasures. See *Purāṇa* XVII. 2 p. 160. The text here omits *nīla* and repeats *Padma*.

The energy Anugraha should be invoked at the central pitcher.

17. "O perfect, unbroken, full-bodied brick, the daughter of the sage Aṅgiras, I am establishing you. You grant me the desired thing."

18-20. The preceptor, having placed the brick with this mystic syllable should do *garbhādhāna*[1]. Having invoked the goddess Padminī at the central pitcher, earth, flowers, minerals, gems, and iron pieces as well as the weapons of deities of quarters (should be placed) in the hole of twelve fingers' width and four fingers' depth.

21-22. The goddess earth should be worshipped in a copper vessel of the shape of a lotus. "O the exclusive mistress of all beings, abound with the summits of mountains as the seats, one surrounded by oceans, O goddess ! You resort to this hole. O rejoicer ! born of sage Vasiṣṭha ! you rejoice with the Vasus and the progeny.

23. O Victorious ! related to Bhārgava (Paraśurāma) Maker of thine subjects victorious ! the perfect ! the relative of Aṅgiras ! fulfil all my desires.

24. O Auspicious one ! related to sage Kāśyapa ! Make my intellect good. One who is accomplished with all seeds ! One who possesses all gems and herbs !

25. May you be victorious ! O beautiful one ! O rejoicer ! Related to Vasiṣṭha ! The daughter of the creator ! O Goddess ! O handsome one ! Stay on here in bliss—O majestic one !

26. Stay thou in this house ! O beautiful and brilliant one ! the daughter of Kaśyapa ! The honoured, most wonderful and bedecked with scents and garlands !

27. O Goddess ! Stay in bliss in this room ! O Bhārgavi (daughter of Śukra) ! Bestower of worldly prosperities ! Possessed by the gods, kings, and masters of the house !

28. May you become the multiplier of animals for the happiness of men and others. Having said in this way one should then sprinkle cow's urine on the pit.

29. Having done so, one should place in the pit (such that) the impregnation would take place in the night. One should

1. Impregnation at the pit.

give away cows and clothes to the preceptor (the officiating priest), and food to other people.

30. Having filled the hole and placing the bricks in the hole, the hole is completely filled. Then one should construct the base of the deity proportionate to the edifice of the deity.

31. An excellent base is that where it is more than half the breadth of the edifice, while a quarter lesser than that would be mediocre and that which is half of the excellent base (aforesaid) would be the lowest (in merit).

32. After completing the base, the rite for the presiding deity (of the ground) should be done again. One who performs the consecration of the base would enjoy in heavens free from sin.

33. One who would mentally think that "I am going to build a temple", the sins which had stuck to his body would get destroyed that day itself.

34-35. No need to speak (about the merits) of one who has built a temple in the prescribed manner. It is impossible for anyone to describe the merits one would accrue by building a temple with eight bricks alone. One should indeed infer from this the (proportionate) fruits (accrued) (from the building) of temples of greater dimensions.

36. The door of the temple at the centre of the village or on the eastern part should face the west, while in other directions the door should be facing the west and in the southern, northern and western parts (the door) should face the east.

## CHAPTER FORTYTWO

### *Construction of a temple*

*Hayagriva said* :

1. Listen to me describing the construction of a temple in general. A wise man should divide a square ground into sixteen parts.

2. One should make the four central squares endowed with wealth. The other sixteen parts are left for the walls.

3. The pedestal should extend over four squares. The length of the cornice should be double that of the pedestal.

4. The path of circumambulation should be a quarter of (the length) of the cornice. Two equal openings having the same width as the latter, should be left on the two sides for projections

5. The extent of the ground should be made at first equal to the length of the tower or twice that such as it may be beautiful.

6-7. One should construct the pavilion in front of the sanctum on the lines running parallel through the sides of its inner chamber, adorned with pillars and being of the same length or longer than the principal temple sanctorum by a quarter of its length. The anti-chamber should then be constructed at 81 steps.

8. The deities at the end of the base should be worshipped before placing the parrots at the front door. In the same manner the thirty-two gods at the end should be worshipped when the outer wall is raised.

9. This is the characteristic of a temple in general. Listen to the description (of raising) a temple proportionate to the (size of the) image.

10. The base (of the deity) should be of the same size as the image. The adytum (of the temple) should be half the size of the base and the walls proportionate to the adytum.

11. The height (of the walls) should be equal to the length of the walls. The pinnacle should be made equal to twice the height of the wall.

12. The path around the temple should be a quarter of the extent of the pinnacle. The entrance chamber in the front should be a quarter of the extent of the pinnacle.

13. The projections of the arches should be one-eighth of the extent of the adytum. The arches should be made proportionate to the circumference.

14. The projections of arches should otherwise be made as one-third of it. Always there should be three projections on the left on the three arches.

15-16. Four upward lines should be marked for (the construction of) the pinnacle. A downward line is marked to fall above the key-stone which is located at the middle part of the pinnacle. A lion is built at the middle part of the pinnacle in a line with the key-stone.

17. Two such lines should be marked on the sides. There should be a small platform above that.

18. (The lion) should not be in a dropping posture or fierce-looking. The conical shaped structure is placed above, proportional to the small platform.

19. A beautiful opening should be made twice the length of the platform. Two globes should be placed above that with beautiful (ornamental) branches.

20-21. (Forms of) Caṇḍa and Pracaṇḍa should be carved on the door-frame occupying a fourth (of its space), (possessing) a staff like that of Viṣvaksena (Viṣṇu) and at the threshhold of the branch beautiful (Goddess) Śrī (Lakṣmī) (should be carved) as being bathed by the elephants of the quarters with (waters from) the pitchers . The height of enclosing wall should be one-fourth of that of the temple.

22. The height of the tower should be a quarter lesser than that of the temple. The pedestal (of the image) of the deity of five cubits should be of a cubit.

23. A shed known as the Garuḍamaṇḍapa and shed for Bhauma (Mars) and other (planets) (should be made). In the eight directions above (the chamber housing) one should make (the images as follows) :

24-25. (The images of) *Varāha* (boar) in the east, *Nṛsiṁha* (man-lion) in the south, *Śridhara* ( a form of Viṣṇu) in the west, *Hayagriva* (horse-necked form of Viṣṇu) in the north, *Jāmadagnyaka* (Paraśurāma, a manifestation of Viṣṇu) in the south-east, *Rāma* in the south-west, *Vāmana* (the short-statured manifestation of Viṣṇu) in the north-west (and) *Vāsudeva* in the north-east. The temple should be decorated with gems all around. Leaving out one-eighth of the door if that is done, it is not defective.

# CHAPTER FORTYTHREE

*Installation of deities in the temples*

*The Lord said* :

1. O Brahman ! Listen to my description (of the mode) of installation (of images) of deities in the temples. (Image of Vāsudeva should be placed at the middle of the five divine) edifices.

2. (The images of) the dwarf-form, man-lion form, horse-headed form, (and) boar form (of Viṣṇu) should be placed in the south-east, south-west, north-west and north-east (respectively).

3-5. (The image of) Nārāyaṇa should be placed in the middle. (The images of) the goddess, sun, Brahmā and the *liṅga* (symbolic representation of Śiva) or of Rudra (Śiva) should be placed in the south-east, south-west, north-west and north-east (respectively). Otherwise, (image of) Vāsudeva should be placed at the centre of the nine chambers and beautiful (images of Indra and the guardian deities of the world (should be placed) in the east and other directions. Otherwise, one should make five chambers and worship Puruṣottama (Viṣṇu) in the centre.

6. (The images of) Lakṣmī and Vaiśravaṇī (Kubera) should be placed in the east, the divine mothers in the south, Skanda, Gaṇeśa, Īśāna (a form of Śiva) and the sun and other planets in the west.

7-8. Otherwise, having installed (the images of) the manifestations (of Viṣṇu) such as the Fish etc., in the north, Caṇḍikā (a form of Goddess Pārvatī) in the south-east, Ambikā in the south-west, Sarasvatī in the north-west, Padmā (Lakṣmī) in the north-east and Vāsudeva or also Nārāyaṇa in the centre. The omni-present form of Hari should be placed in the centre in (the construction of) the thirteen chambers.

9-11. (Images of) Keśava and others (should be placed) in the east and other directions or (the images) of Hari himself in all chambers. The images are of seven kinds—earthen, wooden, metallic, made of gems, made of stones, made of sandal and made of flowers. The images made of flowers, sandal and earth yield all desired fruits when they are worshipped at that moment. I shall describe the stone image (where such practice) prevails.

12. In the absence of hills, the stone lying buried in the earth should be taken out. Among the colours, white, red, yellow, and black are extolled.

13. When stones of the above-mentioned colours are not available (the desired) colour is brought about by the (ceremony known as) *siṁhavidyā*.[1]

14. After (the performance of) the *siṁhahoma* (a piece of) stone (which becomes) tinged with white colour or black colour or produces sound like a bell-metal or emits sparks of fire (is deemed) as male.

15. The female one is that in which these characteristics are present in a lesser degree. If they are devoid of colours they are neuter. (The stones) in which the sign of a circle is found are to be taken as impregnated and should be rejected.

16. One should go to the forest and perform the forest rites for the sake of an image. After having bathed and plastering a shed Hari should be worshipped there.

17. After having made the offering of the victim, the (stone-cutter's) chisel used for the work should be worshipped. Having offered *homa* (pouring of clarified butter into the fire), water mixed with rice should be sprinkled over the image with the implement (chisel).

18. Having made the protective spell it should be worshipped with basic sacred syllable of lord Nṛsiṁha. After having made the offering to fire the final oblation should be made. Then offerings to the goblins should be given by the preceptor.

19. Having worshipped the good (spirits), the demons, *guhyakas* (a class of attendant-gods of Kubera), and accomplished souls and others who may be residing there, should be requested to forgive.

20. (They should be addressed as follows). "This journey (has been undertaken) by us for the image of Viṣṇu by the command of Keśava. Any work done for the sake of Viṣṇu, should also be your (concern)."

---

1. Only *Hayaśirṣasaṁhitā* of the Pañcarātrāgama texts mentions this. The present text does not explain this. See *Vaiṣṇava Iconography*, p. 40.

21. "Being always pleased with this offering (you) repair quickly to some other place quitting this place for good".

22. Being informed thus (these beings) go to another place in good cheer and satisfied. Having eaten the sacrificial porridge along with the sculptors, he should repeat in the night the following sacred syllables (inducing) sleep.

23. "Om ! salutations to (Lord) Viṣṇu, the omnipresent, Prabhaviṣṇu (Viṣṇu) (strong), the universe, and Salutations to the lord of dreams."

24. "O Lord of lords ! I have slept by your side. (Instruct me) in my dreams (how to execute) all the works I have in my mind."

25. "*Om Om* ! *hrūm phaṭ viṣṇave svāhā* ! When the dream (is) good, everything (will also be) good. If it is bad, it becomes good by the performance of the *siṁhahoma*[1]. Having offered reverential waters to the stone in the morning, the implements should be worshipped with (the sacred syllables) (for the worship of) implements.

26. The spades and chisels should have their edges besmeared with honey and clarified butter. (The priest) should think himself as Viṣṇu and the sculptor as Viśvakarman (the divine architect).

27-28. The implement which is of the form of Viṣṇu should be given (to the sculptor) and its face and back should be shown. Having cut a square block of the stone with controlled senses and holding a chisel, the sculptor should make a smaller one for the purpose of the pedestal. Having placed (them) in a chariot and brought to the workspot together with the cloth (one who) makes the image after having worshipped (the form conceived), is a sculptor.

## CHAPTER FORTYFOUR

### *Characteristics of the image of Vāsudeva*

*The Lord said* :

1-2. I shall describe to you the characteristics of the image

1. See VV. 13 and 17 above.

of Vāsudeva and other gods. Having placed the stone to the north of the temple facing either the east or the north and worshipped it, the sculptor should divide the stone into nine parts along the central line after making the offering.

3. In the twelve divisions (of the line) a division is said to be an *aṅgula* (a finger breadth). Two *aṅgulas* are known to be a *golaka*. It is also said to be a *kālanetra*.

4. Having divided one of the nine divisions into three, (with one part) the region of the calves should be made. In the same way a part is to be used for the knees and part for the neck.

5. The crown should be of a measure of a *tāla* (12 *aṅgulas*). In the same way the face (should be) of the measure of a *tāla*. The neck and heart should also be a *tāla* each.

6. The navel and the genital part should be a *tāla* apart. (The length) of the thighs should be two *tālas*. (The length) of the part from the ankle to the knee should be two *tālas*. Listen now to (the description) (of the drawing) of lines (on the body).

7. Two lines should be drawn on the foot, and (two) more in between the calves (and knees). Two lines about the knees and two more in between the thighs and the knees should be drawn.

8. One line should be drawn over the genital part, and one more about the waist. Another (line) (should) then (be drawn) above the navel for accomplishing the girdle.

9. Then (a line) should be drawn on the heart and two lines on the neck. One such line should be drawn on the forehead and one more on the head.

10. One more line should be drawn on the crown by the learned. O Brahman ! seven vertical lines should be drawn.

11. Six lines should be laid in between the armpits and the lower part of the spine. These lines alone should be marked clearly omitting the central line.

12. The forehead, the nose and the mouth should be made (to measure) four *aṅgulas*. The neck and the two ears should be made (to measure) four *aṅgulas* long.

13. The cheeks so also the chin should be made (to measure) two *aṅgulas* broad. The forehead is said to be eight *aṅgulas* broad.

14. Over that the temples (sides of the forehead) should

be made two *aṅgulas* endowed with curbs. The intervening space between the eyes and ears is said to be four *aṅgulas*.

15. The ears should be two *aṅgulas* wide. (The inter-space between) the ears and the ends of eye-lashes (should be) two and a half units. The cavity in the ear is spoken to be in the same line as the eyebrows.

16. A pierced ear (should be) six *aṅgulas* and an unpierced (ear) (should be) four *aṅgulas* equal to the chin. (Or it should be) six *aṅgulas* whether it is pierced or not pierced.

17. Then the external auditory passage with its membranes etc. should be made. The lower lip should be of two *aṅgulas* and the upper lip should be half of it.

18. Then the (breadth) of an eye (should be) half an *aṅgula* and the mouth (should be) four *aṅgulas*. The measurement of its depth is spoken to be one and a half *aṅgulas*.

19-20. The unopened mouth should be in this way. The opened mouth should be three *aṅgulas*. The base of the bridge of the nose should be one *aṅgula* high. From its tip it should be two *aṅgulas* similar to the *karavira* (flower) (oleander). The intervening space between the two eyes should be made to measure four *aṅgulas*.

21. The corners of the eyes (should be) two *aṅgulas*. The space between them (should be) two *aṅgulas*. The pupil (should be) one third of the eye and the iris (should be) one fifth (of it).

22. The breadth of the eye (should be) three *aṅgulas*. The cavity (of the eye) is considered to be half an *aṅgula*. The lengths of the eyebrows are considered to be equal and are proportional to the eye-brows.

23. The middle of the eye-brow should be two *aṅgulas* and its length (should be) four *aṅgulas*. The measure round the head (should be) thirty-six *aṅgulas*.

24. The measurement around the heads of the images of Keśava and other gods should be thirty-six (*aṅgulas*). The head-measure of all those (images) which are short-necked (should be) ten (*aṅgulas*).

25. The inter-space between the neck and the chest should be three times the length of the neck and should be thrice as much broad plus eight *aṅgulas*.

26. The shoulders (should) be made (to measure) eight

*aṅgulas* and the two beautiful shoulder regions (should be) three times those. The arms should measure seven times (the length of) the eyes. The fore arms (should be) sixteen *aṅgulas*.

27. The arms should be three *kalās*[1] in breadth and the fore-arms should also be equal to that. The upper arm should have a circumference of nine *kalās*.

28. It should be seventeen *aṅgulas* at the middle and sixteen *aṅgulas* above the elbow-joint. O Brahman ! the circumference of elbow should be three times that.

29. The circumference of the middle of the forearm is said to be sixteen *aṅgulas*. The circumference of the fore-part of the arm is said to be twelve *aṅgulas*.

30. The palm of the hand is said to be six *aṅgulas* in breadth. The length should be seven *aṅgulas*. The middle (finger) should be five *aṅgulas* (long).

31. The index finger and the ring finger (should be) half an *aṅgula* less than that. The little finger and the thumb should be made to measure four *aṅgulas* each.

32. The thumb should be made to have two *parvans* (joints). The other fingers (should have) three joints. The measure of the nail is laid down as half (the size of the joints) on the respective fingers.

33. The extent of the belly is same as that of the chest. The navel should be an *aṅgula* (in breadth) and proportionally deep.

34. Then the inter-space between the generative organ and the intestines should be made to measure a *tāla*. The girth around the navel (should be) forty-two *aṅgulas*.

35. The inter-space between the breasts should be made to measure a *tāla* in breadth. The nipples should be of the measure of a *yava*[2] (barley grain). The circular space around them should be two *pādas* (two feet).

36. The circumference of the chest should be made sixty-four *aṅgulas* clearly. The girth of the lower portion (of the chest) is said to be four *mukhas*[3] (one *tāla*).

---

1. Equal to two *aṅgulas*. Also called *Golaka*.
2. One eighth of an *aṅgula*.
3. Seems to be a corrupt form for *mukhya* equal to one *tāla* or twelve *aṅgulas*.

37. The circumference of the waist should be fifty-four *aṅgulas*. The breadth of the base of the thigh is said to be twelve *aṅgulas*.

38. It is somewhat greater at the middle (of the thigh) and gradually less (broad) below. The knee-joint (should be) eight *aṅgulas* in breadth and thrice that in its girth.

39. The middle of the leg from the ankle to the knee is said to be seven *aṅgulas* broad. The girth of it (should be) three times that. The top of the leg (should be) five *aṅgulas* broad.

40. The girth of that (the leg) (should be) thrice its breadth. The feet (should) measure a *tāla*. The extent of elevation of the feet (should be) four *aṅgulas*.

41. The front (part) of the ankles should be four *aṅgulas* The extent of the feet should be three *kalās*. The generative organ should be three *aṅgulas*.

42. Its girth (should be) five *aṅgulas*. The fore-finger (should be) of same length. The other fingers are duly lesser by one part of eighth.

43. The height of the toe is said to be one and a half *aṅgulas*. The nail of the two should be made twice that.

44. (Those of other fingers) should be gradually made half *aṅgula* less than the previous. The scrotum should be three *aṅgulas* (long). The generative organ (should be) four fingers (long).

45. The girth of the upper part of the pouch should be made (to be) four *aṅgulas*. The girth of the scrotum is said to be six *aṅgulas*.

46. The image should be adorned with ornaments. This is the exact description of details. The features (of the deities) should be made in this world, as described.

47. A disc on the (upper) right hand, and a lotus on the lower (right hand), the conch on the (upper) left hand, the mace on the lower (left hand) are to be placed according to the characteristic of Vāsudeva.

48-49. (The images of) Śrī and Puṣṭi should be made carrying a lotus and a harp respectively in their hands, (their images) reaching upto the thighs (of that of Vāsudeva). Then the two Vidyādharas (a class of semi-divine beings) holding the garlands (in their hands) should be made in the halo of the principal image). The halo (should also) be decked with the (images) of (celestial) elephants. The pedestal should be radiant like a lotus on which the images (should be worshipped) as follows.

## CHAPTER FORTYFIVE

### *Characteristics of pedestals and details relating to images*

*The Lord said* :

1. I shall describe the characteristics of the pedestal. The length is the same as that of the image. The height (should be) half of it. It should have sixty-four folds.

2. Leaving two rows at the bottom, the other parts should be polished on either side as also inside.

3. Leaving two rows at the top, the other parts are polished evenly on either side and inside.

4. The rectangular space in between these should then be polished. The first two rows should be divided into four parts by a wise man.

5-6. The girdle should be equal to one such part. The indent should be half that. Leaving one such part evenly on either side a wise man should leave on the exterior a breadth of a foot. The water drains should be at the top of each one of the three parts.

7. This auspicious and excellent pedestal (has been described) relating to its manifold ways (of construction). The (images of the)goddess Lakṣmī and other feminine forms should be made (to measure) eight (*tālas* in length.

8. The eye brows should be more than a *yava* (in length). The nose (should be) less than a *yava* (in length). The mouth (should measure) more than a small ball well distributed above and below.

9. The eye should be made long (measuring) three parts of a *yava* less than three *yavas*. The breadth of the eyes should be made half of it.

10. The beautiful ears should be made to be in a line with the corners of the mouth. Then the two shoulders should be made sloping by less than a *kalā*.

11-12. The neck should be one and a half *kalās* long and made beautiful by a proportionate width. The thighs, knee-joints, the pedestal, should be broad. The feet, the hinder part, the bullocks and the hips should be made as prescribed. The fingers should measure less than the seventh part of the above and should be long and not crooked.

13. The shank, thigh and the hip would be one *netra*[1] less in length. The middle part and the sides should have the same roundness. The two breasts (should be) fully developed and plump.

14-15. The beasts should be made to measure a *tāla*. The waist should be one and a half *kalās*. The other marks should be the same as before. A lotus (should be placed) on the right hand and a *bilva* (fruit) on the left (hand). (There should be) two maidens on the sides holding chowries in their hands. (The image of) Garuḍa should have a long nose. I shall then describe those which bear the marks of a disc.

## CHAPTER FORTYSIX

### *Characteristics of different Śālagrāma stones*

*The Lord said* :

1. I shall describe (the characteristics of) the *śālagrāma mūrti*[2] (the different gods represented by different kinds of *śālagrāma* stones) which yield enjoyment and emancipation. (The stone called) *Vāsudeva* is black (coloured) around its mouth and has (marks) of two discs on it.

2. The *Saṅkarṣaṇa* (stone) is red (in colour) and has marks

1. The measurement indicated by this word is not quite clear. Probably equal to two *aṅgulas*.

2. The *śālagrāma* stones obtained from the beds of Gaṇḍakī river in Nepal are associated with the worship of Viṣṇu. The different stones bearing different marks are taken to represent different forms of Viṣṇu.

of two discs (and is considered as) excellent. The *Pradyumna* (stone) has many holes, elongated and is blue (coloured).

3. The *Aniruddha* (stone) is yellow (in colour) and has the mark of a lotus. It is circular (in shape) and has two or three rays. The *Nārāyaṇa* (stone) is black (in colour) with an elevated and deep hole.

4. The *Parameṣṭi* (stone) (has the marks of) the lotus and disc. It is perforated at the back and has dots on the surface. The *Viṣṇu* (stone) has a big disc (mark). It is black (in colour). It has a line in the middle part. It is of the shape of a mace.

5-6. The *Nṛsiṁha* (stone) is tawny. It has (the mark of) a big disc and five dots. The *Varāha* (stone) is of the shape of the female divinity. It has unequal discs. It is of the colour of sapphire. It is large with the marks of three lines and is good. The *Kūrma* stone has an elevated hinder part with circular lines and is black (in colour).

7. The *Hayagriva* (stone) has a line of the shape of a good. It is blue (coloured) and is dotted. The *Vaikuṇṭha* (stone) has (the mark of) a disc and lotus. It has the radiance of a gem. It has tail-shaped lines.

8. The *Matsya* stone is long and has three dots. It is crystalline-coloured and is well formed. The *Śrīdhara* (stone) has a garland of wild flowers and five lines and is circular.

9. The *Vāmana* (stone) is circular and is very short. It is blue (coloured) and has a dot. The *Trivikrama* (stone) is black (coloured). It has a line on the right and a dot on the left side.

10. The *Ananta* (stone) has the mark of the hood of a serpent, it has variegated colours and manifold forms. The *Dāmodara* (stone) is big and has a disc in the middle part with two minute dots.

11. The *Sudarśana* (stone) has (the mark of) a disc. The *Lakṣmīnārāyaṇa* (stone) (is that which has the marks of) two discs. The *Acyuta* (stone) (has the marks of) three discs. Or the *Trivikrama* (stone) may have (the marks of) three discs.

12. The *Janārdana* (stone) has (the marks of) four discs. The *Vāsudeva* (stone) has (the marks of) five discs. The *Pradyumna* (stone) has (the marks of) six discs. The *Saṅkarṣaṇa* (stone) has (the marks of) seven discs.

13. The *Puruṣottama* (stone) has (the marks) of eight discs. The *Navavyūha* form has the marks of nine discs. (The stone representing) the ten manifestations (of Viṣṇu) (is marked) with ten (discs). The *Aniruddha* form (is marked) with eleven (discs). The *Dvādaśātman* (class of *śālagrāma*) (is marked) by twelve (discs). (One is deemed to be) the *Ananta* (class of *śālagrāma*) (if it has) more (discs) than these.

## CHAPTER FORTYSEVEN

### *Mode of worshipping Śālagrāma*

*The Lord said* :

1. I shall describe the mode of worshipping the *śālagrāma* marked with discs for (the sake of) accomplishment. The worship of Hari (in the *śālagrāma*) is of three kinds—

(i) *kāmyā* performed for gaining particular benefit

(ii) *akāmyā* performed with disinterestedness about the benefits

(iii) *śubhayātmikā*, that is of the nature of both of them.

2. (The worship) of the five (manifestations of Viṣṇu) (such as) the Fish[1] etc., is,either *kāmyā* or *ubhayātmikā.* (The worship of the manifestations) of the Boar Man-lion and Dwarf forms (of Viṣṇu is) for emancipation.

3-6. Listen to the three-fold worship of the *śālagrāma* endowed with discs. The excellent worship is that performed without desiring for the fruits. The worship with desire for the fruits is the last (in the rank). The worship of an image is mediocre. In a circular lotus placed on a rectangular seat, having assigned the *praṇava* (the syllable *Om*) to the heart and having assigned (the sacred syllables) to the parts of the body and having shown three *mudrās* (positions of fingers in the practice of worship), the preceptor should be worshipped outside the circle. The attendant gods (*gaṇas*) should be worshipped on the west. Dhātṛ on the north-west,Vidhātṛ on the south-west,the Kartā and Hartā on the south and north, Viṣvaksena (Viṣṇu)should be worshipp-

1. The text does not specify the names of other manifestations.

ed in the north-east, and Kṣetrapālaka (the guardian deity) on the south-east.

7. The *Vedas*, *Ṛgveda* etc. (should be worshipped) in the east etc. (The serpent) Ananta (which is) the support of the earth, the seat of worship, the lotus, the three orbs—sun, moon and fires (should be worshipped).

8. The seat (should consist) of twelve letters[1] (forming the mystic formula of the God). Having placed (the God) there, the stone should be worshipped with the individual syllables and the whole of the sacred syllable in order.

9-10. Then one should worship with the vedic sacred syllables accomplished by the syllables such as the *gāyatri*, etc. and *praṇava* on the east and other directions. Then the three *mudrās* of the Viṣvaksena (Viṣṇu), the disc and the Kṣetrapāla should be shown. This is the first variety of the worship of *śālagrāma*. Then I shall describe the one with no merits.

11. One should draw a circle as before with sixteen radii and with a lotus. One should then worship the preceptor and others with a conch, disc, mace and sword.

12. The bow and the arrows (should be placed) in the east and the north. The seat should be placed with the vedic (syllables). The stone should be placed with the (sacred) twelve syllables[2] of the lord. Listen to the third variety of worship.

13. One should draw a lotus having eight radii and worship the preceptor and others as before. Having offered the seat with the eight sacred letters[3] one should place the stone with the same (formula). One should worship ten times with that (formula). It is then accomplished by *gāyatri* etc.

## CHAPTER FORTYEIGHT

### *Adoration of twentyfour forms of Viṣṇu*

*The Lord said* :

1. Keśava of the form of (syllable) *Om* bears the lotus,

1. *Om namo bhagavate vāsudevāya.*
2. See the previous note.
3. *Om namo vāsudevāya.*

conch, disc and mace. Nārāyaṇa (bears) the conch, lotus, mace and disc. Circumambulation to Him.

2. Then I salute Mādhava, who bears the mace, disc, conch and lotus. Govinda wields the disc, the Kaumodakī (name of a mace), lotus and conch.

3. Viṣṇu, the bearer of the disc, the mace, lotus and conch is the bestower of emancipation. I salute Madhusūdana, who bears the conch, disc, lotus and mace.

4. (I prostrate) with devotion (at the feet of) Trivikrama who bears the lotus, mace, disc and conch. May Vāmana, the bearer of the conch, disc, mace and lotus protect me always.

5. Śrīdhara who holds a lotus, disc, bow and also the conch yields emancipation. Hṛṣīkeśa wields the mace, disc, lotus and conch. May He protect us.

6. And Padmanābha (is one) who yields boons and who holds the conch, lotus, disc and mace, (I salute him). Dāmodara (is one) who holds a lotus, conch, mace and disc. I salute him.

7. May Vāsudeva, who wields a mace, conch, disc and lotus (protect) the universe. May Saṅkarṣaṇa, who holds a mace, conch, lotus and disc protect us.

8. Lord Pradyumna is one who holds a mace, disc, conch and mace as well as a lotus. May Aniruddha, who wields the disc, mace, conch and lotus protect us.

9. May Puruṣottama, the Lord of celestials, who holds disc, lotus, conch and mace (protect you). May Adhokṣaja who wields lotus, mace, conch and disc protect you.

10. I salute that Lord Nṛsiṁha, who wields disc, lotus, mace and conch. May Acyuta, who holds mace, lotus, disc and conch, protect you all.

11. So also (may) Upendra, who is of the form of a child and (who holds) the disc and lotus, (protect you). And (may) Janārdana, who wields lotus, disc, conch and mace (protect you).

12. May Hari, who holds conch, lotus, disc as well as (mace) *kaumodaki* yield me enjoyment and emancipation. May Kṛṣṇa, who holds conch, mace, lotus and disc give enjoyment and emancipation.

13. The first manifestation was that of Vāsudeva. Then Saṅkarṣaṇa manifested. Pradyumna manifested from Saṅkarṣaṇa. Aniruddha appeared from Pradyumna.

14. Each one of the (above) forms was divided into three forms such as Keśava and others.. One who reads or hears this hymn consisting of twelve letters on the twenty-four forms gets free from impurity and gets all things.

## CHAPTER FORTY-NINE

### *Characteristics of forms of 'Fish' etc. of Viṣṇu*

*The Lord said* :

1. I shall describe to you the characteristics of the ten manifestations (of Viṣṇu) beginning with the Fish. The Fish (form of Viṣṇu) should resemble a fish. The Tortoise (form) should resemble a tortoise.

2. The terrestrial boar (manifestation) should have a human body and as carrying a mace and other (weapons) in the right hand, and the conch, (the goddess) Lakṣmī or a lotus in the left.

3. Or (the goddess) (is represented) as resting on the left elbow and the earth and (the serpent) Ananta at the feet. The installation of the figure secures for a person a kingdom and (such a person) gets across the ocean of mundane existence.

4. The Man-lion image (should be represented) as having a wide open mouth and having the killed demon (Hiraṇyakaśipu) on the left thigh. His chest should wear a garland and (his arms) should hold disc and mace.

5. The Dwarf-form may hold an umbrella and a stick or have four arms. The figure of Paraśurāma may hold the bow and arrow, a sword and an axe.

6. (The figure of) Rāma should have the bow, arrow, sword, conch or two hands or may have four arms holding a mace and plough.

7. The plough may be provided on the left half (upper arm) and the auspicious conch on the lower arm. The mace may be

provided on the right half (upper arm) and the auspicious disc on the lower arm.

8. The figure of Buddha (should be made) as calm, having long ears, white complexion, wearing a cloth, and seated on a lotus with its petals upwards and as conferring favour and protection.

9. (The figure of) Kalki is (to be represented as) a twice-born endowed with a bow and quiver and as destroying the foreigners. Or (he should be represented as) seated on the horse and endowed with a sword, conch, disc and arrow.

10. I shall describe the characteristics of nine forms of Viṣṇu commencing with Vāsudeva. The mace (is placed) on the right half (upper arm) and the excellent disc on the left half (upper arm).

11. The image of Vāsudeva may be made as before or as having four hands or two hands, one holding a conch and the other as conferring boons and having Brahmā and Īśa (Śiva) always on either side.

12. (The figure of) Balarāma (is represented) as holding a plough, mace, club and lotus. (The image of) Pradyumna (is represented as having) thunderbolt and conch on the right arm and the bow in the left arm.

13. Or Pradyumna (is represented) as having the mace resting on the navel with pleasure or holding the bow and arrow. Aniruddha may be (represented as) having four arms. In the same way Lord Nārāyaṇa (may also be represented).

14. (The image of) Brahmā is (represented as having) four faces, four hands, big belly, long beards, matted hair, and (having) swan as the vehicle in front (of him).

15. (There should be) a rosary and a ladle on the right hand and a water-pot and vessel to hold the sacrificial clarified butter. Sarasvatī and Sāvitrī (consorts of Brahmā) (should be placed) on the left and right sides.

16. (The image of) Viṣṇu (is represented) as having eight hands, Garuḍa (the vehicle), (holding) a sword, mace, and arrow in the right hand and as conferring gifts and (holding) the bow and mace in the left hand.

17. (The figure of) Narasiṁha (is represented) (as having) four hands holding the conch and disc and piercing (the body) of the mighty demon (Hiraṇyakaśipu).

18-22. (The figure of) Varāha (is endowed with) four arms holding the (serpent) Śeṣa in (one of) the hands and the earth in the left (hand) and (his consort) Kamalā (Lakṣmī). The earth should be made as resting at the feet and (goddess) Lakṣmī as seated at the feet. Trailokyamohana (one who stupefies the three worlds) (should be represented as riding) the Tārkhya (the eagle-vehicle) and possess eight hands, holding the sword, mace and goad in the right hand and the conch, bow, mace and the noose in the left hand. (Images of) Lakṣmī and Sarasvatī should be endowed with lotus and lute (respectively). Then (the form of) Viśvarūpa (of Viṣṇu) (should be endowed) with the club, noose, spear and arrow in the right hand and conch, bow, mace, noose, *tomara* (javelin), plough, axe, staff, sword and leather sling in the left hand.

23-24. The Harihara (Śiva and Viṣṇu) form of Viṣṇu (should be placed) on the right or left (side), (being endowed with) twenty hands, four faces and three eyes. He should either be lying on his left or reclining on the water. (He should further be represented) as his leg being held by the goddess Śrī (Lakṣmī). He should also be shown as being attended to by (the female divinities) Vimalā and others. He should also have the four-faced (Brahmā) in the navel-lotus.

25. The form of Viṣṇu bearing the marks of Rudra and Keśava should hold a spear and sword in the right hand and the mace and disc in the other and be in the company of Gaurī and Lakṣmī (the consorts of Śiva and Viṣṇu).

26. The Hayaśiras (horse-headed) form of Viṣṇu (should be represented) as holding the conch, disc, mace and the *Vedas*. The left foot should rest on (the serpent) Śeṣa and the right on the back of tortoise.

27. The form of Dattātreya may have two arms, the goddess Śrī (Lakṣmī) being seated on the left lap. The Viṣvaksena form of Viṣṇu (may hold) a disc, mace, plough and conch.

# CHAPTER FIFTY

## *Characteristics of an image of the goddess*

*The Lord said* :

1-5. (The image of) Caṇḍī may have twenty hands and may hold the spear, sword, dart, disc, noose, club, *ḍamaru* (a small drum) and spike in the left hands and also (show) protective posture (and) the snake as the noose, club, axe, goad, bow, bell, banner, mace, mirror, and iron mace in the (right) hands. Or (the figure of) Caṇḍī is made to have ten hands, with the buffalo placed below with its head fully severed and the demon as issuing forth from (its) neck with rage and brandishing his weapon, holding spike in the hand, vomitting blood, his hairs (stained) with blood and blood dripping out from the eyes (forming) a garland (on the chest), being devoured by the lion and well-bound by the noose in the neck. (The goddess is represented as) resting her right foot on the lion and the left foot on the demon underneath.

6-12. This form of Caṇḍikā, the destroyer of enemies (is made as) having three eyes and endowed with weapons. (This) Durgā is to be worshipped with the nine elements in order in a diagram of nine lotuses from her own form at the beginning, centre and the eastern and other (directions). (The image should be made as) possessing eighteen arms (carrying) a human head, club, mirror, *tarjani* (a kind of weapon), bow, banner and a little drum in the right hand and the noose, spear, mace, trident, thunderbolt, sword, goad and dart in the left hand. The others (Rudracaṇḍā and other goddesses) should be endowed with the same weapons in their sixteen hands except the little drum and *tarjani* (a kind of weapon).

The nine (goddesses) commencing with Rudracaṇḍā are Rudracaṇḍā, Pracaṇḍā, Caṇḍogrā, Caṇḍanāyikā, Caṇḍā, Caṇḍavatī, Caṇḍarūpā, Aticaṇḍikā and Ugracaṇḍā stationed at the centre. (They are made to be) coloured as the *rocanā* (yellow pigment), red, black, blue, white, purple, yellow and white and as riding the lion. Then the buffalo as a human (form) should be held by the hair by the nine (forms) of Durgā holding weapons.

13. They are in the *ālīḍha*[1] posture. They have to be established for the increase of progeny; as also (the forms) Gaurī, Caṇḍikā and others (as well as the forms) Kuṇḍi, Akṣaradā (and) Agnidhṛk.

14-15. She is the same as Rambhā. (She is) accomplished and devoid of fire. (She is) also Lalitā. (She) holds the severed head along with the neck in the left (hand) and a mirror in the second hand.

(The image of) Saubhāgyā (is made) as holding fruits in the folded palms on the right side. (The image of) Lakṣmī holds the lotus in the right hand and the *śrīphala* (bilva fruit) in the left.

16. (The image of) Sarasvatī (should be made as holding) a book, rosary and lute in the hands. (The image of) Jāhnavī (the river Ganges) (is represented) as holding a pot and flower in the hand (and standing) on the crocodile and of white complexion.

17. (The image of the river) Yamunā is worshipped as mounted on the tortoise and as holding a pot in the hand and of dark complexion. (The image of) Tumburu is represented as white (in colour), holding a lute and trident and riding a bull.

18-19. The four-faced Brāhmī (the female-energy of Brahmā) (is represented) as of fair complexion, riding a swan and as carrying a rosary, different vessels such as *surā* and *kuṇḍa* in the left hand. Śāṅkarī is represented as white, (seated) on a bull holding the bow and arrow in the right hand and the disc and the bow in the left hand. Kaumārī (is represented) as red in colour, riding the peacock and having two arms, holding the spears.

20. (The form of) Lakṣmi should hold the disc, and conch in the right (hand) (and) the mace and lotus in the left (hand). (The form of) Vārāhī should be mounted on the buffalo and hold the stick, conch, sword and goad.

21-25. (The image of) Aindrī conferring success should be represented as having thousand eyes and holding the thunderbolt in the left hand.

---

1. The posture in shooting, in which the right knee is advanced and the left leg is held back.

Cāmuṇḍā may have three eyes deeply sunken, a skeleton form devoid of flesh, erectly standing hair, emaciated belly, clad in tigerskin and holding a skull and spear in the left hand and a trident and scissor in the right standing on the dead body of a man and wearing a garland of bones. (The image of) Vināyaka should have a human body, big belly, elephant face, big trunk and sacred thread. The mouth measuring 7 *kalās* in breadth while the trunk should measure 36 finger-breadths in length. The neck should be 12 *kalās* in girth and 10 *kalās* in height. The throat-region should be 36 finger (in length). The space about the region of anus should have the breadth of half a finger.

26. (The region of) the navel and thigh should be of twelve (fingers) as also the leg from the ankle to the knee and the feet. He should be represented as holding his own tusk made into an axe in the right hand and the *laḍḍuka* (a ball of sweet) and lotus flower in the left.

27. (The image of) Skanda, the lord (of the universe) also known as Śākha and Viśākha, (is represented) as a boy possessing two arms and riding a peacock (with the images of) Sumukhī and Viḍālākṣī[1].

28-29. The god may be represented as having a single face or six faces, six hands or twelve hands carrying the spear and a cock in the right hand. In the village or the forest (it should have) two arms. (He should bear) the spear, arrow, noose, *nistriṁśa* (sword), goad and *tarjani* (a kind of weapon) in the six right hands and the spear in the left hand.

30-31. (The image of) Rudracarcikā (the manifestation of) the goddess may have a bow adorned by the plume of peacock, club, banner, protective posture, cock, skull, scissors, trident and noose in the right and left hands. (She should also be) clad in the elephant hide, with her leg raised up and the little drum placed on the head.

32. Hence she (is known as) Rudracāmuṇḍā, the goddess of dancing and one who is dancing. This (goddess herself), having four faces and in the sitting posture (is known as) Mahālakṣmī.

---

1. The consorts of Skanda. The two names mean good-faced and cat-eyed respectively.

33-34. (The goddess) having ten hands and three eyes (holding) (different) weapons, sword and *ḍamaru* (little drum) in the right hand and the bell, club, staff with a skull at one end and trident in the left (hand) and eating men, horses, buffaloes and elephants held in the hand is called Siddhacāmuṇḍā.

35. That goddess accomplishes everything and is (known (as) Siddhayogeśvarī. She is also represented in another form endowed with the noose and goad and red (in complexion).

36. (The goddess) Bhairavī who has an embodiment of beauty is endowed with twelve arms. These are (all) (spoken as) fierce (forms) arising from the cremation ground. The above are remembered as the eight forms of the goddess.

37. (The goddess) Kṣamā (Forbearance) (should be) surrounded by jackals, old, having two arms, and widely opened mouth. (The goddess) Kṣemaṅkarī (Benevolent) may have protruding teeth and be resting her knees on the ground.

38. The wives of semi-gods should be made to have long and motionless eyes. The Śākinīs (female attendants on Goddess Durgā) should be made to have oblique vision. The Mahāramyas should have yellow eyes. The (images of) nymphs should always be made beautiful.

39. (The form of) Nandīśa the bull, the door-keeper (of the goddess), should carry a rosary and a trident. (The image of) Mahākāla (a form of Śiva as the destroyer) may have a sword, human skull, trident and club.

40. (The form of) Bhṛṅgin (an attendant of Śiva) should have an emaciated body. Kuṣmāṇḍa (another attendant of Śiva) should have a stout and dwarf form dancing. Vīrabhadra and other attendants (of Śiva) should have ears and faces of elephants, cows, etc.

41. Ghaṇṭākarṇa (an attendant of Śiva) form should have eighteen hands crushing the accrued sin, (holding weapons) thunderbolt, sword, club, disc, arrow, mace, goad and hammer in the right hand and *tarjanī* (a weapon), club, dart, human skull, noose, bow, bell and axe on the left and a trident in the (remaining) two hands and wearing a garland of bells and crushing the eruptive diseases.

# CHAPTER FIFTYONE

## *Characteristics of the images of the Sun and other planets*

*The Lord said* :

1. (The image of) the Sun (should be made) to ride a chariot having one wheel and seven horses. (He must) hold two lotuses, ink-stand, pen and a staff in his right hand.

2. Piṅgala, an attendant and gate-keeper of the Sun (should be placed) on the left with the mace in his hand. (Sun-god) should have female attendants bearing chowries (fly-flappers) and the pale-looking consort by his side.

3. Or (the image of) the Sun should be made as riding a horse alone. The guardian deities of different quarters should duly be endowed with weapons, holding two lotuses (in hands) and bestowing boons.

4. (The images of) Agni and other gods bearing the club, trident, disc and lotus should be placed in different directions (around). (The images of) the forms of Sun, commencing with Aryamā are represented as possessing four arms and placed in a diagram of twelve petals.

5-6. Varuṇa, Sūrya, Sahasrāṁśu (one who has thousand rays), Dhātṛ, Tapana, Sāvitṛ, Gabhastika, Ravi, Parjanya, Tvaṣṭṛ, Mitra (and) Viṣṇu are his different names as he moves over the zodiacal signs commencing with the Aries in the course of months commencing with Mārgaśīrṣa and ending with Kārttika.[1]

7-9. Their female energies known by the names—Iḍā, Suṣumnā, Viśvārcis, Indu, Pramardinī, Praharṣaṇī, Mahākālī, Kapilā, Prabodhanī, Nīlāmbarā, Ghanāntasthā and Amṛtā, and placed at the ends of petals are of black, red, pale red, yellow, pale yellow, white, brown, yellow, green, white, grey and blue.

10. Similar colours are given to Varuṇa and others placed at the tips of petals. The form of Tejas (effulgence) should be represented as fierce, extremely crooked, possessing two arms holding a lotus and sword.

---

1. These two correspond to the months December-January and November-December.

11. The form of Moon should be represented as holding a sacrificial pitcher and rosary. (The image of) Mars should be) holding a spear and rosary. (The figure of) Mercury (should be) holding the bow and rosary in his hands. (The form of) Jupiter (should be) holding the sacrificial pitcher and rosary.

12. (The image of) Venus may be holding the sacrificial pitcher and rosary. (That of) Saturn should be endowed with a girdle of bells. (While that of) Rāhu (the ascending node of the moon considered as a planet) (is represented as) holding half of the lunar disc, (that of) Ketu (the descending node of the moon considered as a planet) (is represented as) holding the sword and lamp.

13. (The serpents) Ananta, Takṣaka, Karka, Padma, Mahābja and Śaṅkha are all (represented as) having hooded heads with great radiance.

14. (The image of) Indra is endowed with thunder-bolt and as seated on an elephant, (that of) Agni as riding a goat and holding a spear, (that of) Yama as on a buffalo and carrying a club and (that of) Nirṛti as holding a sword.

15. (The image of) Varuṇa (ocean god) is made as seated) on a crocodile and as holding a noose, (that of) Vāyu (wind god) (as riding) an antelope and holding a banner, (that of) Kubera (god of wealth) as seated on a sheep and bearing a mace, and (that of) Īśāna (as seated) on a bull and having a matted hair.

16. (The images) of the guardian deities of the quarters of the world are endowed with two arms. (The celestial architect) Viśvakarman (should be represented) as holding a rosary. (The figure of) Hanūmat (monkey, devoted to Rāma) may be holding the thunderbolt in his hand and pounding the earth with his feet.

17. (The semi-divine beings) Kinnaras may be (represented) as holding lutes in their arms and the Vidyādharas (semi-divine beings) as having garlands (and moving) in the sky. The goblins may be (represented) as having emaciated bodies and the vampires as deformed faces, the Guardians of the sites as having the tridents and the spirits of the dead people as lean and big-bellied.

## CHAPTER FIFTYTWO

*Characteristics of images of different forms of goddesses*

*The Lord said*:

1. I shall describe (the characteristics) of the eight Yoginīs (female attendants on Durgā) respectively residents of (the eight quarters) east to north-east. (The Yoginīs) Akṣobhyā, Rūkṣakarṇī, Rākṣasī, Kṛpaṇā and Akṣayā (reside in the east).

2. (The Yoginīs) Piṅgākṣī, Kṣayā, Kṣemā, Ilā, Līlā, Layā, Laktā, Balākeśī, Lālasā and Vimalā (dwell in the south-east).

3. (The Yoginīs) Hutāśā, Viśālākṣī, Huṅkārā, Vaḍavāmukhī, Mahākrūrā, Krodhanā, Bhayaṅkarī and Mahānanā (are the residents of the south).

4. (The Yoginīs) Sarvajñā, Taralā, Tārā, Ṛgvedā, Hayānanā, Sārā (khyā), Rudrasaṅgrāhī, Śambarā and Tālajaṅghikā (occupy the south (-west).

5. Raktākṣī, Suprasiddhā, Vidyujjihvā, Karaṅkiṇī, Meghanādā, Pracaṇḍogrā, Kālakarṇī and Varapradā (are the inmates of the west).

6. Candrā, Candrāvalī, Prapañcā, Pralayāntikā, Śiśuvaktrā, Piśācī, Piśitāśā and Lolupā (dwell in the north-west).

7. Dhamanī, Tāpanī, Rāgiṇī, Vikṛtānanā, Vāyuvegā, Bṛhatkukṣi, Vikṛtā and Viśvarūpikā (govern the north).

8. Yamajihvā, Jayantī, Durjayā, Jayantikā, Viḍālā, Revatī, Pūtanā and Vijayāntikā (hold sway over the north-east).

9. (These Yoginīs should be represented) as having eight arms (or) four arms, wielding weapons of their choice and yielding all benefits (on their votaries). (Lord) Bhairava may hold the *arka* plant (Calotropis Gigantee) in the hand and have the face like the knee or elbow bearing the matted hair and the Moon.

10. Kṛttivāsas (should be represented) as holding on one side the sword, goad, axe and arrow and offering protection to the universe and a bow, trident, club with a skull at the top and noose on the other.

11. Or he shall be having five faces and be wearing the elephant's hide and adorned by the serpents. He shall be seated on the dead body. He must be worshipped in the midst of the

mother goddesses.[1]

12. One has to worship him being endowed with the letters of the alphabet upto the letter 'ra' and with (his mantra) having six constituents and the eight long vowel mantras.

13. (He is also to be contemplated upon) as established in the wicks of the flame in the house as endowed with golden ornaments and the *nāda*, *bindu* and *indu*[2] and making the body of the divine mother and the lord radiant.

14. Vīrabhadra (attendant of Śiva) (is represented) as having four faces, seated on a bull in front of the mother (goddesses). (Goddess) Gaurī (consort of Śiva) (is represented) as having two arms and three eyes as endowed with a spear and mirror.

15. (Goddess) Lalitā (a form of Durgā) (should be represented) as having four arms (holding) a spear, a small pitcher, (and another) pitcher (in the hands) and showing boon-conferring hands. (She should) be seated on the lotus. (She should also) be endowed with a mirror, a small stick for applying collyrium and Skanda and Gaṇa (Gaṇeśa).

16. (Goddess) Caṇḍikā may (be represented) as having ten hands having a sword, spear, disc (and) dart in the right (hand) and the magical noose, shield, pike, axe, and bow in the left (hand). (She must) be riding a lion with the buffalo (demon) having been slain with (her) spear in front of her.

## CHAPTER FIFTYTHREE

### *Characteristics of the liṅga (parabolic representation of Śiva)*

*The Lord said* :

1-2. O Lotus-born (Brahman) I shall describe to you the characteristics of the *liṅga* and other things. Listen. Having marked a rectangular (block of stone) as divided into two parts

---

1. They are Brāhmī, Māheśvarī, Caṇḍī, Vārāhī, Vaiṣṇavī, Kaumārī, Cāmuṇḍā and Carcikā.

2. These are the sound, dot and crescent, making up the *Praṇava* or *Om*.

lengthwise, the lower part again being divided into eight parts and three parts of these divisions being left out, the remaining (block) formed by five parts should be divided breadthwise into three parts and the three (gods) should be assigned therein.

3. This is spoken as representing the forms of Brahman, Viṣṇu and Śiva (among) which (the last one) is larger (than the other two parts). Half of the figure is marked at the angular points in the square.

4. An octagonal (block) known as the part of Viṣṇu is certainly obtained (thus). Then a polygon of sixteen sides is made and then a polygon of thirty-two sides.

5. Having made a polygon of sixty-four sides, the circular shape is accomplished. Then the excellent spiritual teacher should chisel the head portion of the emblem.

6. The breadth of the *liṅga* may be divided into eight parts. An umbrella-shaped top portion (of the *liṅga*) is got by discarding half of this length.

7. A *liṅga* which has a breadth equal to three-fourth of its length bestows all the desired benefits.

8. The pillar (part of the emblem) should be a quarter of the length (of the emblem) in the case of those worshipped by the celestials. Listen now (the narration) of the characteristics of all *liṅgas*.

9. The wiseman should divide the *liṅga* measuring 16 *aṅgulas* into 6 parts through the central line upto the Brahman and Rudra parts.

10. The spaces in between two such lines of division should measure eight *yavas* each in the first two cases, each latter measuring a *yava* less than the preceding one.

11. Having divided the lower part into three parts, one part should be left out. Having divided the (remaining) two parts into eight parts, the three upper ones (of these divisions) should be left aside.

12. Those (three sections) above the five divisions should be rotated and the markings lengthened. Having left out one part their union should be brought about.

13. These are the general characteristics of the *liṅga* described by me. I shall (now) describe the most general (characteristics) of the pedestals.

14. After having known the commencing portion of the *liṅga* and height, the part (belonging) to Brahman should be well placed by the learned person on the stone (pedestal).

15. Then having known the height (of the *liṅga*) the different dimensions of the pedestal should be made. The base (of the *liṅga*) should be twice the height and length commensurate with that of the *liṅga*.

16. The central part of the pedestal should be hewn and divided into three parts. Its breadth should be one-sixth part of its length.

17. The girth should measure one-third part of its breadth and the depth (of cavity) should be equal to that of the girth. It should be sloping gradually.

18. Or the depth (of the cavity) should be one sixteenth part of that of the girth. The height of the base should be deviated.

19. One part of the base should remain imbedded in the ground. One part of it will be (the height of) the stool proper. Three such parts (will be the height) of the neck portion. The first step should be one such part.

20. The second step should be of two such parts in height while the remaining steps should have a height of such a single part until one reaches the neck portion step by step.

21. Outlets to the breadth of such a part should be set apart on each one of the steps till the last one. They should be cut into three parts by the three outlets.

22. It should measure a tip of the finger in breadth at the base and one-sixth (of a finger) at their ends. Their beds should be a little inclined towards the eastern side. These are considered to be the general characteristics of the *liṅga* along with the pedstal.

## CHAPTER FIFTYFOUR

### *The dimensions of different varieties of the liṅga*

*The Lord said* :

1. I shall describe the measurement of the *liṅga* in a different way. Listen. I shall (now) speak about the *liṅgas*

made of salt, (and) ghee (which when worshipped) increases (one's) intellect.

2. A *liṅga* made of cloth (is worshipped) for the sake of wealth. It is known as temporal. The one made of earth is either burnt or half burnt of which the former is better.

3. Then, one made of wood is meritorious. One made of stone is more meritorious than that made of wood. (The *liṅga*) made of pearl is more meritorious than that of stone. Then (relatively merit-worthy) are the *liṅgas* made of iron, and gold.

4. The *liṅgas* made of silver, copper and brass yield enjoyment and release from bondage. The *liṅgas* made of red lead and mercury are excellent and confer enjoyment and release from bondage.

5. The installation of a *liṅga* on the earth made of mercury and iron etc or studded with gems increases one's glory and grants success as desired.

6. If desired one can build temples and bases to these (emblems) on the left side. One may worship the image of the sun cast on the mirror.

7. Hara should be worshipped everywhere. The worship gets completed only (by the worship) of the *liṅga*. A *liṅga* made of stone or wood should be of a cubit length.

8. The movable *liṅga* should be of the size of a finger and encircled by the adytum. The *liṅga* worshipped in the house should be of the size of one to fifteen fingers.

9. The *liṅgas* are classified into three groups according to the measure of the doorway or into nine groups according to the measure of the adytum. These *liṅgas* should be worshipped in one's residence.

10. Thus there are thirty-six *liṅgas* in the first class, thirty-six in the second class and thirty-six in the third class.

11. Thus totally there would be one hundred and eight *liṅgas*. The *liṅgas* (measuring) one to five fingers (known as) the short are said to be movable.

12. The movable *liṅgas* measuring six to ten fingers are known as middle. Those measuring eleven to fifteen fingers are known as the best.

13. (Those made) of excellent gems (should measure) six fingers. (Those made) of other gems (should measure)

nine fingers. The golden ones (should be) twelve (fingers). The rest of the *liṅgas* (should be) fifteen (fingers).

14. The four sets of corners from the top should be successively cut into four or sixteen equal sides, and those again into thirtytwo and sixty-four (in turn so as to make it a polygon of sixty-four equal sides).

15. The two sides being thus lopped off, the neck of a solid *liṅga* should be twentysix parts from the rectangular space at its foot.

16. (The face of the *liṅga*) should gradually be decreasing by four, six and eight parts from its base (and similarly) the middle part of the *liṅga* should be gradually less than the height at its beginning by a foot.

17. That which is equal to half (the size of) the adytum is (said to be) the lowest (variety of) *liṅga*. That which is fifteen (fingers in length) is the excellent. Seven equal lines should be drawn in the central portion of these *liṅgas*.

18. In this way there would be nine lines. The middle (variety of *liṅga*) would have five lines. The length of the *liṅgas* should be nine fingers. The opposite side (should be) separated by two intermediate links.

19. The *liṅga* is measured out cubit by cubit till it would be nine hands (length). The *liṅga* is of three kinds—inferior, mediocre and superior.

20-22. A wiseman should mark three *liṅgas* at the centre of every *liṅga* foot by foot at fourteen (places) by a fixed measure of length of the door or the adytum. Four *liṅgas* representing Śiva, Viṣṇu, Bṛhaspati proportionately should be marked by the breadth. The *liṅga* should be (shaped) long to represent the three forms.

23. The *liṅga* should have a circumference of four, eight, eight (inches) representing the three qualities. One should make the *liṅgas* of such lengths as one desires.

24. One should divide the figure (marked) by the banners, celestial gods, elements or cocks. One should know the good or bad from the inches left over.

25. The banners etc., the crows, lions, elephants and goats are excellent. The others are auspicious. Among the primary notes of Indian gamut, the first one, second one and the fifth one confer good.

26-27. Among the elements, the earth is auspicious. Among the fires, the consecrated fire (from the household's perpetual fire) is auspicious. Half of the said length having been divided in order into seven, eight, five, nine and five parts there would be symmetrical representation of Śiva, Viṣṇu and Brahman.

28. The fifth one is known as the *Vardhamāna*. There would be two kinds based on the increase of breadth and length. Many kinds are described according to Viśvakarma (the divine architect).

29. The *āḍhya* class would be of three kinds on account of the size. Measured by the barley grains it would be eight parts, by the arm it would be three parts. The last one endowed equally is known as *jina*.

30-31. (There would be) twenty-five *liṅgas* in the first (variety) which are worshipped by the celestials. Then being divided into thirtyfive there would be 14000 and 1400 varieties. Thus (we have) the eight *aṅgula's* extent from the nine cubit adytum.

32. One has to mark the angular points by means of threads placed at the angular and middle of angular points. Having made the expansion from the middle, three parts should be fixed from the middle.

33. There would be eight angular parts above the division. Two angular parts represent the part of Śiva. From the foot to the knee portion (of the *liṅga*) is Brahmā. (From the knee) to the navel is Viṣṇu.

34. (From the navel) upto the head is the part of Śiva. Similarly, it is in the case of distinct and indistinct forms. In the *liṅga* of five parts, the head part is said to be circular.

35. The images (may be) of the shape of an umbrella, cock or crescent moon. I shall describe the merits of the four varieties in each (class) differing on account of one's option.

36. The head portion (of the liṅga) should be divided into eight parts. The first part of the longitudinal portion should be divided into four parts.

37-39. There (should be) four lines successively drawn in order to divide into parts. We have by one part the lotus, the one called *viśāla* by cutting off, the *śrivatsa* by thinning out and the *śatrukṛt* by elision of the fourth part. In the *sarvasama* class the top portion is the excellent and the cock-shaped in the *sura* class among the *liṅga* of four parts. The top portion of the *anādi* has been described. You listen to (the characteristics of) the crescent of the top.

40. At a corner of a part (there should be) the charming axis (represented) by four parts deficient by one part. By the elision of two, three and four parts in order, (one gets) the full, crescent moon and lotus shape.

41. Listen then to (the description of forms having) four or three faces or one face and *mukhaliṅga*. The part to be worshipped is to be made set with nine parts.

42-43. Having left out twelve parts for the arms and eyes, as before, the head, forehead, nose, face, chin, neck are then to be made. Having covered by the hands, the arms and eyes (are made) with four parts proportionate to the measurement of image.

44. The face should be made equal to one-eighth part of the breadth. I have described the four-faced form. Listen ! The three-faced form is described now.

45. The ear and feet are made. One has to mark the forehead etc. for that. Then the arms should be made with four parts quite strong.

46. The projection of the frontispiece (should be) one-eighth of the breadth. One face has to be made such as to have beautiful eye on the eastern side.

47. It should be made round at the forehead, nose, face and neck. By one-fifth from the arm one should make it round less by one's arm length.

48. It is good to have the projections in the frontispiece as one-sixth of the breadth for all the *mukhaliṅgas* whether it is *trapuṣa* or *kukkuṭa* (?)

# CHAPTER FIFTYFIVE

## *The characteristics of the pedestal*

*The Lord said* :

1. I shall describe (the characteristics of) the pedestal of images. They have the same length as (the height) of the image and have breadth half (the height) of (the image).

2. Or the breadth should be half or one-third of the measure of the height. The girdle should be equal to one-third of its breadth.

3. The cavity should be of the same measure and should be inclined towards the posterior part. A quarter of the breadth (should be left out) for the canal as outlet.

4. (The width) of the forepart (of the channel) should be half of the breadth of the base. The water-course should be one-third of the breadth (of the base).

5. Or else the length of the *liṅga* is said to be equal to half (the length) of the base or equal to the length (of the base).

6. The height (of the pedestal) should be divided into sixteen parts as before. The lower six divisions should be made to comprise two parts. The neck should be three parts.

7. The foundation, projections, joint, seat and other remaining parts should each comprise one part. This will hold good in the case of ordinary images.

8. The door-way (leading) to the image is said to be proportionate to the door-way of the temple. The canopy over the image should be endowed with elephants and tigers.

9. The pedestal of (the image of) Hari also should always be made beautiful. The measures (laid down) for the images of Viṣṇu shall apply to (the images of) all gods. Those measures set forth for the image of Lakṣmī shall apply to all (images of) the goddesses.

# CHAPTER FIFTYSIX

*Five divisions of installation :*

*The Lord said :*

1. I shall now describe the five divisions of an installation. The image is the embodiment of the supreme being, the real principle, the pedestal is the symbol of nature or the Goddess Lakṣmī. The installation is the union of the two.

2-3. Hence, the installation is done by men who desire to have their wishes fulfilled. The officiating priest (has to arrange) sheds (measuring) eight, sixteen or twenty (cubits) in front of the temple for bathing, the pitchers, and things required for the sacrifice by extending the side lines of the adytum.

4. The auspicious sacrificial platform should be made ready with one third (or) half (of the above space). It should be decked with pitchers big and small and canopies etc.

5. All the materials (to be used in the rite) should be cleansed with *pañcagavya* (the five things extracted from a cow). The priest should adorn (himself with ornaments). Having contemplated his own self as (lord) Viṣṇu, he should begin worship.

6. The expert idol-worshippers should be established in front of each pit (intended for the rite). (They should be endowed) with rings, bracelets and other things.

7. Logs of the *pippala*, *udumbara*, *vaṭa* trees (should be planted) at the doorways of the place for the sake of arches. The place may be quadrangular, semi-circular, circular or lotus-shaped.

8. Log of the fig tree should adorn the east, of the *subhadra* the south, of the *sukarma* and *suhotra* the northern and western doorways respectively.

9. The pitchers having young sprouts of mango trees should be placed five cubits apart at the foot of each one of the supporting columns of the arches and be worshipped with the sacred syllables *syonā pṛthivī*[1].

10. The *sudarśana* (disc of Viṣṇu) should be placed at the top. A wise man has to make the banner five cubits long.

1. ṚV. 1.22.15.

11-12. It should be made sixteen fingers broad. O excellent among the celestials ! the height should be seventeen cubits in the alternative. The pit should be duly reddish, flame-coloured, black, white, yellow, deep red, white and (again) white.

13-15. The presiding deities of the banners (hoisted) in the (quarters) east etc., such as Kumuda, Kumudākṣa, Puṇḍarīka, Vāmana, Saṅkarṣaṇa, Sarvanetra, Sumukha and Supratiṣṭhita, who are endowed with countless (divine) qualities should be worshipped. One hundred and eight pitchers resembling the ripe *bimba* fruit (in colour), not having black spots and having been filled with water and gold and having pieces of cloth around their necks should be placed outside the arches.

16. Pitchers should be placed at the east and other directions. Four pitchers should be placed at the corners of the sacrificial altar with the sacred syllable *ājighra*.

17. After having invoked Indra and others in the pitchers in the east etc. one should worship (Indra). O Indra, the lord of celestials, the wielder of thunderbolt, seated on the elephant you come.

18. (You) protect the eastern door in the company of celestials. May salutations be to you. After having worshipped (Indra) with the sacred syllable *trātāram indra*[1], the wise man should invoke him.

19. O Agni ! endowed with a trident, seated on a goat and possessing strength (you) come and accept my worship. You protect the south-east in the company of celestials. Salutations to you.

20-21. One should worship Agni with the sacred syllable *agnir mūrddhā*[2]. Salutations to Agni. O Yama ! seated on the buffalo, wielding the mace, and possessing great strength (you) come. You protect the southern gate. O Yama ! salutations to you. Yama should be propitiated with the sacred syllable *vaivasvataṁ saṅgamanam.*[3]

22-24. O Nairṛta ! carrying a sword accompanied by an army and riding an animal, (you) come. Here is the offering and water for washing the feet. You guard the south-western

1. ṚV. 6.47.11.
2. ṚV. 8.44.16.
3. ṚV. 10.14.1.

direction. Men should worship with the sacred syllable *eṣa te nirṛte*[1] and with offerings. O Varuṇa ! riding the crocodile, holding the noose and possessing great strength (you) come and protect the western doorway. Salutations to you. The preceptor should worship with (the sacred syllable) *uruṁ hi rājā varuṇam* and offerings.

25-27. O Vāyu ! endowed with strength, holding the banner, together with a vehicle you come. You guard the north-western direction in the company of celestials and Maruts (groups of celestial gods). Salutations to you. He should be worshipped with (the sacred syllables) *vāta*[2] etc. or with 'Om ! Salutations to Vāyu'. O Soma ! you come with strength, wielding the mace and riding the vehicle. You protect the northern gate along with Kubera. Salutations to you. One should worship with (the sacred syllable) *somaṁ rājānam* or 'Salutations to Soma'.

28-30. O Īśāna ! (you) come along ! possesser of strength, riding the bull. You guard the north-eastern direction of the ritual pavilion. Salutations to you. He should be worshipped with (the sacred syllable). *iśānamasya*[3] or 'Salutations to Īśāna'. O Brahman ! (you) come. Seated on a swan ! Carrying the sacrificial vessel and ladle ! You defend the direction above the sacrificial place, O unborn ! Salutations to you. (One) should worship with (the sacred syllable) *hiraṇyagarbha* or 'Salutations to Brahman'.

31. O Ananta ! you come. Endowed with the disc ! Seated on the tortoise ! Lord of the *gaṇas*. You protect the bottom (of the sacrificial place). O Lord Ananta ! Salutations to you. One should worship with (the sacred syllable) 'Salutations to serpent' or 'Salutations to Ananta'.

## CHAPTER FIFTYSEVEN

### *Consecration of pitchers*

*The Lord said* :

1. One should do (the ceremony) of taking possession of

---

1. VS. 9.35.
2. ṚV. 10.186.1.
3. ṚV. 7.32.22.

the ground. One should scatter grains and mustard seeds uttering (the sacred syllable) 'Nārasiṁha' which destroys demons. One should sprinkle *pañcagavya* (the five things got from a cow).

2. Having worshipped the earth in the pitcher containing gems as well as Hari and his retinue, worship the eighteen pitchers therein with the sacred syllable of weapons.

3. The rice grains should be purified by an incessant shower (of water) and scattered around. The pitcher should be placed in their midst.

4-5. Lord Acyuta and (his consort) Śrī should again be worshipped in the pitcher (provided with) a cloth. The bed as well as the mattress should be spread on the *kuśa* grass on a drawn circle with (the recitation of) the sacred syllable *yoge yoge*.[1] Lord Viṣṇu, the slayer of (the demon) Madhu and the lord of the three (divisions of the universe) and also the different lords of learning are worshipped on the bed.

6-7. Having worshipped Vāmana, Śrīdhara, Hṛṣīkeśa, Padmanābha (different forms of Viṣṇu) in the north-west and other (corners) of the bathing place and the Dāmodara (form of Viṣṇu) in the north-east and having brought all the materials to the bathing pavilion they should be deposited in the four pitchers and the altar in the north-east.

8. These pitchers should be consecrated in the four quarters with the pitchers containing water for the consecration. The pitchers should be placed with due regard for the purpose of consecration.

9-11. The young sprouts from the *vaṭa* udumbara, aśvattha, *campaka*, *aśoka*, *śrīdruma*, *palāśa*, *arjuna*, *plakṣa*, *kadamba*, *bakula* and mango trees should be brought and put in the eastern pitcher. The lotus, *rocanā* (a kind of yellow pigment), *dūrvā* grass, *darbha* grass, *piñjala* (yellow orpiment), the flowers *jāti* and *kunda*, (pieces of) sandal wood, red sandal, white mustard, *tagara* (a kind of herb), and rice should be put on the southern one.

12-14. Silver and gold and earth from the two banks of rivers flowing into the ocean especially the earth from the (river) Jāhnavī (Ganges), the urine of a cow, barley grains, paddy and sesamum should be placed in another pitcher. The *viṣṇuparṇī* *śyāmalatā*, *bhṛṅgarāja*, *śatāvarī*, *sahadevī*, *mahādevī*, *balā* and *vyā-*

1. ṚV. 1.30.7.

*ghni* (?), the auspicious things are put in the other pitcher in the north-east.

15. The earth from an ant-hill obtained from seven (different places should be put in another pitcher. The sand from the Ganges and its water should be put in another pitcher.

16. The earth loosened by the boars, bulls, and elephants with their horns and tusks as well as earth from the root of the lotus and the *kuśa* grass should be placed in another pitcher.

17. One should put in another pitcher earth got from sacred places and hills. The flowers of *nāgakeśara* and *kāśmira* should be put in another pitcher.

18-19. Flowers together with the sandal wood, agallochum and camphor should be placed in another pitcher. (The gems) lapis lazuli, coral, pearl, crystal, and diamond should be put earlier in one pitcher and placed firmly by the holy priests. Another pitcher should be filled with the waters of the rivers and tanks.

20. Another (set of) pitchers filled with perfumes etc. should be placed at eightyone places and consecrated with the *śrisūkta*[1].

21. Barley grains, white mustard, perfumes, tips of *kuśa* grass, unbroken rice, sesamum, fruits and flowers should be first placed for the sake of worship.

22. The lotus, (the creeper called) *śyāmalatā*, *dūrvā* grass, leaf of holy basil and *kuśa* grass (should be kept) on the right-hand side for being offered at the foot. The *madhuparka*[2] is also placed on the right side.

23. The *kaṅkola*, cloves and nutmeg along with the *dūrvā* grass and unbroken rice (should be offered) in the fire on the north for the sake of rinsing the mouth.

24. A vessel for offering camphor and perfumes to be applied on the body should be placed on the south-east. A vessel containing perfumes and flowers should be placed on the north-east.

25. The *murā*, *māṁsi*, myrabolan, *sahadevā* and *niśā* and sixty lamps should be placed. Eight lamps should be kept for the *nirājana* (showing the light in adoration).

26. The conch, disc, *śrivatsa* (mark on the breast of Viṣṇu), thunderbolt, lotus etc. should be placed in a golden vessel along with flowers of variegated colours.

---

1. Hymn commencing with hiraṇyavarṇāṁ hariṇim. ṚV. Kh. 5.87.1.
2. A respectful offering consisting of five ingredients: curd, clarified butter, water, honey, and candied sugar.

## CHAPTER FIFTYEIGHT

### *Consecration of the idol*

*The lord said* :

1-3. The priest should get ready a pit (for sacrificial fire) in the north-east. The fire relating to Viṣṇu should be kindled with (the recitation) of *gāyatri*[1] one hundred and eight times. Having cleansed the pitchers thoroughly and established (the priest) he should go to the shed where the image has been made ready accompanied by the sculptors and custodians of the idol and along with music of (the instrument) *tūrya*. The woollen thread containing mustard seeds should be tied on the right arm (of the idol) with the syllables *Viṣṇave śipiviṣṭāya*[2] etc. The priest should also have a piece of silk cloth tied (to his arm).

4-5. Having placed the idol in the pavilion and having adored and worshipped the dressed idol (one has to say) "I bow to you the sovereign lady of celestials who has been made (ready) by Viśvakarman (the divine architect)." I make obeisance to you who is resplendant and is the sustainer of the entire universe. I worship in you the healthy Lord Nārāyaṇa.

6. Be thou always prosperous (goddess) devoid of defects due to the sculptors. Having submitted thus that idol should be carried to the bathing pavilion.

7. The sculptor should be satisfied by offering articles (of present). A cow should be given as gift to the priest. Then the eyes of the idol should be made open with (the recitation of) the syllable *citraṁ deva*.[3]

8. The sight should be endowed with (the recitation of the syllable) *agnir jyoti*.[4] Then white flowers, ghee and mustard seeds should be placed on the pedestal.

9. The priest should place *dūrvā* grass and tips of *kuśa* grass on the head of the deity. Then the priest should anoint the eyes (of the deity) with the syllables *madhu vātā*.[5]

10. The syllables *hiraṇyagarbha* and *imam me* should be

---

1. The mantra beginning with 'Om bhūr bhuvaḥ svaḥ consisting of twenty-four letters.
2. VS. 22.20.
3. ṚV. 1.115.1.
4. VS. 3.9.
5. ṚV. 1.90.6.

recited. Then the idol should be anointed with ghee reciting (the hymn) *ghṛtavati.*[1]

11. The flour paste of *masūra* (a variety of grain) should be rubbed on the deity reciting (the hymn) *ato devā.*[2] Then the priest should wash (the deity) with hot water with the recitation of) *sapta te agne*[3].

12. It should be anointed with (the syllables) *Urupadādiva.* (The image) should be bathed with (the waters of) the rivers and sacred places with (the syllables) *āpo hi ṣṭhā*[4] and with the (waters containing) gems (with the) *pāvamāna.*

13. (The image) (should be bathed) with the waters of an earthern pot with (the syllable) *samudraṁ gaccha*[5]. It should be consecrated with *śanno devi*[6] and bathed with hot water (consecrated) by *gāyatri.*

14. The supreme god should be bathed with five (kinds of) earth with (the syllable) *hiraṇya.* With pot made of earth of an anthill and sand waters and (the syllable) *imam me*[7] (it should be bathed).

15. (The image should be bathed) with herbal waters (with the syllable) *tadviṣṇoḥ*[8] and *yā oṣadhi,*[9] with herbal decoctions (with the syllable) *yajñā-yajñā*[10] and then with the *pañccagavya* (the five things got from a cow).

16. (The image should be bathed) with the waters containing fruits (with the syllables) *payaḥ pṛthivyām*[11] and *yāḥ phalini*[12] and with (the contents of) the pitchers (kept in) the north and east with (the syllables) *viśvataścakṣuḥ.*[13]

17. The cleansing (of the image) of Hari (Viṣṇu) should be done with (the recitation of the syllables *somaṁ rājānam, viṣṇo rarāṭamasi*[14] from the right and with *haṁsaḥ śuci*[15] on the west

1. ṚV. 6.70.1.
2. ṚV. 1.22.16.
3. VS. 17.79.
4. ṚV. 10 9.1.
5. ṚV. kh. 5.49.2.
6. ṚV. 10.9.4.
7. ṚV. 1.25.19.
8. ṚV. 1.22.20.
9. ṚV. 10.97.1.
10. ṚV. 6.48.1.
11. VS. 18.36.
12. ṚV. 10.97.15.
13. ṚV. 10.81.3.
14. VS. 5.11.
15. ṚV. 4.40.5.

18. One should offer the *dhātri* and *māṁsi* (herbs) on the head with the sacred syllables *mūrdhānaṁ divā*[1]. (One should bathe the image) with perfumes with the syllables *gandhadvāra* and *mā nas toka.*[2]

19. (One has to pour over its head the contents of the pitchers) placed in the eightyone squares (with the syllables) *idam āpaḥ*. O Lord Viṣṇu ! the bestower of grace on the universe ! you come.

20. (You) accept this share in the sacrificial offerings. O Vāsudeva ! Salutations to you ! Having invoked the lord in this way, the wrist thread (on the hand of the image) should be unfastened.

21. The wrist thread on (the hand of) the priest should also be unfastened with the hymn *muñcāmi tvā.*[3] The water for washing the feet should be offered with (the syllable) *hiraṇmaya*[4] and the offering with *ato devā.*[5]

22. The *madhuparka* (should be offered) with (the syllables) *madhuvātā*[6] and the *ācamana* (the ceremonial sipping of waters at the commencement of any rite) should be done with *mayi gṛhṇāmi.*[7] The learned (priest) should scatter the unbroken rice with (the syllable) *akṣannamīmadanta.*[8]

23. The image should be rubbed part by part and perfumes (should be offered) with (the syllable) *gandhavat*[9], garland with (the syllable) *unnayāmi* and the sacred thread with (the syllable) *idaṁ viṣṇu.*

24. Pair of cloth pieces (should be offered) (with the syllable) *bṛhaspate* (and) the upper cloth (with the syllable) *vedāham.* The herbs and the flower of concluding worship should be placed with the *mahāvrata.*

25. Incense should be offered with *dhūrasi* and the collyrium (to the eyes of the image) with the hymn (called) *vibhrāṭ.* The mark on the forehead (should be made) with (the syllable) *yuñjanti* and the garland (should be offered) with *dīrghāyuṣṭvā.*

---

1. ṚV. 6.7.1.
2. ṚV. 1.114.8.
3. See LXVII. 22.1.
4. ṚV. 10.161.1.
5. ŚB. 14.7.1.12.
6. ṚV. 1.22.16.
7. ṚV. 1.90.6.
8. ṚV. 10.9.

26. (One should offer) an umbrella with (the syllable) *indra cchatra*, mirror with *virāja*, the chowrie with *vikarṇa* and the ornaments with *rathantara*.

27. (One should offer) the fan with (the syllable) *vāyu daivatya* and flowers with *muñcāmi tvā*. One should sing in praise of (Lord) Hari (Viṣṇu) with vedic hymns and (the hymn called) *puruṣasūkta*.

28. All these rites should be performed similarly relating to pedestals of Hara (Śiva) and other gods. The hymn (called) *sauparṇa* should be recited at the time of raising (the image of) the deity.

29. (The image) having been raised (by reciting) (the syllable) *uttiṣṭha*, the lord should be led to the bed in the pavilion with (the recitation of) the hymn *śakuna*[1] and with (the syllable) *brahmaratha*.

30. Then the image and the pedestal (should be laid) in the bed with the hymn *ato devā*.[2] With the (recitation of) *śrisūkta* the rite for Viṣṇu is completed.

31. The eight auspicious things are: the lion, bull, serpent, fan, pitcher, banner, trumpet and lamp.

32-33. (The priest) should show (these) at the foot with the hymn (called) *aśvasūkta* and the *tripād* (*gāyatri*). One should submit a cooking vessel, covering pan, ladle, pestle, crushing stone, grinding stone, groomstick, utensils for eating and other household things should be given to the goddess.

34. A pitcher known as *nidrā* provided with clothes and gems and filled with edibles (should be placed) at the head-side (of the image). This is the mode of bathing (the image).

## CHAPTER FIFTYNINE

### *Preliminary consecration of an image*

*The Lord said* :

1-4. The act of causing the presence of God Hari is said to be the *adhivāsana* (preliminary consecration). Having contem-

1. ṚV. 9.107.
2. ṚV. 1.22.16.

plated on the self as the omniscient, all-pervasive and supreme spirit and having united one's self-conceited conscious energy with (the syllable) *om* and after having drawn it out and identifying one's own self with the all-pervasive lord, (the priest) should unite the earth with the wind, illuminate it with the fire particle (mentally), draw the fire with the wind (particle) and lead the wind into the ethereal space. The wiseman should draw in the same order (the other gross elements) after having made them the receptacles of subtle principles along with the gross principles, the supreme being and the secondary forms such as the *sādhya-s*[1].

5. The ethereal space should be drawn into the mind (principle), the mind (in its turn) should be (drawn) into (the principle of) ego, (the principle) of ego in the (principle of) *mahat* (first principle). The *mahat* should be led into the *avyākṛta* (unmanifest).

6-7. The unmanifest (is led) into the absolute knowledge known as Vāsudeva. Being desirous to create he, the Lord of sound by means of the unmanifest brought into being Saṅkarṣaṇa (the principle) known as touch. He created Pradyumna the form of splendour by agitating the illusion.

8. He created Aniruddha, (consisting of) taste only and Brahmā of the form of smell. That Aniruddha, the Brahmā created water at first.

9. He also laid the golden egg (of the five principles) in that (water). Impregnated with consciousness (this generated) a peculiar force within.

10. The breath united with life force is spoken as existence. The inner being also known as the *vyāhṛti*[2] is a spiritual entity amidst the five winds (*prāṇāḥ*).

11. Then intellect came into being associated with the *prāṇa* and with eight-fold modifications. Egoism was born then and the mind came out from it.

12. Then the five (abstract) things were born possessing determination. They are known as sound, touch, sight, taste and smell.

13. The sense-organs possessing consciousness were brought

1. They are refined secondary forms. See MW. p. 1202a.
2. The mystic syllables *bhūḥ, bhuvaḥ, suvaḥ*.

about by these. The skin, ear, nose, eyes, tongue are the sense-organs.

14. The feet, anus, arms, speech (mouth) and the genitals are the five organs of action. Listen (I shall describe) the five elements.

15. The ether, wind, light, water and earth (are the five elements). The gross body is composed of these elements and becomes the support for all.

16. (I shall presently) describe the mystic syllables signifying these and for being (mentally) placed on (the different parts of) the body. The letter *ma* which is the symbol of the inner self should be located to co-extend with (the body of) the deity.

17. The letter *bha* which is the emblem of life should be lodged in the differentiating individuality of the god. The letter *ba* which represents the intellect should be located in the region of the heart.

18. The letter *pha* representing the sense of ego should also be located there itself. The letter *pa* representing the mind should be located in the mental resolve.

19. The letter *na* which is a symbol of the principle of sound should be placed on the forehead. The letter *dha* which is the symbol of sense of touch should be placed in the region of the face (of image).

20. The letter *da* denoting the gradations should be placed in the region of the heart. The letter *tha* symbolising the sense of taste should be placed in the region of pelvis.

21. The letter *ta* signifying the sense of smell should be located on the shanks. After having located the letter *ṇa* in the ears, the letter *ḍha* should be located on the skin.

22. The letter *ḍa* should be located in the two eyes, the letter *ṭha* in the tongue, the letter *ṭa* in the nose and the letter *ña* in the speech.

23. Having placed the letter *jha* representing the hands in the hands, a wise man should place the letter *ja* in the feet, *cha* in the anus and *ca* in the genitals.

24. The letter *ṅa* symbolising the principle of earth should be placed on the feet. The letter *gha* (should be placed) in the pelvis. (The letter) *ga* representing the principle of lustre should be placed in the heart.

25. The letter *kha* which represents the principle of wind should be placed in the nose. The letter *ka* signifying the principle of ether should be assigned to the forehead by the wise.

26-27. The letter *ya* denoting lord Sun having been placed in the lotus of the heart, the letter *sa* possessing sixteen digits should be placed in the seventy-two thousand (rays) emanating from the (lotus) heart. The priest fully initiated in the mystic syllables should contemplate on the point (*bindu*) representing the region of fire in the middle of it.

28. The excellent letter *ha* along with the syllable *om* (*praṇava*) should be placed there. *Om, ām*, salutations to the *parameṣṭyātman.*[1] *Ām*, salutations to *puruṣātman*[2].

29. *Om, Vām*, salutations to the eternal being ! *Nām*, salutations to the soul of the universe ! *Om, vām*, salutations to the soul of all beings ! Thus the five forms of energies have been described.

30. The first one (of the above five syllables) should be used for the place, the second one for the seat, the third one for the bed, and the fourth one for the drink.

31. The fifth one is used at every worship. These (five mystic syllables) are known as the five *upaniṣads*. The syllable *hum* should be placed in the middle after having contemplated on Hari, composed of mystic syllables.

32. Whichever form of the deity is being installed one should assign the particular principal mystic syllable of that form afterwards. The principal syllable of Vāsudeva is *Om*, salutations to Lord Vāsudeva !

33. (The different forms of the god) should be (mentally) assigned to (the different parts of the body such as) the head, nose, forehead, face, neck, heart, arms, shanks and feet in order. (The manifestation known as) Keśava should be assigned to the head (of the image).

34. Nārāyaṇa should be assigned to the face, Mādhava to the neck, Govinda to the arms, (and) Viṣṇu to the heart.

35. Madhusūdana should be assigned to the hinder part, Vāmana to the belly, Trivikrama to the hip (and) Śrīdhara to the shank.

1. The word *Parameṣṭin* denotes the supreme being or one of the forms of Trinity.
2. This means a supreme being.

36. Hṛṣīkeśa (should be assigned) on the right side, Padmanābha on the ankle, Dāmodara on the feet.

(This is assignment) in the six limbs commencing with the heart.

37-39. O most virtuous one ! This is general mode of assignment of Viṣṇu. In the alternative, the installation of which form of the deity has been begun, one should infuse life into the image with the principal mystic syllable of that form. The first letter of the name of any form of a deity should be used along with the twelve vowels and assigned to the different parts of image such as the heart. O Lord of celestials ! the principal mystic syllable should consist of ten syllables.

40. The principles should be placed in the body in the same order as they are found in the god. Lord Viṣṇu should be worshipped with perfumes etc., in the diagram of a lotus inscribed in a circle.

41. One should contemplate on the seat as before together with the limbs and cover. Then one should imagine an auspicious disc over that as having twelve radii.

42. The circle (should be imagined) as having three concentric naves and two outer circles and filled with the vowels. The wise man should then place the *prakṛti* (the nature, the source of the material world) and other principles.

43-44. The sun god should again be worshipped at the tips of the spokes in the twelve-fold way[1] and the moon possessing three-fold armies and sixteen phases should be contemplated therein. The excellent worshipper should contemplate on a lotus flower of twelve petals.

45. The effulgent energy of the supreme being should be contemplated and worshipped in the centre (of the lotus flower) by the priest. Having located (Lord) Hari in that image, one should worship him as well as the celestials.

46. Keśava and others should be worshipped well with twelve mystic letters[2] with perfumes, flowers etc. and with their attendants and enclosures in due order.

47-48. The twice-born should worship the guardian deities of quarters and others in the circular diagram of twelve radii. The image should then be worshipped with perfumes and

1. Consisting of twelve names of Sun.
2. *Oṁ namo bhagavate vāsudevāya.*

flowers and with the *puruṣasūkta.*[1] The pedestal should be worshipped with the *śrisūkta.*[2] The sacrificial fire relating to Viṣṇu should be kindled in the prescribed manner.

49. Having made oblation unto the fire with the sacred syllables the wise priest should sanctify waters and consecrate the image (by sprinkling waters). Then he should kindle fire.

50. The wise priest should kindle fire in the pit on the south with the mystic syllable *agniṁ hutam*[3] and in the pit on the east with the syllable *agnim agnim*[4].

51. In the fire pit on the north, the fire should be kindled with the mystic syllable *agnim agniṁ havimabhiḥ*[5] and the sacred syllable to be used to kindle fire in general is *tvam agne hyagnirucyase.*[6]

52. One should place one thousand and eight twigs of the *palāśa* tree in each one of the fire pits and offer grains withvedic hymns.

53. Clarified butter and sesamum (should be offered to fire) with the *vyāhṛtis* (*Om bhūḥ*, *bhuvaḥ*, *suvaḥ*) and ghee with the principal *mantra.* One should perform the appeasing oblation with the three sweet things.[7]

54. One should then touch the feet, navel, heart and forehead with (the utterance of) twelve mystic sullables (of the god). After having offered ghee, curd and milk, the head of the image should again be touched.

55. After having touched the head, navel, and feet, (the priest) should make four rivers Gaṅgā, Yamunā, Godāvarī and Sarasvatī present there by pronouncing their names.

56. (The rivers) should be dried up by (the recitation of the *viṣṇugāyatri*[8] and the sacrificial gruel should be boiled with (the recitation of) the *gāyatri*. One should offer oblation, offer the victim and feed the twice-borns afterwards.

57. For the satisfaction of the singer of *sāmans* one should give gold and cows to the spiritual preceptor. Having made offerings to the guardian deities of the quarters, one should spend night in vigil. By singing the praise of the brahman one gets fruits of the consecration rite.

---

1. ṚV. 10. 90.
2. ṚVkh. 5.87.1a.
3. Could not be identified.
4. Cf. ṚV. 1.12.2a.
5. Cf. ṚV. 1.12.2a.
6. Could not be identified.
7. Sugar, honey and clarified butter.
8. *nārāyaṇāya vidmahe vāsudevāya dhīmahi tanno viṣṇuḥ Pracodayāt.*

# CHAPTER SIXTY

*Mode of installation of the image of Vāsudeva*

*The Lord said* :

1. One should divide the length of adytum into seven parts for the installation of the pedestal. The wise man should fix the image on the part of Brahman.

2-3. (One should) never (fix it) in the parts (presided over) by the celestials, mortals and goblins, leaving out the part (presided over by) Brahman. The pedestal should be carefully fixed off the regions of celestials and mortals. Gems should be imbedded in the case of a hermaphrodite stone.

4-5. Having performed oblation with (the *mantra* sacred to) Narasiṁha (the man-lion form of Viṣṇu), the gems should be placed with (the repetition of) the same (mantra). Rice grains, gems, three (kinds of) minerals, iron and other metallic substances, sandal wood etc., should be placed in the nine holes commencing with the east at the centre as one likes. Then the holes should be filled with the *guggulu* (a kind of fragrant gum resin) with (the recitation of) the *mantras—indra* etc.

6. After having performed the insertion of gems, the preceptor should rub the image with sticks of *sahadeva* (tree) and bunches of *darbha* (grass).

7. The outer and inner surface (of the image) should be cleansed and then purified with the *pañcagavya* (the five things got from a cow). Water should be sprinkled with the *darbha* grass as well as with the waters of the river.

8. The ground for kindling the sacrificial fire should be made ready with sand. An excellent site should be of the measure of a cubit and a half on all sides.

9. The pitchers also should be placed in the eight directions commencing with the east. The consecrated fire should be brought in uttering the eight letters (described already).

10. The twigs should be offered into the fire with (the *mantras*)—*tvam agne dyubhiḥ*[1] and *gāyatri*. Clarified butter should be offered with (the recitation of) eight letters, eight hundred times.

---

1. ṚV. 2.1.1.

11. The appeasing water sanctified hundred times by the principal *mantra* should be sprinkled on the head of the image with (the recitation of) the hymn *śriśca te*.[1]

12. The image should be lifted up with (the *mantra*) *brahmajajñāna*[2] and should be led to the temple with the *mantra uttiṣṭha brahmaṇaspate*[3] and *tadviṣṇoḥ*[4].

13. Lord Hari should be placed in a palanquin and carried towards the divine edifice accompanied by songs and vedic hymns. He should be held at the gates of the temple.

14. Lord Hari should be bathed with waters from eight auspicious pitchers by women and brahmins. Then the priest should worship the image with perfumes etc. and with the principal *mantra*[5].

15. Then the dress, the devotional offerings of eight kinds should be offered with (the *mantra*) *ato devā*[6]. (The image) should be fixed on the pedestal at the fixed moment with (the recitation of) *devasya tvā*[7].

16. The learned (priest) should fix the image on the pedestal (with the recitation of the following *mantra*). "O Conqueror of three spaces ! Om ! salutations to you who surpassed the three regions.

17. The image should be bathed with the *pañcagavya* (five things got from a cow) with (the recitation of) the *mantra dhruvā dyauḥ*[8] and *viśvatascakṣuḥ*[9] and bathed again with perfumed water.

18. Lord Hari should be worshipped along with the attendants and paraphernalia. The heavens should be contemplated as his form and the earth as the seat.

19. His body should be imagined as composed of lustrous minute particles. (One should say), "I am invoking his spirit pervading the twentyfive principles."

---

1. VS. 31.22.
2. TS. 4.2.8.2.
3. ṚV. 1. 40. 1.
4. ṚV. 1.22.20.
5. *Oṁ namo bhagavate vāsudevāya.*
6. ṚV. 1.22.16.
7. VS. 1.24.
8. ṚV. 10.173.4.
9. ṚV. 10.81.3.

20-21. O Supreme Lord ! you become firmly established in the image. I invoke you, the spirit of supreme happiness, one devoid of (three states) waking, dreaming and deep sleep, one who is devoid of a body, sense-organs, intellect, life and egoism, and one who resides in the hearts of all beings beginning with Brahman and ending with a dump of grass.

22. You make the image imbued with your soul both inside and outside. You have taken your abode in this image (of the size of) a thumb with attributes.

23. Having invoked (the god in the image), the supreme brahman, lustrous form of knowledge and who is one without a second, that is deemed as alive by the use of (the *mantra*) *Om.*

24. The act of bringing the god near consists in uttering (the *mantra*) and touching the heart (of the image). (The priest) should recite the *puruṣasūkta*[1] and should recite the following (*mantra*) in secret.

25-27. Salutations to the Lord of celestials who is of the form of happiness and fortune, of the form of knowledge and wisdom and who attends on the lustre of the supreme brahman. (Salutations to) the one who is beyond properties, the great being, devoid of decay, old age. O Viṣṇu, you be present here. Whichever is the supreme principle in you and that which is your form verily (made up) of knowledge, all that be present here in this form. May you awake !

28. Stationing oneself in front of the deity, (the priest) should establish Brahman and other attendant gods as well as the respective weapons (by showing) the *mudrā* (different postures shown with the hand).

29-30. (The priest) should infer the presence of the god from the *yātrā*[2] and *varṣā*[3]. Having saluted and sung the glories and recited the *mantras* of eight syllables[4] etc., the priest should come out and worship Caṇḍa and Pracaṇḍa (the two guardians) at the gate. (The priest) should go to the place of sacrificial fire, install the image of *Garuḍa* (the vehicle bird of Lord Viṣṇu) and worship.

---

1. ṚV.10.90.
2. Existence, livelihood.
3. Rains.
4. *Om namo nārāyaṇāya.*

31. Having installed and worshipped (the images) of different presiding deities of the quarters in their respective quarters, the priest should install the image of Lord Viṣvaksena[1] and worship the conch, disc etc.

32. Offerings should be made to the attendant gods and to the goblins. The priest should be given the fees—(which may be of the form of) proprietary right over a village, clothes and gold.

33. The materials required for (the performance of) sacrificial ceremony should be given to the principal priest. The attendant priests should be paid fees half of what was paid to the principal priest.

34. The other priests should be paid their fees. The brahmins should then be fed. Without any restraint the benefits of sacrifice should be extended to the patron-employer by the principal priest.

35. The consecrator of the image of Viṣṇu leads the self, as well as his entire family (to the region of the god). This is the general mode of performance for all gods. Only the principal *mantra* would be different. The other formalities are the same.

## CHAPTER SIXTYONE

### *Consecration of doors of the temple and the erection of banner*

*The Lord said* :

1. I shall describe the purificatory bathing of Viṣṇu. The offering to the fire is made (with the *mantra*) *na tvā*[2]. Having placed eightyone pitchers (at their respective places) Lord Hari should be invoked and installed.

2. He should be worshipped with perfumes and flowers. Having made the offering, the priest should be worshipped. I shall describe the (mode of) consecrating the door. (A piece of) gold should be placed beneath the door (frame).

3. The priest should place shoots of *udumbara* (fig tree) in

1. An epithet of Viṣṇu.
2. One of the many hymns beginning with these words.

the (mouth of the) eight pitchers and worship them with perfumes etc. and vedic *mantras*.

4. Twigs, fried paddy and sesamum should be offered unto the fire in the pits. Having offered the bed etc., the supporting energy should be placed underneath.

5. Gods Caṇḍa and Pracaṇḍa should be located at the bottom of the shoots, Goddess Lakṣmī worshipped by the celestials should be placed above (the shoot of) the fig (tree).

6. Having assigned the four-faced (Brahman) and duly worshipping (him) (by reciting) the *śrīsūkta*[1] the fruits of the *bilva* (tree) should be offered to him and the fees should be paid to the priest.

7. (I shall describe) the consecration of the divine edifice the doors of which have been consecrated and wherein the image of Hari has been duly installed. It is in the consecration of the adytum. Listen.

8-9. Pitcher made of gold, silver or bell-metal filled with eight kinds of gems, herbs, minerals, seeds of grains, iron and water and covered with a cloth should be placed on the *darbha* (grass) in a circle to the east of the altar after the *śukanāsa* (the keystone) has been got ready.

10. Fallen twigs which have been gathered should be offered into fire with (the *mantra* of) Nṛsiṁha. Then (the temple) should be enlivened with the principle known as *nārāyaṇatattva*.

11. (That lord) who is the life of the temple should be contemplated (as) "O Lord of celestials". Then a wise man has to imagine the temple as the god himself.

12. (A piece of) gold should be placed below the golden pitcher. The priests and others should be paid their fees and the brahmins should be fed.

13-14. Threads should be wound round the altar, neck, top and the globe of the temple after that. Then the metallic ring known as the *sudarśana* disc should be placed. It should be known as the form of (Lord) Vāsudeva offering protection from fear.

15. Alternatively a pitcher should be placed (in the place of a globe) and the disc above that. O birthless one ! eight lords

---

1. See above, p. 151 and fn 1 thereon.

of obstacles (Vighneśvara) should be placed around the altar in the temple.

16. Or four images of Garuḍa (vehicle of Lord Viṣṇu) should be placed in the four quarters. I shall describe now the erection of the flagstaff which destroys the evil spirits.

17. One who performs this remains in the regions of Viṣṇu for so many thousands of years as the number of atoms in the image of the god in the temple.

18. O sinless ! It should be known that (a man gets) a crore times more merit by erecting the flag-staff,since it surrounds the neck of the temple and it wafts the wind around the globe, altar and image.

19. The flag should be known as the *prakṛti* and the staff as the *puruṣa* and you know that the temple is another form of image of Vāsudeva (Viṣṇu).

20. (In a temple) the *dharaṇi* (earth) is so called from its ability to hold, its internal cavity stands for the sky, the illumination inside represents the fire, and its touch represents the wind.

21. The earthly waters found in the stone slabs (of the temple) (represent) the earthly attributes. Its echo stands for the principles of sound. Its touch represents roughness.

22. Its colour which may be white or otherwise stands for the subtle principle of colour. The food (and other eatables) offered (to the deity) stand for the sense of taste. The perfumes represent the sense of smell. The sense of speech lies in the down (used in the temple).

23. The keystone is the nose (of the temple). The two apertures (on either side) represent the two hands. The arched terrace above is to be taken for its head and the pitcher on the head.

24. Its neck should be known as the neck. The platform over the fault is spoken as the shoulder. The outlets for water are the anus and genitals. The lime-plaster is spoken as the skin.

25. The door would be the mouth. The image (installed in the temple) is said to be its life. The pedestal should be known as its energy. Its shape should likewise be known as its animation.

26. Its cavity is its inertia. Lord Keśava is its controller. In this way Lord Hari Himself remains in the form of the temple.

27. God Śiva should be known as the shank. God Brahman-

is located in the shoulder. Lord Viṣṇu remains in the upper portion of a temple as it is.

28. Listen to me. I shall describe the consecration of a temple by means of a banner. The demons were defeated by the celestial gods by erecting banners impressed with the signs of divine weapons.

29. The pitcher (shaped part of the temple) should be placed over the top and the flag should be placed over the same. The post should be made to measure a half or one third of the height of the image.

30. The flag should have a mark of a circle of eight or twelve radii. (There should be the figure) of the man-lion (form of Viṣṇu) or the Garuḍa (Târkṣya) (inside the circle) in the middle. The staff of the flag should not have any cut.

31. The length of the staff is spoken as the measure of the breadth of edifice. It should be made either half of the terrace or a third part of it.

32. The staff should otherwise be made twice the length of the door. The flag staff should be planted on the north-east or the north-west of the divine edifice.

33. The flag should be made of a piece of silk cloth, of a single or variegated colours. It should be adorned with bells, chowries and small bells. (It is said to be) destroyer of sins.

34. A flag which touches the ground and measures a cubit in breadth at its extremity or has a breadth equal to one fourth of its length at its base is called a *mahādhvaja*. It grants all things when worshipped.

35. The banner should measure half (the dimension of) the staff. The breadth should measure twenty fingers.

36. All the rites relating to the consentration of an image should be done for (the consecration) of the disc, flag and the staff. They should be bathed in the shed.

37. The priest should duly perform all rites described earlier except that of opening the eyes. The consecration should be done in the prescribed manner leaving them in the resting position.

38. Then the learned priest should assign (mentally) the hymn (called) *sahasraśirṣā*[1] in the disc. Then the *sudarśana mantra*

---

1. ṚV. 10.90.

and the principle of mind should be assigned.

39. It is known as imbued with life by mental formation. O excellent among gods, (the different forms of Viṣṇu such as) Keśava etc. should be assigned to the spokes.

40. The priest should assign twentyfive principles at the navel, and each of the arcs of the lotus. The form of Nṛsiṁha (the man-lion form of Viṣṇu) representing the universe should be assigned to the middle of the lotus.

41. The *sakala* (endowed with parts) forms should be assigned to the staff as the living soul of it. Lord Hari, the supreme being of the *niṣkala* (undivided) form should be contemplated and assigned to the flag.

42. The energies Bala and Abala which manifest in the form of the banner should be contemplated. Having placed it in the shed and worshipped it, oblation should be made in the pit.

43. Having placed the golden pitcher over the pitcher and putting five (kinds of) gems (at the top of the temple) a golden disc should be placed underneath that with the *mantra* of the disc.

44. The disc should be washed with mercury and covered with the eye-cover. The disc should then be placed. Lord Nṛhari (man-lion form of Viṣṇu)should be imagined there in the middle.

45-46. *Om, kṣaum*, salutations to Lord Nṛsiṁha. Lord Hari should be invoked and worshipped. Then the *yajamāna* (the person who has arranged for the consecration) accompanied by his relatives should hold banner and dip the tip of the banner in a vessel full of curd. The banner should be worshipped with the *mantra* commencing with *dhruvā*[1] and ending with *phaṭ*.

47. Holding that vessel on the head and remembering Lord Nārāyaṇa (the *yajamāna*) should go around the temple along with auspicious sounds from the *tūri* (a musical instrument).

48. The staff should then be placed with (the recitation of) the eight-syllabled *mantra*[2]. Then the flag should be (hoisted) and unfurled with (the recitation of) the hymn *muñcāmi tvā*[3] by the learned person.

49. The twice-born (*yajamāna*) should give the priest the

---

1. ṚV.10.173.4a.
2. *Oṁ namo nārāyaṇāya.*
3. ṚV.10.161.1a.

vessel, banner and elephant etc. Mode of consecration of the flag has been thus described in general.

50. The mark which represents a particular god should be planted with the respective *mantra*. By the offer of a banner one goes to heaven and becomes a strong monarch on the earth (in the next birth).

## CHAPTER SIXTYTWO

### *Mode of installation of the image of Goddess Lakṣmi*

*The Lord said* :

1. I shall describe to you the mode of installation of all divine images. At first I shall describe the (mode of) installation (of the image) of Lakṣmī and her attendant goddesses.

2. As before, one should do all rites such as bathing (the image) in the shed. (The image of) goddess Lakṣmī should be placed on the pedestal. One should place eight pitchers.

3. The image should be anointed with ghee with the principal *mantra* and washed with the five things got from a cow. The eyes of (the goddess) Lakṣmī should be opened with (the recitation of the *mantra*) *hiraṇyavarṇām hariṇīm*[1].

4. The three sweet things[2] should be offered with (the recitation of the *mantra*) *tāṁ ma āvaha*[3]. She (the image) should be bathed with (the waters of) the pitcher on the east with (the recitation of) the (hymn) *aśvapūrva*[4].

5. The image should then be bathed with (the waters of pitchers on) the south, west and north with the recitation of hymns *kāmo'smi te*[5], *candram prabhāsām*[6], *āditya varṇa*[7] (respectively)

1. ṚV Kh. 5.87.1.
2. P. 160. fn 7.
3. ṚV. Kh. 5.87.2a, 15a.
4. cf. ṚV. Kh. 5.87.3a.
5. Could not be identified.
6. Could not be identified.
7. VS.31.81b.

6-7. (Waters) from (the pitchers placed in) the south-east, south-west, north-west and north-east should be poured on the image accompanied by (the recitation of the *mantras*) *upaitu mā*[1], *kṣut pipāsā*[2], *gandhadvāra*[3], *manasaḥ kāmamākṛti*[4]. The image should subsequently be bathed with (the waters of) eighty-one pitchers (accompanied) by *āpaḥ sṛjan kṣitim.*[5]

8. (The priest should worship the image) with perfumes accompanied by *ārdrām puṣkariṇim*[6], with flowers accompanied by *tāṁ ma āvaha*[7] and *ya ānanda.*[8]

9. The goddess should be worshipped in the bed with (the *mantra*) *śāyanti*[9] *yena* and her presence is accomplished by *śrī-sūkta*[10]. Her consciousness is invoked and worshipped again with the principal *mantra* of the goddess.

10. Thousand or hundred lotus flowers or *karavira* flowers should be offered in the fire pit at the shed accompanied by *śrīsūkta.*[10]

11. Household furniture should be offered with the *śrīsūkta*[10] itself. Then the consecration of edifice should be performed as described earlier.

12. The pedestal should be made with (the recitation of) the *mantra*. The installation of the goddess is done subsequently. Her presence is accomplished with the *śrīsūkta.*[10] Everyone of the hymns (stated earlier)) should be recited as before.

13. Having invoked consciousness in the image, her presence is accomplished by the principal *mantra*. The priest and the brahmins should be presented with land, gold, clothes, cow and food. The images of all other forms of goddesses should be installed in the same way. One who invokes (and consecrates) in this way is held as going to heaven.

---

1. ṚV. Kh. 5.87.7a.
2. TB.3.4.1.16.
3. ṚV. Kh. 5.87.9a.
4. ṚV. Kh.5.87.10a.
5. Could not be identified.
6. Cf. ṚV. Kh. 8.87.3a, 14a.
7. ṚV. Kh. 5.87.2a, 15a.
8. Not found.
9. Could not be identified.
10. ṚV. Kh. 5.87.1.

# CHAPTER SIXTYTHREE

*Mode of installation of other gods and goddesses, the Sudarśana disc and the writing of books and their installations*

*The god said* :

1. The installation of the (images of) Garuḍa (vehicle of Viṣṇu) Brahman, Nṛhari (man-lion form of Viṣṇu) and of the (*sudarśana*) disc should be done in the same way as that of Viṣṇu with their respective *mantras*. Listen to me.

2. O *Sudarśana* ! The great disc that is tranquil ! Dreadful to the wicked ! Kill kill, pierce pierce, cut through and cut through.

3. Devour devour the incantations of others. Eat up, eat up the evil spirits. Frighten frighten, *hum phaṭ*, salutation to *sudarśana*. Having worshipped the disc with this *mantra* one destroys the enemies in the battle.

*Om kṣaum Narasimha* (man-lion) ! of fierce form ! burn, burn, blaze up, blaze up, *svāhā*. *Om kṣaum* salutations to lord *Narasimha* ! Effulgent like crores of radiant suns ! One armed with mace, claws and teeth ! One who manifests with a sound similar to the trumpet while the dreadful and dishevelled manes wildly dance in the storm and one who has agitated the ocean ! One who rescues from all incantations ! O Lord *Narasimha* (you) come ! Manifest with the divine truth as the universal subjective and objective ! Open thy mouth ! Attack ! Roar and release your lion-like voice ! Cut through ! Drive away ! Pierce into all sorts of incantations ! Kill, cut, heap together, dislodge, cut open, break up, cause to be burst ! A multitude of cluster of flames ! Destroy all nether regions with your disc (showering) flames and thunderbolts in all directions ! Besiege the nether regions with your arrows of thunderbolt discharging endless fire ! Pull out the hearts of all demons residing in the nether worlds ! Burn quickly ! Cook ! Destroy ! Dry up ! Hack them to pieces till they have not been subject to my control ! *Phaṭ* to the nether worlds ! *Phaṭ* to the demons ! *Phaṭ* to all kinds of incantations ! O Lord of the form of Narasimha ! Protect me from all doubts ! Protect me from all calamities and all incantations ! O Viṣṇu ! *Hum Phaṭ* ! Salutations to you ! This is the spell of Narasiṁha representing Hari (Viṣṇu) which grants all desires.

4. The captivator of the three worlds (*trailokyamohana*) (the image of the lord) should be installed with the *mantras* known as *trailokyamohana* (captivating the three worlds) (described above). (The image) should be made to have two or four arms, holding the mace in the right hand and conferring benediction.

5. The disc should be placed in the upper left arm and the (conch-shell) *pāñcajanya* on the lower (arm). (The two right hands) should be provided with *śri* (riches) and *puṣṭi* (nourishment) along with strength and welfare.

6. The images of Viṣṇu, Vāmana (dwarf form of Viṣṇu), Vaikuṇṭha, Hayāsya (horse-faced form of Viṣṇu) and Aniruddha should be installed in a shed or house or edifice.

7-9. (The images of) manifestations (of Viṣṇu) (such as) the fish etc. should be installed in waters. (The images of) Saṅkarṣaṇa, Viśvarūpa, *liṅga*, the form of Rudra, hermaphrodite form (of Śiva) (Ardhanārīśvara), Hari (Viṣṇu), Śaṅkara, Śiva, the divine mothers, Bhairava, Sūrya, the planets, Vināyaka, Gaurī (consort of Śiva) worshipped by Indra and others, Bala and Abala (should also be installed similarly).I shall describe the (mode of) consecration of books and the mode of writing them.

10. Having worshipped the manuscript and the written book on a seat made of *kuśa* grass placed on a *svastika* figure, the preceptor should worship the spell and Lord Hari (Viṣṇu).

11-12. The *yajamāna* (the person at whose instance a rite is performed) should face the east and contemplate the spiritual guide, the spell, lord Hari, the copyist and (the goddess) Padminī after having written five verses on a silver plate with golden pen and *devanāgari* letters. The brahmins should be fed according to one's capacity and fees should be paid as much as one could give.

13. After having worshipped the preceptor, the spell and Lord Hari, one should write the *purāṇas* etc. as before in a figure in an auspicious seat in the north-east.

14. Having seen the book in the mirror in the pitcher it should be consecrated as (described) earlier. After opening up the eyes one should place it in the bed.

15. The *puruṣasūkta*[1] and the Vedas etc. should be (mentally) located in the book. After having infused life to it, it should be worshipped and the porridge offered.

16. Having fed the preceptor and given the fees, the twice-borns should be fed. The book should be carried by men in a car, or on the elephant.

17. The book should be established and worshipped (on its return) in a house or temple. That which is wrapped up in a cloth should be worshipped at the commencement and end of reading.

18. Having resolved to have universal peace a chapter of the book should be read out. The *yajamāna* and others should be sprinkled with water from the pitcher.

19. The merit of presenting a book to the twice-born is unlimited. Three things (are said to be) gifts par excellence. (They are) cows, land and knowledge.

20-21. O sinless one ! the merits of imparting knowledge (is great). One who presents a bundle of written leaves, remains and enjoys in the region of Viṣṇu for so many years as the number of leaves and letters (in the manuscript). One who gives away *pañcarātra*[2], *purāṇas*, *bhārata* (as gift) elevates twentyone generations of his family and gets merged in the supreme being.

## CHAPTER SIXTYFOUR

### *Mode of consecration of tanks and ponds*

*The Lord said* :

1. I shall describe the (mode of) consecration of wells, tanks and ponds. Listen ! Lord Hari (Viṣṇu) as Soma and excellent Varuṇa remains in the form of water.

2. The universe is permeated by fire and water. Viṣṇu in the form of water is its cause. The image of Lord Varuṇa (the presiding deity of waters) should be made of gold, silver or gems.

1. ṚV.10.90.
2. The religious code book of the *Vaiṣṇavas*.

3. (The image should have) two hands, the right conferring refuge and the left should hold the snake-noose and as seated on the *haṁsa* along with the rivers and serpents.

4. There should be an altar at the centre of sacrificial shed having a fire-pit. There should be an arch. A pitcher made of stone for Lord Varuṇa should be placed.

5. Pitchers (should be placed) at the entrance to the fire receptacle which may be of a semi-circular shape or a *svastika* of auspicious nature. Having done the *agnyādhāna* (rite) in the pit for water the final oblation should be done.

6. (The image of) Varuṇa should be touched in the bathing seat with (the *mantra*) *ye te śate*[1]. It should then be anointed with ghee by the priest with (the recitation of) the principal *mantra*.

7. Having washed the eight pitchers with pure water with (the recitation of) *śaṁ no devī*[2] they should be consecrated. Sea water (should be kept) in the eastern pitcher.

8-9. Having kept the Ganges water in the (pitcher on the) south-east, rain water in the (pitcher on the) south, water from waterfalls in the (pitcher on the south-west, river water in the west, water from a masculine river in the north-west, spring water in the north, waters from sacred places (should be kept) in the north-east. In the absence of all the above, river water (should be poured into these pitchers) with the chanting of *yāsāṁ rājā*[3].

10. After having cleansed and anointed the eyes with the three sweet things (honey, sugar and clarified butter) with (the *mantra*) *durmitriya*[4], they should be opened with *Citram*[5] and *taccakṣuḥ*[6].

11. Having invoked lustre in them the priest should be offered a golden cow. (The image of) Varuṇa should be consecrated with the (waters of the) pitcher on the east with (the recitation of) *samudrajyeṣṭhā*.[7]

---

1. Kāt. Śr. Sū. 25.1.11a.
2. YV. 10.9.4a.
3. not identified.
4. VS.6.22 and T.S. 1-4-45-2.
5. ṚV.1.115.1a.
6. ṚV 7.66-16a.
7. ṚV. 7.49.1a.

12-13. The waters of the Ganges should be poured with (the *mantra*) *samudraṁ gaccha*[1], rain waters with *somo dhenum*[2], water from waterfalls with *devirāpa*[3], the water of the masculine rivers with *pañca nadyaḥ*[4], the spring water with *udbhid*[5], the waters from sacred places with *pāvamāni*[6], the *pañcagavya* (the five things from a cow) with *āpo hi ṣṭhā*[7] and from the golden (pitcher) with *hiraṇyavarṇām*[8].

14. (The image should be bathed) with rain water with *āpo asmā*[9], with well waters with the *vyāhṛtis* (*bhuḥ*, *bhuvaḥ*, *suvaḥ*). (Image of) Varuṇa should be consecrated with the waters of the tank with *varuṇādbhiḥ*[10].

15. Waters from the hills (should be poured) with (the *mantra*) *āpo devi*[11] and then with the waters from eightyone pitchers. Then (the image) should be bathed with *varuṇasya*[12] and waters for sipping (should be given) with *tvanno varuṇa*[13].

16-17. The *madhuparka*[14] should be given) with the *vyāhṛtis*,[15] clothes with *bṛhaspate*[16], *pavitra* with *varuṇa*[17], the upper garment with *praṇava* (*Om*).

Flowers etc. chowriee, mirror, umbrella, fan and banner should be offered to (the image of) Varuṇa with (the *mantra*) *yadvāruṇya*[18].

18. The image should be raised up with the principal *mantra* (saying) 'Rise up' and the preliminary consecration is made that night. The presence of divinity is accomplished by *varuṇaṁ ca*[19]. It should be worshipped with *yadvāruṇya*.[20]

---

1. ṚV Kh. 5-49-2.
2. ṚV.1.91-20a.
3. MS. 1.1.11.
4. VS. 34-11a.
5. Could not be identified.
6. Designation of the hymn *svādiṣṭhayā madiṣṭhayā* RV.9.1.1.
7. ṚV.10.9.1.a
8. ṚV Kh. 5-87-1a.
9. ṚV. 10.17-10a.
10. Could not be found.
11. TS. 1-3.8-2.
12. One of the many hymns beginning so. See Bloomfield, Vedic Concordance *C.* 106.
13. Cf. ṚV. 10.147.5a.
14. Curd, clarified butter, water, honey, sugar.
15. Cf. ṚV. 2. 23.15a.
16. Cf. ṚV.9. 83-1a.
17. Could not be identified.
18. Could not be identified.
19. ṚV.1.2.7b.
20. Could not be identified.

19-20. Life should be infused into the image with the principal *mantra* and should again be worshipped with perfume etc. Having worshipped it well in the shed as before after having offered twigs etc. into the fire pits with (the recitation of the *praṇava*) the first word of the *Vedas*, four cows should be milched in the four directions. Then gruel of barley should be prepared and offered to the fire.

21. The invocation should be performed with the *vyāhṛtis*, *gāyatri* and the principal *mantra*. Oblation should be done with the *mantra sūryāya prajāpataye dyauḥ svāhā cāntarikṣakaḥ*.

22. (Ceremony is to be performed) for the earth, Dehadhṛti, Svadhṛti, Rati, Ugra, Bhīma, Raudraka.

23-24. Viṣṇu, Varuṇa, Dhātṛ, Mahendra the furtherer of riches, Agni, Yama, Nairṛta, Varuṇa, Vāyu, Kubera, Īśa Ananta, Brahman and the lord of waters should be propitiated with oblations reciting *svāhā* and (the *mantras*) *idaṁ viṣṇuḥ*[1] and *tad viprāsa*[2].

25. Having made oblation six times with *somo dhenu*[3], oblation should be made with *imaṁ me*[4]. Again oblation should be done thrice with *āpo hi ṣṭhā*[5] (and once) with *imā rudrā*[6].

26. *Bali* (offering) should be made in the ten directions. The image should be worshipped with perfumes and flowers The image should be lifted and placed in a mystic diagram by a wise man.

27-28. (The image) should be worshipped with perfumes and flowers as well as golden flowers duly. The excellent priest should lay eight raised platforms filled with sand after having made ready the water tanks measuring two feet. Then clarified butter (should be given as oblation) hundred and eight times with (the *mantra*) *varuṇasya*[7].

29. Then the barley gruel should be offered in the fire and purificatory water sprinkled over the image. The rite to bring life into the image should be performed.

---

1. ṚV.I.22.17a.
2. ṚV.I.22.21a.
3. ṚV.I.91.20a.
4. ṚV.I.25.19a.
5. ṚV.10. 9. 1a.
6. ṚV.10.1.114.1a.
7. Could not be identified.

30. Lord Varuṇa should be contemplated as being accompanied by goddess Gaurī and the host of masculine and feminine rivers. Then having worshipped with the *mantra* "*om* salutations to Varuṇa", the act of bringing near should be done.

31. (The image) should be lifted and carried around on the back of elephant etc. and along with the eight auspicious things (a brahmin, cow, fire, gold, clarified butter, sun, water and king). With the recitation of *āpo hi ṣṭhā*[1], it should be immersed in the water of the pitcher into which the three sweet things have been put.

32. The image should be placed in the midst of the tank unseen. (The priest)should bathe and contemplate on Varuṇa, the creation known as the primordial egg.

33. Having purified it with the principal letter (of the *mantra*) of the fire, the ashes should be scattered over the earth. The entire world consists of water. Hence, the lord of waters is contemplated.

34. The sacrificial post of a rectangular, octagonal or circular shape should be placed in the middle of the tank.

35. Having worshipped the symbol of the lord, post made of the tree used for the purpose of sacrifice (should be driven) ten cubits into the ground in the case of (consecration of) a well. At the bottom of the post gold and fruit should be placed.

36. It should be driven into the ground in the middle of water fifteen cubits in the case of a well, twenty (cubits) in the case of a tank (*puṣkariṇī*) and twentyfive cubits in the case of a pond.

37. In the alternative, (the post) should be driven in the centre of the sacrificial bed and with the *mantra yūpavraskā*[2] cloth should be put around. The banner should be put at the top of the post.

38. Having worshipped it with perfumes etc., (the rite for)universal peace should be performed. The spiritual preceptor should be given the fees (in the form of) land, cows, gold and water vessel.

39-40. Fees should be paid to twice-borns. Those who are present should be fed. "From Brahman down to (inanimate

---

1. ṚV.10.9.1a.
2. ṚV.I.162. 6a.

objects like) the pillar all those who seek water may get satisfied with the waters of the tank !" (With the utterance of these words) the water should be given as charity. The five things got from a cow should then be thrown (into the water).

41. With the utterance of (the mantra) *āpo hi ṣṭhā*[1] thrice, the sanctified water got ready by the brahmins and the holy waters of the sacred spots should be sprinkled (into the tank) and herd of kine should be given to brahmins.

42-43. Food and other things should be given to all the people without any restraint. One who consecrates a reservoir of water (acquires) in a single day a merit ten crores times more than one who performs thousands of *aśvamedha* (the horse-sacrifice). Such a person goes to heaven in the (celestial) vehicle and rejoices (there). He never goes to hell.

44. The consecrator can never get any sin as the cattle and other (animals) drink water from it. One attains all merits by the endowment of water (tank) and goes to heaven.

## CHAPTER SIXTYFIVE

### *The building of pavilions in front of the temples*

*The Lord said* :

1. I shall describe the mode of building pavilions (in front of temples) and their maintenance. The *vāstuyāga* (rite performed to please the spirits dwelling in a site) should be performed after having tested the ground (intended for building pavilion).

2. Having constructed pavilion as per one's liking, one should install (the images of) gods according to his wish. (Such buildings) should not be constructed at the junction of four roads or at a deserted place in the village.

3. Such a builder being free from sins and raising his ancestors (to heaven), enjoys in heaven. One should build a seven-storeyed building for Lord Hari (Viṣṇu) in the following way.

---

1. ṚV.10.9.1a.

4. The same rule holds good in the building of other (temples of gods), as in the case of erecting the mansions of kings. The banner should be placed in the east. The edifice should be built as a quadrilateral without (having any walls on) the diagonal lines.

5-7. The building should have three or two chambers or one chamber. The *vyaya*[1] should not be much. Excessive *vyaya* is deemed to be harmful. Excessive *āya*[2] is also harmful. Hence the two should be made equal. (The priest) well-versed in the science of Garga (*vāstuśāstra*), should sum up the hand measures of building and multiply it by eight. It should be multiplied by three and the resultant product should be divided by eight and the remainder is known as *vyaya*.

8. Alternatively, having divided the sum of the hand measures of the building by three and multiplying it by eight the resultant is known as the *dhvaja* (banner) etc.

9. Banner, camel, lion, dog, bull, donkey, elephant and crow are said to be eight *āyas*.

10. It is commended if we have three after leaving the north and east in houses having three storeys. Together with the building on the opposite side there will always be two buildings in the south.

11. One-storeyed building may be had in the south or there may be two one-storeyed buildings in the west. The other kinds of buildings cause fear.

12-13. A four-storeyed building devoid of all defects is always commended. One may build a mansion having one-storey or seven-storeys without the door, platform and moulding. The mansions of the images of gods should be consecrated in the prescribed way for the gods.

14-23. The hall should be consecrated with the ceremonies as described (for the installation of an image). The consecrator should bathe in the herbal waters and becoming pure and alert should feed brahmins with sweets. He should then enter the hall decked with pitchers and arches, with his

---

1-2. One of the formulae for ascertaining the right proportion of measurement.

hand placed on the back of a cow, and after having wished prosperity to the brahmins. The householder should then enter the house after having honoured the astrologers. The following *mantra* of prosperity should be repeated.

"*Om*, O Mother Earth ! related to Vasiṣṭha ! you rejoice with the Vasus (semi-divine beings) and people. Glory be to the daughter of Bhārgava[1] (Śukra the preceptor of demons), the giver of success to her offsprings. The accomplished goddess ! relative of Aṅgiras ! You grant me my heart's desire. O auspicious one ! related to (sage) Kaśyapa ! make my intellect good. Endowed with all herbs ! Surrounded by all gems and herbs ! Shining one ! Joyous one ! related to Vasiṣṭha ! May you amuse here ! Daughter of Prajāpati (Brahman) ! O Goddess ! Handsome in all parts ! Noble-minded ! Beautiful one ! The strict observer of disciplines ! One who is related to Kaśyapa ! May you enjoy in this house ! O Adored by the great preceptors ! Adorned with perfumes and garlands ! Bestower of prosperity ! O Goddess ! Daughter of Bhārgava ! May you amuse in this house ! The primordial element ! The inexplicable one ! Accomplished ! O daughter of sage Aṅgiras ! O Goddess of bricks ! I establish you. You confer on me my desires ! One surrounded by the lords of regions, place and the house ! You be furtherer of men, wealth, elephant, horse and cow.

## CHAPTER SIXTYSIX

### *Mode of consecration of other gods*

*The Lord said* :

1-2. I shall describe the mode of consecration (of images) of all gods—the Ādityas (the suns, twelve in number), Vasus (eight), Rudrāḥ (eleven), Sādhyāḥ, Viśvedevāḥ, Aśvins and the sages etc. It is like (the consecration of the image of) Vāsudeva. I shall describe special features (of ceremonies). The first letter of the name of particular deity should be taken.

1. Denotes Lakṣmī.

3. It should be split into syllables. The longer vowels should be split. The mystical letter (of the deity) is first formed by adding a nasal and the *praṇava*.

4. (The images of) all gods as well as those who had led a disciplined life and had observed austerities and atonements and those who had lived in the monasteries should be worshipped and installed with their respective principal *mantra*.

5. I shall describe the mode of fasting for a month and that which concludes on the twelfth day (of a fortnight). One should place a stone slab and pitchers made of bell metal filled with the articles (described earlier).

6. After having collected the *brahmakūrca* (grass), the worshipper should prepare the gruel made of barley and milk of tawny (coloured) cow with (the *mantra*) *tadviṣṇoḥ*.[1]

7. It should be stirred with the ladle holding it with (the recitation of) *praṇava* (*om*). Having got it ready and bringing it down lord *Viṣṇu* should be worshipped and the offering made.

8. The oblation should be done with the *vyāhṛti* (*bhūḥ, bhuvaḥ, svaḥ*), the vedic *mantras* such as *gāyatrī*[2] (*mantra*), *tadviprāsa*[3], *viśvataścakṣuḥ*[4] and *bhūragnaye*[5].

9. Oblations should be given to Sūrya, Prajāpati (the creator), (the lord of) the ethereal region. Oblation to sky ! Oblations to Brahman ! (Oblations should be given upto) the earth and the great king.

10. Oblations should be done with (the *mantras*) *tasmai, somaṁ ca, rājānamidam*. Having offered the remaining part of the gruel as oblation, *digbali* (offerings to the quarters) should be done with due respect.

11. Having made oblation of one hundred and eight twigs of the *palāśa* (tree) along with clarified butter, oblations should be done eight times with sesamum and water along with the *puruṣasūkta*[6].

---

1. ṚV.1.22.20a.
2. *Om bhūr bhuvassvaḥ tatsaviturvareṇyam bhargo devasya dhīmahi dhiyo vo naḥ pracodayāt.*
3. ṚV.1.22.21a.
4. ṚV.10.81.3a.
5. TA. 10.2.1 or 10.4.1.
6. ṚV.10.90.

12-13. Having offered oblations for Brahman, Viṣṇu, Īśa (Śiva), the attendant gods, the planets and the presiding deities of different worlds, oblations should be offered for the mountains, rivers, and oceans. Sacrificial spoon full of clarified butter should be offered thrice as the final oblation with the (recitation of) *vyāhṛtis* (*bhuḥ*, *bhuvaḥ*, *svaḥ*).

14-15. O Brahman after having sipped the gruel along with the *pañcagavya* (five things got from a cow) with the *vaiṣṇava mantra* and the syllable *vauṣaṭ*, the priest should be paid fees, vessel containing sesamum along with gold, cloth and a cow well-adorned. The wise man should complete the austerity with (the utterance of) "May lord Viṣṇu be pleased !"

16-17. I shall describe in full about another mode of consecration other than that of fasting for a month. The lord of the celestials (Viṣṇu) should be worshipped and the gruel pertaining to Viṣṇu should be prepared out of sesamum, rice, *nivāra* grains (rice growing unsown), *śyāmāka* or barley. After adding clarified butter and lifting it up, oblation should be made with that with the *mantras* relating to that form of the lord.

18. Oblation should be made to Viṣṇu and other gods who are the lords of different months then. *Om* ! oblations for Viṣṇu ! Oblations to lord Viṣṇu, the ornament ! Oblations to Lord Viṣṇu, the *śipiviṣṭa* (pervaded by rays) (an epithet of Viṣṇu) ! *Om* ! oblations to Narasiṁha (man-lion form of Viṣṇu). *Om* ! oblations to Puruṣottama (the foremost) (an epithet of Viṣṇu) ! Twelve twigs of the holy fig tree dipped in the clarified butter should be given as oblation.

19. Twelve oblations (should be made) with the *mantra viṣṇo rarāṭa*[1]. Twelve oblations with the gruel should be made with (the *mantras*) *idam viṣṇu*,[2] *irāvati*[3].

20. Similarly, oblations should be made with clarified butter with (the *mantra*) *tadviprāsa*.[4] Having done the remaining oblation, three concluding oblations should be made.

21. Having repeated the hymn *yuñjate*[5] the gruel should be

---

1. TS. 1.2.13.3.
2. ṚV. I.22.17a.
3. ṚV. 7. 99.3.a.
4. ṚV. 1. 22.21a.
5. ṚV. 5. 81.1a.

partaken. With the *praṇava* (syllable *om*) repeated at the end of the respective name the gruel should be placed in a vessel made of holy fig tree.

22. Then twelve brahmins (representing) the twelve presiding deities of the months should be fed. The priest (would be) the thirteenth. The thirteenth place should be offered to him.

23. Thirteen pitchers containing sweet water along with umbrellas, shoes, clothes, gold and garlands should be given to them for the sake of conclusion of the rite.

24. A path-way should be laid out (for the cattle) saying, "May the cows get pleased ! May they move happily !" Then the sacrificial post should be planted there.

25-26. A water-shed in the pleasure grove, monastery and path-way should be of ten cubits. Having done the oblation etc. in the house duly in the prescribed way, the householder should enter the house according to the earlier injunctions. Offering of food etc. without any restrictions should be made on all these (occasions).

27. Fees should be paid by wise men to the brahmins according to one's capacity. Whoever causes to set up a pleasure grove stays eternally in the garden of Indra.

28. One who builds a monastery goes to heaven and remains in the world of Indra. One who sets up a water-shed (lives) with Lord Varuṇa. By (the construction of) a pathway one remains in the heaven.

29. One who builds a bridge of bricks and who constructs a pathway for cows in the cattle stall and one who observes the austerities in the prescribed way dwells in the region of Viṣṇu. One who performs atonements gets rid of all sins.

30. Having constructed a house (for the god) one dwells in heaven so long as the universe exists. The installation and consecration of Lord Śiva etc., the lords of their edifices (have been described).

## CHAPTER SIXTYSEVEN

### *Renovation of decayed images*

*The Lord said* :

1. I shall describe the process of replacing the old images. The priest should bathe the images with their ornaments on them. The fixed class of images should be put in a room and the extremely time-worn ones should be rejected.

2. A broken or mutilated stone (image) (should be cast aside) and a new one the same as the previous one should be installed (in its place) by the priest after merging the principles according to the process of merging (described earlier).

3. Having made one thousand oblations with the Narasiṁha (*mantra*), the priest should lift that image. The old image made of wood should be put into fire and the one made of stone should be thrown into water.

4. The old image made of a mineral or gem should be carried on a vehicle after covering it with cloth etc. and be discarded in the deep waters of the ocean.

5. It should be thrown into waters accompanied by the notes of music instruments. Fees should be paid to the priest.

6. New images of the same size and made of the same material should be installed on the same day. One accrues great merit by the renovation of wells, tanks and ponds.

## CHAPTER SIXTYEIGHT

### *Mode of taking out a procession and celebration of festivals after fixing the new image* :

*The Lord said* :

1. I shall describe the celebration of festival after the image has been installed. It shall be for a night, or three or five nights.

2-3. Without the festival the installation would become fruitless. The festival for the deity should be celebrated when the sun enters the solstitial or the equinoctial points in the bed-chamber or garden or it may be done in favour of the person at whose instance the ceremony is performed with the sowing of auspicious seeds and the notes of sacred music.

4-5. An earthen vessel, a small water pot or an embankment are suitable for the sowing of seeds. Grains of barley, uncultivated rice, sesamum, green gram, wheat, white mustard, horse-gram, and black gram should be winnowed, washed and sown. Offerings should be made in the east and other directions. Lighted lamps should be carried round the edifice in the night.

6. (Offering should be made) to Indra, Kumuda and other deities and spirits. They visit the place assuming shapes of men.

7. (One who carries such lamps) certainly gets the merit of (doing) *aśvamedha* (horse sacrifice) for every step he places. The priest should submit to the lord (as follows) after his return.

8. "O Lord ! best among the Gods ! you have to be taken in a procession tomorrow. By all means you deserve to permit us O Lord ! to commence the same.

9. Having informed the lord in this way the festivities should be undertaken. The platform should be decorated with young shoots of plants and small water-jar.

10-11. Four pillars (should be erected). The image should be placed in a *svastika* (figure) (drawn) in their midst. Or desired objects should be painted and placed there and the act of making the deity present in the image should be done with the *vaiṣṇava mantra*. (The image) should be anointed with ghee with (the recitation of) the principal (*mantra*). Or the wise man should arrange an incessant flow of ghee over the image the whole night.

12. Having shown the mirror, there should be the waving of light, auspicious singing and instrumental music, fanning, worship, and present of light. The deity should be worshipped with incense and flowers.

13. Turmeric, green-gram, saffron and white powders should be put on the head of image. But when ghee (is placed over the head) it gets the merit of all sacred places for the devotees.

14. Having bathed and worshipped the image that is placed in the car for being taken around, the officers of the king should take it to the river-side accompanied by music, umbrella and other things.

15. A platform should be got ready at a distance of a *yojana* (eight or nine miles) before the river. The image should be brought down from the car and placed on the platform.

16. Gruel should be prepared and sweet gruel should be offered as oblation. The sacred waters (of the sacred spots) should be invoked for their presence with (the recitation of) vedic *mantras* symbolising the waters.

17. The image should again be worshipped with the principal oblations uttering the *mantra āpo hi ṣṭhā*[1]. The image should again be carried to the waters and the *aghamarṣaṇa*[2] hymn repeated.

18. (The priest) should bathe with the assembly of brahmins and then the image should be lifted and placed on the platform. Having worshipped it there that day it should then be taken to the temple. The priest should worship it as in the fire which gets him enjoyment and liberation.

## CHAPTER SIXTYNINE

### *Mode of conducting the bathing festival*

*The Fire (Lord) said* :

1. O Brahman ! Listen ! I shall describe in detail (the mode of conducting) the bathing festival. The pitchers should be placed in a drawn figure in the shed in front of the temple.

2. First of all, God Hari (Viṣṇu) should be contemplated, propitiated and offered oblations before doing anything. One should offer oblations hundred or thousand times along with the final one.

3. The materials for bathing should then be brought and the pitchers also should be placed. The pitchers to the necks of which

1. ṚV.10.9.1a.
2. ṚV.10.190—*ṛtaṁ ca satyaṁ cābhidhāt*

threads have been tied should be made fragrant and they should be held in a circle.

4. A square should be drawn and divided into eleven compartments. The gruel should be placed at the centre, the adjacent parts having been cleaned.

5. The nine angular points commencing with east should be filled with powdered rice etc., and the pitcher should be brought by the wise man after having formulated the *kumbha mudrā*[1].

6. *Darbha* grass should be put on them with the *puṇḍarikākṣa* (an epithet of Viṣṇu) (lotus-eyed) *mantra.* A pitcher filled with water and containing all gems should be placed in the middle.

7. The barley, paddy, sesamum, uncultivated rice, *śyāmāka* (grains), horse gram, green gram and white mustard seeds (should be put) in the eight directions in order.

8-9. A pitcher filled with ghee should be placed in the middle of the eastern side in the midst of nine pitchers. The remaining pitchers should be filled with the decoctions of the (barks of) *palāśa, aśvattha, nyagrodha, bilva, udumbara, śiriṣa, jambū, śami* and *kapittha.* The central pitcher in the nine pitchers in the south-east should be filled with honey.

10. The remaining eight pitchers should be filled with the earth taken from loosening by cow's horn, elephant's tusk, horse hoofs, mountains, Ganges bed, sacred spots, rivers and fields.

11-12. In the nine pitchers on the south, the central one should be filled with sesamum. The other eight pitchers should be filled with *nāraṅga, jambira, kharjūra, nārikela* (coconut), *pūga* (arecanut), pomegranate, *panasa* fruits. In the nine pitchers on the south-west, the central pitcher should be filled with milk.

13-15. (The remaining eight pitchers should be) duly (filled with) saffron (*kuṅkuma*), *nāga, campaka, mālati,* jasmine, *punnāga, karavira,* and *mahotpala* flowers. In the nine pitchers on the west, the central pitcher should contain the coconut water. (The other pitchers should contain) waters of the river, ocean, tank, well, rain water, water from the melted ice, waters of the falls, and of the Ganges. In the nine pitchers on the north-west the central one should have banana fruits.

16. The divine herbs *sahadevi, kumāri, siṁhi, vyāghri, amṛtā,*

1. A posture made with the hands representing a pitcher.

*viṣṇuparṇā*, *śataśivā* and *vacā* should be placed in the other eight pitchers.

17-19. In the east and the northern (directions) among the nine pitchers one should place the central one having curd. The other pitchers should duly be filled with the fragrant substances—cardamom, *tvacā*, *kuṣṭha*, *bālaka*, the two varieties of sandal, the *kastūrikā* creeper and the black agallochum. (In the central pitcher among the nine pitchers on the north east) one should fill waters for purification. In the other pitchers we should have (the materials) *candra*, *tāra*, *śukla*, *girisāra* (iron), *trapu* (tin), camphor, *śirṣa* and gems.

20. They should be anointed with ghee and lifted up and bathed with the principal *mantra* with perfumes and worshipped. Having offered oblations into the fire, the final oblation should be offered.

21. Offering should be made to all spirits. After paying fees to (the priest), (the priest and the brahmins) should be fed after having installed the images of deities, sages and other divinities.

22. Having installed (the image of the god) in this way one should conduct the bathing festival. One who bathes (the image) in one thousand eight pitchers gets all fortune.

23. By bathing at the conclusion of the rite, the bathing festival concludes. The marriage and other festivals of (the goddesses) Gaurī (consort of Śiva), Lakṣmī (consort of Viṣṇu) should be celebrated after the bathing festival.

## CHAPTER SEVENTY

### *Mode of planting trees*

*The Lord said* :

1-2. I shall describe the mode of planting trees conferring enjoyment and emancipation. The trees having been smeared with all the herbs and adorned with fragrant powders should be decorated with flower garlands. Cloth should be put around them. (The rite known as) the perforation of the ear should be done for them with a golden needle.

3-4. Collyrium should be applied with a short stick. Seven kinds of fruits (should be placed) on the platform. The pitchers should be consecrated. The offering should be made for (the gods) Indra and others and the consecration should be done. Oblations to the fire should be done for (the sake of) plants. Remaining in the midst of trees a cow should be let off with the (recitation of) *abhiṣekamantra*.

5-6. Brahmins should bathe the trees as well as the *yajamāna* with the waters of pitchers placed in the platform with (the recitation of) the *ṛk*, *yajus*, *sāma mantras* and also that of *varuṇa* accompanied by auspicious music. The *yajamāna* should adorn (himself) and should present the fees as well as a cow, ornament and cloth.

7. Food should be given along with milk (to brahmins) for four days consecutively. Oblation should be made with sesamum and twigs of *palāśa* (tree). The sacrificial priest should be paid the fees double (the value of what is given to other brahmins).

8. The construction of sheds etc. here should be done as laid down earlier. The consecration of trees and a garden destroys one's sins and gets the highest merit.

9. Listen to the (mode of) installation (of the image) of Sūrya (sun), Gaṇeśa, the goddess (Gaurī) and the attendant deities of Lord Hari as described by Īśa (Śiva) to Skanda (earlier).

## CHAPTER SEVENTYONE

### *Mode of worshipping Gaṇeśa*

*The God said* :

1-2. I shall describe the (mode of) worship of Gaṇa (Gaṇeśa) which removes obstacles and confers the desired objects. (The worship of six kinds should be done as follows): The heart with "oblations to Gaṇeśa", the head with "(oblations) to the one-tusked", the tuft with "(oblations) to the one who has the ear like that of an elephant", the armour with "(oblations) to the elephant-faced", the eye with "(oblations) to the big-bellied," the weapons with "(oblations) to one who has his own tusk in his hands".

3-5. One should worship the *gaṇa*, the preceptor, the sandals, the (divine) energy, Ananta, the *dharma*, and the collection of bones in the lower part of the pedestal, the cover, the petals of the lotus, the lotus and the principal letter, (should be worshipped) in the upper part. (The energies) (are) Jvālinī, Nandā, Sūryeśā, Kāmarūpā, Udayā, Kāmavarttinī, Satyā, and Vighnanāśā. The seat (should be worshipped) with perfumes and earth. (With the following letters the appropriate acts should be performed): the drying with *yam*, the burning with *ram*, the agitating with *lam* and making it to nectar with *vam*. The *gāyatrī-mantra* is : *lambodarāya vidmahe mahodarāya dhīmahi tanno dantiḥ pracodayāt.*[1]

6-7. The following are the names of Gaṇeśa to be worshipped : "Gaṇapati (Lord of *gaṇas*), Gaṇādhipa (chieftain of the *gaṇas*), Gaṇeśa (Lord of *gaṇas*), Gaṇanāyaka (the lord of *gaṇas*), Gaṇakrīḍa (one who sports with the *gaṇas*), Vakratuṇḍa (having a bent trunk), Ekadaṁṣṭra (having one tusk), Mahodara (big-bellied), Gajavaktra (elephant-faced), Lambakukṣi (long-bellied), Vikaṭa (dreadful), Vighnanāśana (destroyer of impediments), Dhūmravarṇa (tawny-coloured) and Mahendra.

## CHAPTER SEVENTY-TWO

### *Mode of bathing and daily worship*

*The God said* :

1. O Skanda ! I shall describe the modes of bathing and worship after the installation everyday. Having bathed one should dig up eight fingers of earth with the sword.

1. May we know the Supreme person. For that, we meditate upon lambodara (long-bellied) and महोदर (big-bellied). May Dantin (one who has the tusk) impel us towards it.

2. The pit should be filled with the earth thus removed and it should be carried to the river bed and placed there. It should then be purified with the weapon.

3-5. The grass should be lifted up with the *śikhā* (tuft) (*mantra*) and divided into three with the armour (*mantra*). Having washed upto the navel and foot with one part of them, the other part should be burnt with the *astra mantra* and sprinkled all over the body. Having pressed the eyes with the hands one should remain immersed in the water for some time after controlling the breath. One should contemplate in the heart, the weapon, radiant like the deadly fire. Having finished the mud bath in this way one should rise up from waters.

6-7. Having worshipped the *astrasandhyā* (the union of weapon), one should bathe according to the injunctions laid down. The sacred waters of the rivers Sarasvatī and others should be drawn into the heart with the (formation of) *aṅkuśa-mudrā* (a formation with the fingers resembling the goad). Having established it (there), one should collect the remaining mud formulating the *saṁhāramudrā* (posture with the fingers indicating destruction) and enter the navel-deep water.

8-9. (The remaining mud) should be made into three parts on the left palm facing the north. One part of it on the south once with the *aṅga mantras*, the next part with the (previous *mantra*) seven times and the one on the north with the *Śiva mantra* ten times and duly thus the parts should be sanctified. After having recited the *mantra* for the weapon ending with *huṁ phaṭ*, the first part (of the earth) should be scattered in all directions.

10. Having the part on the north and reciting the *Śiva-mantra* the waters of Śiva should be accomplished. The part on the south (sanctified with the *aṅga mantra*) should be smeared all over the body from head to foot.

11-12. After having recited the four *aṅgamantras* and covered all the (nine) apertures (in the body) with the recitation of the *sammukhikaraṇa mantra* (*mantra* accomplishing the presence), one should contemplate Lord Śiva or Lord Hari or the Ganges and plunge into the waters. Then the *ṣaḍaṅga mantra* (*mantra* for assigning to the limbs of the body) ending with *vauṣat* should be recited and water poured (over the head).

13-15. One should place water in the pitchers in the east (and other directions) in order to prevent any harm during ablution. Having bathed one should apply sweet perfumes such as emblic myrabolans which are (considered as) royal honour. Having bathed and come out, that water should be made to cease to exist with the *saṁhāriṇi* (mudrā). One should then bathe from head to foot with the ashes duly purified by the *saṁhitā* (vedic) *mantras* or concluding rites with (the recitation) of the *mantra hum phaṭ*.

16-17. Having performed the *mala snāna*, (bathing with mud), the *vidhisnāna* (bathing with the recitation of *mantras*), one should besmear the head, face, heart, and the genital organ with the (*mantras* of gods) Īśa (Īśāna), Tatpuruṣa, Aghora, Guhyaka and Jāta (Sadyojāta) in the three twilights, night, and before and after the commencement of rainy season.

18-19. If a person happens to touch a woman, an eunuch, a man of lower caste, a cat, hare or mouse just after getting up from sleep, or eaten food or drunk water one should do the *āgneyaka* bathing, standing up with uplifted arms, the face having turned towards the east, being cleansed by the shower of sun's rays.

20. The *māhendra* bathing (consists in the recitation of the) *Īśa mantra* and walking seven steps in the midst of herds of cows being besmeared with the dust (arising) from the hoofs.

21. The *pāvana* (purifying) bathing (should be done) with the nine *mantras* or the constituent *mantra* and the pouring of water (should be done) with the *mantras sadyojāta*, etc.

22. The bathing with the *mantra* should be done in this manner in honour of (the gods) Varuṇa, Agni and others with (the recitation) of the principal *mantra* being preceded by the regulation of the breath.

23. The mental bathing which has been universally enjoined should be performed in honour of Lord Viṣṇu, by uttering the mantra sacred to him.

24. O Guha (son of Lord Śiva) ! I shall describe the rules (relating to) the twilight (worship) (to be performed) with different *mantras*. After having had a look one should drink the water, the Brahma and Śaṅkara *tirthas* (from the root of different fingers).

25. (One should pronounce) the different principles consti-

tuting one's self ending with the term *svadhā*, touching firmly the (nine) apertures (in the body). After having done the *sakalīkaraṇa* (accomplishing deed) one should remain composed by (the performance of) regulation of breath.

26. The performer should mentally repeat thrice the *Śivasaṁhitā*. After having sipped water and performing *nyāsa* (assigning gods or *mantras* in different parts of the body, one should meditate upon the goddess *brāhmi* and the *sandhyā* in the morning as follows:

27. (The goddess) having red complexion, has four faces, four arms with hanging garlands in the right arms and a stick and *kamaṇḍalu* (small pitcher) in the left arms and seated in the crossed-leg posture on the swan.

28. The midday twilight should be contemplated as Vaiṣṇavī, white (in complexion), seated with crossed-legs on the Garuḍa, holding conch and disc in the left arm and the mace and *abhaya* (*mudrā*) (hand showing protection) in the right hand.

29. Raudrī should be meditated upon as seated on the lotus and as riding the bull, possessing three eyes, decorated by the moon and holding trident and rosary in the right arm and the protective posture (*abhaya*) and mace in the left arm.

30. The twilight is the witness of deeds of men. The soul (should be known) as following its radiance. The fourth twilight is that of the learned and it is meditated upon in the night.

31. The supreme *sandhyā* is declared as that which remains invisible in the cavities situated at the heart, and the upper end of the nose and which secures the realization of Śiva.

32. The root of the fore-finger (is known to be) the *pitṛtirtha* and that of the little finger as that of Prajāpati. The root of the thumb (is known to be) that of Brahmā, while the forepart of the hand is held sacred for all gods.

33. It is the place of sacred fire on the palm of the left hand, and the *soma* on that of the right hand. All the tips and folds on the fingers (are sacred) for the sages.

34. After having got ready the sacred waters for Śiva with the *mantras* pertaining to Śiva, one should sprinkle that water with the *saṁhitā mantras*.

35. The water sprinkled from the right hand should drip

down through the left hand and the head should be sprinkled (with water) with the (repetition of) *mantras*.

36. The water remaining in the right palm should be carried to the tip of the nose and should be conceived as white in colour and as the embodiment of knowledge. The water should then be drawn through the right nostril and retained.

37. That water should then be ejected into the right palm after having conceived it as black in colour because of the redemption of one's sins. It should be thrown on a stone slab. This is known to be the *aghamarṣaṇa* (redeeming from sin) rite.

38. Then one should repeat the *gāyatri mantra* as many times as possible after having offered the respectful *arghya* consisting, of *kuśa*, flowers and unbroken rice to Śiva with the *mantras* of Śiva ending with (the syllable) *svāhā* (oblation).

39. I shall describe the offering of water oblations to the god. One should utter the mantra *Śivāya svāhā* (oblations to Śiva) and offer water. (The syllable) *svāhā* should be repeated in all cases.

40. (The *nyāsa* should be done as) *hrām*, to the heart; *hrim*, to the head; *hrūm*, to the tuft of hair; *hraim*, to the armour and the weapons, (or in the alternative), the eight gods (can be located) in the heart and other limbs).

41-44. (The water oblations should be performed for the following gods) —*hrām*, to the Vasus, Rudras, Viśve (devas), (to the sages)—*hām* to Bhṛgus, Aṅgirās, Atri; salutation to Vasiṣṭha, Pulastya, Kratu, Bhāradvāja; salutations to Viśvāmitra, to Pracetas; *vaṣaṭ* to Sanaka; *hām vaṣaṭ* to Sananda, *vaṣaṭ* to Sanātana, *vaṣaṭ* to Sanatkumāra; *vaṣaṭ* to Kapila, to Pañcaśikha, (the ceremony being done) with the fingers of the right hand placed at the elbow joint of the left.

45. *Vauṣaṭ* to all spirits. One should (offer water of oblations) to the spirits, gods, and manes with the sacred thread placed on the right shoulder and with the tips of the *kuśa* and sesamum.

46. (Oblation should be offered)to the fire, the conveyor of offerings, to Soma, to Yama, to Aryamā, (the manes), Agnimanes), Agniṣvātta (and) Barhiṣada with the addition of *svadhā* (food).

47. (Oblations should be given) to (the manes) Ājyapa, Soma and to all manes as it would be done for the gods.

*Om, hām* to Īśāna, the *svadhā* (food) should be offered to the (manes) (departed) father and grand-father.

48. (Oblations should be offered) to the great-grand-father and the manes in the form of *preta* (the form of the manes during the period of obsequies after one's death), the fathers, grandfathers, and great grand-fathers.

49-50. Food oblations (should be given) to great-great-grand-fathers, mother side relatives such as the maternal grand-fathers, great-grandfathers, great-great-grandfathers and all manes. Food oblation (should be offered) to all departed paternal relatives, preceptors, to different quarters of heaven, to their lords, to the divine mothers and to demons.

## CHAPTER SEVENTYTHREE

### *Mode of worshipping the Sun*

*The Lord said:*

1. O Skanda ! I shall describe the (mode of) worship of Sun preceded by the assignment (of letters) on the body. After having contemplated as "I am the Sun", one should worship by offering waters (*arghya*).

2-4. It (should be conceived) as filled with red colour with the drop (of water) drawn to the forehead. After having worshipped it and after making the protective covering with the limbs of the sun-god, that water should be sprinkled on the materials of worship and the sun-god should be worshipped (remaining) facing the east. (One should recite) the syllables *om am* (*hṛdayāya* etc. and worship Daṇḍi and Piṅgala (attendants of the sun) respectively at the right and left sides of the entrance. (Salutations should be made to the *gaṇa* saying) *am gaṇāya* on the north-east. The preceptor (should be worshipped) in the south-east and the lofty seat (of the deity) should be worshipped in the middle of the altar.

5. One should worship *vimala*, *sāra*, *parama* and *sukha*, (the rays of the sun), which are to be worshipped in the directions

south-east (and should be conceived as) strong as the lion and of the colours of white, red, yellow and blue.

6-8. One should worship (the essences of the energies of the lord) *rā-diptā* (radiant), *ra-jayā* (victorious), *ru-bhadrā* (auspicious), *re-vibhūti* (prosperity), *rai-vimalā* (pure), *rai-amoghā* (profound), *rau-vidyut* (lightning), in the (quarters) east etc. inside the lotus (shaped diagram). The seat of the sun would be at the centre (established by the syllable) *ram.* One should invoke the sun and worship his form with the six-syllabled (*mantra*) *oṁ haṁ khakholkāya.* One should assign the sun-god after having meditated upon the altar with the folded hands lifted to the forehead.

9. One should invoke the god (with the *mantra*) *hrām hrim sa* and salutations to the sun-god, showing the *mudrā.* One should offer him perfume etc. and show the *bimbamudrā*[1].

10. One should show the *padmamudrā*[2] and the *bilvamudrā*[3] (to the god) in all directions commencing with the south-east. *Om am* salutations to the heart. (Salutations) to sun on the head.

11. *Bhūrbhuvaḥ svaḥ* ! Obeisance to the lord of celestials in the tuft of hair in the south-west, *hum* to the armour in the north-west, *hām* to the eyes at the centre.

12. *Va* ! (salutations) to the weapons in the east etc. Then one should show *mudrās. Dhenumudrā* (fingers folded in the shape of a cow) to the heart etc. The *Goviṣāṇa mudrā*[4] should be shown to the eyes.

13-14. The *trasani* (the dreadful) should be added to the *mantra* of the weapon and obeisance should be made to the planets (as follows)—*som* salutations to the Moon, *bum* salutations to Mercury, *bṛm* to Jupiter, *bham* to Venus, *am* to Mars, *sam* to Saturn, *ram* to Rāhu and *kem* to Ketu (to be done) in the petals (of the lotus) commencing with the east. The perfumes etc. (should be offered) with the *khakholka mantra.*

15. Having recited the principal *mantra,* water of oblation from the water-vessel should be offered to the sun-god. Then

1. Intertwining of fingers representing a form.
2. Intertwining of fingers representing a lotus.
3. Intertwining of fingers in a particular way.
4. Formation of fingers representing the horn of a cow.

the worshipper should sing the glory of the lord, pay obeisance to him with his face turned away and say "Pardon me, (taking leave of thee)".

16-17. One should mentally merge the five component principles in the fundamental one with the syllable *phaṭ*. The sun-god should be conceived as identical with lord Śiva in the lotus of the heart. One should offer light to the lord as a garland made of the solar rays. One gets everything by thus worshipping and contemplating the sun-god or by oblation unto fire in his honour.

## CHAPTER SEVENTYFOUR

### *Mode of worshipping Śiva*

*The Lord said* :

1. I shall describe the (mode of) worshipping Śiva. After having sipped water, and repeated the syllable *Om*, one should wash the entrance of the temple with water (consecrated by the) *mantra* of the weapon and worship the guardian deities of the door-ways and of the oblations etc.

2-3. One should worship goddess Sarasvatī (consort of Lord Brahmā), Lakṣmī (consort of Lord Viṣṇu) and Gaṇa at the threshold, Nandin (attendant of Lord Śiva) and the Ganges on the right and Mahākāla (form of Śiva) and the Yamunā (river) on the left imagining himself as having divine sight, and after having driven the spirits and impediments present in the sky by throwing a consecrated flower.

4. One should kick the earth thrice with the right heels and enter the place of worship after leaping across the threshold holding the left door frame.

5. Having entered (the temple) by placing the right foot (first) and placing the weapons at the threshold, one should worship at its centre (repeating the following): *om*, *hām*, (obeisance) to Brahmā, the presiding deity of the dwelling place.

6. Then he should go to the river Ganges silently carrying

pure golden pitchers by means of searching instruments, after having obtained permission from Śiva.

7. One should fill them with waters of the river filtered with the cloth after the repetition of *gāyatri* or the *hṛdayamantra*, and purifying one's body.

8. The materials for worship such as the perfumes, unbroken rice and flowers etc. should be placed in front of the place and the purification of five material components (of the earth) should be done.

9. Having placed (these materials) on the right side of the deity with a pleasing face and having lifted these showing *saṁhāra mudrā* (posture of the fingers representing destruction), one should place them on the head with (the repetition of) the *mantra*.

10-11. One who is desirous of enjoying the fruits of action should meditate upon his soul in the twelve-petalled lotus in the heart by means of showing *pāṇikacchapikā* (a particular way of showing the fingers)[1]. As an alternative one should purify the five elements by meditating upon the apertures in the body from the toes of the feet upwards both inside and outside.

12. One who meditates should control his breath and meditate on the energy which pervades the region of the heart, in the letter *hum* which resembles the fire and which is situated at the centre of the aperture.

13. The breath should then be let out and the fiery image should be led through the heart, neck, palate, the intervening space between the two eye-brows and the seat of the soul in the head (*brahmarandhra*), with the ending (syllable) *phaṭ*.

14. Having broken the knots, the life syllable *hum* should be located on the head and the consciousness should be reflected back in the heart by means of the *pūraka* (filling with air drawn through the nostril).

15. Having placed (the syllable) *hum* on the tuft, one should meditate upon the absolute soul of the form of a speck. Having withheld the breath at a single stretch, one should unite the consciousness with Śambhu (Śiva).

16. After having merged himself with Śiva, by means of drawing his consciousness with the aid of *bijamantras* and the

---

1. Representing the tortoise.

*recaka* (exhalation of the breath), (the worshipper) should purify by carrying in the reverse order the luminous point (in the brain) to the point in (the nerve-complex).

17. One should merge the earth, wind, water, fire and sky, one into the other without any deviation in the order. You hear about it now!

18. The principle of earth is hard, of yellowish colour and bears the mark of thunderbolt. Then its destruction is wrought by the subtle *mantra* of the soul (namely) *haum*.

19. The entire body from foot to head should be contemplated as a four-sided figure, and the principle of wind should be meditated therein by five stretches of retention of breath.

20. This principle which has been established with the principal syllable *hrim* should be contemplated as of half-crescent-shaped in a liquid state, white in colour, beautiful and impressed with (the figure of) the lotus.

21. The reverential principle of fire which is causeless and which is the end of men, should be purified by four stretches of retention of breath along with the *Rāma mantra*.

22. The orb of fire should be conceived as three-sided, red (in colour), marked with (the sign of) *svastika* and as the form of knowledge and endowed with the principal syllable *hūm*.

23. The principle of water should be purified by means of three stretches of awful minuteness. The orb of wind (principle) (should be conceived) as marked with six dots.

24. It should be meditated as composed of tranquility, black in colour and endowed with the principal syllable of *hrim* (and purified) by two stretches (of retention of breath). The principle of earth should be purified.

25. (It should be contemplated) as filled in with ether, as of the form of the speck of ether, uniformly circular, spotless like the pure crystal and adorned by the energy of *bindu*.

26. After having contemplated on the form of the digit that is beyond tranquility by means of the (*mantra*) *haum* ending with *phaṭ*, one should contemplate the pure (thing) by one stretch (of retention of breath).

27. One should then permeate the lotus or circles such as *ādhāra* (base), *ananta* (endless), *dharma* (righteousness) and *jñāna* (knowledge) with the shower of ambrosia with the *principal mantra*.

28. After having contemplated this seat of the heart, one should then invoke the form of essence of Śiva placed inside that (lotus) with twelve petals.

29. Then that form should be permeated everywhere with the divine ambrosia with the *mantra* of the energy ending with *vauṣaṭ* and the *sakalikaraṇa* (accomplishing) rite should be performed.

30. The *sakalikaraṇa* is that by which the *mantras* for the heart etc. are placed in the different parts of the body such as the heart, arms, and the little fingers of the hand.

31. Having protected the enclosure with the weapon and the outer place with its *mantra* the *mahāmudrā* consisting of the energy should be shown below and above that.

32-33. One should worship Śiva in the lotus in the heart from head to foot with the retention of breath and with the flowers of one's own feeling. One should then offer the clarified butter of ambrosia to the fire of Śiva in the sacred pit of the navel with the *mantras* of Śiva. One should contemplate the white figure of the form of *bindu* on the forehead.

34. One of the vessels among the golden pitchers, should be purified by water of nectar got from the speck and by unbroken rice.

35. Having filled the vessel with the six constituents and after having worshipped it, it should be consecrated. After having protected it with the *mantra hā* one should cover it with the armour.

36. After having made ready the water of offering, one should sprinkle the eight constituents (with water) by (showing) the *dhenumudrā* (a particular form of intertwining the fingers representing the cow). One should then sprinkle one's own self on the head with the particles of that water.

37. One should sprinkle water of the weapon on the materials of worship kept there. One should then encircle them with the armour of *piṇḍa* with the *hṛt* (*mantra*).

38-39. After having shown the *amṛtā mudrā* (formation with fingers denoting non-decay) and putting flower on its seat and a mark on the forehead consecrated by the principal *mantra* (of the god) a bold man should remain perfectly silent at the time of bathing, worship of the god, (offering) oblation unto fire, eating, practising *yoga* and repetition of necessary (*mantras*).

40. The *mantra* should be purified by pronouncing the *nāda* (*om*) at the end. That purified *mantra* should then be used in the worship along with the *gāyatri* (*mantra*) and the general water of oblation should be offered.

41. After having repeated the *brahmapañcaka*[1], (the worshipper) should collect the garland from the *liṅga* and offer it to Caṇḍa in the north-eastern direction.

42. The purification of the *liṅga* consists in the washing of the pedestal and the *liṅga* with the water (consecrated) by the *mantra* of weapon and *hṛdmantra* and sprinkle with the water (for washing) from the vessel of *arghya*.

43. All the celestials should be worshipped for the purification of the self, the materials, the *mantra* and the *liṅga*. *Hām*, salutations to God *Gaṇapati* in the north-western direction. One should pay obeisance to the preceptor in the north-east.

44-45. One should worship the goddess of the seat (of the god) in the *kūrmaśilā* (the tortoise form on the stone) as possessing complexion of the tender shoots and the seat of Śiva known as ananta (endless) should be worshipped as seated on the *brahmaśilā* along with the attendants of the god such as Vicitrakeśa, Kṛta and Tretā who form the seat and shoes as they were of divinity.

46. Then the worshipper should worship righteousness, knowledge, detachment and prosperity, towards the south-east as possessing the hues of camphor, saffron, gold and collyrium respectively.

47-48. At the centre of the lotus-shaped diagram and in its petals in the east etc. one should worship the energy goddesses—Vāmā, Jyeṣṭhā, Raudrī, Kālī, Kālavikariṇī, Balavikaraṇī and Balapramathanī in order as holding the chowries and as conferring boons and offering protection.

49. One should worship (the goddesses)—*Hām*, (salutations) to Sarvabhūtadamanī, (salutations) to Manonmanī, to Kṣiti, to Śuddhavidyā at the extremities of the petals (of the lotus diagram) as also the seat as spread over the component parts of the universe.

50-51. The lord of white complexion, possessing five faces and ten arms, all-pervasive, bearing the crescent moon and

---

1. The five *mantras* of the five brahman forms of Śiva.

carrying weapons—spear, sword, lance, and staff in the right hands and a drum, citron, blue lotus, a string and a waterlily in the left hands should be located on the lion-seat.

52-54. The image of Śiva possessing thirty-two characteristics (should be installed) at the centre. *Hām, ham, hām* (salutations) to the image of Śiva. After having meditated upon the self-luminant Śiva, the *mantra* should be led to the spot sacred to Śiva after leaving below the place sacred to Brahmā. Then (the worshipper) having meditated upon that Supreme form of Śiva, effulgent with the splendour of the moon, as a luminous point at the middle of the forehead and being invested with the six constituents, with flowers in folded palms, should deposit (those flowers) on the form of (Goddess) Lakṣmī.

55-57. *Om, hām, haum* salutations to Śiva. (The deity) should be invoked with the invoking *hṛd* (*mantra*). Having established Śiva with the *sthāpani* (*mudrā*)[1], and placed near (that ) should be checked with Niṣṭhurā and Kālakāntī concluding with *phaṭ*. After having removed obstructions by sending them away and making obeisance by (showing) the *liṅga-mudrā*, it should be covered with the *hṛd* (*mantra*). The invocation should follow it. Then standing in front of the image he should repeat. "Let you be located and firmly established. O lord ! I am in your presence."

58. The (rite of) *avaguṇṭhana* signifies the presence and super vision of the God and the exhibition of one's devotion (to the God) from the commencement to the end of the act.

59. After having done the accomplishing act with the six *mantras*, the (rite of) *amṛtikaraṇa* should be performed by mentioning different parts of the body along with the body.

60-61. The worshipper should permeate his heart with the energy of consciousness of Śambhu (Śiva). Similarly, (he should contemplate) the tuft of hair of Śiva as formed of the eightfold glories. The worshipper should contemplate the invincible energy of God as forming his armour, the unbearable prowess of God which removes all impediments (and the words) salutations, *svadhā*, *svāhā* and *vauṣaṭ* (should be appended) in order.

62-65. The water for washing the feet should be offered

1. Formation with the fingers denoting firm establishment.

preceded by the recitation of the *hṛd* (*mantra*). The water (should be offered) at the lotus feet and the water for the rinsing of the mouth at the face of the image, the respectful offering at the head of the lord along with the *dūrvā* (grass), flowers and unbroken rice. Having purified the supreme lord with the ten purifications thus, one should worship with the five kinds of services such as the flowers etc. as laid down (in the code books). Having sprinkled and rubbed (the image) with salt, mustard seed etc., it should be slowly bathed with drops of water, flowers, perfumes, milk, curd, ghee, honey and sugar successively.

66. The defects in the above materials should be rectified by worshipping with materials along with the recitation of Īśa *mantras*. Lord Śiva should be bathed with water and fragrance with the principal *mantra*.

67-68. Having applied the paste of barley, it should be bathed copiously with cold water and also with fragrant water according to one's ability. Having wiped it dry with a clean cloth, the preliminary offering of water should be given. The hand should not be moved over the head (of the image). The *liṅga* should never be left without any flower on its head.

69. Having smeared it with sandal etc. and worshipped with flowers with the *mantras* of Śiva, the vessel for holding the perfumes should be consecrated with the weapons (*mantra*) and worshipped with the *mantras* of Śiva.

70. The bell consecrated by the weapon (*mantra*) should be taken and the incense should be offered. The water for rinsing should be given then (with the repetition of) *svadhā* at the end and with the *hṛd mantra*.

71. Having shown light for the idol in the night, then water for rinsing should be offered. After having made obeisance to god and taking his permission, eatables and other articles of enjoyment should be offered.

72. The heart should be worshipped in the south-east, the moon on the north-east, the golden-coloured Śiva together with the tuft and blood on the south-west, Kṛṣṇa and armour on the north-west.

73. These gods having four faces and four arms should be worshipped in the petals in the east etc. along with the divine weapon similar to thunder and fierce teeth.

74. *Haum* salutations to Śiva at the base, *Om hām hūm him hom* in the head, *hṛm* to the tuft, *haim* to the armour, *haḥ* to the weapons and to one with the attendants.

75-76. Waters for washing the feet, for rinsing the mouth and respectful offering, perfumes, flowers, incense, lamp, food offerings and water for rinsing again, should be given to lord Śiva. Intertwined blades of *kuśa* and unbroken rice should be placed on the head (of the image) of the lord. Perfumes, betel, piece of cloth for wiping the face and a mirror (should also be offered to the deity).

77-78. After having repeated the principal (*mantra*) eight hundred times, the sword of the lord covered by the sheath, protected by the *kuśa* and flowers and consecrated by *hṛd* (*mantra*) along with the unbroken rice and with the *udbhava mudrā* (a formation made with the fingers indicating generation). O most mysterious ! Accept this repetition (of *mantra*) for our welfare.

79-81. "May there be success for me by this by your presence here". Having recited this verse at first, the worshipper should offer to Śambhu (Śiva) the waters of respect with the right hand with (the repetition of) the principal *mantra*. Whatever good or bad that I may do O lord ! let it be cast off from me who am in the region of Śiva. *Hūm kṣaḥ* O Śaṅkara, Śiva is the giver, Śiva is the enjoyer, Śiva is all this universe.

82. Śiva is victorious everywhere. I am identical with Śiva. After having repeated these two verses, the *japa* should be dedicated to the lord.

83. One-tenth (should be dedicated) to the limbs of Śiva. Having offered the waters of respect, one should adore (the deity). After circumambulating (the deity), one should bow to the eight-formed (representing the five elements, sun, moon and yajamāna) deity by prostrating (the eight limbs touching the ground). After salutation (the deity) should be worshipped in a picture or in the fire by meditation etc.

## CHAPTER SEVENTY-FIVE

### *Mode of installation of the fire*

*The God said* :

1. (The worshipper) should enter another room unseen with the vessel containing water for offering in his hand and should look to the arrangements of the materials essential in the performance of a sacrifice, as it were, with a divine eyesight.

2. He should look at the sacrificial pit with his face turned towards the north. The sprinkling and beating the water with the *kuśa* should be done by (repeating) the *mantra* of the weapon and the consecration should be done with the *mantra* of the armour.

3. The digging out (a piece of earth), filling and levelling with the sword should be done with (the *mantra* of) the armour and bathing and division into parts (should be done) with the *mantra* of the arrow.

4. The (rites of) cleansing, anointing, fixing the crescent form, investiture of the sacred thread and worship (should be done) always by the *mantra* of the armour.

5. Three lines should be drawn in the north and one below them (should be drawn) so as to face the east. Whatever defects in them may be made good by touching them with the *kuśa* and the *astramantra* of Śiva.

6. A quadrilateral figure should be drawn with the *kuśa* by the *mantras* of *vajrikaraṇa* (establishing firmly) and *hṛd*. The vessel for the rosaries should be laid with (the *mantra* of) the armour. The seat should be laid with the *hṛd mantra*.

7-8. The Goddess of speech along with the God should be invoked therein and worshipped. The consecrated fire brought from a holy place and placed in a pure receptacle, after leaving aside its parts presided over by the demons and purified by the divine look etc., the three fires *audārya*, *aindava* and *bhauta* should be made into one.

9-10. *Om hūm* (salutations) to god of fire. (The deity) should be established with the principal *mantra* of the fire. The fire which has been invoked with the vedic hymns and made immortal by showing the *dhenumudrā* (formation with the fingers representing a cow), and protected by *mantras* of weapons should be covered by the armour. It should be worshipped by waving over the pit thrice and circumambulation.

11. Having meditated upon (the fire) as an element of Lord Śiva, (the worshipper) should contemplate it as lying dormant in the womb of Goddess of speech and cast by the Lord of speech.

12. The worshipper should have his knees resting on the ground and put the fire in his front with the *hṛd mantra*. Then the seeds of fire in the vicinity should be gathered at the centre.

13. The collection of clothes, purification and offering of water for rinsing the mouth (should be done) with the *hṛd* (*mantra*). Having worshipped the dormant fire, it should be protected by (the recitation of) the *mantra* of the shaft.

14. The embryo fire should be contemplated as tied around the wrist of the goddess as a bracelet. The fire should be worshipped with the *sadyojāta* (*mantra*) for the impregnation.

15. Three oblations to the fire should then be offered with (*hṛdayamantra*. For the *puṁsavana* (rite) (for the determination of the sex of the foetus) (generally performed) in the third month it should be worshipped on the left side.

16. Three oblations containing drops of water should be offered with the head. The *simantonnayana* (rite) (parting of the hair on the head) (performed) in the sixth month should be done after having worshipped the fire.

17. Three oblations should be offered into the fire, after having determined the formation of its face and body by one who wants to restore or open up the face.

18. As before the *jātakarma* (the purificatory rite on the birth of a child) and *ṛtukarma* (the rite after the first menses) (usually performed) in the tenth month should be performed by kindling the fire with *darbha* etc. (Mental) bathing (should be done) to remove the impurities of the pregnancy.

19. After having mentally contemplated the golden bracelet of the goddess one should worship with the *hṛd* (*mantra*). He should sprinkle with water consecrated by the *mantra* of the weapon for the immediate removal of impurities after the birth of a child.

20. The pitcher outside the receptacle for the sacred fire should be touched with the weapon (*mantra*) and (water) should be sprinkled over with the (*mantra*) of the armour. The ends of

the *kuśa* which form the boundary (of the sacrificial pit) and placed on the north and east (should be washed with water) with (the *mantra* of) the weapon.

21. The periphery of a circle around (the fire) should be determined with the *kuśa*, previously consecrated with the weapon and *hṛd mantra* and then the cushions inscribed within it should be spread out by (reciting) the weapon *mantra.*

22. Five sacrificial sticks dipped in clarified butter should be offered into the fire with the repetition of the principal *mantra.* Brahmā, Śaṅkara, Viṣṇu and Ananta should be worshipped with the *hṛd* (*mantra*).

23. The gods located in the periphery (of that circle) should be worshipped in turn with unbroken rice. The gods Indra to Īśāna who are directly facing the fire and are having their places inside the circle should be worshipped in their own regions with the *hṛd* (*mantra*) "Protect this child (fire) by removing all obstacles, that might befall it."

24-28. One should then make them hear this command of Śiva. He should then take the sacrificial spoon and the ladle, heat them on the fire and touch them with the base, middle and tips of the *darbha* with face downwards. In the place touched by the *kuśa* the three principles relating to the soul, knowledge and Śiva should be located duly with the sounds *hām, hrim, hūm* and *sam.* Having located the goddess in the sacrificial spoon and Śambhu (Śiva) in the sacrificial ladle with the *hṛdaya mantra,* their necks being girdled with three strings (of thread) and worshipped with flowers etc., *kuśas* should be placed on them and they should be placed on the right side.

29-32. Having gathered the clarified butter of the cow that has been purified by looking at it and after having contemplated one's own Brahma form and carrying that clarified butter, one should wave it over the pit and move it round and round in the south-east. Again having contemplated the Viṣṇu form, one should hold the clarified butter and carry it towards the north-east, it should be offered to Viṣṇu (into the fire) with the tips of the *kuśa* and with the *mantra* of the head ending with *svāhā.* Similarly, one should conceive the form of Rudra (Śiva) as a point in one's own navel and meditate. One should sprinkle water over that with two *kuśas* of the length of a span and held with the ring finger and thumb.

33. Water should be sprinkled over the fire in front (of the worshipper) (with the two *kuśas*) held (as above) accompanied by the *mantra* of the weapon. Similarly, the worshipper should again sprinkle water (over the fire) in front of him with the *hṛd* (*mantra*).

34. The burnt ashes of *darbha* collected with the *hṛd* (*mantra*) should be purified by striking with the implements and with the other lighted *darbha* it should be taken out and lighted.

35-36. The *darbha* burnt by the *mantra* of the weapon should again be thrown into the fire. Having put the knotted *darbha* of the length of a span in the clarified butter, one should contemplate the two for nights, the three arteries *iḍā* etc. in the clarified butter and offer the clarified butter divided into three parts as oblation unto fire with the sacrificial ladle in order with (the syllable) *sva* and *hā*. The remaining part of the clarified butter should also be offered to the fire successively.

37. *Oṁ hām* oblation to god Agni. *Oṁ hām* oblation to god Soma. *Oṁ hām* oblation to the gods Agni and Soma. (The above oblations should be offered into the fire) for the purpose of opening (as it were) the three eyes of the fire god in his face.

38. The fourth oblation should be offered with the sacrificial ladle filled with clarified butter. *Oṁ hām* oblation to fire-god for the offering of a right sacrifice. After having consecrated in the six parts of one's body, (the fire god) should be invoked with the *dhenumudrā* (posture with the fingers representing a cow).

39. Having covered it with the armour, the clarified butter should be protected by the *mantra* of the shaft. The clarified butter should be purified by sprinkling water and offering a drop of it into the fire along with the *hṛd* (*mantra*).

40. The rites of uniting the mouths of the fire should be performed as follows. *Oṁ hām* oblations to Sadyojāta. *Om hām* oblations to Vāmadeva. *Oṁ hām* oblations to Aghora. *Om hām* oblations to Tatpuruṣa. *Oṁ kām* oblations to *Īśāna*. Thus with oblations to one by one, one should do the union of the (different) faces.

41-42. *Oṁ hām* oblations to Sadyojāta and Vāmadeva. *Oṁ hām* oblations to Vāmadeva and Aghora. *Oṁ hām* oblations to Aghora and Tatpuruṣa. *Oṁ hām* oblations to Tatpuruṣa and Īśāna. Thus the union is done in order with the recitation of these *mantras*. With the flow of ghee from the sacrificial ladle taking it from the fire through the angular points such as north-west, south-west, and ending with north-east, one should unite the faces. Oṁ hāṁ oblations to Sadyojāta, Vāmadeva, Aghora, Tatpuruṣa and Īśāna. Thus its form and other faces should be contemplated in the face of one's liking.

43. Having worshipped the fire in the north-east and offering three oblations with the *mantra* of the weapon, (the worshipper) with his entire soul should contemplate—"O Fire-God! you are the divine essence of Śiva."

44. Having worshipped the parents with the *hṛd* (*mantra*) and left them aside, the final oblation which concludes the rite should be offered as laid down with the principal *mantra* ending with *vauṣaṭ*.

45. Then one should worship the resplendent, Supreme God attended upon by the attendants and retinue, after having invoked him in the lotus of his heart as before. He should offer waters of oblation to Śiva after having requested his permission.

46. Having established a union among the god of the sacrificial fire, god Śiva and his soul situated in his arteries, (the worshipper) should offer oblations with the principal *mantra* befitting one's capacity and using one-tenth of *mantras* as a supplement.

47. A *kārṣika* (a particular weight) of the clarified butter, milk and honey and a *śukti* (twice that of *kārṣika*) of the curd and a handful of sweet porridge (should be) offered.

48-49. The worshipper should offer as deemed fit the oblation with all the eatables, a handful of fried grains, three pieces of roots and an equal number of fruits. Five half-mouthfuls of cooked rice, bits of sugarcane of the length of a span and stems of sacrificial creepers measuring two fingers in length should be offered into the fire.

50. The oblations of flowers and leaves should be according to their own measure. The sacrificial twigs should measure ten fingers in length. The camphor, sandal, saffron, musk and an ointment made of camphor, aggallochum and *kakkola* in equal parts (should also be offered).

51. (The worshipper) should make an oblation of the *kalāya* (a leguminous seed) and *guggulu* (a fragrant gum-resin) of the

size of the kernel of the jujube fruit and eight parts of the roots as laid down.

52. The oblation should thus be completed with the (principal *mantra*) *brahmabija* (*om*) with sacrificial ladles filled with clarified butter holding the ladle in such a way as to have its cup part downwards.

53-56. Having placed a flower at the head of the spoon and then holding it first with the left hand and then with the right hand and (showing) the *mudrā* denoting the conch he should stand up half erect with feet evenly placed and eyes fixed upon the end of the ladle and holding the base of ladle pressed against his navel. Then one should rouse up the stream of his pure consciousness through the *suṣumnā* (nerve centre below the spiral chord) and carry it to the base of his left breast vigilantly and tell the principal *mantra* ending with the *vauṣaṭ* in a low tone. The clarified butter should be offered having a flow of the measure of the barley.

57. Water for rinsing the mouth, sandal, betals etc. should be offered. (The worshipper) should meditate in his greatness with devotion and then offer salutation.

58-59. After having worshipped the fire well with (the *mantra* of) the weapon ending with *phaṭ* and showing the *saṁhāra mudrā* (the posture of the fingers conveying destruction) and uttering "Pardon me", the gods who reside in the periphery (of the mystic circle) should be placed in the lotus of the heart with extreme devotion with the *hṛd mantra* after taking a breath.

60. All the edibles (got ready for the worship) should be taken and kept in two circular diagrams. Offerings should be done both inside and outside in the vicinity of sacrificial pit in the south-east.

61. *Oṁ hām* oblations to Rudras in the east and in the same way to the mothers in the south. *Hām*, oblations to the *gaṇas* on the west. This offering is for them.

62. And *hām* to the *yakṣas* on the north, *hām* to the planets on the north-east, *hām* to the *asuras* on the south-east, *hām* oblations to the *rākṣasas* in the south-west.

63. And *hām* to the *nāgas* on the north-west, and to the stars at the centre. *Hām* oblations to the constellations in the south-east, and then to the *Viśve* (*devas*) in the south-west.

64-65. It is said that the offering for the guardian of the ground is inside and outside in the west. (Oblations should be made) to Indra, Agni, Yama, Nirṛti, Varuṇa, Vāyu, Kubera and Īśāna in the east etc. outside in the second *maṇḍala*. Salutations to Brahmā on the north-east.

66. Oblations to Viṣṇu in the south-west. The offerings for the crows etc. (should be) outside. The *mantras* for the two offerings in one's soul should be by the *saṁhāramudrā* (posture with fingers indicating destruction).

## CHAPTER SEVENTYSIX

### *Mode of worshipping Caṇḍa (attendant of Śiva)*

*Lord said* :

1. (The worshipper) should approach (the image of Lord) Śiva and address as follows: "O Lord ! accept the merits of the worship and the oblations offered by me."

2. We should convey these to the lord with a firm mind along with the respectful offering of water and uttering the principal *mantra* preceded by the *hṛdbīja* (*om*) and the exhibition of the *udbhava mudrā* (a posture of fingers representing generation).

3. Then having worshipped as before and praising with hymns and saluting, (the worshipper) should offer the respectful offering of water with his face turned away (from the image) and should say "Pardon me".

4. The *liṅga* should be discharged by uttering the *mantra* of the weapon ending with *phaṭ* coupled with the divine *nārācamudrā* (formation with fingers representing an iron arrow), it should be merged with the *mantra* of the image.

5. After having worshipped god on the platform and having merged in himself the collection of *mantras* as laid down, the worship of Caṇḍa should be made.

6. *Om* salutations to Caṇḍeśāna. Salutations to the image of Caṇḍa at the centre. *Om, hūm phaṭ* oblations to Dhūlicaṇḍeśvara. Thus he should be invoked.

7. *Hūm phaṭ* to Caṇḍa at the heart. Then *om* to Caṇḍa on the head. *Om hūm phaṭ* to *Caṇḍa* on the tuft, to Caṇḍa, the protector and armour.

8. So also to Caṇḍa as the weapon *hūm phaṭ*. One should meditate on Caṇḍa, born of the fire of Rudra and as carrying the mace, axe, rosaries and the anchorite's pitcher and as having a dark complexion.

9. The four-faced deity should be worshipped in the half-crescent shaped axe weapon (of Caṇḍa). One should repeat (the *mantra*) befitting one's capacity, being one-tenth of the principal worship.

10. Except the offerings such as the cow, earth, gold, clothes, gems and ornaments, the remains of offerings should be offered to Caṇḍeśa.

11. Being ordered by Śiva, I have offered to you these articles of food and drink, betels, garlands and scented pastes, the ramnants of offering.

12. O Caṇḍa ! may all these acts of service (undertaken) by me by your order (be agreeable to you). Any shortcoming or redundancy out of my ignorance may be made complete always.

13. Having submitted to the lord thus and offered the respectful water and contemplated his form, the *mantras* should be merged with the self with the *mantra* of the destructive deity and showing slowly the *saṁhāra mudrā* (formation with the fingers (representing destruction) along with the principal *mantra* and taking a breath. The offering such as flowers etc. should then be removed and that place cleansed with cowdung dissolved in waters. After offering water respectfully one should conclude by rinsing one's mouth and do any other worship.

## CHAPTER SEVENTYSEVEN

### *Mode of worshipping Kapilā (the Cow)*

*The Lord said* :

1. I shall describe to you the mode of worship of *Kapilā* (the cow). The cow should be worshipped with these *mantras*. Om

salutations to you O Kapilā, one makes us rejoice, the abode of bliss. Salutations to you.

2. *Om* salutations to you O Kapilā of good disposition. O Kapilā, as effulgent as Surabhi (the divine cow, daughter of Dakṣa and wife of Kaśyapa). *Om* Kapilā, the good-minded, salutations. *Om* salutations to the bestower of enjoyment and emancipation.

3. O Daughter of Surabhi ! the Mother of the universe ! Giver of ambrosia to the celestials ! Granter of boons ! Accept this morsel of food and grant me all my desires.

4. You had been worshipped by Vasiṣṭha and the learned Viśvāmitra. O Kapilā ! Take away my sins and the bad acts of mine.

5. (Let there be) cows always in front of me. (Let there be) cows behind me. (Let there be) cows in my heart also. I am dwelling in the midst of cows.

6. May you accept the morsel of food offered by me. After repetition (of the *mantra*) let me be pure like Lord Śiva. After having worshipped the books of learning one should bow at the feet of the preceptor.

7. One should bathe (again) at noon and worship (Lord) Śiva with *aṣṭapuṣpikā*. The *aṣṭapuṣpikā* is the worship of the image, seat and the limbs of (the image of) Śiva.

8-9. The cooked food should be brought into the well-cleansed kitchen at mid-day. Then after the recitation of the *mṛtyuñjaya mantra* (that which conquers death) seven times and ending with the *vauṣaṭ*, the food should be sprinkled with drops of water with the *darbha* and conch. The entire food should first be dedicated to Śiva after lifting them up.

10. Then half of the above should be set apart for oblation at the fire-place. After having purified the fire-place as per rules, the oblation (should be done).

11-12. Having made the oblation once in the fire around one's navel one should gather the seed of fire with the breath drawn in and after taking it through the places of the letters, one should meditate on it as "You are the fire of Lord Śiva" and it should be put at the fire-place. *Oṁ hāṁ* obeisance to fire-god—as also *hāṁ* obeisance to Soma.

13. Obeisance to Sun-god, to Jupiter, the lord of people. (Obeisance) to all gods and to all Viśvedevas.

14. *Hām* obeisance to fire-god, for offering a right sacrifice. One should worship these in the east and other directions. After having made oblations ending with the word *svāhā* one should bid farewell after seeking forbearance.

15. One should worship (the god of righteousness) on the right-hand side of the fire-place. "Salutations to the god of righteousness. The lord of unrighteousness (should be worshipped) on the left-handside in a vessel containing sour gruel.

16. Lord Varuṇa (should be worshipped) as the transformer of the sap and as the lord of fire in the waters. Lord of obstacles (Vināyaka) (should be worshipped) at the entrance. Obeisance to Subhagā at the grinding stone.

17. *Om* obeisance to Raudrikā and Girikā. Obeisance; one should worship in the mortar. Obeisance to the pestle, the weapon dear to Bala(rāma). It should be worshipped.

18-19. The two gods mentioned (should be worshipped) in the broomstick and the god of love in the bed. Having offered oblation to the trunk for the presiding deity of the ground at the middle stump one should eat from a golden vessel or in the petals of the lotus etc. The preceptor, the worshipper and the son should maintain silence at the time of this vow.

20-22. (The leaves) of the *vaṭa*, *aśvattha*, *arka*, *vātāri*, *sāla* and *bhallātaka* should be discarded. After having rinsed the mouth with water, five oblations should be offered with the five *prāṇas* (winds in the body) together with the *praṇava* (*om*) ending with *svāhā* (oblations). The fire in the belly should be kindled. With the secondary winds (in one's body) *viz*., *nāga*, *kūrma*, *kṛkara*, *devadatta* and *dhanañjaya*, oblations (should be made). Having offered food with the waters of *āpośāna* (prayer repeated before and after eating), one should drink the rest of the water.

23. You are an ambrosial seat. Oblations for the vital winds should be made as before. Oblations to the *prāṇa*, *apāna*, *samāna*, *udāna*, and *vyāna*. Having eaten food, water should be sipped. (The *mantra* for that) is "you are the ambrosial covering." Thus the food and the winds in the body (are worshipped).

# CHAPTER SEVENTYEIGHT

*Mode of investiture of the sacred thread for the deity*

*The Lord said* :

1. I shall describe the (mode of) investiture of the sacred thread (for the deity) which completes the acts of worship etc. (It is of two kinds), the daily routine (without any motive) and the other being undertaken to be done with a motive.

2. It should be done on the eighth or fourteenth day of the bright or dark fortnights in the months of *āṣāḍha* (July-August) or *śrāvaṇa* (August-September) or *bhādrapada* (September-October).

3-4. Or it should be done on the first day of either fortnights during the (above) months upto *kārttika* (October-November), for (the images of) the fire god, Brahmā, Ambikā, Ibhāsya (Gaṇeśa), Nāga (lord of serpents), Skanda, Arka (Sun), Śūlin, Durgā, Yama, Indra, Govinda (manifestation of Viṣṇu), Smara (God of love), Śambhu (Śiva) and other gods. (The threads should be) made of gold, silver and copper in the *kṛta* (first one among the four eras) and other *yugas* (eras).

5-6. A cotton (thread) or silk thread or the one made of (fibres of) lotus should be used in the *kali* (*yuga*) (the last). The *praṇava* (*om*), moon, fire-god, Brahmā, serpent-god, Guha (son of Śiva), Hari (Viṣṇu), Sarveśa and other gods would reside in the nine component strings (of the thread). The *uttama* (excellent) and other classes (*madhyama* and *adhama*) would be those which contain one hundred and eight (strings) or half of that or a quarter of that.

7. Or it should be made to contain eighty-one or thirty-eight or fifty strings having binding knots at equal intervals.

8. The breadth of the thread should be twelve or eight or four finger lengths or else it should be equal to the breadth of the *liṅga*.

9. (In length) it should be touching the pedestal (of the image) or (should be equal) to a quarter of the length of the deity as a whole. The descent of the Ganges should be accomplished by washing with pure (water).

10-11. The knots should be made with (the *mantra* of) Vāma (deva), purified with that of Aghora, dyed with the paste of saffron, sandal, musk, yellow pigment, camphor, turmeric and red chalk etc. with that of (Tat) puruṣa. There should be ten knots or equal to the number of strings.

12-13. The inter-space between the knots (should be) one, two or four finger lengths in such a way as to make it elegant. The knots are known as sadāśivā, manonmanī, prakṛti (nature), pauruṣī (relating to the *puruṣa*), *virā* (valorous), *aparājitā* (invincible), *jayā* (victorious), *vijayā* (victorious), *ajitā* (unconquered), *sadāśivā* (always auspicious), *manonmanī* (expanding intellect), and *sarvamukhī* (omniscient) which confer good.

14. The sacred thread for the moon, fire-god and sun should be done similar to that for Śiva, in the heart, or in their own image or in a book or in that of the preceptor or the *gaṇas*.

15. In the same way there should be one in each one of the pitchers of the door-keeper and the presiding deity of the directions etc. The sacred thread for the *liṅga* should measure from one to nine cubits in length.

16-18. The number of knots (in a thread) of the *vṛddha* (class) should be twenty-eight, the number for other classes being eighteen and eight respectively, their breadth in all being proportionate with the breadth of the *liṅga*. On the seventh or thirteenth day of a fortnight (one should) become clean and do his daily rites. Then (he) should adorn the place of worship with flowers, cloth etc. in the evening and should perform the *naimittika* (rites done with some motive), especially the waters of oblation.

19. After having taken possession of the sacred ground, the sun-god should be worshipped. After rinsing his mouth, the preceptor should do the rite of accomplishment (mentioning the names of the parts of the body along with the *mantras*). Water should be offered with respect with the *praṇava* (the syllable *om*).

20. The threshold should be sprinkled with water with the *mantra* of the weapon (and) the worship should be duly commenced from the east. *Hām* (obeisance) to the entrance to the *śāntikalā* (digit of peace); (obeisance) to the *vidyākalā* (digit of knowledge).

21. (Obeisance) to the digit of non-action, to the one digit

known as existence. The warden of the god should be worshipped at the top sides of those doors, two at each (as follows):

22. (Obeisance) to Nandin, to Mahākāla, to Bhṛṅgin, to Gaṇa, to Vṛṣabha, to Skanda, to Devī and to Caṇḍa in order.

23. In the case of worship being undertaken without any motive, the preceptor, having entered and worshipped the guardian deities at the western entrance, and after purification of materials, should offer water of respect.

24. After having done the sprinkling (of water) etc., and collected the materials for the rite, consecration with *darbha*, *dūrvā* and flowers should be made with the *mantras* like *hṛd* etc.

25. After having permeated thus with the essence of Śiva, one should place it on his head. I am Śiva, the first being, omniscient and I have the importance in the rites.

26. The preceptor (holding) the sword of knowledge in his hand should deeply contemplate the lord. Subsequently he should go to the south-western direction and pour (the washings etc.) with his face turned towards the north).

27-28. The respectful water offering, the *pañcagavya* (the five things got from a cow) and all other (articles of worship) which have been purified by means of rites at the end of cross-roads and by divine look etc. and put in the sacrificial pavilion, one should collect the bunch of *kuśa* lying scattered, place them over the little jar in the north-eastern direction.

29. The presiding deities of the place should be worshipped in the south-west and (Goddess) Lakṣmī at the entrance. The pitcher is placed on all kinds of grains facing the west.

30. Then the bull-riding God and the pitcher (*varddhanī*) placed on the lion (should be worshipped) with the *praṇava* (*om*). Lord Śiva should be worshipped in the jar with his attendant gods and the weapons in the *vardhanī*.

31-32. Indra and other guardian deities of directions, Brahmā, Viṣṇu and Śiva (should be worshipped) in the (different) directions. Having taken the *vardhanī* (in the hand) behind the pitcher, the preceptor should read out the mandate of Lord Śiva in all directions commencing with the east and ending with the north-east. (The entire ground) (should be made wet) by an unbroken flow of water (along) with the recitation of principal *mantra*.

33-35. This should be moved around in all directions

for the sake of protection as if it were the weapons. Having placed the pitcher in the east, the lord should be worshipped in the pitcher placed foremost at the front firmly, while there should be one for the weapons to the left of it. The weapons located with the *praṇava* (*om*) (should be worshipped with the *vardhani*. Then the union of the two, the base and the *liṅga* should be accomplished by (showing) the *liṅga mudrā* (posture of the fingers representing the *liṅga*). Then the sword of knowledge should be dedicated to the (consecrated) pitcher. The principal *mantra* should then be repeated.

36-37. Protection should be spelled out with a tenth (of the *mantra*) in the *vardhani*. After having worshipped Lord Gaṇeśa (lord of the *gaṇas*) in the north-west and Lord Hara (Viṣṇu) with the five sweet things (milk, sugar, ghee, curd and honey), the fire sacred to Śiva should be worshipped in the sacrificial pit as before and bathed after having made the sacrificial gruel duly purified by the *sampāta* (residual) oblation.

38. It should be divided with the *kuśa* into three parts respectively consecrated to the god, the fire-god, and the soul, of which the former two should be offered to Lord Śiva and the fire-god and the part consecrated to the soul should be kept apart.

39. (The stick for) cleansing the teeth should be offered on the east by (repeating the *mantras* of) the weapon and arrow, and (a piece of) earth on the west or south with the (a) *ghora* and *śikhā* (*mantras*).

40. Water reduced in quantity (should be offered) on the north with the *sadyojāta* and the *hṛd* (*mantras*). Perfumed water (should be offered) on the north-east with the *vāma* (*deva*) and *śiras* (*mantras*).

41. The five things got from a cow and flowers like *palāśa* and lotus (should be cast) all around. Flowers should be offered on the north-east and the yellow pigment on the south-east.

42. The agallochum (should be offered) on the south-western direction and all the articles for oblation in four equal proportions on the north-west with the *sadyojāta* (*mantra*) and with the *kuśa*.

43-44. (An anchorite's) stick, rosary, loin-cloth, alms bowl, collyrium, saffron, oil, a small stick (for applying the collyrium), comb, betel (leaf), and mirror should be offered to the image of the god. The yellow pigment (should be offered) on the north.

45. He should offer a seat, a pair of sandals, a vessel, an upper cloth and an umbrella on the north-east with the mantra of the lord for the satisfaction of Īśāna (one of the five forms of

Śiva). The sacrificial porridge together with the clarified butter and perfumes etc. should be offered on the east.

46. Having gathered the sacred threads and sprinkled them with the waters offered as respect, they should be led to the presence of fire after purifying them with the *saṁhitā mantras*.

47-48. After having covered them with the hide of the black antelope and remembering the eternal blissful one, the witness of all deeds, the protector, the one without any change, that Śiva, with the application of *sva* and *ha* (*mantras*) and *saṁhitā mantras*, the sacred threads should be purified. Twenty-one water vessels (should be got ready).

49. The room (for worship) etc. should be girdled by threads. Perfumes etc. should be offered to the sun-god, (who had already been) worshipped. After having rinsed the mouth, and doing the assigning, the water should be offered with respect.

50. Then (the worshipper should worship) the *vāstu* god along with the weapons, the guardians of the world, Nandin and others by (mentioning) the name of each in the pitcher of (lord) Śiva after adding perfumes.

51-52. Vardhanī, lord of obstacles, the preceptor should be worshipped. Then the sacred thread smeared with (the paste of) all herbs and perfumed with the flowers and *dūrvā* and purified with the *mantras* should be held between the folded palms. *Om* ! (salutation to you) the regulation for rectifying any omission in regulations.

53. O lord ! I invoke you and that which yields the desired boon. O lord of entity and non-entity ! You bless me, one who worships, with that success.

54-55. O Śambhu (Śiva) ! Obeisance to you at all times and by all means. Be pleased with me. O lord of celestials ! You have been invoked along with the goddess, lords of *gaṇas*, lords of *mantras*, guardians of the world and attendant gods. I invoke you. This sacred thread is for you in the early morning.

56. O supreme lord ! By your command I shall do the prescribed routine. Thus one should invoke the lord and do the *amṛtikaraṇa*[1] rite by drawing in the breath.

57. Having recited the principal *mantra* for Śiva, it should be dedicated to (lord) Śiva. After completing the recitation

---

1. Mental identification of the parts of one's body with those of the lord.

(of *mantra*), praises, and obeisance, (lord) Śambhu (Śiva) should be bid adieu.

58-59. Having made oblation with the third part of the gruel in the fire (permeated with the essence) of Śiva, (oblation should be made) for the residents in the quarters, the lords of the quarters, the spirits, the mothers, *gaṇas*, Rudras, guardians of the region. Obeisance. This oblation is given. The oblation is made for the (guardian) elephants of the quarters east etc. and to the regions.

60. After having rinsed the mouth, the oblation should be done for the rectification of omissions in the observances. After doing the final oblation, the fire should be put out.

61-62. Then *om* oblations to fire (god), to Soma, *om* oblations to fire and Soma. So also to fire-god, the accomplisher. After having made four oblations, the union of the gods respectively worshipped in the sacrificial pit and the mystic circle of lord Śiva should be brought about.

63-64. Then the union should be made by the method of assigning in the different parts of the body. Then the sacred threads should be placed in a vessel made of bamboo along with (the *mantras* of) weapons and armour and consecrated with the (*mantras*) of the digits. The six articles of worship should be consecrated with the principal *brahma* (*mantra*) (*Om*). (The *mantras* of) the heart, armour and weapon should also be united.

65. Having girdled the vessel with threads and worshipped it with the (*mantras* of) the parts of the body it should be offered to the lord of the universe with extreme devotion for the sake of protection.

66. After it has been worshipped with flowers, incense etc. and two theological books have been submitted, one should go near the feet of the preceptor and offer the sacred thread with devotion.

67. Having come out of the place and rinsed the mouth, one should worship five things got from a cow, the gruel and the stick for cleansing the teeth on three circles made with the cow-dung.

68. After rinsing the mouth again, one should remain awake singing songs and repeating hymns and should sleep at the end after fasting on a bed of *darbha* all the while contemplating on the lord.

69. Even one, who is desirous of cessation of births and deaths, should undertake in this way lying only on a bed of ashes, fasting and self-controlled.

## CHAPTER SEVENTYNINE

### *Investiture of the sacred thread*

*The Lord said* :

1. Having got up early in the morning, and finishing bathing the worshipper should enter the sacrificial shed after completing the twilight worship and remaining composed.

2. Having collected the sacred thread, and the deity not being given farewell, the sacred thread should be placed in a spotless vessel within a mystic diagram in the north-east.

3. Then the lord of celestials should be bid farewell and the materials of worship should be removed (from the body of the deity). He should again perform the two rites as before on the cleaned ground.

4. Then the gods—sun, the guardian deities of the entrance and of the directions the pitcher, Īśāna, Śiva and the fire-god should specially be worshipped, as usually done in the *naimittiki* (done with some motives) rites, elaborately.

5. (Having done) the *tarpaṇa* (appeasing) rite with the *mantras* and the oblation of expiation one hundred and eight times with (the *mantras* of) the arrows, the final oblation should be made slowly.

6. Having offered the sacred thread to the sun god and rinsing the mouth, (the worshipper) should offer it to the guardian deities of the entrance and of the directions, the sacrificial pitcher and *vardhani* etc.

7. Then having sat in his own seat in the presence of lord Śambhu (Śiva), (the worshipper) should offer the sacred thread to one's own self, the *gaṇa*, the priest and fire-god.

8-9. *Om* O lord ! soul of the time, whatever has been ordained by you in my observances that which has been done. contradictorily, and omitted, and that which has been done secretly O Śambhu let the contradictory thing become normal, the contradictory deed become refined, by this omniscient sacred thread and by your wish.

10. *Om* ! Complete this sacrificial observance ! Oblations to the lord of regulations, the principle of the soul, that which underlines the natural principle that is protected by the lotus-born Brahmā.

11-15. Having recited the principal *mantra* upto the end, lord Śiva should be worshipped with the sacred thread. Again in the principle of knowledge which is the end of all the learning and which is governed by Viṣṇu, one should invest the sacred thread having recited the *mantras* of Viṣṇu. Similarly, in the principle relating to Śiva, he should recite the *mantras* of Śiva and invest that deity with the sacred thread. O man of good practices ! In the case of those governed by all the deities one should recite the principal *mantra* upto the end after having recited the *mantras* of Śiva and the descent of the Ganges should be accomplished. In the case of those who desire to get release (from the cycle of births) it is said that the sacred thread should be invested with the *mantras* of Śiva relating to the knowledge of the soul. For those who desire to get enjoyment it has been pointed out (that the sacred thread should be invested) duly with (the *mantras* of) the principles of Śiva. The *mantras* should be uttered ending with 'oblation' or 'obeisance'.

16. *Oṁ hāṁ* oblations to lord Śiva, the lord of the principle of soul. *Oṁ hāṁ* oblations to (lord) Śiva, the lord of the principle of learning. *Oṁ hāṁ* oblations to (lord) Śiva, lord of the principle of Śiva. *Oṁ hāṁ* oblations to lord Śiva, the lord of all principles (of the universe). Having made obeisance to the descent of the Ganges, he should pray to it with folded palms. "You are the refuge for all beings. You reside in the movable and immovable beings."

17. "O Supreme lord ! You are the witness (of the acts) of beings by pervading inside the beings. By deed or thought or words I have no other being to resort to except you."

18-19. "O Great lord ! Whatever has been done defective in the *mantra* or deeds or in the materials (of worship) or in the repetition and worship in the daily (observances), may you complete them. O Supreme lord ! You are well-purified. You are pure and destroyer of sins. Every being in the universe, the immovable and movable have been purified by you.

20-22. "O lord ! Whatever has been made defectively by me in my observances (let it be free) from becoming useless. By your mandate let all of them become united, being tied in a string." Having conveyed the recitation (of the *mantras*) to the lord and praising him devotedly, one should take up the vow after saluting the preceptor and as directed by him. (It should be) for four months, (or) three months, (or) three days or one day.

23-24. After having saluted the lord and seeking excuse, the votary should go near the sacrificial pit and cast four sacred threads for Śiva located in the fire, and worship with flowers, incense, unbroken rice etc. The oblation and holy thread should be presented to the Rudras.

25-26. Having entered inside and praising Śiva (the lord) should be bid adieu with salutations. After having made the expiatory oblation and oblation of sweet porridge, the final oblation should be offered and (lord) Śiva located in the fire should be bid farewell. Having performed oblations with the *vyāhṛtis* (the syllables *om bhūḥ, om bhuvaḥ* etc.), the fire should be obstructed with *niṣṭhurā* (scornful goddess).

27-31. Then four oblations should be offered to the fire-god and others. Oblation should be given outside along with a sacred thread to the guardian deities of all directions. Two theological books and a sacred thread should be offered. *Om, hām, bhūḥ* oblations. *Om, hām, bhuvaḥ* oblations. *Om, hām svaḥ* oblations. *Om, hām, bhūrbhuvaḥ svaḥ* oblations. After having done the oblations with the *vyāhṛtis*, four oblations should be made (as follows). *Om, hām* oblations to the fire-god. *Om, hām* oblations to the fire-god, one who accomplishes all desires. The preceptor should be worshipped as lord Śiva with clothes, ornaments and bed. All annual rites etc. of the performer (become) fruitful if the preceptor gets satisfied. The Supreme lord had said so. After having placed the thread on the body of the preceptor thus, the brahmins should be fed and offered clothes etc. with devotion. "O lord of celestials ! May lord Śiva get pleased by this gift of mine."

32. After having bathed in the morning (the investor) should perform his daily rites of prayer and worship and take

leave of (god) Śiva after having worshipped him and the sacred threads with eight flowers.

33. After having performed the *nitya* and *naimittika* rites as before in full, the sacred threads should be placed and lord Śiva should be worshipped in the fire after obeisance.

34. The expiatory oblation should then be done with the *mantras* of the weapons. The final oblation should then be given. One who is desirous of enjoyment should then submit the fruits of his acts to lord Śiva.

35. "May this rite of mine become fruitful by your grace !" One who is desirous of release (from the cycle of births) should do this act (as follows): "O lord ! May there be no bondage for me."

36. (Lord) Śiva located in the fire should be united with lord Śiva (in the solar plexus of the investor) by *nāḍiyoga* (assignment on limbs). The essence of fire should be drawn in one's heart and the fire should be discharged.

37. After having rinsed the mouth well, (he) should enter inside (the shed) and permeate the water of the pitcher with the essence of Śiva and bid farewell (after saying) "Pardon (me)".

38. After having taken leave of the guardian deities of the world, the sacred thread should be taken from the lord and placed on the Caṇḍeśvara (form of the lord) after worship.

39. The materials of worship along with the sacred thread should be submitted to him. In the alternative lord Caṇḍa should be worshipped on the sacrificial ground in the prescribed manner as before.

40. "Whatever annual rite has been done by me defectively, may that become perfect by your mandate, O lord ! Caṇḍa ! my master !"

41. Having thus submitted to the lord of celestials, he should be given farewell after obeisance and praise. After having removed the materials of worship (from the images) and becoming pure, the votary should bathe (the image) and worship (lord) Śiva. A man who remains even at a distance of five *yojanas* (a *yojana* is equal to about eight miles) from the preceptor (is deemed to be) pure.

# CHAPTER EIGHTY

## *Mode of investiture with the fibres of Damanaka*

*The Lord said*:

1. I shall describe the mode of investiture with *damanaka* fibres for the lord. It has to be performed as before. Once, the celestials were harassed by Bhairava, a form born of the anger of lord Hara (Śiva).

2-5. Hence, he was cursed by the foe of Tripura (Śiva) (saying), "Become a stum". Being pleased (after propitiation) the lord said, "Whoever propitiates you would get full benefits and not otherwise." The votary should address the tree by the (following) words of Bhava (Śiva) after having worshipped it with the vedic hymns on the seventh or thirteenth day (of a fortnight). "O (tree) born of the grace of (lord) Hara (Śiva) ! You be present here. For the sake of work of Śiva you have to be carried (home) as per the mandate of lord Śiva." (The tree) should be invited home and the consecration should be done in the evening.

6. Having worshipped the sun-god, Śaṅkara (Śiva) and fire-god as prescribed, the root (of the tree) should be placed on the west of the lord alongwith the (clump of) earth.

7. The stump (may be placed) on the left or on the head (of the image), the *dhātri* (myrabolan) on the north, the broken leaves on the south and its flower on the east.

8. The fruits and roots should be placed in a cup. Lord Śiva should be worshipped in the north-east. The lord should be invoked after having placed the five articles of worship in the folded palms and (later) placing them on one's head.

9. "O lord of celestials ! You have been invoked by me in the early morning ! O lord ! the merit of this penance has to become fully fruitful by your mandate."

10. After having kept the sacred remnants in the vessel covered, (the votary) should worship the lord of the universe with flowers etc., after having bathed early in the morning.

11-12. After having performed the *nitya* and *naimittika* rites, he should then worship with the *damana*. After having kept the remnants in the folded palms, lord Śiva, fire-god and the preceptor should be worshipped with (the mantras) of the lord of the principle of knowledge of soul, the principal *mantras* of the lord ending with (the names of) Īśvara, with four handfuls (of offering). "*Oṁ haum* (obeisance) to the lord of sacrifice. Complete the sacr ifice. Obeisance to the holder of the spear."

13. "O lord ! Whatever has been in excess or in short in my acts let all that be complete by this investiture of the *damanaka* by me". (Whoever performs this) would go to heaven after having obtained the benefits of all that is got in the month of *Caitra* (April-May).

## CHAPTER EIGHTYONE

### *Mode of spiritual initiation*

*Lord said* :

1-3. I shall describe the spiritual initiation for the sake of enjoyment and release from bondage, destroying one's sins and shattering bondages of impurities and illusion; by which, knowledge is gained by the disciple, that initiation (is considered) as yielding enjoyment and release. It is considered to be of three kinds. The first one is *vijñātakala* (cognisant of the beatitudes). The second one is *pralayakala* (a psychic state from which one can be cognisant of those attributes). The third one is *sakala* (clouded by worldly impurity). These deserve initiation in scriptures. The first (category) among these is free from all mental impurities, while the second is free from sinful acts.

4. The third variety can (hold communion) by prayer with the region from *kalā* to the earth. The initiation is also considered to be of two kinds—devoid of any hold and possessing a hold.

5. (The initiation) independent of any (external) aid is for the first two categories (among the three) and that which is dependent on any (external) aid is for (the third category) *sakala* (endowed with a form). (The initiation in the first sort) is done by the worship of Śambhu (Śiva) alone without any dependence.

6. That which is remembered as independent (is achieved) by an impact of strong piercing force by resorting to the image in the form of the preceptor and by rending asunder the (veil of) illusion.

7-8. That (initiation) in which Lord Śambhu (Śiva) does it, is spoken as dependant. The spiritual initiation is said to be of four kinds—*sabijā* (together with imparting of some *mantra*), *bijavarjitā* (without any *mantra*), *sādhikārā* (with some governance), *anadhikārā* (without any governance). They are described (now). A *sabijā* (type) is that in which the disciple is subject to the control of code of conduct laid down in the scriptures.

9-10. The *nirbijā* (variety) is intended for the incapable which is devoid of any code of conduct of the scriptures. The *sādhikārā* type of initiation shall be in the case of rites of daily nature and those done with a motive for the disciple and the preceptor. The nirbījā type of initiation is in those cases (where the disciples) possess characteristics as my two sons.

11. The *niradhikārikā* type of initiation allows one to undertake rites in which the disciple does not aspire for the fruits. This (initiation) may be of two kinds marked by the individual characteristics.

12. One consists of performance of acts preceded by (preparations of) sacrificial pits and mystical diagrams. The other one is composed of knowledge which is achieved by the operation of the mind.

13. In this way an initiation may be made by a preceptor who has the right (to administer). The *skandadikṣā* may be done by the preceptor after doing daily rites.

14-17. (The preceptor) should purify the place from the spirits remaining in his own seat, having the *arghya* (waters of respect) in the lotus palm and worshipping the guardian deities of the threshold with *praṇava* (*mantra*) and after removing the obstacles and placing the weapons at the threshold. The special *arghya* offering should consist of sesamum, rice, white mustard, *kuśa*, *dūrvā*, unbroken rice, mixed with water, barley, milk and water. Then the materials (for worship) (should be done) pure with that water. (After putting) the mark and the worship of the self and of the seat, the materials (of worship) such as the five things got from a cow, fried paddy, sandal, white mustard, sacred ashes, *dūrvā*, unbroken rice and *kuśa* should be purified as before with *mantras*.

18. The pure fried paddy which has been scattered should be consecrated with mantras of weapons along with incense and consecrated with waters with the *mantras* of implements and covered by armour.

19-21. Having made *darbhas* into different shapes of missiles so as to number thirtysix bunches, each measuring (the length of) a palm, which are capable of warding off multitudes of obstacles,and after having repeated the *mantra* of the weapon of Śiva seven times on the sword of knowledge continuously and having located in one's self, lord Śiva, the basis of all creation, the most sought after, and devoid of any form, one should deem himself as "I am (lord) Śiva". After having placed turban on the head one should adorn his body (in the following way).

22. He should besmear his right arm with the sandal paste. The lord should be worshipped in the prescribed way. This is how the head of Śiva is got ready.

23-25. Having located the luminous lord on one's own head with the *mantras* of Śiva, the doer should conceive himself as not different from (lord) Śiva as follows: "(He is) the witness of all deeds in the mystic diagram, the protector of sacrifice in the pitcher, the recipient of oblations in the fire and the liberator of the disciple from the bonds and the benefactor in one's own self," such that the lord is of six kinds of basis. One should consider (himself) as "I am he". (Lord) Bhava (Śiva) should again be made firmly established (in one).

26. (Then) that person should remain facing the south-west holding the sword of knowledge and sprinkle the sacrificial shed with the waters of respectful offering and the five things got from the cow.

27. By purification at the crossroads and by (divine) look, (*darbhas*) should be purified. Having thrown the scattered *darbhas* there, (*darbhas*) should be gathered.

28. A seat should be made ready with them in the north-east (direction) for the pitcher. The presiding deity of the place and the celestials should be worshipped in the south-west and (Goddess) Lakṣmī at the entrance (of the sacrificial shed).

29-30. (Goddess) Pūrayantī of the form of sacrificial shed should be worshipped in the west with gems and with the *hṛd* (*mantra*). Lord Śambhu (Śiva) should be worshipped in a pitcher placed in the north-east over the grains and containing water, gems and a piece of cloth (over the mouth) with the face of the worshipper turned towards the west. (Goddess) Śakti (should be worshipped) in the south of the pitcher. (Goddess) Vardhanī, in the form of a sword and riding a lion should be worshipped in the west.

31-32. Having worshipped (with their respective names and the *hṛd* (*mantra*) the (gods) Indra and the guardian deities of the directions ending with Viṣṇu placed on the *praṇava* (*om*), riding their respective vehicles and holding their respective weapons, that (the sacrificial jar) should be carried round in front of pitchers and an uninterrupted flow of water (should be made) after making a circumambulation.

33. After having recited the principal *mantra*, the mandate of (Lord) Śiva should be conveyed to the guardian deities. The jar should be duly consecrated and it should be held.

34. After having worshipped lord Śaṅkara (Śiva) in the pitcher placed on a firm seat along with the retinue, the weapon should be worshipped in the *vardhanī* after being placed to purify the path.

*Oṁ haḥ* to the seat of the weapon *hūm phaṭ*. *Om Om* Salutation to the embodiment of weapon. *Oṁ hūm phaṭ* obeisance to the Pāśupata weapon. *Om Om* obeisance to the heart. *Oṁ śrīṁ hum phaṭ* obeisance to the head. *Oṁ yaṁ hum phaṭ* obeisance to the tuft. *Oṁ gūṁ hum phaṭ* obeisance to the armour. *Om phaṭ hum phaṭ* obeisance to the weapons.

35. The weapon should be meditated upon as possessing four faces and having teeth in the company of the Goddess Śakti, effulgent like crores of suns and wielding a mace, spear and sword.

36. By (showing) *liṅgamudrā* (a posture of fingers denoting *liṅga*), the union of the *bhaga* (base) and the *liṅga* is accomplished. The pitcher should be touched with the little finger, the weapon with the heart and *vardhanī* with the clenched fist.

37. The *vardhanī* should first be touched with the clenched fist for the sake of enjoyment and release (from worldly existence).

The sword of knowledge should be offered for protecting the mouth of the pitcher.

38. After the repetition of the principal (mantra) hundred times, the weapon should be placed in the pitcher. A tenth part of it should then be conveyed to the *vardhani* for the sake of protection.

39. "O lord of the universe ! This sacrificial shed has been raised with great effort. O lord ! the sustainer of all sacrifices ! This has to be protected by you."

40. The lord Gaṇa placed on the *praṇava* (*om*) and having four arms should be worshipped in the north-west by offering water. Having worshipped lord Śiva on the ground, the worshipper should proceed near the pit.

41-42. Remaining in contemplation for the sake of pleasing the *mantras*, and having placed the water of respectful offering, perfumes, ghee etc. on the left and the twigs, *darbha*, sesamum etc. on the right, and having purified the pit, fire, ladle etc. as before, (the worshipper) should think of the greatness of the elevated-faced (god) in the heart and worship lord Śiva in the sacrificial fire.

43. After having performed *sṛṣṭinyāsa* (assignment representing creation) in one's body, in the pitcher of lord Śiva, on the sacrificial ground, in the hṛd and (the body of) the disciple, purification and meditation (should be done) in the prescribed way.

44. Having contemplated the face of the (same) measure of the pit, the *hṛd bīja* (*mantras*) are repeated and oblations made for the seven tongues of the fire.

45-46. The principal *mantras* for the tongue (should have) the last letters without (the letter) 'ra', and should have the sound of six 'ra's and the moon, a point and the tuft. Hiraṇyā, Kanakā, Raktā, Kṛṣṇā, Suprabhā, Atiriktā and Bahurūpā should in order (be placed) in the directions north-east, east, south-east and west.

47. Oblations should be done with the sweet things such as milk etc. in the rites to appease (god) or seeking welfare and with oil-cakes, flour, one's dress and sour-gruel in the rites performed for harming some one.

48. An angry man should offer oblations of salt, goat's

curd, pungent oil, thorns and crooked twigs along with vedic syllables.

49. Yakṣiṇī (a goddess) becomes certainly favourable by doing oblations with the buds of *kadamba*. One should offer oblations with *bandhūka*, *kiṁśuka* and other (flowers) for attracting and subjugating another person.

50. The *bilva* leaves (sacred in the worship of Śiva) are offered for getting kingdom, the *pāṭala* and *campaka* (flowers) for the sake of wealth, lotus flowers for the sake of (becoming) a sovereign (and) eatables for wealth.

51. *Dūrvā* (is offered) for the cure of diseases, flowers *priyaṅgu* and *pāṭalī* for exercising sway over all beings, and the *Āmra* flower for arresting fever.

52. (An oblation made with) the *mṛtyuñjaya*[1] *mantra* would conquer death. By the oblation of sesamum there would be prosperity. Propitiation of Rudra (Śiva) (should be made) for all sorts of appeasement. Then the subject of (present) discussion is narrated.

53. Eight hundred oblations with the principal *mantra* and a tenth of it with the subordinate ones should be made. Appeasement should be made with the principal *mantra*. The final oblation should be offered as before.

54. Then the repetition (of *mantra*) should be made hundred times for each disciple for the entry of the disciple and for the sake of good omens after the removal of bad omens.

55. As before oblation should be made two hundred times with the principal *mantra*. One oblation should be made with the principal (*mantra*) and the *mantras* of eight weapons concluding with (the syllable) *svāhā* (oblation).

56. The illumination (rite) should be done with the repetition of mantras of the tuft ending with (the syllable) *phaṭ*. Oblation should be done with the *mantras* like *Om*, *hrim*, oblations to Śiva.

57-58. Then the illumination should be done with (the *mantras*) like *Om*, *hrūm*, *hraum*, *hrim*, to Śiva, *hrūm*, *phaṭ*. Then the vessel for preparing the gruel should be washed with waters (made sacred by the *mantras*) of Śiva and covered by an armour. It

1. Beginning with Tryambakaṁ yajāmahe etc.

should be besmeared with sandal paste and a girdle of *darbha* consecrated with the (*mantra*) of armour and weapon.

59. After having placed the seat with (the *mantra* of the) armour, in a semi-circular mystic diagram, Śiva, whose presence is accomplished in the form of an image, should be worshipped with flowers of sentiment.

60-62. (Worship should be made) alternatively in the vessel whose mouth has been covered with a cloth with flowers got from outside. Over the oven placed to the right of the pit and having its mouth facing the west and previously consecrated with the syllables of *ahaṅkāra* (egoism) and (the two sides of the oven) having been contemplated as made up of righteousness and unrighteousness over which (the *mantra*) of the soul of man has been repeated, the vessel should be placed after having repeated (the *mantra*) of the weapon and sprinkled with the urine of cow. The vessel (should have been) cleaned with the milk of cow and (the *mantra*) of the weapon and repetition of the *prāsāda* (*mantra*) hundred times.

63. Rice and grains such as the *śyāmāka* etc. should be cast into it. If (the initiation) is to be given for a single disciple five handfuls (of grains) (should be thrown).

64. A handful of grains should be added. The above grains should be protected with the *mantras* of the fire or that of the armour.

65-66. The gruel should be cooked in the flame of Śiva on the eastern face with (the recitation of the) principal (*mantra*). Then having filled the ladle with the clarified butter and heated in the oven, it should be offered (to the fire) with the *saṁhitā mantras* ending with (the expression) "oblations for the sake of satisfaction". The vessel should be placed in the mystic circles after having consecrated with the *darbha*.

67. Having covered it by the (uttering of) *praṇava* (syllable *om*), it should be besmeared with the *hṛd* (*mantra*). Thus it would become cool after having received a cool plastering.

68-69. (Oblations) should be offered with the recitation of *saṁhitā mantra* once towards the disciple. After having made oblation for the sake of seats etc. on the west of the sacrificial pit and the mystic diagram, the residual offering should be made with the ladle and purification should be performed by (the recitation of) *saṁhitā* (*mantras*). The gruel should be taken out from the vessel with (the recitation of) the (syllable) *vauṣaṭ*.

70. The act of making the gruel into ambrosia should be done by showing *dhenu-mudrā* (formation made by fingers resembling the cow) and it must be allowed to cool on the ground. A part of the gruel consisting of clarified butter (should be set apart) for the disciples and a part for the lord Fire.

71. A part containing honey and clarified butter should be made over to the guardian deities of the worlds. These are three parts. These should be offered to them with the *hṛd* (*mantra*) ending with obeisance. The water for rinsing the mouth (should also be given) with the same (mantra).

72-73. The final oblation should be offered as laid down after having made hundred offerings with clarified butter along with the recitation of *mantra*. Having drawn a mystic diagram on the east of the sacrificial pit or in the midst of pitchers of Lord Śambhu (Śiva), Rudra, the divine mothers and the *gaṇas* (attendant gods of Śiva) and after having made offerings with the *hṛd* (*mantra*), the worshipper should identify himself with God Śiva in the pitcher sacred to Śiva even though he has not received a command.

74-76. He should think himself as the omniscient who stands above all things around. (He should also think) "The place of union is a part of mine and I am the presiding deity at the sacrifice. I am lord Śiva". Thus the performer should come out of the sacrificial shed with the sense of I-ness. Having made the disciple to be seated on the seat of *darbha* already placed on a mystic diagram with the *mantra* of the weapon and duly consecrated with the *praṇava* (syllable *om*), and (providing him) with white upper garment after the bath, (the disciple) should be made to face north for emancipation and the east for enjoyment.

77. Having made (the disciple) to sit erect and face the east, (the preceptor) should look at him from foot to tuft if (the initiation) is for emancipation and in the reverse direction if it is for enjoyment.

78-79. (The preceptor) should look (at the disciple) graciously extending the splendour of Śiva. Having sprinkled water with (the *mantra* of) the weapon in order to accomplish purification by (means of) consecrated water, the disciple should be struck with the ashes (accompanied) by (the *mantra* of) the weapon for the purpose of bathing with the ashes and for the destruction of obstacles and sins by the union of creation and destruction.

80-81. Having sprinkled him again with the water of the weapon for the sake of consummation and having repeated the bathing (*mantra*) of the weapon above the navel with the tip of *kuśa*, one should touch thrice under the navel with the (recitation of the) principal (*mantra*) for the destroyal of sin and with the *mantra* of the arrow for the breaking of bonds.

82. Then (the preceptor) should locate lord Śiva in the body (of the disciple) along with his seat and attendants by offering worship with flowers and by looking into his eyes or by the heart.

83-84. Having tied the seat with a white cloth with (the recitation of) *mantra*, (and) having made him enter by means of circumambulation of Śiva, the seat along with the cloth should be given. (The preceptor) should exhibit the *saṁhāra mudrā* (posture with fingers indicating gathering) and communicate his own self with that form in the lotus of the heart (of the disciple).

85. Having retained that (form of Śiva) in the purified body and having located (it there), it should be worshipped in the east facing the forehead of the disciple with the principal *mantra*.

86. The hand of the disciple should be converted into a hand sacred to (lord Śiva) and permeated with the essence of (lord)Śiva by telling the Śiva *mantra*, such a hand being known to convey (the worshipper) to the region of (lord) Śiva, and to supply him with the only means of worshipping (lord) Śiva.

87. Then after having removed all other materials of worship, one should cast flowers on lord Śiva in the company of attendant gods of lord Śiva invoking his presence with *mantras*.

88-89. The preceptor should name brahmins in the usual order or as desired. After having made (the disciple) to bow to the pitcher and the *vardhanī* (a kind of vessel), (the preceptor) should make (the disciple) seated on the right near the sacred fire facing the north. He should then meditate on the *suṣumnā* (an artery in the body) as emerging out of the body of disciple.

90-93. Having placed the tip of *darbha* on the right hand duly consecrated by the base of *darbha* and resting on the symbol of one's own self, that base (of *kuśa*) should rest on one's own knee while the tip (should rest) on the cock-banner. Having entered the heart of the disciple by breathing out the wind while repeating the *mantra* of the tuft and re-entered his own heart by breathing in and having thus established communion again with the fire of lord Śiva, the preceptor) should offer three oblations with the *hṛd* (*mantra*) for the accomplishment of that communion. One should make hundred oblations with the principal *mantra* for the sake of making the hand (of the disciple) permeated with the essence of Śiva. Being thus initiated in religious practices one would become eligible to perform the worship of lord Śiva.

## CHAPTER EIGHTYTWO

*Mode of performing the purificatory initiation* :

*The Lord said* :

1. "O Ṣaṇmukha (six-faced one)[1] ! Listen to me ! I shall describe the mode of performing the purificatory initiation. The great god Śiva situated in the heart and in the fire should be invoked.

2. Having worshipped those two (God Śiva situated in the heart and the sacrificial fire) and having appeased them with the *hṛd mantra*, one should offer five oblations in their presence with the same *mantra*.

3. That babe (of fire) should be struck with a flower consecrated by (the *mantra* of) the weapon with (the repetition of) the *hṛd* (*mantra*). One should contemplate the starry-like effulgent form therein.

1. Son of the divine pair Śiva and Pārvatī.

4. Having placed the syllable *hum* in it by exhalation of breath and having drawn it by means of *saṁhāriṇi* (*mudrā*) (formation with fingers representing gathering), it should be placed in the heart by the inhalation of breath.

5. Then (the above-mentioned essence of fire) should be cast in the generative organ of goddess *Vāgiśvari* (goddess of speech) with the *mudrā* known as *udbhava*[1] and the repetition of *hṛd mantra*.

*Om hām, him, hām* obeisance to the soul.

6. Oblation should be offered in the smokeless sacrificial fire fully ablaze (with the above *mantra*) for the fulfilment of desires. Oblation made in undeveloped and smoky fire does not get the desire fulfilled.

7. A fire which is pleasing, circling upwards and sweet smelling is commended. So also is the fire which touches the ground and which emits sparks in the contrary direction.

8. Having offered oblations in this way, the impurities of the disciple should be destroyed by doing the sin-consuming oblation or it may be burnt with the syllables of Śiva.

9-10. Five hundred oblations should be made with the principal *mantra* and *vauṣaṭ* etc. in one-tenth of proportion for the sake of getting the characteristics of a twice-born (for the disciple) and to permeate him with the essence of Lord Rudra (Śiva) as well as for the purification of the food etc. and for the (rites of) *garbhādhāna*, *simanta*, and *nāmakaraṇa*.[2]

11. The *garbhādhāna* is spoken as that which elevates the soul of the disciple by breaking the bonds and making him gain the sonship of Lord Rudra (Śiva).

12. The *puṁsavana* is considered as the manifestation of independant attributes of the soul in the initiated. The dawn of knowledge by means of discrimination in the disciple clouded by illusion is the *simantavardhana* (growth of *sīmanta*).

13. One's birth is considered to be the evolution out of the principle of absolute bliss etc. The wakening (of consciousness) is by means of the principle of supreme bliss in the initiated which has become equal to the Supreme Being in the spiritual perfection.

---

1. Posture of finger indicating evolution.
2. See Ch. 75 Verses 13-17.

14. (Then the preceptor) should carry into the lotus of his heart his own soul resembling a spark of fire by (exhibiting) the *saṁhāra mudrā* (formation with the fingers denoting gathering).

15. Then the principal *mantra* should be uttered along with the retention of breath and the union of God Śiva and his own soul should be brought about in his heart.

16-17. (Then the preceptor) well-versed in the procedure (relating to the performance of sacrifices) should carry his pure consciousness to the region of Śiva from the sacrificial performances which are the cause of Brahmā (and others) by means of exhalation of breath and collect it by showing the *udbhava mudrā* (formation with fingers denoting generation) and (repeating) the *mantra* of the heart and exhaling the breath he should locate it in the petals of lotus of the heart of the disciple.

18. The preceptor should duly propitiate Lord Śiva and the fire-god. The disciple (should be made) to bow down to the self (preceptor). (He) should then make the disciple hear conventions.

19. One should not blaspheme scriptures or God. One should not leap across the materials of worship. One must propitiate Lord Śiva, the fire-god and the preceptor as long as one is alive.

20. One has to impart these instructions to children, old people, women, people addicted to pleasures, and sick people according to their capacity (to preserve them) and in entirety to those who can practise them.

21-22. After having consecrated in a vessel the symbols of discipline—tuft, ashes, staff and loin cloth in order with the *iśāna*, *hṛd* and *saṁhitā mantras* ending with (the syllable) *svāhā* (oblation) as before, (the preceptor) should show them to the presiding deity of sacrificial site after having quickly cast in the fire the residual offering.

23. Having kept them for a while under the pitcher for the sake of protection, the preceptor should give them to the person who takes the vow after having obtained permission of Lord Śiva.

24. Thus in this special spiritual initiation a child especially becomes fit to have a scriptural knowledge about the fire and oblation unto the fire.

## CHAPTER EIGHTYTHREE

*Mode of spiritual initiation that removes one's bondage:*

*The Lord said* :

1. The principal *mantra* should be stimulated in the spiritual initiation. In order to gain strength (to break) the bonds (of worldly existence) one may do it by the rites of *tāḍana* (striking gently).

2. (Oblations should be offered) with each one of the (principal) *mantras* or thrice with (them). The principal *mantra* together with half the tuft *mantra* (should be repeated) along with (the syllables) *hūm*, *phaṭ*, etc.

3. The principal *mantra* should be stimulated by (the syllables) *Om*, *hrūm*, *hraum*, *haum*, *hrūm*. (assigning) to the heart as well as the tuft and face with (the syllables) *Om*, *hrūm*, *hraum*, *hrūm*, *phaṭ*.

4. One should do the rite of stimulation for each part of the principal *mantra* in all ceremonies performed to cause injury (to one's enemy) while the (syllable) *vaṣaṭ* is appended to the principal *mantra* in ceremonies intended to bring peace and prosperity.

5. In all instances of annual rites, oblations should be done with religious acts for all desired results along with (the syllables) *vaṣaṭ* (and) *vauṣaṭ*.

6. Then after having worshipped the disciple having a pure body and seated on a circle on the right side of one's self, (the preceptor) should contemplate upon a thread as the *suṣumnā* (an artery of human body).

7. The tuft of hair (of the disciple) should be tied with the principal (*mantra*) and (one end of the string) should be led to (touch) the toe. In the case of (the disciple) yearning for salvation (the string) should be tied on the body of the disciple showing the *saṁhāra* (*mudrā*) (posture of fingers denoting gathering).

8. (The String) should be attached on the right side in the case of males and on the left side in the case of females. The female deity should be worshipped with the *mantra* of the deity on the head.

9. The thread should be collected with the *saṁhāra mudrā*

and placed with the same (*mudrā*). The *nāḍi* (artery) should (be mentally) collected with the principal (*mantra*) and placed on the string and worshipped with the *mantra* of the heart.

10. Having covered it with the Rudra (*mantra*), oblations should be offered thrice with the *mantra* of the heart for accomplishing the presence. It is the same way in the case of female deity also.

11-13. *Om*, *hām* obeisance to the path of letters, *hām* obeisance to the path of residence (*bhavana*), *Om*, *hām* obeisance to the path of phases. Having located the path of purification on the thread and sprinkled water on the disciple with the weapon and beaten gently the heart (of the disciple) with flower consecrated by (the *mantra* of) the weapon, the preceptor should (mentally) enter the body of the disciple (by pronouncing) the syllable *hūm* and exhaling the breath. The spirit situated in the *haṁsa-bija* should be separated by (the *mantra* of) the weapon: *Om*, *haum*, *hūm*, *phaṭ*.

14. Having covered the same with the *śaktisūtra* (the thread of energy) by (uttering) the *mantra hāṁ ham* oblations, it should be joined with the thread which has become artery, by (showing) the *saṁhāramudrā* (posture made with the fingers indicating gathering) *Oṁ hāṁ haṁ hām* salutations to the soul.

15. It should thus be conceived as pervasive. It should then be covered by the *mantra* of the armour. Oblations should be made thrice with (the *mantra* of) the heart for the sake of invoking the presence.

16. Having located the principle of knowledge (in the thread), one should look at it as beyond the state of bliss. Other principles which have become *mantras* as they were should be located in that. One should look at it with (the *mantra*) "*Oṁ*, *hāṁ*, *haum* obeisance to the *kalāpāśa* (the bondage of phases) beyond absolute bliss".

17-18. Two principles (out of the twentyfive), *mantra* of single word, sixteen letters, eight worlds, two (principal) arteries (*iḍā* and *piṅgalā*), (letters) *ka* and *tha*, the one object (of sense-perception, the one fundamental attribute, the one fundamental cause and the eternal blissful one (*śadāśiva*) should be contemplated as having been located in the (phase of) white colour beyond the absolute bliss.

19. *Om hauṁ huṁ phaṭ* to the *katapāśa* beyond the region of absolute bliss. Having collected the latter by (showing) the *saṁhāramudrā* (posture of fingers denoting gathering), it should be placed over the thread. It should then be worshipped and three oblations (of clarified butter) should be made for its presence (in the thread).

20-21. Two principles (out of twenty-five), two letters *ka* and *tha*, two principal arteries (*iḍā* and *piṅgalā*), two qualities, two *mantras* and one supreme lord situated in the lotus (of the heart), twelve terms (denoting god), seventeen worlds, one of the objects (of sense-perception) should be conceived as merged in the dark phase which is beyond the region of bliss. (Lord) Acyuta should be meditated upon therein.

22. Having gathered it after a gentle stroking, it should be placed at the mouths of the nerve. Oblations should be made thrice with the respective *mantras* for the sake of its presence.

23-24. The seven (fundamental) principles, twentyone words, six letters, one path-way, twentyfive worlds, three qualities and an object for which Rudra is the cause should be located in the principle of knowledge and the *mantras*, artery, (the latters) *ka* and *tha* higher above.

25-26. Having taken the weapon, twenty-two words, six worlds, six *kalās* (phases), four qualities, three *mantras* and an object for which (Lord) Viṣṇu is the cause should be meditated at the base. The (rites of) beating should be done in the white (phase).

27-29. Then having placed (the same) in the nerve in the navel (region), one should offer oblations for the sake of its presence. (The preceptor) should then locate (the syllable) *hrim*, hundred worlds, twentyeight words, twice each of the *mantras*, artery, the winds as well as senses, the principle of the letter, the five objects of sense-perception and the (first) cause governed by the *brahmāṇḍa-mantra*, four times the *śambaras* (a religious observance) in the principle of non-action of yellow colour. It should then be beaten.

30. The principles which were left out at the outset should be located on the thread and worshipped. Three oblations should be offered unto the fire for the sake of its presence.

31. Thus having gathered the principles from the body of the disciple, they should be located in the thread. In the initia-

tion with the *mantras*, it should be done accompanied by religious-sacrificial performances.

32. Other rites (should be undertaken) for the sake of initial protection of the body (of the disciple) until the *mantra* accomplishes the desired fruits.

33-34. The subtle soul awakening (*mantra*) should be meditated in the principles of beatific knowledge. (The rites of) *arpaṇa* (pleasing) and *dipana* (stimulation) should be performed in the same way with three oblations with their respective *mantras* (such as) "*Om, haum* oblations to the phase of beatitude beyond that of absolute bliss" which is (the *mantra* for) the rite of pleasing; "*Om, hām, ham, hām, hum, phaṭ* to the phase of beatitude beyond that of absolute bliss" which is (the *mantra* for) stimulation. Then that thread should be considered as pervading the five nerve centres.

35. (The thread) should be smeared with saffron and clarified butter and (Lord) Śiva should be worshipped therein along with his attendants with the *kalā-mantras* ending with *hum phaṭ* after having pierced the bondage through the occult nerve.

36. Having (mentally) entered inside (with syllables) ending with obeisance, (the preceptor) should take hold of (the thread) and tie it. *Om, hūm, hām, haum, hām, hum, phaṭ*, I take hold of the phase exceeding that of pure bliss.

37. (The preceptor) should place that thread on the shoulder of the disciple after having made him seated for the sake of successful completion.

38. One hundred oblations should be made with the principal *mantra* for the expiation of all the sins (of the disciple). (The oblation should be made) in a covered shallow saucer (if the disciple) is a male and in a saucer of enlarged belly (in the case of a) female (disciple).

39-42. The thread which has been covered with the *mantra* of the heart should be placed and worshipped with (the *mantra* of) the heart. After having been made pure by the worship of Śiva and his attendants the thread should be placed under the pitcher (saying), "let protection be announced". After having placed a flower in the hands (of the disciple) and having worshipped the pitcher and other things, the disciple should be made to bow down and led outside the sacrificial shed. After having drawn three circles, the disciple should be made to sit facing the north in the case of aspiration for emancipation and made to sit facing the east in the case of aspiration (for enjoyment). Three handfuls of *pañcagavya* (the five things got from a cow) should be sipped at the outset.

43-44. After that, three or eight morsels of gruel unpolluted by the touch of the teeth should be offered with the hand holding a *kuśa* with the leaf of *palāśa*, if desirous of emancipation and with the leaf of *pippala*, if desirous of enjoyment.

45-47. Having offered profuse feeding with (the *mantra* of) the heart, the pure water should be given for rinsing the mouth. After having given the teeth stick (for cleansing the teeth) with (the repetition of the *mantra* of) the heart, one hundred and eight oblations should be offered with the principal (*mantra*) for the removal of defects such as deficiency etc. After having dedicated all acts to the lord of the ground, the deity should be given adieu after worship and Lord Caṇḍeśa should be worshipped. Then the materials of worship should be removed and the remnants of the gruel should be offered to the fire.

48. After having worshipped the pitcher and the protectors of the world and bidding them adieu, one should bid adieu to the attendant God and fire if they have been retained on the periphery of the mystic circle.

49. Then having offered oblations in a condensed way to the protector of the world at the periphery, one should enter the sacrificial shed after bathing with ashes or pure oil.

50. (If the disciples are) householders, (they) should be seated) on a bed of *darbhas* with their heads facing the east and protected well (and if the disciples are) monks, (they should be seated) on a bed of ashes with their heads facing the south with (the repetition of the *mantra* oi) the heart.

51. (Then the preceptor) should bathe the disciples who had tied-up their tufts into knots along with the *mantras* of the weapon and *sapta māṇavaka* and walk out of the place again.

*Om, hili, hili,* oblations to the trident-bearer.

52. After having sipped five things got from a cow and the gruel and having collected sticks for cleansing the teeth, and having rinsed the mouth (with water), and contemplated on (Lord) Śiva and having reached the pure bed, the preceptor

should enter (again) remembering the rites performed in connection with initiation. Thus, the mode of preliminary consecration relating to initiation has been described briefly.

## CHAPTER EIGHTYFOUR

### *Mode of Initiation for Emancipation*

*The Lord said* :

1. Then the preceptor having got-up early in the morning should bathe and finish worship. (Seeing in the dream) curd, ginger, meat and wine as being consumed is commended.

2. So also riding on an elephant or horse as well as seeing a white cloth in the dream is auspicious. (Seeing in the dream) as smearing the body with oil is inauspicious. Oblation (should be done) with the *aghora mantra* for the sake of appeasement.

3. After having performed two daily rites (the two twilight worships) and entering the sacrificial shed, (the preceptor) should rinse (his mouth) and perform duties as in the daily routines as laid down for the incidental rites.

4-5. After having purified his self and (the part of the fore-arm known as) the *śivahasta* and having located in his inner being the Gods Indra and others in order and worshipped the pitcher, Śiva worship should be done at the shed or on the ground. Worship of fire and the (rite of) *mantratarpaṇa* (offering oblations along with the recitation of *mantras*) (should be done) until the final oblation is done.

6. After having offered one hundred and eight oblations with the *mantra* of the weapon, for the removal of defects due to bad dreams, one should activate the *mantra* with the subtle syllable *hum*.

7. Having made the *antarbali* (the rite of middle offering) in between the (sacrificial) pitcher and the ground for the entry of the disciple, and having obtained permission, the preceptor should walk out of the shed.

8. One should do (the acts of) placing on a mystical diagram (and other acts) in the religious initiation. The preparatory

oblation (should be done) with the end of *darbha* which should be looked upon as the umbilical chord of the latter.

9. Having offered three oblations with the principal *mantra* for accomplishing its presence, (the preceptor) should worship lord Śiva in the pitcher and take hold of the thread.

10. It should be tied on the tuft of the disciple who would remain standing on the right-hand-side (of the preceptor) in the manner that the thread hangs down upto the toe of the foot.

11. Having placed it and looked at it mentally as pervading the non-action, one should know that more than one hundred and eight worlds are in it.

12-25. Kapāla, Aja, Buddha, Vajradeha, Pramardana, Vibhūti, Avyaya, Śāstā, Pinākī, Tridaśādhipa, Agni, Rudra, Hutāśī, Piṅgala, Khādaka, Hara, Jvalana, Dahana, Babhru, Bhasmāntaka, Kṣapāntaka, Yāmya, Mṛtyuhara, Dhātā, Vidhātā, Kāryarañjaka, Kāla, Dharma, Adharma, Saṁyoktā, Viyogaka, Nairṛta, Māraṇa, Hantā, Krūradṛṣṭi, Bhayānaka, Ūrdhvāṁśaka, Virūpākṣa, Dhūmralohita, Daṁṣṭravān, Atibala, Pāśahasta, Mahābala, Śveta, Jayabhadra, Dīrghabāhu, Jalāntaka, Vaḍavāsya and Bhīma are known as (the manifestations of) Varuṇa. Śīghra, Laghu, Vāyuvega, Sūkṣma, Tīkṣṇa, Kṣapāntaka, Pañcāntaka, Pañcaśikha, Kapardī, Meghavāhana, Jaṭāmukuṭadhārī, Nānāratnadhara, Nidhīśa, Rūpavān, Dhanya, Saumyadeha, Prasādakṛt, Prakāśa, Lakṣmīvān and Kāmarūpa, the latter ten; Vidyādhara, Jñānadhara, Sarvajña, Vedapāraga, Mātṛvṛtta, Piṅgākṣa, Bhūtapāla, Balipriya, Sarvavidyāvidhātā, Sukhaduḥkhahara are the ten. Ananta, Pālaka, Dhīra, Pātālādhipati, Vṛṣa, Vṛṣadhara, Vīrya, Grasana, Sarvatomukha and Lohita known as the ten (manifestations of) Rudra seated on the hoods of snakes; Śambhu, Vibhu, Gaṇādhyakṣa, Tryakṣa, Tridaśavandita, Saṁhāra, Vihāra, Lābha, Lipsu (and) Vicakṣaṇa; (and) Attā, Kuhakakālāgnirudra, Hāṭaka, Kūṣmāṇḍa, Satya, Brahmā, Viṣṇu and Rudra are the eight Rudras who all remain in the interior of hemisphere (of the universe). The names of these (Gods) as well as the names of worlds should be remembered.

26. Bhavodbhava, Sarvabhūta, Sarvabhūtasukhaprada (Granter of felicity to all), Sarvasānnidhyakṛt, (all pervasive) are worshipped by Brahmā, Viṣṇu and Rudra.

27. O Adored one ! Existing prior to all beings ! *Om* ! The Witness ! *Om* ! The Destroyer of Rudra ! *Om* ! Sun ! *Om* ! The Sound ! *Om* ! The Subtle ! *Om* ! Śiva ! The Granter of all things to all beings ! The pervading life-force of all things ! The Creator of Brahmā, Viṣṇu and Rudra ! *Om* ! Salutations to Śiva.

O Guha (son of Lord Śiva and Pārvatī) ! (in the thread described above) the principle of non-action should be contemplated as impregnated with the twenty-eight beatific states, together with the eight letters of which the *sadya*, *hṛd*, *astra*, and *netra mantras* are composed.

28. The letter *ma* is the emblem of the mystic seed, the two occult nerves known as *iḍā* and *piṅgalā*, the two vital winds *prāṇa* and *apāna* and the organs of smell and generation.

29. Among the five qualities smell etc., the quality of smell is spoken as the matter. The principle of matter is yellow (in colour) symbolises thunderbolt and is square-shaped.

30. Its extension is one hundred crores of *yojanas* (a *yojana* is equivalent to eight miles). It should be known that the fourteen creative principles are lying concealed in this (zone).

31. It is the first being and the source of the four-fold existence of all celestial beings, Manu, etc. animals and birds and crawling insects.

32-33. (It is also) spoken (as the source of things born of) the fifth, the immovable things, the sixth, the beings other than human (such as) goblins, demons, *yakṣas*, *gandharvas* and Indra, the seventh, the God of life (Yama) and the eighth, Brahmā. The earthly principle is considered as controlling the eighth.

34-35. Having contemplated the absolute dissolution (of the universe) in the *prakṛti* (the original source of the material world) and the intellect and Brahmā, the enjoyer, as the cause, (as well as) the non-action located along with all the worlds continuing through his waking-state, one should unite the appropriate *mantras*.

*Om*, *hām*, *hrūm*, *hām* to the thread standing for the beatitude of non-action *hūm*, *phaṭ*, *tat*. *Om*, *hām*, *ham* oblations to the thread standing for the beatitude of non-action. Having drawn in breath along with (the above *mantra*) and shown the *aṅkuśa-mudrā* (posture made with fingers denoting a goad), and having withheld the breath and carrying it up by showing the *saṁhāra-mudrā* (formation with fingers representing gathering)and with (the *mantra*) *Om*, *hrūm*, *hrām*, *hram* to the thread of beatitude of non-action *hūm*, *phaṭ* and having placed it in the pitcher by showing the *udbhavamudrā* (formation with fingers denoting generation) and discharging the breath and repetition of (the *mantra*) *Om*, *Om*, *hram*, *hām* obeisance to the thread of beatitude of non-action and having offered the respectful offering with (the *mantra*) *Om*, *hām*, obeisance to the thread of beatitude of non-action and worshipped, (the preceptor) should offer three oblations with face turned away ending with (the word) "Oblation" for the sake of accomplishing its presence and then offer the concluding three oblations. (Lord) Brahmā should be invoked with (the *mantra*) *Om*, *hām*, obeisance to Brahmā and worshipped. (He) should be appeased (with oblations) with (the word) "Oblations". (The preceptor should say), "O Brahman ! I initiate (this disciple) in this (world) over which you hold sway".

36-37. One should submit (to the lord) "you should be propitious to him". Goddess Vāgīśvarī, the deity of protection, who is of the form of desire, knowledge and action and is of six kinds and is the sole cause (of the universe) should be invoked with (the *mantra* of) the heart. One should worship and satisfy the Goddess as follows :—

38-40. (Goddess) Vāgīśvarī, the cause of agitating the receptacles should gently be struck (against) the chest (of the disciple) with the repetition of the *hṛt* (*mantra*) and the principal *mantra* concluding with *hūm phaṭ* and the *mantra* of the arrow. (The preceptor) who knows the procedure (of these rites) should then enter into the inner self of the disciple and then divide the effulgent consciousness (of the disciple) in the heart endowed with the thread located in the beatitude of non-action and resembling a spark of fire, with *jyeṣṭhā* (*mantra*) as follows:— *Om*, *hām*, *hūm*, *haḥ*, *hūm*, *phaṭ* and with (*the mantra*) *Om*, *hām*, oblations and then with the *aṅkuśamudrā* (posture with fingers denoting the goad).

41-43. Having drawn it with its appropriate (*mantra*) and seized it, it should be united with his soul. *Om*, *hām*, *hrūm*, *hām* obeisance to the soul. Having imagined the union of his own soul with discharge of the breath, it should be led to the abode of

Śiva after having gradually discarded with discrimination the cause such as Brahmā, etc. One should cast it in the womb of (Goddess) Vīgīśvarī with the (exhibition of) *udbhava-mudrā* (posture with fingers denoting generation) after having carried it for impregnation in all the principles simultaneously. *Om, hām, hām, hām*, obeisance to the soul. One should worship with this (*mantra*) and after oblations five times.

44. One should do the purification of the body with the *mantra* of the heart in the case of all other principles. The *puṁsavana* (the rite of determining the sex) is not done, as there can be a feminine form also.

45. The *sīmantonnayana* (parting of the hair) and the divine limbs (should be treated) as the body. (The purificatory rite) at the birth for all human beings should be done with the *mantra* of the head with aversion.

46. (The preceptor) should similarly contemplate upon the regions over which they have control, with the *mantra* of Śiva. The objects of sense pleasure (should be contemplated) with the *mantra* of the armour and the worldly objects with (the *mantra* of) the weapons.

47-48. One should contemplate on that one which is known as dissolution, as the form of delusion and unbreakable. Streams should be purified by (contemplating) the *mantra* of Śiva and the purification of the principles should be done with (the *mantra* of) the heart. Five times five oblations should be made in respect of the rites of *garbhādhāna* and others in order for the sake of cessation of the bonds due to sinful acts.

49. One hundred oblations should be made with (the *mantra* of) the heart after having accomplished expiation. By obstructing the force of sins one can severe the bonds.

50. Five times five oblations should be offered with the *mantra* of the weapon ending with oblations. By the repetition of the (*mantra* of the) weapon seven times one gets free from bonds ending with illusion.

51-53. The accomplishment by the *mantra* kalpa of the weapon is like cutting with a scissor. *Ām, hūm*, to the thread of the beatitude of non-action, *hūm, phaṭ*, Having accomplished the cessation of bondage with the hands and with the *mantra* of the arrow, the thread should be untied and laid in a circular form on the sacrificial ladle filled with clarified butter. One should then burn it with the *mantra* of the weapon and reduce it into ashes with the weapon after having offered five oblations for the removal of the goad of bondage. *Om*, *haḥ*, to the weapons *hūm*, *phat*. Expiation should then be made with eight oblations made with (the *mantra* of) the weapon.

54-56. After having invoked (Lord) Brahmā, he should be worshipped and appeased. Then *Om*, *hām*, O Brahman, whom soul and touch cannot perceive, you take (these oblations). Oblations. He should be informed of the authority invested in him by offering three oblations. "O Brahman ! you should not again bind this being whose sins have all been burnt. You listen to the mandate of Lord Śiva." After having bid farewell to Lord Brahmā, (the preceptor) should slowly fill ir the soul of the disciple by his own soul with retention of breath and exhibiting *saṁhāramudrā* (posture with fingers representing collection). (That soul) would then look like the disc of the moon at the beginning of the eclipses at a particular spot.

57. After having taken it out, it should be located in the thread with the discharge of breath and with *udbhavamudrā* (posture with fingers denoting generation). After having worshipped it, the preceptor should place the drop of water in the offering vessel resembling the nectar, on the head of the disciple for the purpose of completion.

58. After having bid farewell to the (divine) parents, the final oblation should be made with the *mantra* of Śiva ending with *vauṣaṭ*. Thus the mode of completion has ended. The non-action principle is thus purified.

## CHAPTER EIGHTYFIVE

### *Mode of purifying the Beatific principle of establishment*

*The lord said* :

1-2. The union of the two principles good and bad should be brought about by the application of short and long (vowels) associated with sound. *Om, hām, hrūm, hām*, water, effulgence, wind, sky, the subtle principles, organs, intellect, the three qualities and ego (are) the twenty-four principles (and) the *puruṣa* (the soul) (is the twenty-fifth).

3. (The preceptor) should imagine the letters beginning with *kha* and ending with *jya* as merged in the above twenty-five principles.

4. The number of Rudras is equivalent to the *bhuvanas* (Worlds), which are known to be fifty-six. They are as follows:

5-12. Amareśa, Prabhāva, Naimiṣa, Puṣkara, Pādi, Daṇḍi, Bhavabhūti, Nakulīśa the eighth, Hariścandra, Śrīśaila the tenth, Anvīśa, Abhrātikeśa, Mahākāla, Madhyama, Kedāra, Bhairava, spoken as the second (group of) eight. Then Gayākurukṣetra-khalānādikanādika, Vimala, Aṭṭahāsa, Mahendra, Bhīma, Vasvāpada, Rudrakoṭi, Aviyukta, Mahābala, Gokarṇa, Bhadrakarṇa, Svarṇākṣa, Sthāṇu Ajeya, Sarvajña, Bhāsvara, Sūdanāntara, Subāhu, Mattarūpī, Viśāla, Jaṭila, Raudra, Piṅgalākṣa, Kāladaṁṣṭrī, Vidura, Ghora, Prājāpatya, Hutāśana, Kāmarūpī, Kāla, Karṇa, Bhayānaka, Mataṅga, Piṅgala, Hara, Dātṛ (saṁjñaka), Śaṅkukarṇa, Vidhāna, Śrīkaṇṭha and Candraśekhara.

13. Their attributes (to be used) along with their names are also described then. O (All) pervasive ! *Om*, Formless ! *Om*, Conqueror ! *Om*, Lustre ! *Om*, Light ! *Om*, (Supreme) Being ! *Om*, Fire ! *Om*, Smokeless ! *Om*, Not reduced to ashes ! *Om*, One without a beginning ! *Om*, Of manifold forms ! *Om*, The Agitator ! *Om*, The Earth ! *Om*, the Atmosphere ! *Om*, Heavens ! *Om*, Deathless ! Born from dissolution ! Auspicious ! Killer ! Absolute Soul ! Supreme Deity ! Lord of celestials ! Lord of Good will ! Supreme lustre ! Presiding deity of yoga ! (Your) release ! The first soul ! All in all ! Lord of all beings ! are the thirty-two[1] attributes. Vāmadeva, Śiva, and Śikhā are the three *mantras* in the subtle form.

14. The two occult sychic nerves *gāndhāri* and *suṣumnā*, then the winds *samāna* and *udāna*, the organs of taste and reproduction (are also worshipped).

15-22. The sentiments are the material objects. The quali-

1. But, actually only twentynine have been given.

ties are perception, hearing, touch and taste. The mystic diagram should be circular and bear the mark of a white lotus.

After having contemplated on the worlds as well as those established along with the eagle-bannered god who is the cause for the establishment in the dreamy state, the thread should be placed on the body with (the recitation) of the appropriate *mantra* and retained (by the preceptor). "*Om*, *hām*, *khūm*, *hām*, to the thread of the beatitude of consecration *Om*, *phaṭ*". With this (*mantra*) and ending with 'oblations' it should be drawn while drawing in breath and exhibiting *aṅkuśa-mudrā* (formation with fingers denoting a goad). Then "*Om*, *hām*, *hrūm*, *hrām*, *hrūm* to the thread of the beatitude of consecration *hrūm*, *phaṭ*". With this and retention of breath and showing *saṁhāramudrā* (formation with fingers denoting gathering) it should be taken from the occult nerve below the heart. *Om*, *hām*, *hram*, *hrām*, *hām*, obeisance to the thread of the beatitude of consecration. With this (*mantra*) and showing the *udbhavamudrā* (formation with fingers denoting generation) and discharge of breath, it should be placed on the pitcher. Having worshipped with the *mantra* "*Om*, *hām*, *hrīm* obeisance to the thread of the beatitude of consecration" ending with 'oblations', and offered three oblations for ensuring its continuance (lord) Viṣṇu should be invoked (with the *mantra*) "*Om*, *hām*, obeisance to Viṣṇu", worshipped and offered oblations O Viṣṇu ! I initiate the disciple who is desirous to get liberation herein under your authority". You should be propitious. Thus Lord Viṣṇu should be informed. Then the (Goddess) Vāgīśvarī and Lord Vāgīśa should be invoked as before, worshipped and offered oblations and the disciple should be gently struck on the chest. *Om*, *hām*, *hām*, *ham*, *phaṭ*. (The preceptor) should enter with the same (*mantra*) and severe the consciousness in the above-said thread with the (*mantra*) of weapon and (showing) the *aṅkuśamudrā* (formation with fingers denoting a goad) and *jyeṣṭhā* (*mantra*) *Om*, *hām*, *ham*, *hom*, *hrūm*, *phaṭ*. Having drawn it with (the *mantra* of) the heart ending with "oblations", it should be lodged in one's own soul repeating the same (*mantra*) and ending with "obeisance". *Om*, *hām*, *ham*, *hom* obeisance to the soul. The union of divine parents should be imagined as before with the *udbhavamudrā* (posture with fingers denoting generation) and (the seed of the soul) should be cast into the womb of the goddess by exhibiting the same (*mudrā*) from the left. *Om, hām, ham, hām* obeisance to the soul. the birth of the body should be (accomplished) by (the *mantra* of) the heart, the postnatal (ceremony) by (the *mantra* of) the head.

23. Otherwise its possession (could be accomplished) by (the *mantra* of) the tuft. For the sake of enjoyment of pleasures it should be done by the *mantra* of the armour. In regard to the purity of principles (it should be done) with (the *mantra* of) the heart and in the case of impregnation it is in the same way as before.

24-25. For cutting bonds (it should be) accomplished by (the *mantra* of) the head. Having cut the bonds thus, the preceptor should repeat (the *mantra*)hundred times. Even after having cut the bonds thus, (the preceptor) should cut it with the repetition of the *mantra* of the weapon and with a scissor over which the *mantra* of the beatific principles has been repeated. *Om, hrim,* to the thread of the beatitude of consecration *haḥ phaṭ*. The thread should be removed and kept in a circular shape as before (described in the previous chapter) with (the repetition of the *mantra* of the weapon.

26. Having placed it over the sacrificial ladle filled with clarified butter, oblations should be done with the *mantra* of the beatific principles and weapons. Five oblations should be made with (the *mantra* of) the weapon for the cessation of shoots of bondage.

27. Eight oblations should be made for the sake of expiation. *Om, haḥ* to the weapons *hrūm, phaṭ*. Lord Hṛṣīkeśa should be invoked and worshipped and offered oblations.

28. As laid down earlier investiture of authority should be made "*om, hām* accept this fees of sentiment, oblations" (is the *mantra* which should be repeated). O Hara ! (you) should not remain as a bond of this being (the disciple) whose bondage has completely been burnt away. Listen to this mandate of Lord Śiva. Having bid farewell to Lord Govinda (Viṣṇu) and united the soul of knowledge which resembles the moon's disc half uncovered by the band by exhibiting the *saṁhāramudrā* (posture with fingers denoting gathering) and having bid farewell by showing the *udbhavamudrā* (formation with fingers denoting generation), the drop of water should be placed on the thread as before. Having bid farewell to the (divine)

parents and having worshipped the fire with flowers, etc. the final oblation should be made as laid down. Thus the consecration also gets purified.

## CHAPTER EIGHTYSIX

### *Mode of Purification of scriptural knowledge*

*The Lord said* :

1. The union of the beatific principle of knowledge and that of ancient one should be done as before, after having located the principles. The union should be done with (the *mantra*) *Om, hom, hṛim.*

2. Attachment, pure knowledge, fate, time, illusion and ignorance together with beatific principle are (known as) the seven unions.

3. The six letters, ra, la, va, śa, ṣa, and sa are said (to represent) the branches of learning. The terms beginning with *praṇava* (*Om*) are twenty-one (in number) (as below)—*Om* obeisance to Śiva, who is the Lord of all (created) things. *Ham,* to (Lord) Śiva, to Īśāna at my head, to Tatpuruṣa at my face, to Aghora at the heart, to Vāmadeva at the anus, to the form of Sadyojāta. *Om* obeisance again and again to the extremely secret form, to the protector, to the deathless one, to the Lord of all beings, to the form of effulgence, to the Supreme Lord (one who pervades) the sky by thoughts *Om.*

4-8. *Om* the forms of Rudras and the *bhuvanas* (worlds) are described now. The first one is Vāmadeva (Lord of irascible nature), next Sarvabhavodbhava (the source of all beings), Vajradeha (possessing a strong body), Prabhu (lord), Dhātā (the supporter), Krama (order), Vikrama (conquest), Suprabha (resplendent), Vaṭu (youth), Praśānta (tranquil), Paramākṣara (supreme knowledge), Śiva (auspicious), Saśiva (endowed with auspiciousness), Babhru (tawny-coloured), Akṣaya (unperishable), Śambhu (one who begets peace), Adṛṣṭarūpa (having an invisible form), Adṛṣṭanāma (having an unseen name), Rūpavardhana (promoter of beatuty),

Manonmana (one who agitates the mind), Mahāvīrya (the mighty one), Citrāṅga (one who is variegated) (and) Kalyāṇa (the blessed one). Thus (the Rudras) are known by the twenty-five names (together with) Mantra (the controller of mind), Ghora (the dreadful one) and Amara (the immortal one). Pūṣā and hastijihvā are the two occult nerves in that (above-said) beatific phase. Vyāna, nāga and prabhañjana (are the vital winds).

9. The only object is that of the form. The feet and the eyes are the organs. Sound, touch and sight are known as the three qualities.

10. Here the state is that of deep sleep. Lord Rudra is the cause. All the worlds should be looked upon as located in this (beatific principle of) knowledge.

11. Gentle beating, cutting and entry into it should also be done. Having pulled it from the region of the heart by means of knowledge, it should be seized.

12. It should be super-imposed on one's own soul. The beatific principle should be firmly held and then placed in the fire-pit, after having invoked (lord) Rudra, the cause, and submitted (to him) the (new born) child.

13. Having invoked the divine parents, (the preceptor) should gently strike the (new-born) child in the heart (of the disciple). After having entered it with the *mantra* spoken earlier, one should unite it with his own soul.

14. After having drawn it out and taking it, it should be united with his own soul by the method described already. It should be united in the womb from the left side. After (the repetition of) the *dvādaśa* (twelve) letters of *mantra* it should be taken out.

15. The rites relating to the birth and post-natal purification of the body, enjoyment, deep absorption, purification of the stream and of the principles should be performed.

16. One hundred oblations should be made as expiation as laid down for the removal of all bondages due to impurities.

17. The severance of bondage (should be done) with (the *mantra* of) the weapon. The vanishing force of impurities

should be cut and pounded. Then the thread should be placed in a circular form[1].

18. Its burning and the absence of those letters as well as expiation should then be done. The invocation of(god) Rudra, (and his) worship and the submission of sensibles of sight and smell (should be done).

19. *Om, hrīm* O Rudra ! take this fee of the sensibles of sight and smell. Oblations. After having conveyed the mandate of lord Śambhu (Śiva) and bidding farewell to (lord) Rudra, the cause, the pure spirit should be located (first) in himself and then located in the thread of bondage.

20. The subtle speck (of the soul) should be placed on his head and the divine) parents should be bid farewell. Then the final oblation should be made, as laid down, which completes all formalities.

21. The act of gently beating and other acts should be done in the beatific knowledge as described earlier. Here the speciality is the location of (the soul as a) speck. Thus the beatific knowledge is purified.

## CHAPTER EIGHTYSEVEN

### *Mode of purification of the principle of peace*

*The Lord said* :

1-2. The beatific knowledge should be united now with the (principle of) peace as laid down. The two principles lie in the (principle of) peace. Bhāveśvara and Sadāśiva are spoken as the two letters *ha* and *kṣa*. The Rudras are equal in number to the worlds. They are as follows :

3. Prabhava (valiant), Samaya (time), Kṣudra (little), Vimala (free from impurity), Śiva (auspicious), Ghana (heavy), Nirañjanākāra (unstained form), Svaśiva (auspicious to himself), Dīptikāraṇa (cause of brilliance), Tridaśeśvara (lord of

1. This act and the succeeding ones are same as those described in the previous chapter.

the thirty (gods), Tridaśa (representing the thirty), Kālasaṁjñaka (known as the time), Sūkṣma (minute), Ambujeśvara (lord of the lotus). These are the Rudras firmly established in the principle of peace.

4. (Obeisance) to the one who pervades the ether, to the form which manifests as the ether, to the all-pervasive, to the auspicious one, to the endless, to one who has no master, to one who is not having any hold, to the firm one, to the eternal, to the one firmly established in the seat of *yoga*, to the eternal yogin, and one who partakes of such meditation (of votaries) are the twelve terms (used in their invocation).

5. The preceptor should meditate with the two protective *mantras* (known as) *bindu* and *upakāraka*, the two occult nerves *alambuṣa* and *syasa* and the two vital winds *kṛkara* and *kūrmaka* in the subtle phase.

6. The organs of skin and hand are considered as the two senses of perception for this beatific principle. The attributes of touch and sound are the only two attributes. lord (Śiva) is the only cause of thesc.

7. Having contemplated upon the different worlds which are located in the beatific principle of peace as the fourth state (of consciousness) (in which the soul gets united with the Supreme being), (the preceptor) should do the (acts of) gentle beating, division, entry and union.

8. Having drawn the (beatific principle of) peace from the string of the face, it should be held (by the preceptor). Having merged it in one's own self, the beatific principle should be held and projected in the receptacle.

9. "O Lord ! I am initiating this disciple desirous of release (from bondage) subject to your control. You have to be beneficial to him." The appeal should thus be made.

10. After having invoked the divine parents and doing the gentle beating of the disciple etc. and collecting the soul-force, it should be united with his preceptor's own soul.

11. Having invoked the divine parents as before by (showing) *mudrā* known as *udbhava* (formation with fingers denoting generation), it should be located in the womb of the goddess by repeating the principal *mantra* of the god preceded by the *mantra* of the heart.

12. A corporeal frame for the beatitude should be done with the (repetition of the *mantra* of the) heart five times. (The *mantra* of) the head (should be repeated) for bringing it into being. Its authority (is accomplished) by (the *mantra* of) the tuft and the enjoyment by (the *mantra* of) the armour.

13. Its repose (is accomplished) by (the repetition of) the *mantra* of weapons. The purification of the currents (is achieved) by (that of lord) Śiva. In (the case of) purification of the principle, (the rites of) *garbhādhāna* etc. (should be done) in the same manner as before.

14. The thread is untied with that of the armour. Having completed the purification thus, one should repeat the *mantras* hundred times. In order to compensate the mitigation of the power of *mantras* five oblations should be made with (the *mantra* of) the weapon.

15. After having untied the thread, it should be severed with a knife by the repetition (of the *mantra*) of the weapon seven times just as the bondage is cut off with the principal *mantra*.

16. (The *mantra* is): "*Om, haum*, to the thread of the beatific principle of peace *haḥ, hūm, phaṭ*. After having untied and made into a circle, the chord should be placed as before in the sacrificial ladle filled with clarified butter with (the repetition of the *mantra* of) the weapon. Oblation should be done with (the *mantra* of) the weapon and of the beatific principle.

17. Five oblations should be made with (the *mantra* of) the weapon for the sake of ending the fresh shoots of bondage. To remedy the obstruction in expiation, eight oblations should then (be made). *Om, haḥ* to the weapon *hūm phaṭ* (is the *mantra* for the same).

18. Having invoked god with (the *mantra* of) the heart, and offered worship and appeasement, the appropriate fee should be offered to him in the prescribed way: "*Om, hām*, O lord ! accept this fee of intellect and ego, oblations."

19. O lord ! You should not remain as a bondage for this being whose all bonds have been burnt away. Thus the mandate of (lord) Śiva should be made to be heard.

20. The god should be bid adieu and the crescent-like soul should be united with the lord Rudra. Then it must be united with one's own (preceptor's) soul in the prescribed way.

21. The same should be united with the thread by showing pure *udbhavamudrā* (formation with fingers denoting generation). The drop of nectar should be put on the head of the disciple with (the repetition of) the principal (*mantra*).

22. Having taken leave of the (divine) parents after worshipping them with flowers etc., (the preceptor) should offer the final oblation to the fire as a concluding rite.

23. Even here the acts of gentle beating etc. should be done as before. The distinctive feature is (the use of) its principal *mantra*. Thus the purification (of the beatific principle) of peace is done without any impediment.

## CHAPTER EIGHTYEIGHT

*Mode of initiation which secures nirvāṇa (liberation from existence)*

*The Lord said* :

1. (The preceptor) should blend the beatific principle surpassing peace with the pure beatific principle of peace and write the principles of letters with that as before. *Om*, *hrīm*, *kṣaum*, *haum*, *hām* (are the syllables used for) the union.

2-5. (Goddess) Śakti and (God) Śiva which are the two principles (of the universe), the eight perfections of the universe (known as) *dipaka* (illuminating), *rocika* (brightening), *mocaka* (delivering from bonds), *ūrdhvagāmi* (ascending up), *vyomarūpa* (of the form of ether), *anātha* (not having any master), *anāśrita* (not being dependent) and the eighth the syllable of *om*, the *mantra* of (lord) Īśāna, the sixteen letters beginning with the letter '*a*' and ending with *visarga* (aspirated sound), the principal *mantra*, the two (occult nerves) *kuhū* and *śaṅkhinī* which are the cause for the body and the two winds *devadatta* and *dhanañjaya* (should be contemplated as pervading the above). The senses of touch and hearing are considered as the materials of sense perception. The principle of sound is the predominating attribute. Its state is the fifth state exceeding that of the fourth state (the state in which the soul becomes one with the supreme soul).

6. Lord Sadāśiva should be known as the sole cause. Having meditated upon the collective beatific principles known as beyond (the beatific principle) of peace, (the rites of) stroking gently etc. should be performed.

7. Having gently beaten the beatific principle of the thread and dividing it (mentally) with (the recitation of the principal *mantra*) ending with *phaṭ*, (the preceptor should penetrate inside the noose (with the recitation of the above *mantra*) ending with (the pronunciation of) salutations and loosen (the beatific principle with the recitation of the above *mantra*) ending with *phaṭ*.

8. Then (the beatific principle of) the thread should be consecrated with (the recitation of) the *mantras* of the tuft (and) heart ending with "oblations" and should be drawn out of the head of the thread with the inhalation of breath and showing the *sṛṇimudrā* (posture with fingers denoting a goad).

9. Having gathered it with the retention of breath, it should be projected into the fire-receptacle with the exhalation of breath (and showing the *mudrā* known as) *udbhava* (posture with fingers denoting generation), after having consecrated with (the *mantra* of) the heart ending with "obeisance".

10. All the worship etc. of this should be accomplished as (it would be done) for the beatitude of non-action after having invoked lord Sadāśiva and worshipping him and making offerings.

11. (The lord should be addressed by the preceptor as follows) :

"I initiate this person (disciple) desirous of emancipation in this well-known mode of life. You should be beneficial (to him)". I am submitting to you with devotion.

12. After having invoked the (divine) parents and having made offerings and achieving their presence, the disciple should gently be struck on the chest with the syllable consecrated by (the *mantra* of) the heart.

13. *Om, hām, hūm, ham, phaṭ*. Having entered (the heart) with (the repetition of) this (*mantra*), the psychic energy should be divided by showing the *aṅkuśa mudrā* (formation with the fingers denoting a goad) and with the weapon along with the noose.

14. *Om, hām, haḥ, hrūm, phaṭ.* Having drawn it (with this *mantra*) duly consecrated and ending with "oblations", it should be united with his own soul by concluding with "obeisance", after having seized it.

15. *Om, hām, ham, him*, obeisance to the soul. After having meditated on the union of the (divine) parents as before by (showing) the *udbhava mudrā* (posture with the fingers denoting generation), (the preceptor) should place (the psychic principle) in the womb of the goddess with the same (*mantra*) and by the left.

16. The (rites of) *garbhādhāna* etc. should be done as laid down earlier. One should repeat (the *mantra* of) release and the bondage is cut off with that of the principal (*mantra*).

17. As before five times five oblations should be done with (the *mantra* of) weapons for the sake of cutting the bonds and to destroy the evil forces in the disciple.

18. With the repetition of the *mantra* of weapons seven times the principal *mantra* of beatitude the bonds should be cut, with the scissor.

19. *Om, hām*, to the noose of beatitude beyond that of peace *haḥ, hūm, phaṭ.* (Then the preceptor) should bid farewell to the noose as described earlier, make it into a circle, place it in the ladle filled with clarified butter and cast it into fire with the (*mantra* of) weapons and of beatitude.

20. Five oblations should be made with (the *mantra* of) the weapon for the removal of the goad of bonds. Eight oblations should be made for compensating atonements.

21. Having invoked lord Sadāśiva with (the *mantra* of) the weapon and done appeasement, one should submit suzerainty as laid down before.

22. "*Om, hām*, Sadāśiva, accept fees (in the form of) the principle of mind. Oblations. O (lord) Sadāśiva ! You should never remain as a bond for this being whose all shackles have been destroyed. You hear the mandate of lord Śiva."

23-24. The final oblation should be made with the principal (*mantra*). (Lord) Sadāśiva should be bid adieu. Then the preceptor should unite in his soul, the pure soul in the body of the pupil just risen like the autumnal moon by showing the *saṁhāramudrā* (posture made with the fingers denoting gathering), after having collected the same by (showing) the *udbhava-mudrā* (posture made with fingers denoting generation).

25. Then (the preceptor) should place drops of water of *arghya* (offered for washing) on the head of the disciple as completion. Having requested the divine parents with great devotion to forgive they should be bid adieu.

26. "O Parents ! You have been put to trouble for the sake of initiating this disciple. Having discarded that gracefully depart with pleasure to your own place."

27. (The preceptor) should then cut off the tuft (of the disciple) of the form of knowledge to a length of four finger-breadths with the scissors, the weapon of lord Śiva, (duly) consecrated with the *mantra* of the tuft.

28. "*Om, klīm*; to the tuft, *hūm, phaṭ, om, haḥ*, to the weapon, *hūm, phaṭ*." Then those (cuttings) should be set in a ladle full of clarified butter in which a ball of cow-dung is kept in the middle and cast into fire with (the recitation of) the *mantra* of weapon ending with *phaṭ*.

29. After having washed the two kinds of ladles and after bathing the disciple, the self (preceptor) should sip waters and gently beat the soul thus blended with the *mantra* of the weapon.

30. It should be disjoined, drawn and worshipped as before to the end of twelve (kinds of worship) and placed in the petals of the lotus of his own heart.

31. The ladle is filled with clarified butter. The ladle should be held (in such a way that the cup of the ladle) faces downwards according to the rules of daily rites of worship and by showing the *śaṅkhamudrā* (posture made with fingers denoting a conch).

32. He should have his head and neck expanded in unison with the pronunciation of the nasal sound (*om*), having his sight fixed and (the heart) filled with contemplation of the Supreme Being.

33. Having gathered the six paths[1] in the form of nerves from the pitcher, the sacrificial pit, the pupil and from one's own soul, (the preceptor) should place them at the head of the sacrificial ladle.

1. The six paths are *mantra, pada, varṇa, bhuvana, tattva* and *kalā* of which the first three are related to the sound and the rest to the objects according to *saṁhārakrama* and the reverse way according to *sṛṣṭikrama*. See Śāradātilaka 5.79.86.93.

34-35. Having contemplated the soul-energy as a point it should be united with the (following) seven (principles) in turn. The first one is the union of the soul. Then follows the next one consisting of repetition of the *mantras* of the heart etc. after having done the inhalation and the retention of the breath with the mouth open a little.

36. The form of the sound (*om*), which has permeated the *suṣumnā* (an artery of human body), is the third one. There would be calm absorption of the mind in the seventh cause by one's renunciation.

37-38. The movements above the energy and the sound known as the discordant (are the fifth one). (The sound emitted) by the universal life, which cannot be measured by energy and which is the discordant of time is the sixth one. The seventh one is that beyond the (region of) energy. This is the proper place for union and is known as the discordant principle.

39. After having inhaled the breath and retaining it while keeping the mouth little open, (the preceptor) should utter the principal (*mantra*) and (accomplish) the repose of the soul of the disciple.

40. The letter *ha* (should be deemed as resting) in the lightning stream which is the life force of six paths. The letter *u* remains pervading above the navel for a length of twelve *aṅgulas* (an *aṅgula* is equal to four finger breadths).

41. Then above that the letter *ma* (should be made to occupy) four finger breadths over the heart. The syllable *om*, expressive of lord Viṣṇu, occupies the region of the heart for eight *aṅgulas* still above.

42. The letter *ma*, expressive of (lord) Rudra, occupies the region of the palate for four *aṅgulas*. Similarly, the nasal phonetic sign, expressive of lord Īśvara should occupy the middle of the forehead.

43. The syllable *om*, (the essence of) Lord Sadāśiva, should rest in the aperture on the head. The female energy should be located in the aperture on the head. These should always be rejected one by one.

44-45. After having experienced the divine minute contact therein, the preceptor should contemplate the soul of the disciple in that supreme twelfth principle, characterising extreme happiness, devoid of feelings, beyond the reach of mind, auspicious and giving rise to eternal qualities.

46. After having offered an oblation of clarified butter into the fire for lord Śiva with the *mantra* of lord Śiva ending with *vauṣaṭ* for the sake of stability of the union.

47-52. Having offered final oblation as laid down, (the preceptor) should do for the attainment of qualities. "*Om, hām*, oblations to the soul ! Be omniscient ! *Om, hām*, oblations to the soul ! Be satisfied ! *Om, hrūm*, oblations to the soul ! Be cognizant of originless existence ! *Om, haum*, oblations to the soul ! Be self-dependent ! Om, *haum*, soul ! Oblations ! Be undiminished in energy ! *Om, haḥ*, oblations to the soul ! Be of endless energy !" The self, possessing six qualities, should thus be taken out of Supreme Being and with contemplation united in the body of the disciple as laid down. Drops of ambrosia from the water-offering should be placed on the head of the disciple to alleviate sufferings due to the projection of powerful soul force (into the disciple). Having made obeisance to the sacrificial pitcher relating to lord Śiva, situated to the right of (lord) Śiva, and placing the disciple to the right of his self with a pleasing face, (the preceptor) should submit to the lord (as follows) : "This (disciple) has been favoured by you only ! Being present in this form of mine, increase his devotion to the lord, fire-god, and preceptor." Having paid obeisance to the lord, the preceptor should himself bless the disciple affectionately by saying, "May you have bliss". The sacrifice should be concluded after having offered eight flowers to the lord with extreme devotion and bathing the disciple with (the waters of) the pitcher of lord Śiva.

## CHAPTER EIGHTYNINE

### *Initiation of principles*

*The Lord said* :

1. Then the initiation in the principles is imparted as it is concise. Binding with the thread should be done suitably with one's soul.

2. The fundamental principles should be contemplated as pervading time, fire etc. concluding with pure bliss. They should be like the bead of rosaries, the principles distributed evenly on the whole thread.

3. After having invoked the principle of bliss etc., the rites of *garbhādhāna* etc. (should be done) as before. But the offer of all fees should be done with the principal (*mantras*).

4. Then the final oblation endowed with the sound-essence of all principles should be offered by which alone the disciple gets emancipation.

5. After having offered another such final oblation to lord Śiva for the sake of union and for securing firmness, (the disciple) should be bathed with the waters of the pitcher (consecrated) for Śiva.

## CHAPTER NINETY

### *Anointing the disciple after worshipping Śiva*

*The Lord said* :

1. Having worshipped lord Śiva, the (rite of) bathing should be done for the welfare of the disciple. Nine pitchers should duly be placed in the directions of north-east etc.

2. The preceptor should invoke the eight oceans of alkali, milk, curd, ghee, molasses, wine, sweet water and sour water in those pitchers.

3-4. The following eight Rudras should be duly located in them :— (1) Śikhaṇḍin, (2) Śrīkaṇṭha, (3) Trimūrta, (4) Ekarudrākṣa, (5) Ekanetra, (6) Śivottama, (7) Sūkṣma, and (8) Ananta.

5. Lord Śiva, the ocean and the *mantra* of lord Śiva should be located in (the pitcher at) the middle. Sacrificial sheds (are erected) for the deities of the quarters within the pavilion.

6. A platform measuring eight inches in height and two cubits in length should be erected wherein an endless seat should be made as also a seat of *bel leaves*.

7-14. Having made the disciple face eastwards, and doing the *sakalīkaraṇa*[1], (the preceptor) should worship (the pupil). His body should then be rubbed with sour gruel, earth, ashes, *dūrvā* (a kind of grass), cowdung balls, white mustard and curd mixed with water. Then the pupil should duly be bathed with the waters of the pitchers starting with that of alkali with the repetition of (the *mantras* of) the heart, *vidyeśa* and *śambara* with pleasure and devotion. Having clad him in white dress and placed him to the right of lord Śiva, the disciple should again be worshipped as before in the cushion mentioned already. (The preceptor should address him as follows): "From this day onwards you shall test well the recipient of the dress of an anchorite such as the turban, cloth on the body while in meditation, crown, knife, pot, rosary, book etc., initiation, exposition and installation before you favour him. You hear the command." After having saluted the disciple and prostrating (in front of lord) Maheśvara, the following submission should be made for the removal of all impediments. "I have been commanded by you in the form of a preceptor for doing *abhiṣeka* (anointing) ceremony. This (disciple) who is well-versed in the scriptural lore has been anointed by me O (Lord) Śiva." Five times five oblations should be made for the propitiation of the chain of *mantras*.

15-16. Then the final oblation should be made. The disciple should then be made to sit on the right side of one's self (preceptor). Then (the preceptor) should mark the fingers of the right hand of the disciple beginning with the thumb with the burnt edge of *darbha* with the *śambara* (*mantra*) for the sake of establishing contact. After having placed flowers on the hand, he should be made to bow down.

17-18. The merits of performance of this rite should be assigned to (lord) Śiva, the fire, the pitcher and his own self. (The preceptor should address him as follows): The disciples who have been well examined in the scriptures should be blessed by you. Like a monarch the desired objects are gained by men by this anointing (with the *mantra* of) the weapons—*Om*, *śrām*, *śrim*, *paśum*, *hūm*, *phaṭ*.

---

1. The act of assigning the different parts of the body to the different deities with the different *mantras*.

## CHAPTER NINETYONE

*Different kinds of mantras for the worship of God* :

*The Lord said* :

1. One should worship lord Śiva, (lord) Viṣṇu and other gods such as Bhāskara (Sun) after being anointed, accompanied by the sounding of the conch, *bherī* (a kind of kettle-drum) and bathe (the images) with five things got from a cow.

2-3. Whoever (worships) gods (in this manner) goes to heaven and elevates his departed manes. Whatever sin has accrued to him in the course of millions of years gets reduced to ashes in the fire by anointing gods with ghee. Whoever bathes gods with an *āḍhaka* (two maunds) of ghee etc. becomes a celestial.

4-6. After having applied sandal paste, (the lord) should be worshipped with perfumes etc. The gods praised with hymns with little effort always confer ability to know past and future events, proficiency in *mantra*, enjoyment and emancipation.

7. Having taken principal letters of the *mantras*, if they are divisible by two, (one should know) (whether they are) auspicious or inauspicious. (If divisible) by three (they denote) *jiva*, *mūla* and *dhātu*, (and if divisible) by four (they denote the four castes) brahmin etc. (Divisible) by five denote the five principles (elements) (earth etc.). So also for muttering (the *mantras*) etc. (one should find whether they are auspicious or inauspicious). If the *mantra* consisting of groups of three letters happens to have the letters *pa*, *ma* and *ka* and letter *ma* comes in the middle it is inauspicious. Lord Indra and a king occurring in the middle are auspicious.

8-9. One should write the *mantras* of Sūrya, Gaṇapati, Śiva, Durgā (śaivite goddess), Śrī (consort of Viṣṇu) and Viṣṇu in a lotus. One should write on that the *mantras* commencing with a three-letter unit to those having four letters in the form of the *gomūtra* (a particular form of writing letters) with a consecrated stylus.

10. In the same way (one should know) the auspiciousness etc. of (*mantras*) of sixtyfour letters from the fall on or contact of the dice with the odd place.

11. Commencing with one unit of three-lettered (*mantras*) to eight units of three-lettered (*mantras*), denoting the *dhvaja* (flagstaff) etc. even ones are inauspicious and odd ones are auspicious.

12. The *mantra* known as *tripurā* is composed of the letter '*ka*' amplified by *ā*, *i* etc., and preceded by the sixteen letters along with their vowel sounds.

13. The *mantras* having for its principal part (the syllable) *hrim*, preceded by *praṇava* (*om*) and concluding with "obeisance" used in worship are twenty-thousand one hundred and sixty.

14. The mantras '*ām*, *hrim*' are for (goddess) Sarasvatī (goddess of learning), Caṇḍikā, Gaurī and Durgā (different forms of consort of Śiva). So also *ām*, *śrīm* are the *mantras* for Śrī (goddess Lakṣmī).

15. Then *kṣaum*, *kraum* are the *mantras* for Sun, and *ām*, *haum* for god Śiva. *Ām*, *gam* are the *mantras* for lord Gaṇeśa and *ām* for lord Harī (Viṣṇu).

16-17. The preceptor should after anointing repeat one hundred and fifty times the letters '*ka*' etc. as well as the sixteen vowels. With three '*ka*' at the beginning along with the vowels and ending with '*ka*' all the *mantras* are formed. After contemplation (the preceptor) should initiate the disciples.

## CHAPTER NINETYTWO

### *Mode of installation of the image of lord Śiva*

*The Lord said* :

1. O Guha (a name of the son of lord Śiva and Pārvatī)! I shall briefly describe the (mode of) installation of the *liṅga* (representing) Śiva and the pedestal (representing) the female energy. Their union (is accomplished) by (the repetition of) the *mantras* of Śiva.

2. There are five different ways of installation. I shall describe to you their characteristics. Where there is union of the *brahmaśilā*, that installation is worth that name.

3. The *sthāpana* (fixing) is the proper manner in which (the *liṅga*) is placed in the pedestal. The installation in which (the *liṅga*) is placed in pedestal with a cleave it is called *sthitasthāpana* (installation on a pedestal already existing).

4-5. It is (known as) *utthāpana* (re-installation) in which the removal (of the old *liṅga*) precedes. It is known as *āsthāpana* in which the new *liṅga* is placed and consecration is done by wise men. (The installation of the images) of (lord) Viṣṇu etc. are of two kinds. In all these cases supreme lord Śiva should be made the soul-energy.

6. There are five divisions in the case of the temples also on the basis of the above differences. The ground should be examined according to the requirements for the respective temple.

7. The earth is white (coloured) having the smell of clarified butter, blood-coloured, possessing the smell of blood, the yellow one having sweet smell and black one having the smell of wine, which are respectively known as the brahmin etc.

8. Among these the earlier ones are commendable than the later ones. If the ground of this type is dug upto a cubit and filled again it would be in excess of the pit.

9. The kind of earth which is moist with water is also to be known as excellent. The preceptor should purify well (the ground) which is impure because (of the presence) of bones, charcoal etc.

10. The ground where a city, village, fort, house or temple is to be constructed (should be purified) repeatedly by digging or by erecting cattle sheds or by ploughing.

11. The worship of the (sacrificial) shed (should be done) as also the concluding (rite) for the satisfaction through the *mantras*. Having concluded the rites, (the preceptor) should offer one thousand oblations with the *aghorāstra* (*mantra*) in the prescribed manner.

12. After having levelled the ground and plastering the ground, the preceptor should purify it. Encircling lines should be drawn with gold, curd and unbroken rice.

13. (Lord) Śiva should be worshipped in the filled up pitcher at the north-east corner from the centre. After having worshipped the presiding spirit, those waters should be sprinkled on the spades etc.

14. Having offered oblations to the groups of demons in the prescribed manner, they should be scattered in (different) directions. Having sprinkled (water) over the ground, the spades (and other implements) should be washed and worshipped.

15-16. Having placed a pitcher (filled with water) and covered by a pair of clothes on the shoulder of a brahmin, being accompanied by the sounding of musical instruments, it should be placed at the south-east corner (of the shed) and worshipped at the auspicious moment. The ground should be excavated with the spade duly consecrated and sprinkled with honey.

17. The earth dug out should be deposited on the south-west corner and water from the pitcher should be put into the pit. The eastern boundary of the edifice should be extended as far as desired.

18. Then having stood there for a while, the preceptor should make the excavations carried around and sprinkle water over the same until the north-eastern corner of the ground is reached.

19-20. This is spoken as the *arghyadāna* (offering of waters) (accomplished) by taking round the pitcher. The ground should thus be taken possession of. After that, (the preceptor) should cause the ground to be excavated, if it is a virgin one, until the stone or water (is reached), in order to ward off evils due to the extraneous matter. The extraneous matter should be dug out in the prescribed manner.

21. If (the extraneous matter) relates to a human being, the (presence of) extraneous matter could be known by writing letters, *a, ka, ca, ṭa, ta, pa, ya, śa and ha* for query and casting the die. If it falls on the flagstaff etc. at the south-east corner, it indicates the presence of extraneous matter.

22. The existence of that (matter) could be validly known from the changes noticed in the body of the questioner or from the wailing of animals in (different) directions or from their entry (and movement) into the ground.

23. In the alternative, the presence of extraneous matter could be known by writng the letters of the alphabet on a plank or on the ground, dividing them into eight groups and from the presence of the group (of letters) in the directions east to north-east in order.

24-25. One should declare the presence of (a piece of) iron in the eastern part if the letter of the '*a*' group is met. Similarly, the presence of charcoal in the south-eastern part from '*ka*' group, of ash in the southern part from '*ca*' group, of bones in the south-western part from '*ṭa*' group, of bricks in the western part from '*ta*' group, of skull (in the north-western part) from '*pa*' group, of a corpse from '*ya*' group and of (a piece of) iron from '*śa*' group (could be declared).

26-28. So also, (the presence of) silver, from '*ha*' group and (the presence of) something causing harm (could be known) from '*a*' group. (After removal of these extraneous matters) and after taking eight inches of earth and sprinkling water with (the *mantra* of) the soul, three-quarters of the pit should be filled with water and earth broken by a club. Having made the ground levelled, the preceptor should go to the sacrificial shed with the general *argha* offering in the hand. After having worshipped the two guardian deities of the entrance, the preceptor should enter the temple through the western door.

29-30. (Then the preceptor) should purify his self as well as the sacrificial shed and sacrificial pit. The sacrificial pitcher along with the small sacrificial pitcher (should be placed) there. The worship of (lord) Śiva and the guardian deities of the world and the generation of the fire and its worship and other acts should all be done as before. (The preceptor) should go to the bathing shed of the stones along with the *yajamāna* (at whose instance the sacrifice is performed).

31-32. The stone slabs of a temple for the *liṅga* are known as the *pāda* or *dharma* etc. They are commended if they are square shaped, eight inches in height and one cubit in breadth. Those made of bricks should be half (the size) of those made of stones. If the temple (is built of) stones the images (should be made of) stones and if (it is) of bricks the images (should be of) bricks.

33. (These statues) (should be) marked with nine faces and lotus flowers known as *nandā*, *bhadrā*, *jayā*, *riktā*, and the fifth (*pūrṇā*).

34. *Padma*, *mahāpadma*, *śaṅkha*, *makara* and *samudra* the five treasures; the presiding deities of these should be located in pitchers.

35. The names of stones are *nandā*, *bhadrā*, *jayā*, *pūrṇā*, *ajitā*, *aparājitā*, *vijayā*, *maṅgalā* and *dharaṇi*, the ninth.

36-37. *Subhadra, vibhadra, sunanda, puṣpanandaka, jaya, vijaya, kumbha, pūrṇa* and *uttara* are the nine pitchers of treasures. Having offered the cushion to them, (the preceptor) should (gently) beat and write on them with the *mantra* of the weapon.

38-39. All the stone slabs should be covered without exception with the mantra of armour. They should be bathed with perfumed waters mixed with earth, cow-dung and cow's urine with the recitation of *mantra* of weapon ending with *hūm phaṭ*. Then they should be bathed with the five things got from a cow and also the five sweet things (milk, sugar, ghee, curd and honey) as laid down.

40. Then they should be immersed in perfumed water with the repetition of *mantra* containing their own names. Then (they should be bathed) with water containing fruits, gems, gold and cow's horn.

41-48. After having applied sandal paste, the slabs should be wrapped up with clothes. After having provided a seat made of gold and led them to the sacrificial shed circumambulating, they should be laid on a bed or on a mattress of *kuśa* with (the recitation of the *mantra* of) the heart. After having worshipped, the principles commencing with the intellect and ending with the earth should be located therein. The three principles permeating the three divisions should be located in order. (The first group consists of) principles beginning with intellect and concluding with mind, (the second group consists of principles beginning with) thought and concluding with the subtle principles and (the third group) begins with the subtle principles and concludes with the earth. These principles should be taken as location of pure bliss, knowledge and soul. The principles should be worshipped with their respective *mantras* and their lords with the *mantra* of the heart in their respective places marked with garlands of flowers in order (as follows): "*Om, hūm*, obeisance to the principle of absolute bliss ! *Om, hūm* obeisance to (lord) Rudra, the lord of the principle of absolute bliss ! *Om, hāṃ* obeisance to the principle of knowledge ! *Om, hām* obeisance to (lord) Viṣṇu, lord of the principle of knowledge ! *Om, hām* obeisance to the principle of soul ! *Om, hām* obeisance to (lord) Brahmā, lord of the principle of soul !" Each one of the principles—earth, fire, the sacrificer, sun, water, wind, moon and ether of the eight forms (of the lord) should be located in each one of the slabs along with their presiding deities Śarva, Paśupati, Ugra, Rudra, Bhava, Maheśvara, Mahādeva and Bhīma in order. "*Om* obeisance to the image of the earth ! *Om* obeisance to the presiding deity of the earth !" are the *mantras* for duly locating the guardian deities. The pitchers should be worshipped with their own *mantras* or with these *mantras*. The principal *mantra* for (lord) Indra etc. are as narrated below : *lūm, rūm, śūm, ṣūm, vūm, yūm, mūm, hūm, kṣūm.*

49. (The procedure for the installation) in the case of nine images has been told. (The procedure for installation) in the case of five images is being told now. Each one of the five principles of creation such as the earth etc. of the images should be located (in the slabs).

50. As before the five presiding deities of these, Brahmā, Viṣṇu, Rudra, Īśvara and Sadāśiva should also be worshipped in them.

51-54. "*Om* obeisance to the image (of the principle) of earth ! *Om* obeisance to Brahmā the presiding deity (of the principle) of earth" ! are the *mantras*. Having worshipped the five pitchers in order with their own names, the rite of location should be done as laid down, duly commencing with the central image with the *prākāra mantra* as well as auspicious *darbhas* and sesamum. After having located the supporting *cārikā* (energy) in the sacrificial pit and worshipping it, the principles, the presiding deities of the principles, the images and the presiding deities of the images should be pleased with ghee etc. Then the slabs should be sprinkled with waters of propitiation after having offered hundred oblations upto the final one for the purification of the part (of the slab known as) Brahmā, after having touched each one of the principles with *kuśas* in order and worshipped.

55. Having done the rites of invoking the presence and union, (the principles) should be located again (in the slabs) after purification, in the same way one should do these rites for the three groups (of principles).

56. "*Om, ām* and *im* obeisance to the principles of soul and knowledge." (Reciting this *mantra*, the preceptor) should duly touch the three parts (of the stone), *Brahmā* etc., with the base of the *kuśa* etc. The union of the fundamental principles

should be done by the applications of short and long (*mantras*).

57-59. "*Om, hām, um* obeisance to the principles of knowledge and absolute bliss." Oblation should be made in the presence of pitchers filled with clarified butter and honey and into which gems have been put and on which the five things got from a cow have been sprinkled, after having worshipped them with their respective *mantras* being presided over by the guardian deities of the world. The presiding deities of all the slabs should then be contemplated as of the form of knowledge, as having bathed, gold-coloured, and wearing the dress in the form of knowledge. Hundred oblations should be offered with the *mantra* of the weapon and the *mantra* of the head for the purification of the sacrificial site and for the removal of defects of deficiency etc.

## CHAPTER NINETYTHREE

### *Mode of worshipping the presiding deity of a ground*

*The Lord said* :

1. Strings should be laid in the sacrificial shed so as to enclose it. The ground should be divided into sixty-four squares of equal measurements.

2. Two bamboo poles should be fixed at each one of the four corners. Strings (should be laid down) across the eight angular points. They should enclose two squares and six squares. The presiding deity of the ground should be worshipped therein.

3. At the time of worship, one should meditate on the presiding deity of the ground in the fire-pit, as the form of a demon with curled locks and head held raised up from the ground and facing north.

4. The knees, knee-joints and thighs (of the deity) should be taken as lying in the directions of north-west and south-east, the two soles of feet in the south, the head in the north and the two folded palms in the heart.

5. The auspicious gods located in the body of this person are worshipped. The presiding deities of the eight angular points,

situated in the eight half chambers of the angular points (should also be worshipped.) .

6. The sages Marīci etc. should be located in the six squares commencing with the east, Brahmā in the four squares at the centre. The rest of the gods are known to occupy one square each.

7-8. The twelve joints such as the trident, *svastika* (a kind of figure), thunderbolt, *mahāsvastika*, *sampuṭa*, *trikaṭu*, *maṇibandha* and the pure square among all the joints of the presiding deity of the ground should be left in the walls etc.

9. Oblations of unbroken rice along with clarified butter, for (lord) Īśa, offering of water with lotus flowers for lord Parjanya (god of rain), and a bright saffron-coloured banner should be offered for Jayanta (son of Indra).

10. Gems (should be offered) to Mahendra (lord of the celestials), smoke-coloured canopy for the Sun, wheat and ghee for (the god of) truth and clarified butter alone for (lord) Bhṛśa.

11. Unclean meat (should be offered) to (the lord of the sky) and the flour of barley (first fried and then ground) for all those gods commencing with the east. A ladleful of honey, milk and clarified butter should be given to the fire-god.

12. Fried paddy put in golden waters should be offered to (god of) untruth. Honey should be offered to the destroyer of the house and *palaudana* for Yamarāja (god of death).

13. Perfumes (should be given) for the lord of the gandharvas (semi-divine beings), a bird's tongue for Bhṛṅga (one who wards) and lotus leaves for the beast on the south. Thus the eight deities (should be offered offerings).

14. Sesamum mixed water and milk (should be given) for the manes. Sticks from the trees for cleansing the teeth should be given to the lord of the entrance by showing the *dhenumudrā* (posture with fingers indicating a cow).

15. Cakes should be offered to Sugrīva, *darbha* to Puṣpadanta (a *yakṣa*), red lotus flowers to Pracetas (lord of waters) (and) wines to demon.

16. Ghee and rice mixed with jaggery (should be given) to Śeṣa (serpent-god), ghee mixed with baked flour or fried paddy to disease. Thus the mode of offering for gods in the western direction has been told.

17. A yellow banner (should be offered) to Māruta (wind god), *nāgakesara* (a kind of fragrant flower) to serpent-god and eatables and well-cooked gruel of green gram to Mukhya.

18. Sweet gruel mixed with clarified butter should be given to Soma, root of lily flower to (goddess) Dawn, *lopī* to Aditi, and *pūri* to Diti. These are the gods placed in the northern direction.

19. Sweet meats (should be offered) to Brahmā on the east and to (sage) Marīci in the six squares. Red flowers (should be offered) to (god) Savitrā situated below the angular square (assigned to) the fire-god.

20. Waters along with the *kuśa* should be presented to goddess Sāvitrī below that square. Red sandal should be offered to (god) Vivasvān occupying six squares on the south.

21. Turmeric mixed rice (should be offered) to lord Indra in the corner square below that of the demon. Mixed rice should be presented to Indra-jaya below that of Indra.

22. Rice mixed with jaggery (should be offered) to (lord) Mitra occupying six squares on the west. Rice cooked with ghee should be offered to (lord) Rudra at the square below the angular point in the north-west.

23. Meat (should be offered) to the servant of Rudra below that. An offering of black-gram should be offered to the mountain (god) occupying the six squares on the north.

24. One should duly offer curd and milk to *āpas* and its progeny below the angular point (dedicated to lord) Śiva after worshipping in the proper way.

25. Brahmā located at the four squares in the middle of the place should be presented gruel along with clarified butter and the five things got from a cow.

26. Outside the sacrificial ground the four demonesses Carakī etc. should be worshipped in the angular points commencing with the north-east and ending with the north-west in order.

27. Meat with ghee should be offered to Carakī, curd with lotus flowers to (demoness) Vidārī and meat, bile and blood to (demoness) Pūtanā.

28. Bones, blood, biles and meat (should be offered) to demoness sin. Lord Skanda should be offered rice mixed with black gram on the east.

29. Sweet cakes along with *kṛsara* (rice and peas boiled together) (should be offered) to (lord) Aryaman in the southern direction), meat along with blood to Jambhaka in the western direction.

30. Rice mixed with blood and flowers (should be presented) to Pilipiñja (monster-maiden) on the north. Otherwise all the presiding deities of the ground should be worshipped with water along with unbroken rice and *kuśa.*

31. In the case of a residential building or town, worship should be done in eighty-one squares. The lines (drawn across the cardinal points of the diagram) should be made to occupy (the breadth of) three squares and comprise (the breadth of) six such squares at the other angular points.

32. The gods Īśa and others should occupy one square each in that (diagram), the serpents and others two squares each, (sages) Marīci and others six squares each, Brahmā is known to occupy nine squares.

33. The above diagram may comprise hundred squares in the case of a city, village or hamlet. Two bamboo poles (are known) as 'invincible' and irresistible always.

34. The location (of the deities) in the hundred squares is commended if the rite is done as in the case of a divine edifice. The planets and gods such as (lord) Skanda are known to occupy six squares in that (diagram).

35. Demoness Carakī and others should be located in five squares. The lines and bamboo should occupy spaces as described earlier. In the case of a sacrificial ground relating to the founding of a country, it should comprise one hundred and thirty-four squares.

36. (In that diagram) Brahmā occupies sixty-four squares, as also (sages) Marīci and others. The eight gods, *āpas* etc. should occupy fiftyfour squares.

37. (Gods) Īśāna and others should occupy nine squares. (The gods) Skanda and others should occupy eight squares. (Demonesses) Carakī and others, lines, bamboo should also be located as before.

38. In a sacrificial ground comprising twenty-thousand squares, the location of the deities should be such that they occupy nine times more than what has been enjoined in the founding o country.

39. The diagram which is divided into twentyfive squares is known as the *vaitāla* . The other diagrams are known to have nine squares and sixteen sub-divisions.

40. There may be a square figure inscribed in a sexagon or triangle. The location (of the gods) in the case of excavation around should be done as in the case of (the stone slab known as) *brahmaśilā*.

41. An offering of sweet gruel to all gods should be made at the installation of the image of a deity or the burial of a dead body.

42. In the absence of any specified measurement, the sacrificial ground should measure five cubits. The sacrificial ground proportional to the measure of the house or divine edifice is always held as excellent.

## CHAPTER NINETYFOUR

### *Mode of placing the stone slabs*

*The lord said :*

1. (Demonesses) Carakī and others should be worshipped in the angular points of north-east etc. and outside as before. Three oblations should be done to each one of the gods in succession.

2. After having offered oblation to the presiding spirit, the placing of stone slab (is done) thereafter. (Goddess of) energy and the excellent pitcher known as *ananta* should be located in the middle line.

3-5. The stone slab should be held in this pitcher with (the recitation of) the principal (*mantra*) coupled with the letter '*na*'. Having placed the eight pitchers known as Subhadrā etc. in order in the directions east etc. with the recitation of the *mantra* of the guardian deities of the world and having located the goddesses in each one of the holes, the stone slabs such as Nandā etc. should be duly placed in them by repeating the *śambara* (*mantra*) sacred to the presiding deities of the different images, in such a way that they are in order from the middle of the ground. The eight (deities) such as the guardian deities of virtue etc. should be located in the different angular points in order.

6. The four pitchers Nanda etc. out of Subhadrā etc. are placed in the south-eastern corner. Ajitā etc. out of the group commencing with Jaya should be located in the east etc.

7. (Lord) Brahmā should be invoked in them and (lord) Maheśvara (Śiva) should be contemplated as pervading the internal space (of the shed) which would serve as a receptacle of these.

8. After having offered oblation one should repeat (the *mantra* of) the weapon for warding off impediments. The procedure in the case of five stone slabs is now described a little.

9. (The preceptor) should locate the stone slab Pūrṇa in the pitcher (known as) Subhadra half-immersed. The stone slabs respectively known as Nandā etc. should be placed in the pitchers Padma etc. at the different angular points south-east etc.

10-17. Four slabs should be contemplated as located in the middle with the exuberance of mother's affection. "*Om* Pūrṇa ! You are the great learning ! Possessor of all divine attributes ! O Daughter of Aṅgiras ! You make all (this undertaking of mine) here as complete. *Om* ! Nandā ! you make men rejoice ! I establish you here. You remain in this temple as fully satisfied as long as the moon, sun and stars shine. O Nandā ! Daughter of Vasiṣṭha ! You grant long life, fulfilment of) desires, prosperity to men. You have to strive to protect in this temple always. *Om* Bhadrā ! Daughter of Kaśyapa ! You always do good to the people. O Goddess ! You be granter of long life, of desired (objects) (and) prosperity always. *Om* ! Jayā ! O Goddesss ! You be granter of prosperity (and) long life always. *Om* ! *Jayā* ! Being established by me you remain here for ever. O Daughter of Bhṛgu ! You become the governess of prosperity and success. *Om* ! Riktā ! Destroyer of excessive defects ! O Auspicious one ! Granter of accomplishment and emancipation ! One who is of the form of the universe and one who underlies all the world, you remain here always." After having contemplated upon the ethereal mansion, (the preceptor) should locate the three principles therein. Then the sacrifice should be completed in the prescribed manner after having offered the expiatory oblation.

# CHAPTER NINETYFIVE

## *Mode of installation of the liṅga*

*The Lord said* :

1. I shall describe the mode of installation of a liṅga in temple which yields enjoyment and emancipation. One should always do it for the purpose of enjoyment and emancipation on the day of the god.

2. The installation ceremony should be performed in the five months commencing with *māgha* (February-March) except (the month of) *caitra* (April-May) and in the first three *karaṇas* (one of the eleven divisions of the day) at the rising of the Jupiter and Venus.

3. (The ceremony should be undertaken) especially in the bright fortnight or in the dark fortnight omitting the fifth, fourth, ninth, eighth and fourteenth days (of the fortnight).

4-5. (All) the other days are auspicious except those falling on the days of inauspicious planets. Commencement during (the rule of) the stable stars of *śatabhiṣak*, *dhaniṣṭā*, *ārdrā*, *anurādhā*, the three *uttara* (*uttarā*, *uttaraphālguni* and *uttarabhādrapada*), *rohiṇi* and *śravaṇa* yield good results. (The days fixed for the rite should possess) the rising points of aquarius, leo, scorpion, libra, virgo, taurus and sagittarius.

6. Jupiter is always commendable in the above nine stars and seven constellations. Mercury (is commendable) in the sixth, eighth, tenth, seventh and fourth, from the *lagna* (rising point in the east), while Venus (is commendable) in all the places except the fourth.

7. The Moon is always strengthening if located in seventh, fourth, third or tenth, the sun in the tenth, third, and sixth places and *Rāhu* (ascending node of the Moon) in the third, tenth and sixth places.

8. The Saturn, Mars, Sun and Ketu (the descending node of the Moon) are commendable in the sixth, and third places. Both the good and bad (planets) in the eleventh place are cruel.

9. Their aspect full in the seventh place, half in the ninth and fifth places, one fourth in the first and tenth places and one fourth less in the fourth and eighth places.

10. (The two constellations) pisces and aries have a duration of three and three-fourth *nāḍis* (two and a half *nāḍis* are equal to one hour). The (constellations) taurus and acquarious have a duration of three and three-fourth *nāḍis*.

11. Capricorn and gemini have a duration of five (*nāḍis*), sagittarius, scorpion, leo and cancer have a duration of five and three-fourth (*nāḍis*) and libra and virgo have a duration of five and a half *ghaṭikās* (synonym of *nāḍi*).

12. (The constellations) leo, taurus and acquarius are stationary and yield success. (The constellations) sagittarius, libra and aries are movables. The third (constellations) have both the characteristics.

13-14. The constellations aspected by auspicious planets or associated with them are auspicious and are commendable. Jupiter, Venus and Mercury in the *lagna* confers abundant strength, long life, sovereignty, valour, strength, progeny, fame and virtue. The first, fourth, seventh and tenth (places from *lagna*) are known as the *kendras*.

15. Jupiter, Venus and Mercury in these (houses) yield all perfections. The presence of wicked planets in the third, fourth and eleventh houses from the *lagna* are beneficial.

16-17. The learned should combine these with the *tithis* (the days reckoned by the phases of the Moon) for good performances. (The preceptor) should raise a square shed in front of (the temple) leaving a space equal to or five times that (of its measurement) at twelve cubits from the flight of steps with four entrances. (The shed) for (sacrificial bathing) should be half the size of that shed).

18. The shed should be constructed) in the north-east, east or north, (measuring) one or ten or twelve cubits respectively and having a single entrance or four entrances.

19. The remaining eight sheds should be measuring two cubits more than that (shed). The sacrificial altar (should measure) four *kara* lengths in the middle and should have pillars at the angular points.

20. Leaving apart a quarter of the platform nine or five fire pits or a single pit (should be dug up) in the north-east or east. (The digging of one pit) is done only in the case of the worship of the preceptor.

21-24. (The fire pits) should be a span, an *aratni* (a cubit of the middle length, from the elbow to the tip of the little finger), a cubit, a yard, four cubits and eight cubits respectively depending on fifty, hundred, thousand, hundred thousand, lakh or a crore oblations (are offered in the pits). (The pit) in the south-east (should be of) the shape of the female generative organ, in the south (of the shape of) the crescent moon, in the south-west (of the shape of) a triangle, in the north-west (of the shape of) a hexagon, in the north (of the shape of) a lotus, in the north-east (of the shape of) an octagon. The pit made at an inclined angle with a border above is auspicious. There should be three borders around that respectively measuring four, three and two fingers in breadth. Alternatively there should be a single border measuring six fingers in breadth or the borders (should be) of the shape of sacrificial pit.

25. The aperture should be above that. It should resemble the leaf of the holy fig tree in its shape. (The aperture should be) an *aṅgula* in height and eight *aṅgulas* in breadth.

26. Its length (should be) half the length of the pit and (should be) in the same level as the neck. The apertures of the fire pits on the east, south-east and south should face the north.

27. It should face the east (if the fire pits have been located) in other directions, while those situated at the other points of compass should have their outlets turned towards the north-east. The twenty-fourth of the fire receptacles is called the *aṅgula* (finger breadth).

28. The four entrances (to the sacrificial shed) on the east etc. should be made of (woods of) *plakṣa*, *udumbara*, *aśvattha* and *vaṭa* (trees) which duly (stand for) peace, prosperity, strength and health.

29. (The sheds) should be eighteen cubits in length, one cubit high and half (the length) in breadth and should be decorated with mango leaves.

30. The banners should have (colours) resembling (the colours) of a rainbow (or be) red, black, tawny, (or) of the colour of the moon, (or be) white, golden coloured or resembling that of a crystal.

31. (The banner) dedicated to the lotus-born (Brahmā) in the east (should be) red (and that) which belongs to Ananta

(lord of the serpents) in the south-west (should be) blue. The banners (should be) five cubits long and half as much broad.

32-33. The rods should be commensurate with the five cubits of banners being a cubit for every cubit. Twelve kinds of earth from (the places such as) the ant-hill, the tips of the tusk of elephant, horns of the bull, bunch of lotuses, pastures of boars and cows and the cross-ways of roads should be taken in the case (of installation of an image) of Vaikuṇṭha (Viṣṇu) and eight (kinds) in the case (of installation of an image) of Pinākin (Śiva).

34. The decoctions made up from the barks of *nyagrodha*, *udumbara*, *aśvattha*, *cūta* and *jambū* and eight *palas* (a measure of weight) of the essence of flowers should be taken.

35-36. The waters of the sacred pools, fragrant waters and the waters mixed with the herbs (should be taken). I shall describe the (names of) auspicious flowers (and) fruits (afterwards). Waters mixed with five kinds of gems, cow's horn and also five things got from a cow should be taken for bathing. A piece of cloth in which the paste has been put should be taken for rubbing.

37. A pitcher having thousand holes should be used for bathing and the yellow pigment for decoration. Roots of hundreds of herbs (are needed). Therein (the roots of) *vijayā*, *lakṣmaṇā*, *balā*, *guḍūci*, *atibalā*, *pāṭhā*, *sahadevā*, *śatāvari*, *ṛddhi*, *suvarcalā* and *vṛddhi* have been prescribed separately for bathing.

38-41. (Either) an incessant pouring of waters together with the sesamum and *darbha* (or) merely the bathing with the sacred ash (has been prescribed) for protection. A wiseman should prepare a paste of powders of barley, wheat, *bilva* (fruit), along with camphor. (He should also make ready) the pitcher and *gaṇḍa* (a small vessel with a narrow tube like outlet for pouring). The bed-stead along with two mattresses, pillow bed and cloth should be made ready suited to one's aim and in accordance with his means. The vessel filled with ghee and honey and a golden brush should be made ready.

42. The sacrificial small pitcher, the pitcher (sacred to Lord) Śiva, and the pitchers for the guardian deities of the directions, (should be made ready). One pitcher for each of the sacrificial fire-pits, should be set apart for inducing sleep and for peace.

43-44. The pitchers for the attendant deities at the door, god of virtue, for Praśānta (a deity), *vāstu* (presiding deity of the ground), (goddess) Lakṣmī (consort of Viṣṇu), (Lord) Gaṇeśa (son of the divine pair Śiva and Pārvatī) and pitchers for others should be placed on heaps of grain along with the cloth and garland and gold should be put and they should be filled with fragrant waters.

45-51. They should be supported by vessels filled with (rice),fruits and decorated by tender leaves and should be covered by cloths. White mustard seeds and fried paddy should be brought for scattering. As before the sword of knowledge should be made ready. Sacrificial twigs, the vessel (for cooking) porridge, the sacrificial ladle made of copper and the vessel filled with ghee and honey for anointing the feet, four seats made of three hundred *darbhas* and of the measure of two cubits long, *palāśa* twigs for enclosure, and vessel for sesamum, vessel for *havis* (food offering), vessel for water which can respectively hold one, twenty and eight *palas* and the sacred thread (should be made ready). A pitcher, an incense-burner, *sruk* and *sruva* (the two kinds of sacrificial ladle), a box, a seat, a chowrie, dry firewood, flowers, leaves, scented gum resin, lamps with ghee, incense, unbroken rice, sacred thread, clarified butter from the cow's milk, barley and sesamum stems of *kuśa*, the three sweet things (honey, sugar and clarified butter), sacrificial twigs of the length of ten *parva* (the interspace between the folds on the fingers) are all needed for appeasement. The sacrificial ladle (*sruva*) of a length of one cubit is required for the appeasement of the sun and other planets.

52. There should be one hundred and eight sticks of *arka*, *palāśa*, *khādira*, *amārga*, *pippala*, *udumbara*, *śamī*, *durvā* as also green *kuśa*.

53-54. In their absence barley and sesamum (are used). So also the household articles, a *sthālī* (a kind of vessel), a sacrificial ladle, lid etc. and two pieces of cloth for the gods, coins, crown, apparels, necklaces, earrings and bracelets should be made ready for the worship of the preceptor. One should avoid making them costly.

55. Worship of the custodians of images should be a quarter less than that stated before and that of those who repeat (the *mantra* of) the weapon is still a fourth less than that. Worships

of brahmins, astrologers and sculptors are as done for those who repeat (the *mantras*).

56. The diamond, sun-stone, sapphire, *atinila*, pearl, topaz, ruby, lapis lazuli are the eight gems.

57. *Uśira* (the fragrant root of a plant), *mādhavakrāntā*, red sandal, agallochum, sandalwood, *sārika*, *kuṣṭha*, and *śaṅkhinī* are the (eight) kinds of herbs.

58-60. The metals (are) gold, copper, silver, bell-metal, lead and iron. Yellow orpiment, red arsenic, red chalk, *suvarna mākṣika* (honey-like mineral), mercury, *vahnigairika*, sulphur, and mica are the eight kinds of minerals. The eight kinds of grains are stated to be wheat, sesamum, black-gram, green-gram, barley, short term paddy, śyāmāka. All these things should be gathered.

## CHAPTER NINETYSIX

### *Mode of initial consecration of an image* :

*The Lord said* :

1. After having bathed and performed the two daily (worships), the preceptor should enter the sacrificial shed with the *argha* offering in his hand and accompanied by the brahmins who are the protectors of the idols.

2. The doors (of the sacrificial shed) (known as the doors) of peace should be worshipped duly as before and also the warder-gods (located) in the branches (of the sacrificial trees) by the (performance of) circumambulation.

3. (The warder-gods) Nandi and Mahākāla (should be worshipped) at the east, Bhṛṅgi and Vināyaka at the south, Vṛṣabha and Skanda at the west, (the warder) goddess and Caṇḍa at the north (of the sacrificial shed).

4-5. Then the preceptor should worship two pitchers each at the base of the branches (of the sacrificial trees)—*praśānta* (tranquil) and *śiśira* (cool), *parjanya* (rain-cloud ) and *aśoka* (griefless), *sañjivana* (reviving) and *amṛta* (ambrosia), *dhanada* (bestower of wealth) and *śriprada* (bestower of prosperity) one after another with (the repetition of) their names ending in the fourth case preceded by (the syllable) *om* and ending with 'obeisance'.

6-7. The worlds, planets, warder gods and rivers, two in each one of them, three suns, two *Vedas*, (goddess) Lakṣmī and (lord) Gaṇapati are the gods who stay in the sacrificial shed at each one of the doors for warding impediments and guarding the sacrifice.

8. The thunder-bolt, spear, club, sword, noose, banner, mace, trident, disc and lotus should be duly worshipped in the banner with the *mantras Om hrim phaṭ* obeisance. *Om hrūm phaṭ* to the spear at the door, *hrūm phaṭ* obeisance.

9-10. The eight presiding deities of the banner such as Kumuda, Kumudākṣa, Puṇḍarīka, Vāmana, Śaṅkukarṇa, Sarvanetra, Sumukha and Supratiṣṭhita should be worshipped in the east etc. with (the offering of) oblation to all beings and with the *mantras om kaum* obeisance to Kumuda etc.

11-12. In the same manner the eight guardian deities Hetuka, Tripuraghna, Śakti, Yamajihva, Kāla, Karālin, Ekāṅghri and Bhīma should be worshipped in the (different) directions with offerings, flowers and incense. (The preceptor) should contemplate them as satisfied.

13. The five fundamental principles earth etc. should be worshipped in *kakṣitṛṇa* (a kind of fragrant grass), bamboos, pillars and other things in order with the *mantras sadyojāta*[1] etc.

14. The preceptor should look at the sacrificial shed as permeated by the essence of (god) Sadāśiva, hallowed by his presence and endowed with the banners and spears in the form of fundamental principles.

15. After having warded off the divine ethereal and earthly obstacles as (laid down) before, (the preceptor) should enter (the shed) through the western door and look at the other remaining doors.

16. After having walked around (reverentially) and seated on the southern side of the altar and remaining facing the north, one should perform the purification of elements as before.

---

1. Sadyo jātam prapadyāni, Vāmadevāya namo jyesthāya namaḥ, tatpurnṣāya Vidmahe, aghorebhyo, the ghorebhyaḥ and īśānaḥ sarvavidyānām.

17. Then the internal sacrifice, the purification of the *mantras* and the materials, and the worship of one's own self (should be done). The five things got from a cow (should be applied) as before.

18. Then the sacrificial pitcher should be placed therein along with the receptacle, especially for the principle of Śiva and the three fundamental principles (soul, body and matter) in order.

19. The preceptor should locate by means of his psychic force, the supreme principle of Śiva along with the presiding deities Rudra, Nārāyaṇa and Brahmā in his body from the forehead and trunk to the foot.

20. *Om, ham, hām,* The images of the god and their presiding deities should be located therein as before (and contemplate himself) as covered by the essence of Śiva along with his constituent members and forearm of Śiva on his head.

21. (The preceptor) should then contemplate the effulgence (of Śiva) (which has permeated his body and) which has entered the cavity of the brain as coming out dispelling darkness and illuminating the inter-space between directions.

22. Having decked himself with flowers, garlands and cloth along with the custodians of deities (the preceptor) should contemplate as "I am Śiva" and draw out the sword of knowledge.

23. The sacrificial shed should be purified with the fourfold rites of purification. After having scattered the *kuśa* all around, they should again be gathered.

24. After having seated the guardian deity of the ground etc. in the big pitcher (vardhanī) as before, (the preceptor) should worship them. The pitcher sacred to god Śiva and the weapons and the *vardhani* (pitcher) should be worshipped in the fixed seat.

25. Then the guardian deities of the worlds along with their weapons and vehicles should be worshipped in order in the pitchers situated at the different directions as laid down.

26. (The preceptor) should contemplate (god) Indra as having a golden complexion, thousand eyes, wearing the crown, and wielding the thunderbolt.

27. (God) Saptārcis (Fire god) (should be contemplated) as holding a rosary, *kamaṇḍalu* (a small water pitcher), and a

spear in the hand, red (in complexion), engulfed by garland of flames and as riding the goat.

28. (God) Yama (god of death) should be remembered as riding a buffalo, carrying a club in his hand and of the form of destructive fire and (lord) Nirṛti as riding an ass, carrying a sword in the hand and having red eyes.

29. (The preceptor) should then meditate (lord) Varuṇa as seated on a crocodile and having white complexion holding a noose of serpent in his hand and (lord) Vāyu (wind god) as riding an antelope and having blue complexion and Kubera (god of wealth) as seated on a sheep.

30. (Lord) Īśa (Śiva), the trident-bearer should be contemplated (as seated) on a bull, (god) Ananta, the disc-bearer (as seated) on a tortoise, and (lord) Brahmā, the four-faced and four-armed as riding a gander.

31. (Lord) Dharma (god of virtue) and others should be worshipped in the pitchers located at the base of the pillars at the corners. Some also worship (the gods) Ananta and others in the pitchers placed at the corners of different directions.

32. The injunction of (lord) Śiva should be made to be heard. The pitcher placed behind one's own self should be gently turned around. Then as before the pitcher should be firmly put first and then the pitcher *vardhanī*.

33. After having worshipped (lord) Śiva (seated in) a firm seat and (again in) a firm seat for the sake of weapons, (the preceptor) should as before touch with the *udbhavamudrā* (posture made with the fingers denoting generation).

34. "O lord of the universe you protect this sacrifice of thy own self out of compassion for the devotee". After having addressed these words, (the preceptor) should place the sword in the pitcher.

35. After having worshipped the lord in the pitcher or on the ground or in the shed relating to initiation and establishment, (the preceptor) should go in front of the fire-receptacle.

36. The custodians of images who are seated in front of the centre of the pit should purify the respective pits as directed by the preceptor.

37. The reciters (of *mantras*) should recite (the *mantras*) as many times (as laid down). Others (should recite the *saṁ-*

*hitā mantra*. The brahmins, well-versed in their respective branches should read the appeasing *mantras*.

38. A follower of the *Ṛgveda* should recite the hymns *śrīsūkta*, *pāvamāni*, *maitraka* and *vṛṣākapi* on the east.

39. A follower of *Sāmaveda* should recite the hymns—*devavrata*, *bhāruṇḍa*, *jyeṣṭha* and *rathantara* on the south.

40. A follower of *Yajurveda* should recite the hymns *rudra*, *puruṣasūkta*, *ślokādhyāya* especially and the *brāhmaṇas* in the west.

41. An *Atharvavedin* should repeat the hymns—*nīlarudra*, *sūkṣmāsūkṣma* and the *atharvaśirṣa* in the north.

42. After having ignited the (sacrificial) fire, the preceptor should fill the eastern part of each one of the pit from the east in order.

43. Incense, lamps and sacrificial porridge should be offered to them. Then the fire should be offered. After having worshipped Śiva as before, offering unto fire should be made (accompanied by the chanting of) *mantra*.

44. After having made the oblation for making the place and time of the sacrifice as auspicious and to ward off omens portending evil, the knower of *mantras* should offer the final oblation which brings forth good.

45. After having prepared the sacrificial porridge as before, it should be offered to each one of the pit. Then the *yajamānas* (persons at whose instance a ceremony is performed) should go to the bathing shed well-adorned.

46. (The image of) the god should be placed on the auspicious seat and covered with the essence of the *mantra* after gently stroking it. After having worshipped, it should be bathed with mud and herbal waters.

47. The image should be bathed in between with the urine of a cow and cowdung, sacred as and perfumed water with (the recitation of the *mantra* of) the weapon ending with (the syllable) *phaṭ*.

48. The preceptor, after having purified the casual principles, should cover (the image) with a yellow coloured cloth (sanctified) by the repetition of the *dharma* (*mantra*) in the company of the protectors of the image.

49-51. After having worshipped (the image) with white flowers it should be carried to the sacrificial platform at the north. After having laid (the image) on a seat placed over the bed, the preceptor should mark (on the image) with lines of saffron-smeared strings and mark (the position of) the eyes with a golden stick. The collyrium should be put on (the eyelids) and then the sculptor should carve out the eyes with an implement at the spot as laid down in the technical works.

52. The eyes should be carved into a spot just at half of one third or half of one fourth or half of half the length, for accomplishing all desires and it is auspicious.

53. Taking one-fourth part of the length of the *liṅga* and having divided it into three parts, one such part should always be the breadth of the body.

54. In the *liṅga* of a cubit length, the cavity of the eyes should be a ninth part of one eighth of a *yava* (measure) both in depth and breadth.

55. In the *liṅga* of one and a half cubit length, the sockets of the eyes would measure an eighth part of a *yava* (measure) more (than that of the preceding). In that (the *liṅga*) of a cubit length (the cavity of the eyes) would be eight *yava* (measure) in depth and breadth.

56. In all the *liṅgas* of Śambhu (lord Śiva) where the length would increase by the *pāda* (measure), the measures of the cavities of the eyes would also correspondingly increase by a *yava* (measure).

57. The lines (on the top of the *liṅga*) would also increase by three parts both in depth and breadth. In all the cases the top of the *liṅga* would be narrow and tapering.

58-59. The region of the eyes should be divided into eight parts and the lower part of the head into two. The two lower parts (of the region of the eyes) should be left out. The remaining six parts should be carved into three lines taken round and joined at the back (of the emblem). The line at the top should be made to measure a *yava* (measure) in the case of (a *liṅga*) made of gem as well as of gold.

60. The form and characteristic features of these are that the radiance of those made of gem is spotless. (The emblem) should be endowed with the eyesight by carving the above mark (into the part indicated above).

61. After having worshipped the lines bringing out the characteristic features of the emblem with ghee and honey with (the

repetition of) the *mṛtyuñjayamantra*[1] in order to remove the defects due to the sculptor, the *liṅga* should then be worshipped after having bathed it with mud and other things. After having gratified the sculptor, a cow should be given to the preceptor.

62-64. After having worshipped the *liṅga* with incense and other things, married women should sing (in praise of the lord). After having touched the (*liṅga*) on the left and right with the string or with the *kuśa*, and rubbing with *rocana* (pigment), the women should be sent away after giving gifts of molasses, salt and brains.

65-67. The preceptor along with the custodians of idols should bathe (the *liṅga*) with mud, cow-dung, cow's urine, ashes and water with the (recitation of) *hṛdayamantra* or *praṇava*. Then (it should be bathed) with the five things got from a cow preceded by (bathing with) the five sweet things. After the smearing (of decoctions) of herbs (it should be bathed) with all herbal waters. (Then it should be bathed) with waters mixed with white flowers, fruits, gold, gems, horn and barley. Then (it should be bathed) with thousand pourings of divine herbal waters.

68. Subsequently, the *liṅga* should be bathed with sacred waters, waters of (river) Ganges, waters mixed with sandal and from the pitcher representing milky ocean and that pitcher of water sacred to lord Śiva.

69-71. Rubbing and besmearing should be done with fragrant sandal and other things. After having worshipped (the *liṅga*) with flowers with the recitation of *brahma* (*mantra*) and with red garments with (the *mantras* of) armour and after having shown a red flower preceded by the offer of protective mark, the *liṅga* should be worshipped with the *mantra* of *puruṣa*, after having appeased it with jets of ghee, water, milk, *kuśa*, other articles of worship and praises. After having rinsed the mouth with (the *mantra* of) the heart (the preceptor) should say, "O lord ! May you rise up !"

72. Then the lord should quickly be led to the shed along with the articles (of worship) in a divine chariot and placed in the bed (made ready) at the western door (of the shed).

73. At the western door itself a pedestal should be placed on

1. addressed to lord Śiva praying for deliverance from death. Tryambakaṁ yajāmahe sugandhim puṣṭivardhanam urvārukamiva bandhanān mṛtyor mukṣiya māmṛtāt.

an auspicious seat permeated with the goddesses beginning with Śakti and ending with Mati. The *brahmaśilā* should also be bestowed therein.

74-75. The sacrificial pitcher in which the psychic sleep had been induced should be converted into the fixed seat. After having placed it in the north-east corner of the shed and offered waters for washing with (the *mantra* of) the heart, the *liṅga* should be lifted (from the bed) and deposited on the seat with the head turned towards the east and obeisance to *Dharma* (god of virtue) and others (should be done) with (the *mantra* of) creation.

76. Incense should be offered. After having worshipped the *liṅga*, garments and household articles should be offered with (the *mantra* of) the heart befitting one's capacity.

77-78. A vessel filled with ghee and honey should be placed near the foot as unguent. The officiating priest who is present therein should locate the thirtysix principles beginning with energy and ending with the earth along with their respective presiding deities and divide (the above body) into three parts with garlands of flowers.

79-83. After having located the fundamental principles beginning with the principle of illusion and ending with that of the absolute energy, together with the principles of soul, knowledge and pure bliss, in the order in which they were created, in the different parts of the body such as the square, octagon or circle and the presiding deities of the above three principles such as the gods Brahmā, Viṣṇu and Śiva having been projected into each of the above said divisions and also the different embodiments of gods such as the earth, fire, the person for whom the sacrifice is done, sun, water, air, moon, sun, sky together with their respective deities such as Śarva, Paśupati, Ugra, Rudra, Bhava, Maheśvara, Mahādeva and Bhīma and these letters respectively sacred to them such as *la*, *va*, *śa*, *ṣa*, *ca*, *ya*, *sa* and *ha* should be located therein. The *praṇava* of three parts or the *mantra* of the heart or some other principal *mantra* (are also located).

84-85. (The preceptor) who knows the *mantra* should locate five deities of (the five fundamental principles earth, water, lustre, wind and ether along with their five presiding deities, and

Brahmā, Dharaṇīdhara, Rudra, Īśa and Sadāśivain the order of creation in the case of a sacrifice having five fire-pits.

86. (The principles of) non-action, and other things, and their presiding deities Ajāta and others or the three principles should be located as the cause of pervading in the case of a seeker of release (from bondage).

87. Gods known as Vidyeśas (lords of learning) should be meditated upon in the case of one's own soul being pure and the Lokanāyakas (lords of the world) in the case of one's own and being impure and also the protectors of images, enjoyers and lords of the *mantras*.

88. (The fundamental principles numbering) twenty-five[1], eight[2], five[3] and three[4] and their lords such as Indra and others (should be worshipped) in order as follows:

*Oṁ hāṁ* obeisance to the principle of energy etc. *Oṁ hāṁ* obeisance to the presiding deity of the principle of energy etc. *Oṁ hāṁ* obeisance to the image of *kṣmā* (earth). *Oṁ hāṁ* obeisance to (lord) Śiva, presiding deity of the image of earth etc. *Oṁ hāṁ* obeisance to the image of *pṛthivī* (earth). *Oṁ hāṁ* obeisance to *Brahmā*, the presiding deity of the image etc. *Oṁ hāṁ* obeisance to (lord) Rudra, the presiding deity of the principle of Śiva (auspiciousness) etc.

89-91. (The preceptor) should recite (the above *mantras*) from the region of the navel, spreading like the sounds of bell, rejecting the causes such as Brahmā and others and meditate on the *mantra* resting in (the lotus of) twelve petals and which is different from the mind and which resembles the sentiment of bliss obtained. Having collected filaments from the twelve (petalled lotuses) (lord Śiva), who pervades (everything) and is devoid of *kalās*, should be contemplated upon as shining resplendent with thirtyeight *kalās*, effulgent with thousand rays, consisting of all energies and accompanied by the attendant gods; (he) should be then projected in the *liṅga*.

92. The *jīvanyāsa*[5] in the *liṅga* will be accomplished in this

1. The *avyakta, mahat, ahaṅkāra, pañcabhūtas, pañcatanmātrās, pañcakarmendriyas, pañcajñānendriyas, manas* and *yajamāna*.
2. The five elements, sun, moon and *yajamāna*.
3. The five elements.
4. The three qualities *sattva, rajas* and *tamas*.
5. The projection of vital energy.

manner. It yields all fruits. The location in the pedestal etc. will be described now.

93-94. After having been washed and besmeared with sandal paste etc., the pedestal should be covered by a good cloth. Then the stone set ready just like the *liṅga* and placed at the north of the *liṅga* should be endowed with the five gems in its aperture resembling the female organ of generation and should be worshipped as laid down.

95. The (pedestal) stone which has been bathed again should be deposited at the foot of the *liṅga*. So also the bull and (others such as the goddess of) energy should be located after doing the rites of bathing etc. (to them).

96-97. It should be done being preceded by the *praṇava* (syllable *om*) and (followed by) any one of (the mystic letters) *hum*, *pum* and *hrim*. The pedestal stone which is of the form of the base and which is endowed with the energy of action (should be worshipped) with sacred ashes, *darbha* and sesamum. Then the three outer walls should be set up. The guardian deities with their weapons should be worshipped outside for the sake of protection.

*Oṁ hūm, hrām* obeisance to the energy of action. *Oṁ hūm, hrām, haḥ* oblation to Mahāgaurī, the consort of Rudra—this (being performed) on the pedestal. *Oṁ, hām* obeisance to the energy of support. *Om, hām* obeisance to the bull.

98-101. The (female deities) Dhārikā, Dīptimatī, Ugrā Jyotsnā, Balotkaṭā, Dhātrī and Vidhātrī or the five goddesses Vāmā, Jyeṣṭhā, Kriyā, Jñāna, Vedhā or the three Kriyā, Jñāna and Icchā should be located as before. So also the female goddesses should be located in the benefic forms of gods. The five energies Tamī, Mohā, Kṣamī, Niṣṭhā, Mṛtyu, Māyā, or Bhava Jvara, Mahāmoha, Ghora, Tritayajvara or the three presiding female deities Kriyā, Jñāna and Bādhā should be located in the three indomitable principles of soul etc.

102. Even in this case the pedestal (should be worshipped) in the Brahmā--part (of the *liṅga*) in the order. All routines should be performed as before with (the goddess) Gaurī and others.

103-105. Having located in this manner, (the preceptor) should go near the (fire) pit and invoke (lord) Maheśvara at the centre of the pit and on the borders, the goddess of action in the other border and the sound (*om*) at the lip. Then the union of the occult psychic force with the sacrificial pitcher, the ground, fire and (lord) Īśa (should be brought about).

106-107. The preceptor should contemplate his psychic energy resembling the fire of a lotus rejected upwards by the rising wind, entering by the path of the sun, emerging out and again entering by the path of void. In this manner mutual union with (the psychic forces of) the protectors of guardians should be brought about everywhere.

108. After having worshipped the energy (known as) Dhārikā (ability to hold), duly the fundamental principles along with their presiding deities, and the images (of gods) along with their presiding deities with ghee etc. and offered oblation duly in the fire-pit in their presence with the *saṁhitā mantras*, oblation should again be made hundred or thousand or five hundred times (concluding) with the final oblation.

109. Similarly, the guardians of deities should also satisfy the fundamental principles along with their presiding deities, and the images (of gods) along with their presiding deities and offer oblation.

110-111. After having satisfied the (goddess of) energy with Brahma *mantras* befitting one's capacity and time and sprinkled the waters of the pitcher with the ends of the *kuśa* and touched the base of the *liṅga*, one should repeat (the *mantras*) as many times as (the number of) oblations. The presence of the god should be accomplished by (repeating) the *mantra* of the heart. The act of covering (the image) should be done by (repeating) the *mantra* of the armour.

112-13. After having performed (the rites) thus for the purification of (the parts of the *liṅga* presided over by) the gods Brahmā to Viṣṇu, (the preceptor) should complete the oblation and repetition of the *mantras* as many times (as mentioned above). The middle and tip of the *liṅga* should be touched with the middle and tip of the *kuśa*. The mode of achieving the union is described now:

*Om, hām, ham, om, om, om, em, om, bhūm, bhūm* obeisance to the image outside. *Om, hām, vām, om, om, om, ṣām, om, bhūm, bhūm, vām* obeisance to the image of fire-god.

114. Similarly, the images of the *yajamāna* and others should be contemplated (in the *liṅga*). So also in the case of the five

manifestations of the god, union must be brought about with (the repetition of the *mantra* of) the heart etc.

115. It should be known that (the union) in the case of the three fundamental principles (soul, knowledge and bliss) with the *liṅga*, pedestal and bull is brought about by the principal (*mantra*) or with their own fundamental (letters) completely and without any omission.

116-19. Hundred oblations should be made for the purification of the different parts (of the *liṅga*) and hundred and eight (oblations) with the *mantra* of (lord) Śiva for the removal of any deficiency (in performing the sacrifice). After having made oblation, whatever act has been done that should be uttered in the ear of (lord) Śiva: "This act has been completed by me by your grace ! O lord ! *Om*, obeisance to lord Rudra ! Obeisance to (lord) Rudradeva ! Whether this act is complete as laid down or incomplete, you complete it by your power and accept it. Then the learned (preceptor) should locate in the *liṅga* and the act in the pedestal of the image.

120-121. The energy of the form of support should be located in the Brahmā (part of the) stone. The (rite of) *adhivāsana* (staying together) should extend over seven nights or five nights or three nights or a single night or be done immediately. The sacrifice performed without (the performance of) *adhivāsana* does not yield any benefit even if performed.

122. Hundreds of oblations should be offered everyday with the respective *mantras*. Worship of the pitcher of (lord) Śiva and offering to the quarters should be conveyed.

123. The *adhivāsa* is so called because the disciple stays with the preceptor practising vows. It is said to be the attitude till the end of the stay.

## CHAPTER NINETYSEVEN

### *Mode of installation of the image of (lord) Śiva*

*The lord said* :

1. After having performed the daily rites in the morning and worshipped the guardian deities, the preceptor should enter (the temple) as described already and purify his body.

2-3. After having worshipped the lords of the quarters, the sacrificial pitcher of (lord) Śiva and the small pitcher and having satisfied the *liṅga* and the fire duly with eight handfuls (of oblation), (the preceptor) should enter the temple reciting (the *mantra* of) the weapon by the command of (lord) Śiva. The obstacles therein should be removed by (the repetition of) the *mantra* of the arrow ending with (the syllables) *hum*, *phaṭ*.

4-7. The *liṅga* should not be established at the middle (of the temple) to avoid the defect of injury. Hence the stone slab should be established having left half of a *yava* (a measure) or a *yava* from the centre a little towards the north-east.

That slab (known as) *ananta* (literally without end) and which is of the form of support of all (should be established) with the principal (*mantra*). The stone slab known as *Acalā* (without movement) which is all-pervading and is of the form of the seat of (lord) Śiva should be placed by the use of (the *mantra* of) creation or by (the repetition of) the following *mantra* :—"*Om* ! All pervading goddess ! Firm and unmovable (goddess) Acalā ! obeisance. *Hram*, *lam*, *hrim*, oblations. You must always remain here by the command of (lord) Śiva."

8-16. After having spoken thus and having worshipped (the *liṅga*), (the preceptor) should arrest its movement by showing the *raudramudrā* (a posture made with the fingers). After that, (the preceptor) should place the diamond and the other gems, fragrant root, metals like gold and bronze yellow orpiment etc., cereals and grains described already and respectively representing lustre, beauty, strength and valour duly in the holes in the (directions) east etc. after having devotedly contemplated with the *mantras* of guardian deities of the world. A tortoise or bull made of gold or silver (should be located) along with earth from the banks of a river or from the peaks of a mountain in the central (and other) holes facing the entrance. Otherwise a golden image of a *meru* along with honey, unbroken rice and collyrium (should be located). Otherwise a golden or silver image of the earth should be located along with syllables of all the *mantras* and gold. Then a lotus stalk made of gold or silver or all metals together with a dish consisting of sesamum and grains should be located. After having located the seat of the lord representing the energy it should be anointed with sweet porridge or *guggulu* (an aromatic) and covered with a cloth protected by (the recitation of) the (*mantra*) of the armour and weapon.

17-21. After having offered oblations to the presiding deities of the quarters and rinsing the mouth, the preceptor should offer hundred oblations either with (the repetition of) (the *mantra* of lord) Śiva or with (the *mantra* of) the weapon along with the final (oblation) for the removal of defects in the cavity of the stone slab on account of contamination. After having appeased the presiding deities of the ground by offering an oblation, the preceptor should lift the deity along with the seat with (the recitation of the *mantra* of) the heart and the sounding of auspicious notes. Then the preceptor should walk ahead of the deity and behind the sacrificial ground of the lord along with the four custodians of the image standing in the (different) directions and the person at whose bidding the rite is performed. After having done the circumambulation, the *liṅga* should be established in front of the door known as *bhadra* (welfare). After having offered waters for washing, (the *liṅga*) should be taken to the temple through the door, the door frame and the region of the door.

22. The great lord should be taken only through the door without contacting the door (in the case of an unfinished temple) if the door frame has unfinished edges or incomplete or is half done.

23-24. In the case of the construction of a temple being begun, (the *liṅga*) should be taken in through the corner also. This is the general rule even in the case of a manifested *liṅga* as the worldly practice for entry into the temple through the door. It is known that if the entry into the temple is made through the side door it causes destruction of the race.

25-33. After having placed the *liṅga* in the seat facing the door with the sounding of auspicious *tūrya* (a kind of musical instrument) and (offerings of) *dūrvā* (a kind of grass) and unbroken rice, (the preceptor) should recite the great *pāśupata* (*mantra*) after uttering 'Rise, O lord' with (the recitation of the *mantra* of) the heart. After having removed the sacrificial pitchers from the holes, the preceptor in the company of the guardians of the image should mentally repeat the *mantra* and contemplate (the *liṅga*) besmeared with saffron and other things and the union of the god and goddess as protected. After having recited the principal (*mantra*) till deep concentration (is gained), (the preceptor) should touch (the *liṅga*) and place it in the hole. Either a portion of the Brahmā-part (of the *liṅga*) or two parts (of the same) or half of it or one-eighth of the whole (*liṅga*) should be under (the earth). After having covered (the *liṅga*) with lead upto the waist with concentration, (the preceptor) should fill the cavity with sand and say, "(You) be firm". Then after the *liṅga* has become firm, (the preceptor) should contemplate him who is of all the forms (of beings), recite the principal (*mantra*) and locate the *niṣkala* (devoid of attributes) upto the energy by the (order of) creation. If the *liṅga* that is being established leans towards the south, the preceptor should offer oblations with the *mantras* of the respective presiding deities of the directions until the final (oblation) along with the fees. (The preceptor) should offer hundred oblations either with the principal *mantra* or (the *mantra*) of manifold forms if (the *liṅga* leans) to the left or slips down or cracks. Even in the case of other defects (the preceptor) should similarly perform the blissful appeasing rite.

34. A *liṅga* associated with the rites of location etc. in this manner does not bring any harm. The pedestal should be consecrated as possessing a part of the characteristic (mentioned already for the *liṅga*).

35. After having projected the *mantra* of (the goddess) Gaurī (consort of lord Śiva) in the pedestal, the pedestal should be consecrated with (the *mantra*) of creation. The sides (of the *liṅga*) should be smoothened and binding cement and sand should be put.

36-37. Then the preceptor in the company of the custodians of the image should bathe the images (with the waters) from the pitcher of peace and other pitchers placed there as well as the *pañcāmṛta* (a composition of the milk, sugar, curd, ghee and honey) and other things. It should then be besmeared with sandal paste and other things. After having worshipped the lord of the universe (Śiva), (the preceptor) should touch the parts (represented by lord Śiva and his consort Umā) with the recitation of the *mantras* of (goddess) Umā and (lord) Maheśa (Śiva) and showing the *liṅgamudrā* (a posture made with the fingers).

38-39. Then (the preceptor) should (mentally) project

the three (fundamental) principles[1] in that preceded by the six kinds of worship. After having located the image along with the presiding divinities of the (different) parts as also (lord) Brahmā in the seat of action, the learned person should bathe it. After having besmeared it with fragrant (pastes) and showing fragrant fumes, it should be located as the sole pervading principle of (lord) Śiva.

40-44. After having offered to (lord) Śiva the garlands of flowers, incense sticks, lamps, edible offerings and fruits with (the recitation of the *mantra* of) the heart befitting one's capacity and sipping waters (thrice), water should be offered to the lord for cleansing. After the recitation (of the *mantras* sacred to the lord) and assigning the merits of the same on his right hand (the preceptor) should address the lord in the company of the custodians of (the image of lord) Śiva as follows: "O lord ! You should stay in this temple by your own wish as long as the sun, moon and stars (would shine in the sky)." After having made obeisance thus, (the preceptor) should go outside (the temple reciting) either (the *mantra*) of the heart or the *praṇava* (syllable *om*). After having established (the image of) the bull, (the preceptor) should make the offering as before. One hundred oblations should be made with the *mṛtyuñjaya* (*mantra*) (that which conquers death) for the removal of defects like omission etc. In order to appease the lord oblations with sweet porridge should be done with (the recitation of the *mantra* of) the heart. "O great lord ! Whatever thing has been done by me through ignorance or inadvertance you make it good."

45. One should dedicate all things to the lord of the goddess who is the cause of gold, animals, earth, songs and musical instruments with devotion and within one's means.

46. Gifts (should be given) and then festivities should be celebrated for four days. The preceptor should offer oblations for three days at the three conjunctions (of time) (the morning, midday and evening) in the company of the custodians of the image.

47-48. And the final oblation composed of sacrificial porridge should be offered in all pits purified with the obla-

1. Soul, knowledge and bliss.

tion (known as) *sampāta* (fulfilling oblation) on the fourth day with (the recitation of) the *bahurūpi* (*mantra*). The flowers used should be kept for four days after that and removed afterwards. After having bathed the image, it should be worshipped.

49-52. Worship in the case of ordinary *liṅgas* should be done by (the repetition of) the general *mantras*. Except consciousness of the *liṅga*, the lord should be bid adieu. In the case of *liṅgas* of extraordinary nature (lord) should be bid adieu (with the repetition of words), "Pardon (us O lord ! )" Invocation, manifestation and dismissal (are done) befitting one's ability. According to some it has been stated that seven oblations for the steadiness etc. (should be cast)at the end of installation. Steadiness, immeasurableness, cognisance of the originless existence, eternity, all-pervasiveness, deathlessness, seen as manifested are spoken as the characteristics of (lord) Śiva for the manifestation.

53-54. "*Om* ! obeisance to (lord) Śiva. Be thou steady." This is the order offering oblations. After having accomplished this in this manner and having permeated the two pitchers with the essence of lord Śiva, the (lord) Bhava (Śiva) should be bathed with (the waters of) the one and the other should be borne for bathing the performer.

55-57. After having made the offering, (the preceptor) should do the *ācamana* (sipping of waters thrice) and go outside with the permission of lord Śiva. (The god) Caṇḍa should be located on a seat over a good pedestal in the north-eastern direction outside the sacrificial ground and worshipped with the *brahma mantras* preceded by contemplation, and rites of location and offering of oblations. The worship using the *brahma mantras* is that in which the components are mentioned at first.

*Om*, *hūm*, *phaṭ* obeisance to Sadyojāta. *Om*, *hūm*, *phaṭ* obeisance to Vāmadeva. *Om*, *Vum*, *phaṭ* obeisance to Aghora. *Om*, *vaum*, *phaṭ* obeisance to Tatpuruṣa. *Om*, *hūm*, *phaṭ* obeisance to Īśāna.

58-59. After having conveyed the (merits of) repetition (to the lord) and appeased him, (the lord) should be addressed as follows preceded by bowing. O (lord Caṇḍa) ! Stay (in this temple) as long as the lord (Śiva) stays here. O (lord) Caṇḍeśa ! Whatever has been omitted or made in excess by me out of ignorance, make it complete by your grace.

60. Lord Caṇḍa should not be invoked in cases where a *bāṇaliṅga* (a kind of stone representing lord Śiva) or a *liṅga* placed on the *bāṇa* stone or an accomplished *liṅga* or self-originated *liṅga* or images of all gods (are established).

61-66. Even in the case of rites relating to the presiding deity of the sacrificial ground in which there is the mental attitude of union with the lord, the preceptor should worship (lord) Caṇḍeśa, and the *yajamāna* (the person for whom the work is done) along with his son and wife and should bathe himself with (the waters of) the pitcher already placed. The *yajamāna* should also worship the preceptor as (the lord) Maheśa (Śiva) and make gifts of earth, gold and other things without any distinction whatever. After having satisfied befittingly the protectors of images, those who repeat (the *mantras*), the brahmins, astrologers and sculptors, the destitutes, forlorns and others should be fed. "O lord ! Ocean of compassion ! Forgive me for all the sufferings you had in being present here." To the *yajamāna* who has spoken thus, the preceptor should offer with his own hands the merits of consecration resplendent like the glowing star along with the *kuśa*, flowers and unbroken rice.

67. After having then saluted (lord) Parameśvara (Śiva) endowed with the *pāśupata* (*mantra*), (the preceptor) should address the attendant gods (of the lord) with offerings for their presence.

68-71. "You should stay here in as long as (the lord) Hara (Śiva) is present here. Then the preceptor should take possession of the sacrificial shed along with the cloth etc. Then the sculptor (should take possession of) the bathing shed along with the articles (found therein). All other gods should be established with the repetition of the *mantras* as given in the *āgamas*[1]. (In these establishments of other gods) the splitting of the first letter of the (respective) names (of the gods) and the location of fundamental principles pervading these (should be made). The gods commencing with Sādhya, the rivers, herbs, the guardian deities of the ground, *kinnaras* (semi-divine beings) and others should lie in the principle of earth. In some places the location of the (goddesses) Sarasvatī and Lakṣmī (are) in the waters.

1. Texts relating to worship of deities in the temples.

72. The presiding deities of the world (should be established) in those places where they remain firm. The place of Brahmā is the three fundamental principles which extends to the important cause of expansion of the (primordial) egg.

73. The place of Hari (Viṣṇu) is the triad (of worlds) which has the subtle principles as the main. The places for the lord of dancing (Nāṭyeśa, a form of Śiva), *gaṇas* (attendant gods), mothers (goddesses), Yakṣeśas (semi-divine beings) and (lord) Subrahmaṇya (are as described above).

74. The place of Gaṇapati is that upto the principle of pure knowledge. (The place) of splendours emitted by (lord) Śiva and (his consort) Śivā (Pārvatī) extends to the energy in the region of a part of the illusion.

75-77. In the case of manifested images, the place is spoken as upto the lord (Śiva). Some forms like the tortoise as well as the five things such as the gem etc. should be put in the hole of the pedestal except in the case of (the image of) the five brahman forms (of lord Śiva). In the hole divided into six parts one part from the end is left out and fixing is made in the fifth part. If it is divided into eight parts, the fixing is done in the seventh part. This fixing in the case of images brings forth happiness.

78-79. Purification is done by meditation when the images are fixed. In the case of plastered and painted images bathing, placing on a pedestal, placing gems (underneath), opening of the eyes, the (placing of) *mantras*, and the offer of seats etc. (should be done) mentally. Worship should be done with flowers without water in them so that the picture may not get spoilt.

80-82. "The mode (of fixing) the movable variety of *liṅga* is described now." (The *liṅga*) should be divided into five or three parts separately and three or two parts (should be set apart for fixing). On account of the different fundamental principles, the purification of the pedestals as well as the *liṅgas* made of crystals (should be done) with the *mantra* of creation as laid down. In those cases there is no need to place the *brahmaśilā* and the gems etc.

83. The placing of the image on the pedestal should be done mentally. There is no special procedure for purification in the case of self-originated *liṅgas* and *bāṇaliṅgas* (*liṅgas* made of a kind of stone).

84. (The movable *liṅgas*) should be bathed with (the recitation of) the vedic *mantras*. So also the (rite of) assigning an oblation should be done (with the same *mantras*). The (sacred) rivers, oceans and mountains are installed as before.

85-86. The *liṅgas* made of earth and flours are known as *aihika* (relating to this world) and *kṣata* (perishable). After having made such a *liṅga* pure, one should worship as laid down with the rites of initiation etc. Then after having withdrawn the *mantras* into himself in its presence, the preceptor should cast that *liṅga* in the waters. It yields one's desires within a year. The installation of (the images of) Viṣṇu etc. should be done with separate *mantras*.

## CHAPTER NINETYEIGHT

### *Mode of installation of the image of goddess Gaurī*

*The Lord said* :

1. Listen ! I shall describe the mode of installation together with the worship (of the image) of (goddess) Gaurī (consort of lord Śiva). The sacrificial shed etc. should be erected and (the image of the goddess) should be placed therein.

2. O Guha (son of lord Śiva and Pārvatī) ! After having placed the goddess on the bed, the *mantras* of the images (should be located therein), and the principles commencing with the knowledge of the soul and ending with Śiva as also lord Īśāna (Śiva) should be located.

3. After having located the goddess of absolute energy, offered oblations and recited (the *mantras*) as before, the pedestal of the form of the energy of action should be placed.

4-5. After having contemplated it as pervading the same place and having put the gems etc., the goddess of the form of supreme energy should be fixed therein with her own *mantras*. The energy of action should be located in the pedestal and the energy of knowledge in the image (of the goddess).

6. Then the pervading energy should be invoked and located therein. Then the mother goddess known also as Śivā should

also be invoked and worshipped. *Om*, obeisance to the sustaining energy. *Om*, obeisance to the tortoise (supporting the universe). *Om*, obeisance to (lord) Skanda (son of lord Śiva and Pārvatī). *Om*, *hrim* obeisance to (lord) Nārāyaṇa (Viṣṇu). *Om*, obeisance to sovereignty. *Om*, *am* obeisance to the undercover. *Om*, obeisance to the lotus seat. Then (the gods) Keśava (Viṣṇu) and others should be worshipped. *Om*, *hrim* obeisance to the pericarp. One should worship here with (the *mantras*) "*Om*, *kṣam* obeisance to the lotus eyes". *Om*, *hām* obeisance to nourishment, *hrim* (obeisance) to knowledge, *hrim* (obeisance) to action. *Om*, obeisance to the stalk of lotus. *Rum*, obeisance to virtue. *Rum*, obeisance to knowledge. *Om*, obeisance to indifference to the world. *Om* obeisance to impiety. *Om*, *Rum* obeisance to ignorance. *Om* obeisance to attachment to the world. *Om* obeisance to indigence. *Hum*, obeisance to speech, to the passionate, *kraim* to the fiery. *Om*, *hraum* obeisance to tranquility. Then *hrum* obeisance to the elder (goddess). *Om*, *hrum*, *raum*, *kraum* (obeisance) to (goddess) of fresh energy, *gaum* to the seat of Gaurī. *Gaum* obeisance to the form of Gaurī. Then the principal *mantra* of (goddess)Gaurī is told. *Om*, *hrim*, *sāḥ*, mahā Gaurī, consort of Rudra (Śiva), oblations ! Obeisance to (goddess) Gaurī. *Gām*, *hrūm*, *hrim*, *Śivaḥ*, *gūm*, to tuft, to armour. *Gom* to eye and *gom* to the weapon, *om*, *gaum* to the energy of wisdom, *om Gūm* obeisance to the energy of action. (Gods) Indra and others (are worshipped) in the east and other directions. *Om*, *sum* obeisance to Subhagā (favourite wife). *Hrim* bīja lalitā then. And *om*, *hrim* obeisance to Kāminī (an affectionate woman). *Om hrūm* Kāmaśālinī. After having established (goddess) Gaurī with the *mantras*, worshipping (her) and repeating (the *mantras*), one may get everything.

## CHAPTER NINETYNINE

*Mode of installation of the image of the sun-god.*

*The lord said* :

1-2. I shall describe (the mode of) installation of the sun-god. The sacrificial shed (and other things) should be (made ready) as before. Then after having completed the rites of ablution etc., as prescribed before, and having located the sun-god with his attendants and (goddess) Vidyā in the seat and bed, (the preceptor) should locate the three (fundamental) principles (of soul, knowledge and bliss) and the five (principles of) sky etc. along with chants.

3. After having done the purification etc. as before and having purified the pedestal as before, (the preceptor should locate the five principles upto their own place.

4-5. After having established (the pedestal) then along with the (goddess of) energy (called) Sarvatomukhī as laid down, the preceptor should establish (the image of) the sun (god) as laid down with the (utterance of) its *mantras* as permeated with the energy or the master. The name should be borne upto the end of the foot. The *mantras* which have been described already should be seen at (the time of) establishment also.

## CHAPTER ONE HUNDRED

### *Rites of consecration of doors of a temple*

*The Lord said* :

1. Then I shall describe the mode of consecrating the doors (of a temple). After having washed the door frames with decoctions of herbs, they should be laid on the bed.

2-3. The three fundamental principles—the soul etc. together with their lords should be located in the lower, middle and upper parts. After having offered oblations, and repeated the *rūpa mantras*, the *vāstu* (the presiding spirit of the place) should be worshipped there itself with the *mantra* of Ananta (an important serpent chief). After having placed the five things gem etc., the rite of appeasement should be done.

4-5. Barley, white mustard, *krāntā*, *ṛddhi*, *vṛddhi*, *mahātila*, *gomṛt*, mustard, *rājendra*, *mohani*, *lakṣmaṇā*, *amṛtā*, *rocanā*, *rug*, *vacā*, *dūrvā* and *pāṭali* should be placed on the threshold under the temple in their natural form for the sake of protection after the recitation of (the syllable) *om*.

6. The northern door should be consecrated after sprinkling water. The fundamental principle of the soul should be located under that and the principle of knowledge on the sides.

7. The principle of bliss (should be located) in the region of the sky as permeating the entire region. Then (lord) Maheśanātha (Śiva) should be installed with (the recitation of) the principal *mantra*.

8. The turrets etc. resting on the door (should be located) with their respective names appended. Oblation to fire should be made hundred times or half the number of times or twice that or according to one's ability.

9. One hundred oblations should be made with the *mantra* of the weapons to ward off defects of omission etc. After having offered oblations for the quarters, the fees etc. should be paid.